Islamic Modern

PRINCETON STUDIES IN MUSLIM POLITICS

Dale F. Eickelman and James Piscatori, Editors

Islamic Modern

RELIGIOUS COURTS

AND CULTURAL POLITICS IN MALAYSIA

MICHAEL G. PELETZ

PRINCETON UNIVERSITY PRESS

PRINCETON AND OXFORD

Library of Congress Cataloging-in-Publication Data

Peletz, Michael G.
Islamic modern: religious courts and cultural politics in Malaysia / Michael G. Peletz.
p. cm. — (Princeton studies in Muslim politics)
Includes bibliographical references and index.
ISBN 0-691-09507-8 (cloth : alk. paper) — ISBN 0-691-09508-6 (pbk. : alk. paper)
1. Courts, Islamic—Malaysia.   2. Malaysia—Social conditions.   ⌐I. Title.   II. Series.
KPG3474 .P45 2002
340'.115'09595—dc21   2002020107

British Library Cataloging-in-Publication Data is available

This book has been composed in Times

Printed on acid-free paper. ∞

www.pupress.princeton.edu

Printed in the United States of America

1   3   5   7   9   10   8   6   4   2

FOR ZACHARY AND ALEXANDER

CONTENTS

LIST OF MAPS

LIST OF TABLES

OSAMA BIN LADIN's statement of October 7, 2001, dated the current troubles of the Muslim world to eighty years before. It is likely that this refers to the demise of the Ottoman empire and the abolition of the caliphate in 1924. So significant has the demise of the caliphate been that Muslim political debates since then have urgently focused on how to construct an Islamic state, or at least on how to proceed with the Islamization of society. Although no firm consensus exists as to what either entails, Islamic law is generally thought to be at the heart of the modern Islamic project. If only Islamic law were implemented, it is argued, the waywardness of Muslim societies would be checked. This pious aspiration obscures, however, a number of fundamental questions: Which parts of the *shari'a* would be implemented? What relationship would Islamic law have to civil law? Who would be the authoritative interpreters of the law?

Each of these issues is contentious, pointing to the symbolic and boundary-setting dimensions of Muslim politics. The law itself becomes a symbol of political rectitude but is predictably invested with variable meanings. Constitutional debates over whether the *shari'a* constitutes "a," "the principal," or "the (sole)" source of law, such as has occurred in Egypt, point to underlying differences on the nature of the state itself. Secularists, official *ulama*, Islamists, and the government put forward understandings of the term that suggest sharply delineated visions of the future and programs of action. Nowhere is this more powerfully seen than in the controversies over family or personal status legislation. Precisely because women are placed at the center of civic order, the law governing marriage, divorce, and inheritance has often become the subject of high politics. As societies seek ways to reconcile these differing interpretations, lines—implicit and explicit—are drawn between the right and enjoined, and the immoral and forbidden. Legal rules naturally formalize such distinctions, but they also invoke tacit hierarchies of power and authority in Muslim societies. In Indonesia, the normally compliant religious officials protested when the government attempted a substantial reform of family law. The objection may have been cast in legalistic, even moralistic, terms, but it was clear that the *ulama* regarded the government's position as an encroachment on their prerogatives.

In some circles, the *shari'a* has acquired the reputation of being tradition-bound or inflexible, yet, as the above suggests, the politics of Islamic law is anything but static. It is integral to the ongoing social construction of authority in Muslim societies. Contenders for authority manipulate law as a symbol of the constancy of faith, but this contention in the long term is also constitutive of normative regulative patterns; the law represents a religiously validated order, but also allows for evolution. Moreover, what makes up "legal" conduct, while ostensibly prefigured in the classical ethical and legal teachings of Islam, is subject to modification. The reality of "Islamic law" is often, in fact, far from the Weberian image of *qadi*-imposed, conservative judgment.

By taking us into the workings of Islamic courts in contemporary Malaysia, Michael Peletz convincingly documents this legal dynamism. Rather than appear as neutral institutions, the courts are themselves caught up in the related processes of self-conscious religious resurgence and concentrated social-economic transformations. Islamic law and its apparatus emerge as part of a rationalized Islam—a concrete arena of activity and dispute—that, inevitably, becomes a critical component of the search for authenticity. Two important features of the search emanate from this rich ethnographic study. First, as all appears to be in dizzying flux, the need for apparent and strong goalposts is keenly felt. Islamic courts may well seem to provide these bearings, particularly as they are associated with a strong state, but they too are resisted and challenged.

Second, the boundaries between permissible and impermissible conduct, the "said" and "unsaid," are debated anew. On the one hand, new standards of "criminality," particularly in sexual and gender matters, have risen whereby the Mahathir regime seeks to impose conformity and control dissent. On the other hand, Islamic courts are active agents of social change. Far from being antiquated and out of touch, Islamic courts are helping to make a "modern" Malaysia in which an urban Malay middle class is privileged over other groups, and individualism, largely unintentionally, is promoted. Women especially have found in Islamic courts a forum in which to advance some of their claims while subverting anticipated understandings of their own and men's social roles. In so doing, they often compel men and the state to accord them greater respect, but recent controversies over homosexuality are a reminder that social tolerance is constructed and variable. The manipulation of Islam from the top—whether by the secular branches of the government or the courts—has the ironic long-term effect of encouraging the re-imagination of associational life, even as it, expectedly, consolidates state power.

This volume speaks to the larger concerns of civic life that go beyond the particular case of Malaysia. Like other books in this series, *Islamic Modern: Religious Courts and Cultural Politics in Malaysia* assesses the potential for the opening of public space in Muslim societies. It is compelling in its argument that there is a "cultural logic" of negotiation and persuasion that becomes encapsulated in the Islamic judicial process. Far from being an inherent bar to civil society development, then, these courts are an ineluctable part of an uncertain, though conceivably liberalizing, process. Much, as always, depends on the state, but Michael Peletz has presented a vivid depiction of culturally grounded possibilities. His substantial contribution is to demystify Islamic law and institutions, highlighting their connections to an official modernizing program as well as their ability to induce consequential social and cultural change.

James Piscatori
Dale F. Eickelman

ACKNOWLEDGMENTS

ETHNOGRAPHY IS A collective enterprise and I am deeply indebted to a great many people and institutions at home and abroad for help in seeing this project through to its completion. I am particularly grateful to the numerous Malaysians who kindly allowed me into their homes and lives and graciously endured what must have seemed like incessant questioning on virtually every topic imaginable. The residents of the village that I refer to as Bogang deserve special mention again for their hospitality and warmth during my extended stays in their community. I employ pseudonyms for the name of that village and its inhabitants, in accordance with established anthropological practice designed to help protect the anonymity of those who shared their thoughts and views with me. I thus apologize to my adoptive parents and like-minded residents of Bogang who would prefer that I identify their community and use their real names.

Kala Kovan, program officer of the Malaysian-American Commission on Educational Exchange, has aided me during each of my trips to Malaysia, and I would like to emphasize again how much I appreciate her advice, help, and friendship. Manogaran Maniam, Shamsul A.B., and Siti Shariah binti Haji Shaari also shared their passionate love and extensive knowledge of things Malaysian with me and helped make my stays in their country not only productive but also extremely enjoyable. Haji Musa (aka Harun) bin Haji Ibrahim, the judge (*kadi*) in charge of the Office of the Islamic Magistrate (Pejabat Kadi) in Rembau, Negeri Sembilan, was also exceedingly helpful, as were members of his staff. Employees of the (secular) Magistrate's Court (Mahkamah Majistret) in Rembau also provided invaluable assistance, as did officials at the District Office of Rembau (Pejabat Daerah Rembau) and the Office of Islamic Magistrate and the Department of Islamic Religion (Jabatan Agama Islam) in Seremban. In Kuala Lumpur I benefited from the cooperation afforded me by many individuals and organizations: Dato' Sheikh Ghazali bin Haji Abdul Rahman, the chief judge (Ketua Hakim) of the Islamic Court of the Federal District of Kuala Lumpur; Dato' Abdul Monir bin Yaacob, the assistant director general/director of the Centre of Syariah, Laws, and Political Science, Institute of Islamic Understanding Malaysia (IKIM); Tuan Haji Ahmad Zawawi bin Muhammad of the Islamic Center (Pusat Islam); Zainah Anwar, Sharifah Zuriah Aljefri, and other members of Sisters in Islam; Marina Mahathir, the president of the Malaysian AIDS Council and the Malaysian AIDS Foundation; and the staff of Pink Triangle, a vibrant outreach organization designed to assist the transgendered community and those at risk for HIV/AIDS. Thanks also to the many lawyers, journalists, activists, artists, and others in Kuala Lumpur, Selangor, and elsewhere who kindly gave their time and shared their perspectives and expertise with me; and to Ellen Walker, who provided help of all kinds during the first two stints of fieldwork and also drew the maps for this volume. Portions of the present volume have been adapted from previous publications (Peletz 1988b, 1993a, 1996, 1997) and are included here with the permission of the publishers.

A variety of institutions have contributed financial support to my research and writing. My early (1978–80) fieldwork and archival research in Malaysia were made possible by the National Science Foundation and the University of Michigan (the Center for South and Southeast Asian Studies and the Rackham School of Graduate Studies). The 1987–88 fieldwork was underwritten by a Fulbright Research Fellowship, a grant-in-aid from the Wenner-Gren Foundation for Anthropological Research, and a Picker Research Fellowship from Colgate University. Fellowships from the National Endowment for the Humanities and the Social Science Research Council enabled me to spend the 1991–92 academic year as a visiting scholar in the Department of Anthropology and the Program in Southeast Asian Studies at Cornell University, where I began preliminary analysis of some of the material presented here. The Southeast Asian Council of the Association for Asian Studies helped defray expenses of my 1998 trip to Malaysia, as did the Research Council of Colgate University. Funds from the Pacific Basin Research Center and Colgate University financed the January 2001 research in Kuala Lumpur.

Most of this book was written during a two-year research/sabbatical leave (1999–2001) supported by fellowships from the National Endowment for the Humanities, the National Humanities Center, the Pacific Basin Research Center, the Erasmus Institute at the University of Notre Dame, and the Research Council of Colgate University. I had the good fortune of spending the first year at the National Humanities Center (NHC), which offers its visiting fellows a great range of scholarly opportunities and experiences. For friendship and intellectual inspiration during the tenure of our NHC fellowships and throughout the twenty-odd years since we first began discussing anthropology at the University of Michigan, I am grateful to Sherry Ortner. Thanks also to the other members of the Late Modernity Study Group for deeply engaging conversation, and to Karen Carroll for expert typing and good cheer.

I spent the second year of my leave (2000–2001) as a senior fellow of the Erasmus Institute at the University of Notre Dame, which proved to be a wonderful environment in which to my pursue my scholarly interests. James Turner and Robert Sullivan, who run the institute with administrative expertise and good humor, deserve special thanks. The camaraderie and wit of Paul Kollman and Kristin Schwain added a great deal to my experience at Notre Dame, as did the memorable meals we shared. Those who participated in my faculty/graduate-student seminar on Islam, modernity, and civil society helped me formulate thoughts for this book; in this regard I am pleased to acknowledge Paul Kollman, Patrick Gaffney, and Asma Afsaruddin.

At Colgate University, Adrienne Ruffle and Kim Wolf proved to be research assistants extraordinaires, for whom I am most thankful. I am also grateful to Trudy King for help with the bibliography and other parts of the manuscript.

A number of friends and colleagues have read parts or all of the manuscript and offered their wisdom and advice. On this score I owe much to Barbara Watson Andaya, Bruce Lawrence, David Pinault, James Piscatori, Sharifah Zaleha Syed Hassan, Tan Beng Hui, and Richard Thompson. Donald Horowitz provided an especially close, incisive, and technically informed reading of the manuscript and encouraged me to rethink, clarify, or expand a good many passages, as did Robert Hefner, whose insights suffuse the book and have inspired me throughout my career. Susan Henry read an early version of the manuscript at a critical stage in the fall of 2000 and offered much needed perspective and many sensible suggestions; her support and assistance have been much appreciated.

At Princeton University Press, I am grateful to Mary Murrell for her initial interest in the project and her encouragement and help as the book moved toward publication. Sarah Green, Linny Schenck, Jennifer Backer, and other members of the editorial staff also lent their professional skills along the way to help make this a better book.

I dedicate the book to my children, Zachary and Alexander, who (like me) will be glad to see it completed so that we can spend more time together. I thank them for their patience and wonderful humor, and for the many ways they have enriched my life.

NOTE ON SPELLING, TERMINOLOGY, AND CURRENCY

THROUGHOUT THE TEXT I introduce various Malay terms, most of which I have spelled in accordance with the conventions of "standard Malay," as set out in Awang Sudjai Hairul and Yusoff Khan's *Kamus Lengkap*, 3RD ed., [1977] 2000. Such spelling conventions are not always followed in contemporary Malaysia; earlier practices still prevail in some cases, especially with regard to the rendering of places and honorifics, people's names and titles, and certain aspects of Islamic law and religion. Many Malay terms relevant to Islamic law and religion derive from Arabic, but in most instances I do not provide the Arabic origin or equivalent. When quoting historical, published, or official sources, I retain the original spelling, which is sometimes at variance with standard Malay. For example, *kadi* (Islamic judge or magistrate) sometimes appears in historical and contemporary sources as *kadzi, qadi*, and so on, just as *syariah* (Islamic law) is occasionally rendered as *syariat, shari'a, shari'ah, shariah*, etc. Since Malay nouns do not usually change for the plural, the term *kadi* can refer either to a single Islamic judge or to two or more such judges. Both in the Malay language and in this book the intended meaning is clear from the context of the discussion. Readers unfamiliar with the Malay language may find it useful to consult the glossary of frequently used Malay terms.

The Malaysian unit of currency is the *ringgit*. One *ringgit* (M$1) was worth approximately US $0.46 at the time of my 1978–80 fieldwork and US $0.39 during my 1987–88 fieldwork. Subsequent years witnessed extreme fluctuations in the value of the *ringgit*, which was pegged to the US dollar in fall 1997. From that time through this writing (October 2001) one *ringgit* has been worth approximately US $0.26.

INTRODUCTION

THIS BOOK WAS moving toward publication when the World Trade Center and the Pentagon were subject to the attacks of September 11, 2001, that resulted in the deaths of more than 3,000 civilians, damage to the American economy currently estimated to be at least in the hundreds of billions of dollars, and terrible losses and disruptions of other kinds that ramified throughout the nation and the world. In the hours, days, and weeks following these horrific tragedies, politicians as well as religious leaders and media figures in the United States consistently directed the attention of Americans and others to an extremist fringe group of Muslims (the Al Qaeda network) that understandably engages the imagination and emotions and thus makes for captivating copy. One of the many questions we must ask, however, is whether the images and symbols of Islam presented to us in connection with the awful events of September 11 are in any way representative of the sentiments, practices, or aspirations of the world's Muslim community in its entirety, which numbers over one billion people, or even a majority or numerically significant minority of Muslims in the world. It is well to bear in mind that Muslim (and other) leaders worldwide condemned the attacks as barbaric and unequivocally beyond the pale of Islam, as did large numbers of "ordinary Muslims" throughout the world. And many ordinary Muslims offered prayers, observed moments of silence, or held candlelight vigils for those who lost their lives or suffered other tragedy.[1] These reactions alone make clear that there is far more variability and diversity in the world's Muslim community than is suggested in most venues of contemporary American culture and that areas of common ground and precious opportunities for meaningful dialogue clearly exist.

For a variety of reasons it will not be easy for politicians in America and elsewhere to establish or maintain constructive dialogue of the sort necessary to help create a safer, saner, or more sustaining world. One reason for this, though certainly not the only one, is that the thrust and specifics of U.S. policies toward the Muslim world reflect not merely the understandings and agendas of sometimes well-informed national leaders and their advisors, but also pressures from congressional leaders and the American public, distressingly large numbers of whom are ill informed about and unabashedly hostile to Islam (Gerges 1999). It is no exaggeration to say that especially with the winding down of the cold war and the collapse of various socialist regimes in the former Soviet Union and elsewhere, the world's Muslim communities and their religious traditions have come to be defined in the minds of Americans and Westerners generally as *the* major threat to world order and security. This is obvious from the way Hollywood films represent Islam in its entirety as a transnationally conspiratorial menace to Western (especially Christian) bodies and minds and to all that they hold dear and sacred. Contemporary television, print media, and popular literature alike are also saturated with images depicting virtually *all*

Muslims as swarthy terrorist bombers, ragtag mountain-dwelling "soldiers of God," sclerotic bearded mullahs, dour albeit capricious jurists of the "hanging judge" variety, or veiled, cloistered women who are subject to compulsory genital mutilation, polygynous unions, and other patriarchal excesses and misogynist perversions. That said, imagery of this nature has a long established genealogy in modern European literature and elsewhere and is in certain respects nothing new (Southern 1962; Said 1978, 1993; Daniel 1993; Caton 1999). Such should be readily apparent from the ninth-century European view that "the rule of Islam was a preparation for the final appearance of Antichrist," coupled with the fact that in "a Crusading appeal of 1213, addressed to every part of Europe except Spain, [Pope] Innocent III expressly identifies Mahomet with the Beast of the Apocalypse."[2] The theme of Islam as the principal threat to world order and security is also evident from the "civilizational discourses" embedded in the contemporary writings of exceedingly high-profile public intellectuals and presidential advisors like Samuel Huntington (1996), who, much like the media and the culture at large, presumes a monolithic, eternally unchanging, and otherwise essentialized Islam that transcends both time and place.

Many myths pertaining to Islam have been debunked by scholars engaged in research on cultural and geopolitical areas beyond the gaze of conventional Orientalist studies, such as South and Southeast Asia, home to more than half of the world's Muslim population (see, for example, Bowen 1993; Eickelman and Piscatori 1996; Lawrence 1998; Hefner 2000). Needless to say, however, much work remains to be done. Indeed, one could plausibly argue that some of the recent scholarship on Islam in Southeast Asia has inadvertently contributed to an essentialization of Islam that is in some ways similar to what one finds in American culture and the West at large. This argument is not as far-fetched or as ungenerous as it sounds, especially when one stops to consider the outpouring of scholarly interest in movements that involve what is variously referred to as the "resurgence" or "revitalization" of Islam (for example, Peacock 1978; T. J. S. George 1980; Nagata 1984; Madale 1986; Husin Mutalib 1990; Abaza 1991; Evers and Siddique 1991; Nash 1984, 1991; cf. Fischer 1980; Ali Hillal Dessouki 1982; Bakhash 1984; Munson 1988; Hiro 1989). It is generally well known that these movements entail resistance of various kinds and, no less important, that studies of resistance have captured the scholarly imagination to the point where they have become a major academic industry. What is not sufficiently emphasized in the flurry of recent scholarship is the fact that those involved in movements of the sort at issue here typically make up a small minority of the population of the countries in which they exist. One consequence of this critical oversight is that we are left with the erroneous impression that the entire Muslim population of Southeast Asia is centrally involved in the resurgence, or at least squarely behind it. More generally, the literature provides little sense of the range of variation as regards what it means to be a Muslim in present-day Southeast Asia and for the most part does not address the comparative or theoretical implications of such variation.[3]

These latter comments are particularly true of the literature on Malaysia. A good deal of scholarly attention has been devoted to Malaysia's Islamic resurgence and state-sponsored efforts to promote or reactualize Islam (see, for example, Kessler 1980; Muhammad Abu Bakar 1981, 1987; Shamsul A. B. 1983, 1997; Nagata 1984; Milner 1986; Chandra Muzaffar 1987; Zainah Anwar 1987; Banks 1990; Nash 1991; Jomo K. S. and Ahmad Shabery Cheek 1992; Husin Mutalib 1993; Sharifah Zaleha Syed Hassan 2000). To date, however, scholars have largely neglected to consider how the resurgence, along with state initiatives to bolster Islam, have affected Malaysia's Muslim population as a whole. Similarly, scholars have focused relatively little attention on the culture, operations, and overall political economy of Malaysia's Islamic legal system.[4] This is especially surprising and regrettable for two related reasons. First, Malaysia's Islamic courts are critical sites in the creation and policing of new Malay-Muslim families and subjectivities that state policies have singled out as the basis for a modern-day citizenry and national polity that will hopefully be competitive—economically and otherwise—both in Southeast Asia and globally. Second, the Islamic courts are key sites in struggles involving ethnic and religious groups, social classes, political parties, and many others with a major stake in defining the role of Islam with respect to the maintenance of sovereignty and the achievement of modernity and civil society in an age of ever-increasing globalization.

In the latter connection I should perhaps be more explicit. An important reason to conduct research on institutions such as Islamic courts that are both highly localized and simultaneously implicated in the global circulation of legal and other discourses is that such research can help ground by instantiation and ideally advance the oftentimes highly abstract discussions and debates that have developed in recent years on various aspects of Islam and modernity, globalization, sovereignty, and "Asian values." Some of the current anthropological writing on these topics is highly provocative and insightful and in some respects brilliant. In another context[5] I have used such language to describe Aihwa Ong's *Flexible Citizenship: The Cultural Logics of Transnationality* (1999), which, as Ashraf Ghani notes on the book's back cover, is "remarkable in its theoretical . . . breadth . . . and for its redefinition of analytic terrain and . . . new directions of research." But I also have to acknowledge that as an anthropologist, I am at times frustrated by *Flexible Citizenship* in much the same way that I am occasionally frustrated by the scholarship of Arjun Appadurai (1996). I say this because their great strengths notwithstanding, such works sometimes err on the side of being "ethnographically thin" when it comes to doing one of the most valuable things that anthropologists are ideally suited to do. I refer here to our capacity to provide "thickly descriptive" accounts of the interpenetration of local, regional, national, and global dynamics—of the ways that different schemes of Islamic modernity, "Asian values," and "good governance," for example, are played out in local and contingent arenas "on the ground."

This book provides "thickly descriptive" accounts of the culture and political economy of Malaysia's Islamic courts and various developments bearing on Islam in Malaysia since the late 1970s. It analyzes the ways Islamic magistrates, religious leaders, public intellectuals, and other strategically situated social actors incorporate, put into practice, and at times effectively subvert state policies and directives concerning Islamic law and other aspects of Islam. It also examines the framing and unfolding of different types of disputes (variably cast in local, nationalist, and/or transnational discourse); the cultural logic of judicial discretion; the creation of new legal orders; the history and politics of rationalization in both the institutional and cultural senses of the term; and the ways that these and other phenomena contribute to—or, alternatively, undermine—the achievement of modernity and civil society in an age of ever-increasing globalization.

This study owes a great deal to the interpretive anthropology of law developed by Clifford Geertz (1983a), Lawrence Rosen (1980–81, 1989a, 1989b), and others who have been concerned with law primarily as a system of symbols and meanings. I also build on traditions of political and legal anthropology, cultural studies, subaltern studies, and feminist scholarship that view law as both a resource and a constraint that figures into the elaboration of discourses in a multitude of paradoxical, contradictory, and unintended ways (for example, Bourdieu 1977, 1984; Foucault 1977, 1978, 1980; Comaroff and Roberts 1981; Scott 1985, 1990, 1998; Chakrabarty 1988; Starr and Collier 1989; Conley and O'Barr 1990; Merry 1990; Lazarus-Black and Hirsch 1994; Hirsch 1998; Dirks, Eley, and Ortner 1994; Guha 1994; Eickelman and Piscatori 1996). I emphasize the importance of incorporating analyses of transnational events and processes into my study, and of attending to religious and secular courts as key sites in the reproduction and transformation of symbols and meanings of nationhood and cultural citizenship as well as mutually determined identities framed in the symbols and idioms of kinship/gender, race, and class. As such, I devote special attention to the processes by which litigants, legal experts, and others attempt to construct persuasive narratives and otherwise use the law not only in the creation, distribution, and transmission of knowledge, power, and meaning but also in their efforts to bring about cultural cleansing, alternative forms of kinship/gender, sexuality, and sociality, and new societies as a whole. I also bring into focus the variable ways in which groups of Muslims deal with social differentiation, religious division, and ideological diversity, including relations with non-Muslims and tensions between the sensibilities of national and transnational elites on the one hand and those associated with "ordinary Muslims" (and/or national popular culture) on the other. This involves analyses of dispute management and conflict resolution; the cultural logic of judicial process; the role of law in reproducing and transforming systems of inequality associated with kinship/gender, race, and class; and the options available to people when the courts and other legal institutions that have jurisdiction over them fail to protect their rights and interests.

More generally, I seek to enhance our understanding of Islam, law, and cultural politics in two ways. First, I provide ethnographic, historical, cross-cultural, and transnational perspectives on recent developments in Islam and laws concerning Islam in the rapidly shifting landscapes of a strategically important region of the contemporary Muslim world. Second, I attend to the ways in which the contestations over symbols and meanings in Malaysia and other societies are informed by and in turn inform patterns of political and economic relations among the various groups and classes making up such societies—in short, what I have elsewhere referred to as "the political economy of contested symbols and meanings" (Peletz 1996).

Concerning the first of these general objectives I would emphasize that the Malaysian case is of much greater significance than the country's territorial expanse (329,573 square kilometers) and demographic girth (approximately 23,263,600 million people) might suggest at first glance.[6] One reason for this is that Malaysia is among the most prosperous of the "non-Confucian" Asian tigers and has also sustained a pace of rapid development that is probably second to none in the Muslim world. Another is that Malaysian Prime Minister Mahathir Mohamad, far more than any of his predecessors, has successfully projected both the Malaysian case and his particular ideas on political-economic modernization as an emulable model for other regions of the world; he has frequently claimed, for example, that the Malaysian model is a viable, indeed, preferred alternative to Western-style development in other Muslim-majority nations and in much of the southern hemisphere as a whole. Such claims have been well received in many quarters, both at home and abroad. Very much related to the warm reception accorded them, and to my assertion that the Malaysian case is of deep, broadly generalizable significance, is that in the course of a mere generation or so Malaysia has catapulted itself into the slender ranks of Muslim countries with appreciable middle classes and burgeoning if still precarious civil societies. Circumstances such as these help explain why Malaysia has become a locus of nationalist, transnational, and academic discourses concerning "Muslim modernities," "Asian modernities," and "alternative modernities" generally (see, for example, Ong and Nonini 1997; Ong 1999a; see also Eickelman and Piscatori 1996; Rofel 1999; Englund and Leach 2000; Hefner 2000).

Of further relevance here is that many of the diverse organizations associated with Malaysia's Islamic resurgence (the *dakwah* movement) are embroiled in struggles with different groups of national elites concerning the role, scope, and force of Islam in Malaysia's modernity project. So, too, is the main Islamic opposition party (PAS), which, like certain *dakwah* groups, seeks the imposition throughout the land of Islamic law and the creation of an Islamic state. Also centrally involved or at least directly implicated in such struggles are activist-oriented Muslim feminists (such as Sisters in Islam), many of whom reject PAS–style Islamization as misguided; and "ordinary Muslims" (or "ordinary Malays"; the two terms are used here interchangeably) who are not in the forefront of contemporary religious or political developments but are among the more enduring targets of resurgents' efforts at cultural cleansing. Ordinary Muslims make up the majority of the Muslim population and are clearly most directly affected by the changes in procedural and substantive law that have occurred or are sought in the Islamic courts. The more germane points to note for present purposes are the pluralistic nature of Malaysian Islam and the unsettled and highly contested nature of the Islamic courts and their role in modernity in contemporary Malaysia.

BACKGROUND AND CONTEXT

Travel brochures and academic treatises frequently describe Malaysia as "the crossroads of Asia." This is partly because of Malaysia's strategic location along the waterways that have long facilitated the flow of people, ideas, and goods among China, India, the Middle East, and points far beyond (see map 1). Another (related) reason has to do with the rich cultural diversity of the various ethnic groups living in Malaysia. The ethnic mosaic is usually discussed in terms of four major categories. "Malays," all of whom are Muslims, constitute 50.8 percent of the total population; "Chinese," who are usually described as practicing a syncretic blend of Buddhism, Confucianism, and Taoism, make up 26.3 percent; "Indians," most of whom are Hindus (though some are Sikhs, others Christian), account for about 7.4 percent; and "Others," including hill-dwelling aborigines following animist traditions, Eurasians, etc., make up the remaining 15.5 percent.[7] The legal system is frequently glossed as pluralistic to highlight the diversity and variegated provenance of its three major traditions of law (*hukum*): Malay customary law (*hukum adat*), which pertains to Malays; Islamic law (*hukum syariah*), which is relevant to Malays and all other Muslims[8] albeit to a limited range of their affairs; and third, national (statutory) law, sometimes referred to as government law (*hukum kerajaan*), introduced by British colonists in the nineteenth century, which bears on all citizens and others in Malaysia. Malaysia's political institutions include a system of parliamentary democracy and a constitutional monarchy, much like the British system on which it is modeled. They also include an indigenous (Malay) polity of precolonial origin, which has been stripped of most of its power but is nonetheless formally intact.

All Malays speak the Malay language, identify themselves as Sunni Muslims who adhere to the Shafi'i legal school of Islam, and order various aspects of their social relations in accordance with a body of social and cultural codes glossed *adat*. English translations of the term *adat* have included "tradition," "custom," and "customary law," but none of these or any others that come to mind adequately convey the cultural meanings, moral force, or social relevance of *adat* as a unifying, broadly hegemonic construct. Suffice it to say that the concept of *adat* refers to "something half-way between 'social consensus and moral style'" (Geertz 1983a: 185), is a core or key symbol in many areas of Malay society and culture, and has ethnographic analogs in the Chinese notion of Dao and the aboriginal Australian notion of the Dreamtime.

The concept of *adat* symbolizes important similarities among all Malays, but it also highlights some significant contrasts, for there are two major variants of *adat* in the Malay Peninsula (also known as West Malaysia; see map 2), which

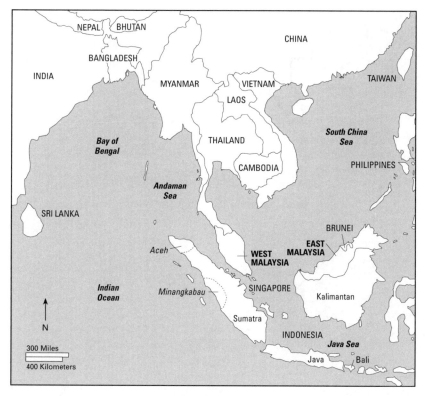

Map 1. Malaysia and Surrounding Regions

is where most Malays live. The first, referred to as *adat perpatih*, is found primarily among Malays in the state of Negeri Sembilan, the Naning district of Melaka, and a few other enclaves scattered about the Peninsula. It is associated with a social organization usually characterized as matrilineal as it includes descent units of matrilineal design, which reflect the Minangkabau (West Sumatran) ancestry of the area's earliest permanent settlers. The second, known as *adat temenggung*, prevails among Malays living in most other regions of the Peninsula and is linked with a social structure usually referred to as bilateral (or cognatic).[9]

One of the most frequently encountered truisms in the literature on the region is that ethnic distinctions and antagonisms in Malaysia are infused with far-reaching religious, political, and economic significance and have been exacerbated by development strategies of the postcolonial government. This is most evident with the New Economic Policy (NEP) implemented in 1971, which sought to eradicate poverty among all Malaysians and to "restructure society" by undermining the material and symbolic connections between ethnic categories on the one hand and economic standing and function on the other. By aiming its policies at enabling the predominantly rural and agricultural Malays

Map 2. The States of West Malaysia

to "catch up" economically with Chinese and Indians, the government has placed tremendous emphasis on "race" (on being a Malay or a non-Malay) as a criterion in allocating government loans and subsidies and other scarce resources (university scholarships, contractor's licenses, start-up funds for businesses, and so forth). These policies have heightened the awareness of distinctions between Malays and non-Malays and made them all the more politically and economically salient.

The NEP has also exacerbated class antagonisms within the Malay community. Although its policies have helped create a Malay middle class and have enriched some Malays substantially, those policies have left other Malays no better and in some cases much worse off than before. Reactions to the NEP have taken many forms, including active and passive resistance to the Green Revolution implemented as a key feature of the NEP in many areas and disaffection from the central clique of the ruling political party and from the party in its entirety (Kessler 1980; Scott 1985; Shamsul A. B. 1986).

Dissatisfaction with the government's commitment to modernity and with the NEP in particular has further significance because it is among the many factors fueling Malaysia's Islamic resurgence, known as the *dakwah* movement. The term *dakwah* means to invite or call one to the Islamic cause, or to respond to the invitation or call (see Nagata 1984; Shamsul A. B. 1997), hence missionary work, including making Muslims better Muslims. The resurgence is usually said to date from the late 1960s or early 1970s, even though it is most appropriately viewed as an outgrowth of earlier developments in Islamic nationalism and reform, such as those associated with the Kaum Muda (Young Group) movement of the 1920s and 1930s (Roff 1967). The Kaum Muda movement was thoroughly homegrown, but it was animated and sustained in part by the activities and organizations of Muslims in Indonesia, Singapore, and elsewhere. The same is true of *dakwah*, which has been inspired in part by Islamist groups and Islamic revivalism in Indonesia, Pakistan, Egypt, Libya, and other parts of the Muslim world.

Most scholars approach the resurgence as a response, indeed, a form of resistance, to one or more of the following analytically related and culturally interlocked sets of developments. The first development concerns the postcolonial state's Western-oriented modernization policies (noted above), which entail a heavily interventionist role for the state with respect to economic planning, distribution, and capitalist processes as a whole. These policies are widely seen as contributing to Malaysia's overdependence on foreign (particularly Western) capital; to the economic success of Chinese and Indians relative to Malays; and to upper-class corruption as well as deracination and moral and spiritual bankruptcy throughout the Malay community. The second development involves the simultaneous shifting and hardening of class interests and animosities, especially between the newly emerged middle class and an entrenched (aristocratic) ruling class. The third development is the tightening of ethnic boundaries, particularly those separating Malays and Chinese. These boundaries have become increasingly salient in recent decades, owing in no small measure to NEP–era (1971–90) practices highlighting race in the allocation of scarce and highly prized government resources. The NEP is commonly regarded as having encouraged a certain cultural assertiveness—some would say chauvinism—among Malays (Chandra Muzaffar 1987; Zainah Anwar 1987). This cultural assertiveness is especially pronounced as regards Islam, the practice of which, along with speaking the Malay language and observing Malay "custom" (*adat*), is a defining feature and increasingly *the* key symbol of Malayness. More broadly, whatever else the *dakwah* movement is, scholars generally view it as a powerful vehicle for the articulation of moral opposition to government development policies, traditional as well as emergent class structures, other ethnic groups, or some combination of these or related phenomena (see Kessler 1980; Nagata 1984; Milner 1986; Chandra Muzaffar 1987; Zainah Anwar 1987; Muhammad Abu Bakar 1987; Husin Mutalib 1993).

Dakwah organizations are highly diverse and their objectives are in certain respects mutually incompatible. However, they all share an overriding concern to revitalize or reactualize (local) Islam and the (local) Muslim community by encouraging stronger commitment to the teachings of the Quran and the *hadith* to effect a more Islamic way of life (*din*). The main organizations have included the following: Darul Arqam, a communal, land-based organization that enjoined its members to emulate the life of the Prophet and that strove for economic self-sufficiency (it was banned by the government in 1994); ABIM (Angkatan Belia Islam Malaysia, the Malaysian Islamic Youth Organization), which emphasizes formal education and is extremely popular among university students, former student leaders, and youth generally, and encourages lobbying efforts, active participation in party politics, and otherwise "working within the system," though it is also suspected by the government of "socialist leanings" (Kessler 1980: 9); and PERKIM (Pertubuhan Kebajikan Islam Malaysia, the Malaysian Islamic Welfare and Missionary Association), a moderate if not conservative charitable organization sponsored by the government geared toward assisting recent converts to Islam.

Also worthy of mention here is PAS (Parti Islam Se-Malaysia, the Pan-Malayan Islamic Party), the major (Malay) opposition party, which has a decidedly populist orientation and has been a key player in Malaysian politics since shortly after its formation in the early 1950s (Kessler 1978; Safie bin Ibrahim 1981; Firdaus Haji Abdullah 1985). Strictly speaking, PAS is not part of the *dakwah* movement, though many of its objectives are espoused by some segments of the movement. The most basic of these objectives is the creation of an Islamic state with the Quran and the *sunnah* as its constitution.

The relationships between the various segments of the movement and the state merit careful consideration, for they have fueled many of the political and religious dynamics characteristic of contemporary Malaysia. As far as most scholars are concerned, Darul Arqam and PERKIM have never posed appreciable threats to the state (the government ban on Darul Arqam in 1994 notwithstanding). But ABIM and PAS clearly have, particularly since their leaders have on numerous occasions publicly charged that the ruling party (UMNO, the United Malays National Organization) has failed to safeguard the interests and well-being of the Malay community, especially with regard to Islam. PAS in particular has also claimed that the ruling party has sold out to local Chinese and Indians, as well as foreign capitalists, all of whom are said to have contributed both to Malaysia's underdevelopment and ongoing dependence on foreign markets and to its decadence and spiritual bankruptcy.

In such a religious and political climate the ruling party has to work overtime to validate its Islamic credentials—relegitimize the party and the state—and thus co-opt, or at least undercut, both the Islamic resurgents and the opposition party. This means going forward with its own far-reaching but ultimately rather moderate Islamization program, which is simultaneously both a consequence of the *dakwah* phenomenon and a key factor in its promotion along certain lines. This program to "out-Islamicize" the opposition, which does at times have those qualities of an arms race that Gregory Bateson (1936), in a very different context, referred to as "schismogenesis," has included: the creation of an international Islamic university, an Islamic research center, and a nationwide system of Islamic banking and insurance; the sponsoring of a plethora of Islamic seminars and conferences; the building and refurbishing of prayer houses and mosques; and last but not least, the passage of myriad legislative measures bearing on Islam and Islamic law specifically. Broadly speaking, these moves have succeeded in undercutting PAS and ABIM and in retaining the support of urban middle-class Malays who constitute the segment of the population most responsive to *dakwah* appeals. But they have also seriously alienated non-Malays, who make up nearly half of Malaysia's multiethnic population, and they have intensified ethnic antagonism. Indeed, Chinese and Indians see the Islamic resurgence as an overtly political movement with strong xenophobic overtones bent on eroding the rights and privileges of non-Muslims and subjecting them to the dictates of Islam. More important, these measures have also clearly alienated significant numbers of ordinary, especially rural, Malays, who perceive them as direct attacks on their basic values and key features of their cultural identities.

These, then, are some of the dynamics that inform the roles and operations of the Islamic courts as well as the ways they are viewed by different segments of the Malaysian population. Needless to say, many of these same dynamics informed my research experiences in the field.

METHODS

Since the late 1970s I have conducted approximately two and a half years of fieldwork and archival research in Malaysia; I have also spent about six weeks studying archival collections from the colonial era that are housed in British institutions in London and its environs (the Public Records Office, the British Museum, the School of Oriental and African Studies, etc.). Almost all of the fieldwork and archival study in Malaysia was carried out in the Malay language (*bahasa Melayu*, also referred to as "Malaysian" [*bahasa Malaysia*]), which I studied at various universities in the United States before going to the field. Much of the early research focused on Malays residing in the state of Negeri Sembilan, located in West Malaysia. The first period of research involved twenty months of fieldwork and archival study from 1978 to 1980; it concerned patterns and dynamics of social organization from 1830 to 1980 and focused on the transformation of kinship and property relations in the face of British colonialism (1874–1957), modern market forces, and Islamic nationalism and reform.

In the years following my initial research, I completed a book[10] and a number of articles on kinship, property, and social history in Negeri Sembilan, with particular emphasis on the district of Rembau.[11] In preparing both the book and the articles, I realized the value of broadening my perspectives by conducting additional research on topics that I had initially and, in retrospect, mistakenly viewed as more or less separate and distinct from the domains of kinship and social structure. I realized, for example, that I knew a fair amount about gender roles and the autonomy of women but that I had a relatively limited understanding of "underlying" issues, such as the way Malays in Negeri Sembilan and other parts of the Peninsula represent or "construct" not only similarities and differences between males and females, but also gender inequality and domination. I also recognized that I needed to gain a better understanding of meaning and experience, of the ways constructions of gender varied according to context and situation, and of the political economy of contested symbols and meanings. Similarly, though I was fairly knowledgeable about continuity and change in norms and laws concerning property relations, marriage, divorce, and related matters, I did not know much about the ways individual litigants and legal specialists deal with property and inheritance issues and various types of disputes in the local Islamic courts and in Malaysia's pluralistic legal system as a whole. Nor was I familiar with the cultural logic of judicial process or the ways the state uses the courts to effect social control and sociocultural change.

I subsequently designed a program of research concerning legal procedures, especially the handling of disputes within the Islamic legal system. The proposed research would enable me to collect data both on the relevant legal and political issues and on topics of gender, since the Islamic courts are one of the principal arenas in which gender differences and inequalities are institutionalized and given formal, state-sanctioned backing. I took a leave of absence from Colgate University during the 1987–88 academic year to conduct field research on this project. The research, which extended over a period of nine months, was carried out mostly in the Rembau district of Negeri Sembilan, though I also spent some of my time in the neighboring, predominantly urban district of Seremban, which includes the state capital of the same name, and in Kuala Lumpur, the federal capital, to acquire a broader perspective. In conducting this research I was struck both by the ways in which court officials and litigants alike invoked contrasting representations of gender (and kinship) in their interpretations of the cases in which they were involved, and by the deeply perspectival nature of cultural knowledge. Since an understanding of these latter issues is a prerequisite for a proper analysis of the cultural logic of judicial process, I decided to write up the material on gender before embarking on a separate monograph on the Islamic courts.[12]

Elsewhere I have provided detailed descriptions of the research methods employed during the two major periods of fieldwork that I have undertaken (Peletz 1988b, 1996). The latter book in particular provides a chapter-length discussion of participant observation with respect to most ritual, religious, political, economic, and other domains of village life; the survey data I collected from each household in the village (concerning, for example, household composition, property ownership, sources of income, and the numbers of marriages and divorces of all ever-married individuals); the land and other archival records I studied in various district offices; my experiences in the village in which I resided throughout much of the fieldwork (including my informal adoption by the village headman, his wife, and her lineage branch; and how villagers and others reacted to me in different ways in accordance with changes in my life course [moving from bachelorhood, to newlywed, to parent]); and various other issues bearing on "how I know what I know."

In light of the foregoing and since I discuss some of the relevant issues at various points below, I will simply add here that during the second period of research I spent much of my time at the office of the Islamic magistrate in Rembau, sitting in on hearings, discussing the details of cases with the Islamic magistrate and members of his staff, and studying marriage, divorce, and other court records going back to the early 1960s. Most of these cases concerned civil matters relating to marriage and divorce (such as men's failure to support their wives and children), though I encountered some criminal cases as well. I also attended court hearings at the District Office, which handles matters of inheritance and other types of property transactions. Finally, I attended hearings at the (secular) Magistrate's Court, which deals with most civil and criminal offenses (traffic violations, theft, assault, and the like), in accordance with the specifications of national (statutory) law.

By sitting in on formal court sessions and on the informal processes of mediation, especially those run by the Islamic magistrate and his staff, I was able to acquire important insights into Malaysia's legal system and other issues on which I sought additional information. These activities proved especially helpful in shedding light on conflict and contradiction both in marriages and other types of relationships and in terms of gender relations more generally. The courts, after all, are one of the few contexts in which Malays are inclined to air their grievances openly and directly. Though procedures for doing so are in theory laid out in *adat*, these are not the quiet, consensus-oriented affairs about which Geertz (1983a) has written in his discussions of legal sensibilities in the Malay-Indonesian world. I was repeatedly struck by the strident nature of some of these disagreements, having been conditioned by the rounds of village life, where restricted speech codes are "pressed into service to affirm the social order" (Douglas 1970: 22), to view Malays as rather averse to conflict and litigation.

One of my objectives in sitting in on court hearings and counseling sessions was to try to determine the extent to which the cultural understandings that Islamic magistrates and their staff bring to bear on the disputes that come before them are comparable to those of the disputants themselves. I was especially interested in ascertaining whether court officials' notions of equity, justice, and due process, as well as their notions of personhood and gender, were similar to or at variance with those of villagers who appear before the court. I also wanted to find out if court officials' understandings of the dynamics and tensions of marriage and of the patterns and causes of divorce corresponded with villagers' understandings of these phenomena. Finally, I wanted to see if men and women used and experienced law and legal knowledge—as both a resource and a constraint—in broadly similar or different ways.

Information on marriage, divorce, and gender that I obtained from the study of court sessions and records of past cases was supplemented by data collected in the course of a household survey conducted by my research assistant—a twenty-five-year-old man who had helped me during my previous study—at all of Bogang's houses (which numbered 115 in 1987). This survey was intended to update the similar survey I conducted in 1979 and thus covered many of the topics dealt with in the earlier survey, though it was far more focused. One of the advantages of having my research assistant conduct the time-consuming survey is that it allowed me to spend my time on other tasks. One of the disadvantages is that much of the information my assistant collected but may not have written down due to his viewing it as irrelevant was lost. Another, less concrete disadvantage is that it reduced my social field in ways that probably offended villagers whose houses I never visited during the second period of research.

Data acquired from observation of court sessions and from discussions with the judge and his staff concerning the hearings and the written records relevant to them were also supplemented by open-ended interviews on gender and kinship (including marriage and divorce) that I conducted with twenty individuals (ten men, ten women), mostly from Bogang. Since I have analyzed these interviews elsewhere (Peletz 1996: chap. 6), it should suffice here to note three points. First, the interviews illustrate that villagers do not necessarily speak in a single voice when it comes to gender or kinship/marriage (or anything else). Second, they reveal the ways in which understandings and representations of gender are informed by understandings and representations of kinship (including marriage and divorce), and vice versa. And third, they demonstrate that women's experiences with their husbands—and in marriage and divorce in particular—are of central importance not only in the ways they think about husbands and marriage in general but also in their feelings, attitudes, and representations concerning men and masculinity as a whole. In short, as with women and femininity, men and masculinity are defined in relational terms. This has important implications in societies with high rates of divorce (or abandonment), especially when divorce (and abandonment) tend to be attributed to male faults. Perhaps most relevant is that this situation poses potentially serious challenges both to ideologies of male supremacy and to the various institutions (Islamic courts, secular political hierarchies) in which that supremacy is instantiated and enshrined.

Much of the material contained in this book derives from the two periods of research noted above. But I also draw in important ways on the brief trips I made to Malaysia in 1993, 1998, and 2001, during which time I resided primarily in Kuala Lumpur. These trips helped familiarize me with political, legal, religious, and other developments that had occurred since the completion of my second period of fieldwork in 1988. The (late May) 1998 visit was especially valuable insofar as it afforded me the opportunity to interview not only the judge who presides over the Islamic legal system of the Federal Territory of Kuala Lumpur (and others associated with the Islamic courts) but also scholarly administrators and other officials in the employ of government-sponsored Islamic think tanks (such as IKIM) as well as members of local human rights groups and Muslim feminist organizations (like Sisters in Islam).[13] These experts, along with journalists and others with whom I exchanged ideas, provided highly pertinent information on recent developments bearing on women's sexual and other rights (and the rights of various ethnic and other minorities) and, more generally, on religious and legal culture, civil society, and the body politic as a whole.

This trip also enabled me to acquire a firsthand albeit highly partial sense of the local-level impact of the Asian financial crisis that began in Thailand in July 1997 and quickly spread throughout the region (and beyond). In Malaysia, this crisis dealt a devastating blow to currency trade, the stock market, the banking industry, and other aspects of the local economy (the prices of many consumer goods skyrocketed, and large numbers of immigrant workers were abruptly deported). But the dislocations in an otherwise booming and prosperous economic climate struck me as comparatively mild since I had just come from a two-week tour of desperately poor Vietnam, where living standards and per capita incomes are but a fraction of those in Malaysia. Also relevant is that the dislocations that occurred in Malaysia were extremely mild compared to the widespread devastation that occurred in Thailand and Indonesia. Indonesia, for example, had just experienced the tumultuous downfall of President Suharto and seemed on the brink of complete political and economic collapse. What was not at all clear to me (or to most anyone else) at the time was that within a few short months Malaysia would be in the midst of its own devastating political turmoil—arguably the most severe since the Second World War. The latter turmoil is generally viewed as at least an indirect result of the economic chaos and political tensions engendered by the financial crisis; it was in any case precipitated by Prime Minister Mahathir Mohamad's jailing of his heir apparent, Deputy Prime Minister and Minister of Finance Anwar Ibrahim, on charges of sodomy, corruption, and bribery.

The research I undertook in Kuala Lumpur in January 2001 was in many ways a continuation of my earlier work there and elsewhere in Malaysia. During this time I interviewed lawyers, journalists, activists, artists, academics, and other professionals, as well as staff of organizations involved in various types of community service and outreach programs geared toward meeting the needs of the transgendered community and those at risk for HIV/AIDS. One of my objectives was to see how such communities had fared during the protracted Anwar trial and in recent years generally. Others involved gaining a better sense of contemporary legal and political developments and enhancing my understanding of Malaysian views and experiences of the Asian financial crisis and the dynamics of sovereignty in an age of globalization.

What follows, then, is an example of what George Marcus (1995) has referred to as "multi-sited ethnography," though not simply because it incorporates findings from ethnographic research carried out in various parts of Negeri Sembilan on the one hand and Kuala Lumpur on the other. It is also multisited in the sense that I draw on research carried out in connection with my role as an "expert witness" in four cases that involved Malaysians residing in the United States. The first was a child-custody case heard in Los Angeles in 1993. The other three involved Malaysians who self-identified as homosexuals (one gay man, two lesbian women; all three Chinese) and were seeking political asylum in this country on the grounds that if they returned to Malaysia they would face persecution by virtue of their sexual orientations and "lifestyles" or, in the relevant legal terminology, by virtue of their "membership in a particular social group," such as that of homosexual, "subject to persecution" in their home country. These cases were heard in New York and Boston in 1999 and 2000. (All three were found in favor of the Malaysians.) More relevant for present purposes is that I learned a great deal about Malaysian and American variants of gender, sexuality, law, and "Asian values" in the course of reviewing the multitudes of documents submitted for these cases, in talking and corresponding with both the Malaysians and others involved (lawyers, judges, domestic partners, etc.), and in conducting the library and other research necessary to provide affidavits, depositions, and other relevant information. I do not discuss these specific cases in the present volume. But the findings of the research that I conducted for these and similar (pending) cases—concerning recent political, legal, and other developments in Malaysia bearing on gender, sexuality, and homosexuality in particular (including Anwar's arrest and pilloring on charges of sodomy)—are central to chapter 5 and to the volume as a whole.

As for the organization and narrative flow of this work, the book is composed of two parts. Part 1 deals with the culture, political economy, and history of the Islamic courts and consists of three chapters. Chapter 1 establishes some of the groundwork necessary to provide a historical genealogy of Islamic magistrates and their courts in the Malay world and Southeast Asia generally since the 1400s. This entails clearing away various myths enshrined in Western scholarship—past and present—many of which stem from the religious and other cultural biases and civilizing agendas of British imperial observers. Although numerous questions remain unanswered, one of my basic arguments is that we need to distinguish among Islamic laws, Islamic magistrates, and Islamic courts throughout the period in question; failure to do so leads to confusion and distortion. The references to Islamic laws that exist in fifteenth-century texts such as the Laws of Melaka (*Undang-Undang Melaka*), for example, should not be taken as evidence that such laws were widely known let alone systematically enforced in Melaka and its environs or throughout the Peninsula. Nor does the mere existence of individuals bearing the title of *kadi* (Islamic magistrate) necessarily mean that there were Islamic judges or officials of any sort who presided over formal courts or advised political leaders as to the proper implementation of Islamic law. Building on but also departing in significant ways from the pioneering historical work of Anthony Reid (1988, 1993), I also argue that data from Aceh, northern Sumatra (present-day Indonesia), bearing on crime and punishment during the seventeenth century are not representative of Indonesia, Malaysia, or Southeast Asia as a whole before, during, or after that century.

In this connection I also advance three interrelated arguments. First, there is much more to justice and law than crime and punishment. Second, if we endeavor to understand how people manage disputes and resolve conflicts (the two are not quite the same), we need to recall that in virtually all societies in which formal adjudication is an option, people tend to prefer to deal with disputes and conflicts by "lumping it," "exiting" (or avoidance), negotiation, mediation, and/or arbitration, rather than by pursuing the more formal, costly, and punitive processes of adjudication (see Nader and Todd 1978). And third, in the case of Islamic areas of Southeast Asia, even when formal adjudication was sought out or did occur, it did not necessarily involve the draconian physical sanctions (amputation, capital punishment) that so mesmerized British and other European observers in the nineteenth century and before who were, in any event, given to comparing their own lofty judicial *ideals* with Malay *practice* (rather than, say, British judicial ideals and Malay judicial ideals, or British judicial practice and Malay judicial practice). That said, such comparisons are of considerable significance inasmuch as they informed the colonial-era reorganization and rationalization of the Islamic courts which began in the 1890s and has continued through to the present, as this chapter also discusses.

In this chapter and elsewhere in the volume I am particularly interested in "rationalization," a concept of central importance in much of Max Weber's work on comparative history and politics and the sociology of religion. Like Weberian interpretive social science generally, the concept of rationalization has a subsequent genealogy that bears careful examination. Weber employs the term to refer both to institutional changes involving differentiation, specialization, and the development of hierarchical, bureaucratic forms of social organization and to intellectual or attitudinal trends entailing, in negative terms, "the disenchantment of the world" (the displacement of "magical elements of thought"), and, in positive terms, processes by which "ideas gain in systematic coherence and naturalistic consistency" (Gerth and Mills 1958: 51; Wrong 1970: 26; Turner 1974: 151–56; Schluchter 1979: 14–15; Alexander 1989: 74). Many of Weber's ideas on rationalization were introduced into the English-speaking social science community by Talcott Parsons, who was Clifford Geertz's mentor, as well as the source and filter through which Geertz developed not only Weber's ideas on rationalization (see, for example, Geertz [1964] 1973b) but also his highly influential variant of interpretive anthropology (Geertz 1973b; 1983b; see also Ortner 1999). Geertz focuses on rationalization as processes of cultural—especially religious—change that entail a standardization, systematization, and more self-conscious sense of doctrine, belief, and/or ritual. More precisely, for Geertz, rationalization involves a rethinking and reconfiguring of key symbols and their meanings so as to better accommodate them to one another and to changing social and cultural realities; and institutional or social organizational changes that help motivate, buttress, or sustain this rethinking/ reconfiguring. Geertz concentrates on the first set of entailments and, unlike Weber, is in many ways (analytically, for example) relatively unconcerned with the second.

In this and subsequent chapters I build on Geertz's insights, but I devote more attention to the institutional contexts and stimuli of rationalization that were of such importance to Weber in light of his concern to develop the foundations for a comparative historical sociology of domination. It will be clear as well that my approach to religion and law differs from that of Geertz and those who have developed Geertzian paradigms (for example, Rosen 1980–81, 1989a, 1989b)—and is in some ways more similar to that of Weber—in at least three ways: I accord political variables a very specific and determinate role in shaping the direction and content of cultural change and of religious (and legal) rationalization in particular; I attend to the darker, apocalyptic side of rationalization and of modernity in general; and I devote greater attention to the political economy and cultural psychology of ambivalence, which, following Andrew Weigert (1991: 21), I define as "the experience of [co-mingled] contradictory emotions toward the same object."

Chapter 2 addresses the roles, jurisdictions, and operations of Malaysia's Islamic courts both during the period of my second fieldwork and to a certain degree, since, and is especially concerned with the cultural logic of judicial process in the Islamic court of Rembau. The first parts of the chapter present material relevant to the state-defined roles and operations of the courts (including their domains and jurisdictions) and the nature of the criminal and civil cases that come before them. Subsequent sections of the chapter, which are concerned primarily with judicial process, focus on the ways that Rembau's Islamic magistrate and his staff interpret the cases brought before them and devise and deploy strategies to effect outcomes that are compatible with their interpretations and objectives. One goal of this chapter is to provide a close look at the "localized offices, institutions, and practices in which the state is instantiated" (Gupta 1995: 375–76); a second is to speak to a central theme in Weber's (1925 [1968]) work on Islamic law. Elaborating and codifying extant views of East-West differences (Turner 1974: 14), Weber avers that judicial process in Islamic courts is relatively arbitrary, ad hoc, and irrational and that it reveals a relatively unelaborated concern with procedural regularities and doctrinal consistency of the sort one sees in Western-style courts. Weber has had a profound impact on Western scholarship concerning Islamic legal systems. The material in this chapter supports Weber's contention that there are some marked differences between Islamic and Western-style courts. But it also makes clear that Weber overstates and misrepresents such contrasts; that there are readily discernable regularities in the workings of Islamic courts in Malaysia and elsewhere; and that the regularities reflect broadly shared cultural understandings bearing on social relatedness, human nature, gender, and the like. A major objective of this chapter is thus to show how local cultural concepts inform the ways in which officials of Malaysia's Islamic courts handle issues of legal liability, moral responsibility, and guilt. A related objective is to illustrate that a good many of these concepts are contextually variable and contradictory and that the anthropology of law needs to be especially attentive to the political economy of contrasting cultural representations and their contextually variable realization.

Chapter 3 views the courts from a different set of perspectives. Here I am concerned with the men and women who use the courts to help them resolve disputes, and I am particularly interested in litigant strategies and patterns of resistance. The first section of the chapter discusses nine case studies and other data illuminating how and why women utilize the courts. The second provides eight cases and other material bearing on men's use of the courts and then examines gendered similarities and differences with respect to the strategies and tactics employed by women and men as plaintiffs and defendants. Here and in the third section of the chapter, which focuses on oppositional discourses and patterns of resistance, we will see that men can more easily exploit the often-times ambiguous and contested symbols and meanings of time, space, language, law, and "custom"; a corollary is that this easier manipulability of such symbols flows from and further enhances gendered powers that women do not have.

Part 2, which focuses on modernity and governmentality in Islamic courts and other domains, consists of two chapters. Chapter 4 elucidates how the narratives of court officials aim to reinforce certain symbols, idioms, and meanings of local kinship, gender, and sexuality—and to transform others—and, more generally, how the courts help produce and legitimize modern middle-class families and subjectivities and simultaneously endeavor to assure that allegiances beyond the household be largely restricted to the global community of Muslim believers (the *ummah*) and the state. With respect to kinship and marriage, we will see that the sanctity of (heterosexual) conjugal bonds and parent-child relations are accorded highest priority in terms of the explicit content of morally corrective exhortations and pronouncements to troubled couples and others, and that this same priority is evident from what is noticeably absent from morally corrective discourses, such as positive references to collateral relatives and kin groupings like kindreds, lineages, and clans. A partial explanation of these dynamics lies in the implicit assumption that the smooth operation of the courts, like that of modern states generally, necessitates narrowly defined (nuclear) family units, not a broadly construed, hence encompassing and always potentially unruly kinship. The more general point is that while the court officials' practices and narratives (including their silences and elisions) sometimes subvert state agendas, they are key components of the discourses on kinship, gender, and sexuality—and citizenship, authenticity, and alterity—that are promoted by the state. These latter discourses reflect concerns to bolster certain types of political legitimacy and political stability, as well as the economic, religious, and overall cultural development that help sustain political legitimacy and political stability alike. State discourses on kinship are thus geared toward undercutting the extended kinship long characteristic of rural Malay society, partly because of the widely held belief that such kinship impedes the development of the narrowly cast political loyalties that are central to the state's patronage machine. Extended kinship formations, like other "backward" excesses of rural society, are also seen as a drag on economic effort, hence an obstacle to the economic development of the Malay community, which, though politically and numerically dominant, continues to lag behind the Chinese and Indian minorities in terms of overall economic standing. We will see that such development has been central to the national political agendas of the ruling party (UMNO) for a full thirty years and that UMNO has long been quite explicit in its twofold goal of eliminating rural Malay social and cultural formations as "traditionally" constituted and "replacing" them with a newly created sector of middle- and upper-middle-class urban Malay capitalists.

Chapter 5 expands the discussion of authenticity and identity—or, put differently, of new ways of understanding, experiencing, representing, and otherwise being in the world—by examining nationalist (and transnational) discourses on "Asian values" that have been expounded in recent years in Malaysia, elsewhere in Southeast Asia, and beyond. I should perhaps clarify here that in the course of my two main periods of fieldwork these latter narratives were not disseminated in the Islamic courts in a register of specifically "Asian values," though I did hear them articulated in the frequently overlapping and in some instances more or less synonymous registers of Islamic and/or Malay values. These narratives are nonetheless implicated in the very same reinscription of authenticity and identity that we see in the Islamic courts and do in these and other ways (for example, as elements of discursive strategies to constitute "good subjects" and define new types of criminality) resonate with the narratives produced by the courts. For that matter, some of the political and cultural crises that have fueled the discourse on "Asian values" in recent years have resulted in the enactment of Islamic laws bearing on sodomy, homosexuality, and the like. Such developments thus enable us to observe a legal and more encompassing cultural "discourse in the process of constituting itself" (Foucault 1980: 38)—or more precisely, a variety of such discourses in the making. For reasons such as these, they are highly relevant to the work and missions of the Islamic courts during the last few years and well into the foreseeable future. In terms of case material, this section of the chapter draws mainly on two celebrated criminal cases that have rocked Malaysia in recent years. The first involves a young Malay woman from the state of Kelantan, who in 1996 was discovered to have "passed" as a male in order to marry her female lover and who created public controversies on such a scale that various media accounts referred to her as "the woman who shook the nation." The second case involves former Deputy Prime Minister and Minister of Finance Anwar Ibrahim, who has been held in prison since the latter part of 1998, which, as already noted, is when he was stripped of his official titles and duties and charged with numerous counts of sodomy, corruption, and bribery.

The concluding chapter summarizes and elaborates on some of the main points covered in preceding chapters, especially those relevant to scholarly (and public) debates bearing on Islam, modernity, and civil society. One of my main concerns here is to pull together and comment on material illustrating that the Islamic courts are not "backward looking" and do not by any means pose fatal obstacles to the rational modes of government, economy, and social organization that are held to be conducive to modernity's "holy trinity": urbanization, industrialization, and bureaucratization.[14] To put this in more positive terms, I underscore that the Islamic courts are relatively forward looking; that they are strategic loci in the projects of modernity that leaders of Malaysia have set for themselves and their countrymen since the latter part of the nineteenth century and during the last three decades in particular; and that they are implicated in a certain type of modernity and civil society that is characteristically Asian and distinctively Malaysian. I argue that the courts help lay the groundwork for Malaysian-style modernity and civil society in a variety of ways, one of which involves providing a legitimate and relatively confidential forum that both enables and encourages people to air intimate experiences and to thrash out certain of their deeply felt differences and views about moral injustice, all in a relatively unfettered, "no holds barred" sort of way. The mere existence of such fora both allows for and helps motivate and induce the type of direct verbal exchange and impassioned airing of difference that is discouraged and prohibited in most other contexts in Malaysia but is nonetheless vital to a modern-day, rights-bearing citizenry, a state that is responsive to democratic sentiment and civil pluralism and a vibrant marketplace alike.[15]

The courts also encourage modernity and civil society by valorizing the contractual responsibilities (though not so much the rights) of the individual, by emphasizing, for example, that while individuals are enmeshed in status- and identity-conferring groups of various kinds such as households, more encompassing groups of kin, and village communities, they can and should enter into written, contractual relationships (like marriage) of their own volition, albeit with the consent of a father (or another male kinsman) in the case of women. More generally, the courts contribute to the further erosion of extended kinship as well as the democratization of family groups, household relations, and marriage in particular. The attainment of these goals is sought partly through morally corrective advice and discourses designed to help free individuals from some of the constraints of extended kinship. The realization of these goals is also pursued through the court's efforts to "even out" certain of the gendered inequalities that obtain in Islamic law, efforts premised on the assumptions that men create most of the problems in marriage, are at fault in much (if not most) divorce, and are much more likely than women to resort to dishonesty. In these and other ways the courts are contributing to the erosion, however partial, of one of the most basic cornerstones of Islamic and state-sanctioned inequality. And they are simultaneously making space for the emergence and florescence of sentiments, dispositions, and embryonic ideologies that are at variance with—and a direct challenge to—one of the most rudimentary and fundamental of the official lines shared by Islam and the state. More broadly, by moving toward policies and practices that make more room for the individual to exercise choice and initiative (to go against one's parents' wishes in selecting, remaining with, or leaving a spouse; to get out of a marriage if it does not meet one's emotional needs), the courts are bestowing sanctified legitimacy on the exercise of theoretically uncoerced judgments and initiatives of the sort that are vital to modernity and civil society.

In the course of this (arguably celebratory) discussion I also emphasize that projects of modernity need not entail liberatory movements or even small steps toward the positive features of civil society. Moreover, we need to bear in mind the Janus-faced nature of civil society. For example, in Malaysia and other contexts, such as Indonesia, recent years have also seen the emergence of decidedly "uncivil" associations whose agendas are very much out of keeping with the pluralistic visions usually associated with the concept. Of equal if not greater analytic concern here are the ways in which concepts of kinship are implicitly and uncritically invoked in definitions and discussions of the concept of civil society. I argue that kinship is (variably) central to definitions of civil society but woefully ignored in the actual investigation and theorization of civil society and that static, Rousseauean, and otherwise essentialized views of "the family" inform much of the relevant literature. Finally, I contend that we need to devote much more analytic attention to state-mediated dialectics of kinship and civil society; in much the same vein, we need to better appreciate that what states (via their agents, policies, discourses, and internal cleavages) do to—and with—the symbols, idioms, practices, and institutions of kinship is of great significance both for the efficacy and meanings of state operations at the local level and for civil society as a whole.

PART ONE

The Culture, Political Economy, and History of the Islamic Courts

CHAPTER ONE

Locating Islamic Magistrates
and Their Courts in History

People do the history of law, and the history of the economy, but the history of
the judicial system, of *judicial practices* . . . this is rarely discussed.
   —*Michel Foucault,* Power/Knowledge *(emphasis added)*

Of all branches of Malay research the study of jurisprudence is the one that presents the greatest difficulties. Malay laws were never committed to writing; they
were constantly overridden by autocratic chiefs and unjust judges; they varied in
each State; they did not harmonise with the doctrines of Islam they professed to
follow; [and] they were often expressed in metaphors or proverbs that seem to
baffle interpretation.
   —*R. J. Wilkinson, "Malay Law"*

Of all the [British imperial] criticisms of Malay misgovernment, the most persis-
tent had been criticisms of the administration of justice. There has been no systematic study of judicial *practice* in the independent Malay states, and it is a
question whether the material for such a study now exists. The scanty, uniformly
disparaging references by contemporary British observers are suspect, since they
are the observations of administrators committed to the introduction of a rival
system, and prejudiced in any case in favour of written codes and procedures.
   —*Emily Sadka,* The Protected Malay States, 1874–1895 *(emphasis added)*

[The difficulties] . . . of the elucidation of early [Malay] religious institutions,
and the operation through them of the *Shari'a,* . . . remain formidable . . .
[partly] . . . owing to the absence of even descriptive materials for the *Shari'a* in
action for (say) most of the nineteenth century. [B]ut equally serious problems
arise from the recognition that the *Shari'a* itself, . . . and those institutions associated with it, formed one part only and that a changing and uncertain one, in
the system of law and belief that characterized Malay peasant society.
   —*William Roff, "The Origin and Early Years of the Majlis Ugama"*

ISLAMIC MAGISTRATES, ISLAMIC COURTS, AND ISLAMIC LAW
THROUGH THE 1830s

The origins and early development of Malaysia's Islamic courts are obscured by
the religious and other cultural biases and civilizing agendas of imperial observers. It is nonetheless clear that while Malaysia's Islamic courts appear to be
relatively recent phenomena, their precedents and genealogies qua religious
symbols and judicial institutions can be traced back to the early modern period
(which extends from the fifteenth to the eighteenth centuries).[1] A good deal of
material relevant to judicial institutions and various aspects of religion in early
modern times is presented elsewhere (Peletz 1988b, 1996; Hooker 1978; Andaya and Ishii 1992; de Casparis and Mabbett 1992; Reid 1988, 1993; Andaya
and Andaya 2001), so I will confine my introductory comments to a few central
points. Most important to note is that from a contemporary and cross-cultural
perspective, Islamic—and many other—institutions of the early modern era,
though in some cases highly developed, were relatively undifferentiated and
"multifunctional." Thus, although Islamic institutions such as mosques (*mas-
jid*), prayer houses (*surau*), and religious boarding schools (*pondok*), certainly
did exist, they were far less specific in terms of their personnel, operations,
functions, and goals than they are at present. (The same is true of syncretic
complexes reflecting the animist and Hindu-Buddhist traditions of pre-Islamic
times.) This will not surprise anyone familiar with Weber's work on the history
of rationalization and the development of institutional differentiation in particular, but the theme is worth emphasizing nonetheless.

Islamic magistrates and their courts are key components of Islamic legal
institutions, as of course are Islamic laws. But we need to bear in mind that
these are analytically distinct phenomena and that the mere existence of references to Islamic laws in historical texts of one sort or another need not imply
the existence of Islamic magistrates, functioning Islamic courts, or the widespread or systematic application of Islamic law. An historically oriented discussion of the larger framework of such institutions might thus begin by acknowledging that references to Islamic laws and other aspects of Islam are abundantly
evident in various legal codes of the early modern era, such as the Laws of
Melaka (*Undang-Undang Melaka*), which are generally believed to have been
compiled during the period 1424–58, the height of Melaka's glory as an international entrepôt.[2] These codes dealt extensively with matters crucial to the
business of thriving maritime-based empires: the commercial, ceremonial, and
other prerogatives of rulers; the consequences for those who fail to acknowledge and honor such prerogatives; the details and varieties of taxation; the
jurisdiction of harbormasters and other port officials; the proper conduct of
commercial transactions; systems of currency, weights, measures, and other
standards; the nature of debt bondage and slavery, including the treatment to be
accorded runaways; the status of women, children, and other minors; and the

contracting of marriage, divorce, etc. We shall have more to say about the *Undang-Undang Melaka* in due course. The point to underscore here is that it is difficult to determine the precise extent to which such codes were systematically or even sporadically enforced either within the confines of Melaka itself or in outlying areas ostensibly subject to the jurisdiction of the Melaka sultanate. Significantly, some foreign observers lamented that in 1500 the port of Melaka was almost lawless; one consequence of this state of affairs was that foreign merchants took to sleeping on their ships to ensure their personal safety (Reid 1988: 145). Even if we allow for a measure of hyperbole in such complaints, they certainly suggest that the enforcement of key provisions of the Melaka codes (concerning, for example, the security of person and property) was less than systematic.

Also unclear are the precise mechanisms and the full range of sanctions available to rulers, their proxies, and concerned citizenry for the enforcement of the legal (and more encompassing moral) codes at issue here, some of which were highly detailed in terms of specifying severe and, in certain cases, gruesome punishments for violations of the law. Eminent historian Anthony Reid and various other scholars of early modern Southeast Asia correctly underscore that justice was "administered by the ruler . . . and seen as a vital aspect of his kingship," such that even when advised by legal specialists, the ruler in principle gave the judgment (1988: 138). But some of these scholars also emphasize the draconian penalties that were supposedly meted out by central authorities on a regular basis for transgressions of some of the more sacrosanct of these laws in certain parts of the Malay Peninsula and in neighboring regions such as Aceh (northern Sumatra), especially in the seventeenth century. This focus on the state-sponsored and otherwise highly organized imposition of exceedingly formal sanctions in the form of harsh physical punishments (whipping, maiming, amputations, etc.) is misleading. It does, in any event, divert attention from the fact that throughout the Islamic areas of early modern Southeast Asia, most conflicts and disputes were undoubtedly handled informally—through processes of negotiation, mediation, arbitration, and the like—without recourse to processes of formal adjudication and the threats of harsh physical punishment that such processes could bring.

In this regard we might note that in a discussion of Southeast Asia during the "Age of Commerce" (1450–1680) that is presented under the heading of "Justice and Law," Reid observes that "the great majority of crimes were punished by fines or by stiffer penalties which were commuted to fines" (1988: 141). He also remarks that

> [e]xecution was the prescribed punishment for a wide range of offenses, particularly those which touched royal sovereignty. Treason was everywhere a capital offense, and usually also murder, . . . [as was] the counterfeiting of money or theft of royal property [at least] in the Malay world. . . . In Aceh four royal concubines were brutally killed in 1636 for stealing silver plates from the palace, and a man was executed in

1642 for stealing a horse. . . . Adultery with the wife of an upper-class Malay was
also punished by death; . . . the honorable form of execution was to be stabbed with a
kris to the heart. (140–41)

Execution of the latter variety is said to have been a daily occurrence in Java
and common in Melaka as well. "For those traitors and others of whom a
ghastly example was to be made, however, there were many more horrible
deaths—decapitation, impaling on a stake, dismembering, burning alive, exposure in some excruciating position, trampling by elephants, or devouring by
tigers" (Reid 1988: 141). Thus, Iskandar Muda, "the strongest of Acehnese
kings (r. 1607–1636)," who is reported to have enforced the Islamic religion by
forbidding gambling and the drinking of alcohol and by requiring (among other
things) that his subjects pray five times daily, executed at least two drunken
Acehnese by "pouring molten lead down their throats" (Reid 1988: 143). He
also cut off the hands of two Englishmen in 1642 "for having tried to distill
arak," the more general points being that "under Iskandar Muda the practice of
maiming went far beyond Islamic prescriptions, extending to the removal of
noses, lips, ears, and genitals from subjects who displeased him" (Reid 1988:
143 [see Mundy 1667 [1919]: 135]), and that "Aceh had an Islamic court which
sentenced thieves to amputation throughout the seventeenth century" (see Bowrey [1680] 1905: 314; Dampier 1699: 96, cited in Reid 1988: 143). More generally, Reid suggests that the Islamic penalty for theft (amputation) "was applied
in a number of Southeast Asian sultanates at the height of Islamic influence—in
Banten between 1651 and 1680 . . . in Brunei in the sixteenth century, . . . and
in some Malay states and Magindinao at a later period" (1988: 143).

In a similar vein, Reid contends that "there is surprisingly widespread evidence to suggest that the law of God, the *shari'a*, was applied" in much of
Islamic Southeast Asia (1993: 183), adding that the *syariah* differs from the
general Southeast Asian pattern that he describes, "especially in the frequency
of such punishments as maiming and whipping, the absence of any concept of
ordeal, and the punishments for moral lapses such as gambling, drinking, and
sexual misconduct" (1988: 142). And by way of further emphasizing his points
concerning the nature of Islamic justice in the region, his exposition includes a
three-quarter-page line drawing reproduced from Thomas Bowrey's *A Geographical Account of Countries Round the Bay of Bengal, 1669 to 1679*, depicting a pathetic cripple on crutches with the caption, "An Acehnese criminal after
having his hands and feet amputated"—this being the only drawing or plate of
any kind in the entire discussion of Southeast Asian "justice and law" during
the period in question (1450–1680) (1988: 144).

But—and more important—Reid also registers a number of exceedingly significant observations that do not simply temper or otherwise qualify the portrait
presented thus far, but actually go a long way toward vitiating it in its entirety.
He concedes, for example, that *"the only definite evidence for a functioning
shari'a court outside Aceh . . . is in Banten [northwestern Java] under Sultan
Ageng"* (r. 1651–1680; 1993: 184); that *"the extent to which . . . [Islamic law]*

was imposed varied greatly with time and place" (1988: 142); and that *even
"when the state itself became Muslim [and] there was some incorporation of
Muslim law into that of the state, . . . [the] process never displaced the indigenous law completely,* though it went furthest in seventeenth-century Aceh"
(1993: 142; emphases added). He notes as well that in the broadly conceived
domain of sexual morality, "The Melaka . . . [laws] tend to give *a milder local
alternative* as well as the Islamic penalty" and, more generally, that *"the effectiveness of these systems of law was extremely varied,"* depending much on the
strength of the ruler, his humanity, notions of collective responsibility, etc.
(1988: 142–143, 44–45; emphases added).

During this period (the sixteenth and seventeenth centuries) "Islamic law
books were becoming influential"; on the other hand, *"local oral tradition continued to be interpreted by the village elders . . . in many areas each village
and ethnic community maintained its own judicial system;* . . . and even the
laws decreed by Malay sultans . . . acknowledged *that sentencing should be
determined by the 'law of the city or the villages'"* (1988: 137–38; emphases
added).

What remains unexplored here, even in very broad terms, are a great many
issues: a general sense of the extent of the variation in the imposition of Islamic
law; the nature of indigenous law; the "milder" local penal alternatives in question; the relevant oral traditions bearing on law; the contours of village-level
judicial systems; the laws of the city and village; and so forth. Another problem
with the characterizations at issue is that while they are ostensibly about "justice and law," they are in actuality, concerned almost exclusively with crime
and punishment in the domains of criminal as opposed to civil law and, as
regards the latter (criminal law), with the most severe, draconian, and sensationalistic punishments meted out in one particular place—Aceh—at one particular point in its history, which happened to be a time when Islamic fervor
was at its peak. Questions of the typicality or atypicality of Aceh aside—and,
as mentioned earlier, Reid is careful to acknowledge that there is much variation here, with Aceh at one end of the continuum and Java at the other (1993:
173–81)—there is no discussion of the culture or social organization of dispute
management or conflict resolution or, more specifically, of the informal sanctions that typically came into play to preclude, minimize, or punish transgression: for example, shaming, shunning, ostracizing, etc. Nor, for that matter is
there any mention of the fact that negotiation, mediation, arbitration, and the
like were undoubtedly far more common than adjudication at the hands of central authorities, as is almost always true at present as well.[3] Note, finally, that
Reid's fascinating and richly detailed discussions of marriage, sexual relations,
festivals, amusements, and gaming, which make up over a third of his first
(1988) volume on Southeast Asia's Age of Commerce, make it quite clear that
many of the Islamic codes at issue were commonly honored in the breach.

Rather than according descriptive and analytic centrality to "crime and punishment" in an inquiry that concerns "law and justice"—or the history of
Islamic (or other varieties of) magistrates and their courts—it seems more pro-

ductive to begin with questions bearing on the social organization and administration of "custom" and (religious) law, *adat* and Islam. In this connection it should first be noted that in the Malay context and Southeast Asia generally, senior kin, village elders, and local rulers were responsible for the administration of religious law and other matters bearing on religion and custom alike. Referring to the importance of kinship and communal sanctions throughout early modern Southeast Asia, Barbara Andaya has recently written that

> [t]he family and the community had a vested interest in insuring compliance because it was commonly accepted that they could suffer when a member of the group offended. In the words of [an eighteenth-century] Malay text, "parents and children, brothers and sisters, share the same family fortune and the family repute. If one suffers, all suffer" (*adat orang anak-beranak dan adik-beradik semalu se-aib rugi bersama rugi*). Embedded in . . . written documents [such as the fifteenth-century Laws of Melaka] was the state['s] realization of the power of communal oversight: "God has left all human beings to their rulers and ministers; the subjects are like roots and the rulers the trees; roots and trees should stand firmly together. Do not be reluctant to go to the *balai* to investigate the families [*keluarga*] who have committed offences so that your trial will be lightened by Allah Almighty on the Day of Resurrection." . . . A major element in this state-family jural chain was the universal recognition that fines and compensation in goods or money could make restitution for virtually any crime. It was the family and the community who were the channels which oversaw this kind of restitution. Indeed, it may be one feature which particularly marks off regional legal systems. . . . The words of a [seventeenth-century] Malay code convey something of the same message. "The use of money (*emas*) and the reason for its having been given to us by Allah is so that those who possess it should live in comfort (*senang*) and be free of the consequences of their misdoings. If it were otherwise, what would have been the use of Allah sending it into the world for his servants?" (2000b: 33–34, 38)

Similarly, the Laws of Dato Sri Paduka Tuan of 1667 specify that village elders (*tuah-tuah*) were to report to the headman all "thieves, robbers, cockfighters, opium smugglers, gamblers, worshippers of trees and rocks and drunkards, and everyone who 'sins against Allah'" (Yegar 1979: 61). Headmen and elders were also charged with enjoining villagers to observe the five daily prayers, to fast during the month of Ramadan, and (at least in the case of males) to attend Friday services at the local mosque (Yegar 1979: 61).

Local elders, headmen, and their superordinates were assisted in the management of Islamic (and other) affairs by village-level Islamic functionaries, especially since there were no district-level or other supra village-level organizations of *ulama* (learned men, scholars of Islam), nor any *mufti* (juriconsults) capable of issuing opinions with the authority of law or anything approaching law-like status. (Ironically, such had to wait for the era of British colonialism, as discussed below.) As Newbold put it with reference to the Rembau/Naning area, "Their criminal laws are founded on the precepts of the Koran, but by no means so exclusively as are those which the Indian followers of the prophet have adopted," and "they have no Maulavis or Ulemas like the Mussulmans of India" (1839, 1:246, 247). The village-level Islamic officials in question exercised a fair degree of autonomy and served various functions that were later assumed by *kadi* and other religious specialists. In Newbold's words: "There are four officiating priests [*sic*] attached to each mosque besides the Kali or Kazi who presides over a number of mosques; viz. the Imam, the Khatib, the Bilal or Meuzzin, and the Panghulu Momkin or Mukim. The immediate religious care of the inhabitants of the mukim or parish to which the mosque belongs, devolves upon the Imam, Khatib, and Bilal" (1:247).

As for the roles and specific functions of these figures, Newbold remarks of the *imam* that his duties included washing and shrouding the dead and pronouncing prayers over the corpse before internment (1:248). *Imam* in particular served as spiritual leaders and as sources of guidance and advice on numerous matters; presumably they were involved in a fair range of dispute resolution as well, though such matters also fell within the domain of local headmen and their aides. More specifically, *imam* helped ensure that interpersonal conflict of various kinds was resolved through informal mechanisms of mediation, arbitration, and the like rather than formal adjudication, particularly since mutual agreement, consensus, and conciliation were highly valued in the Malay context and were in fact enshrined in various myths, aphorisms, and other elements of local culture (see Gullick 1958; Sadka 1968; see also Geertz 1983a). The roles and functions of the *khatib*, for their part, included recitation of *khutbah* during Friday mosque services and the performance of *nikah* or marriage ceremonies. Finally, the duties of *panghulu momkin* or *mukim* seem to correspond to those that presently devolve on those referred to as *siak* (caretakers of the mosque) (Newbold 1839, 1:249). All such officials were apparently elected after examination of their fitness and capabilities by *kadi* and elders.

Although transgressions defined as offenses in Islam are evident (in the sense of referenced) in early modern legal digests such as the Laws of Melaka, legal codes of the early modern era pertain mainly to status, etiquette, sumptuary matters, and commerce and are only minimally taken up with matters of Islamic law or other aspects of Islam. Even so, "royal *kadi*," who were appointed by— and served—local rulers, did exist in various parts of the Peninsula, despite the assertions of some specialists, such as Yegar, that "there were no *kathis* . . . until the era of British protection, not even at the royal courts" (1979: 20). Caution is warranted in interpreting facts relating to the existence of such *kadi*, however, for as Malaysian specialist Sharifah Zaleha Syed Hassan (1985: 72) has remarked of the early modern period in Kedah and Malaya generally, the existence of such *kadi* reflected the ways in which the "historically Islamicized system of kingship and the more encompassing polity had absorbed symbols and principles of Islamic legal institutions" and should *not* be taken as evidence that such polities necessarily implemented Islamic law. "[W]hich . . . of the neatly codified Syariah rules [actually] became law was dependent on and became a function of the discretionary powers of the ruler and chiefs;" the more general point being that "whatever legal authority . . . [*kadi*] possessed was determined by the ruler" (72). Other established scholars of the precolonial era are much more emphatic: "Islamic legal doctrine appears in the Malay legal codes but *there is no evidence to show that this doctrine, or any part of the codes, was effective law*" (Gullick 1958: 139; emphasis added; see also Milner 1983: 27 and the historical sources cited there). Circumstances such as these are partly responsible for the numerous references to "the weakness of the *syariah*" prior to and during the nineteenth century one encounters both in the colonial-era literature and that of more recent times (see, for example, Yegar 1979: 20; see also Hefner 2000: 29–30).[4]

In the case of Rembau and many other areas in the Malay Peninsula, there is considerable disagreement concerning the date for the emergence of the office of *kadi*. With reference to Rembau, some scholars point to the year 1889, others to 1839 (or before). Parr and Mackray (1910: 31, 52) claim that no such office existed before 1889, even though they also refer to the existence of a "royal *kathi*" associated with the court of the *yang dipertuan besar* during the first half of the nineteenth century. Hooker (1972: 145) appears to accept the 1889 date (cf. *NSAR* 1899: 6; Gullick 1958: 139), but Roff (1967: 88) and Yegar (1979: 92) contend that the office dates from the 1830s, if not earlier.

The lack of consensus seems to stem from differing interpretations of inconclusive statements contained in the previously cited 1839 publication by T. J. Newbold, Esq., a lieutenant in the twenty-third Regiment of the Madras Light Infantry, who was also aide-de-camp to Brigadier General Wilson, C.B., member of the Asiatic Society of Bengal and Madras and corresponding member of Madras Hindoo Literary Society. This text merits particular attention for a variety of reasons to be noted in due course and will serve as the basis for the remainder of the discussion of the historical period under consideration.

Newbold was a British chronicler and gatherer of military and political intelligence who journeyed throughout the Malay Peninsula in the 1830s. In the course of his travels and investigations into local conditions he interacted with numerous Malays (whose language he spoke); upon his return, he published a massive two-volume account of the findings, which bore the matter-of-fact title, *Political and Statistical Account of the British Settlements in the Straits of Malacca, viz. Pinang, Malacca, and Singapore; With a History of the Malayan States on the Peninsula of Malacca*. In the second volume of his encyclopedic study, which, much like subsequent Orientalist scholarship, covered a great deal of obvious strategic importance to Europeans but also almost everything from "penis pins in Borneo to the shape of Chinese coolies' hats in Malaysia" (Sullivan 1983: 74), Newbold mentions that during the 1830s "a Kazi" by the name of Haji Hashim Sri Lummah "presided over" Rembau's seven mosque districts—"each with a distinct establishment of priests [*sic*], as in Naning" (a neighboring region Newbold had described in the first volume of his study), that is, an *imam*, a *khatib*, and a *bilal* (2:126). But material presented by Parr and Mackray (1910: 31) suggests that the individual thus titled was attached to the court of the *yang dipertuan besar* rather than that of the *undang*. In light of the fact that prior to British-engineered administrative reorganization in 1889 the *undang* rather than the *yang dipertuan besar* performed many if not all of the civil and other functions commonly associated with the office of *kadi*, the "royal *kathi*" at issue appears to have been accorded considerable prestige—he did, in any event, enjoy the exalted status associated with the title of *haji*—but few if any of the prerogatives and responsibilities usually entailed in the office.

Ellipses and silences in Newbold's work, and in the written record as a whole, preclude greater specificity as to the *kadi*'s official and unofficial duties—to say nothing of actual judicial practice—at least with respect to Rembau. However, one can draw reasonable inferences about such matters from the neighboring district of Naning, which has long been part of Melaka and was thus understandably of greater strategic and other interest to Newbold, who did in fact speak with the two *kadi* in Naning—Selaho and Sulong Juman—and did, moreover, acknowledge his indebtedness to them "for much of the information collected on the religious usages of the Naningites." In addition to telling his readers that the "religious customs . . . and festivals" in Rembau are similar to those observed in Naning, as are the varieties of "priests" attached to each mosque, Newbold writes that the *kadi* in Naning is the "*arbitrator* of all knotty religious points, which the four inferior ["priests" or officials] may not be able to decide," as well as the "guardian to all orphans who have no near male relations" (1:248; emphasis added). The *kadi* is also said to "confirm marriages" (1:248), though exactly what is meant by this reference—and the others mentioned earlier—is unclear. For example, in what specific sense(s)—other than, say, registering them—did the *kadi* "confirm" marriages? In what specific senses did the *kadi* either serve as guardian to orphans with no close male kin, or arbitrate "knotty religious points" or other matters? In the latter connection, did he simply mediate potentially conflicting views or serve as an arbitrator of such points in the sense of offering advice or perspective on matters that parties voluntarily brought before him? Did he instead or in addition, issue *mufti*-like pronouncements that were in some sense binding upon the *ummah*, even though they did not necessarily have the formal status of law? In some ways more important, did the *kadi* have the authority to intervene in disputes whether or not the principals involved in the disputes sought such intervention? And finally, if circumstances of the latter sort did prevail, did the *kadi* (or his assistants) have the authority to administer sanctions that he (or those to whom he was beholden) thought appropriate whether or not the principal parties in the dispute felt the sanctions were warranted?

Unfortunately, Newbold provides no information on matters of the latter sort. He does, however inform his readers that in exchange for services rendered, the *kadi* received certain payments or offerings. In the month of Ramadan, for example, he was given "*fitrah*, in the shape of small donations of rice." And "at sacrifices [when animals were slaughtered for a feast], the head of the victim" (1:248).

Newbold tells us very little about the form of judicial hearings in which *kadi* may have been involved, and he says next to nothing about the relative autonomy that *kadi* in Rembau or neighboring regions may have enjoyed. While fearing that his readers may find Malay customs "puerile and absurd" (2:175), he nonetheless emphasizes that the qualities indispensable in "monarchs" include "mercy, generosity, valour, and vigour in enforcing the laws" (2:233); and he goes on to provide some key observations bearing on matters of religion and on styles of greeting and address, especially in encounters involving status superiors, which are relevant to our understanding of *kadi*. He notes, for example, that "The Natives of the peninsula are well aware of the extensive schemes for their conversion, and manifest much jealousy and sensitivity on religious points" (1:44). More relevant, perhaps, are Newbold's comments that Malays in Rembau and elsewhere in the Malay Peninsula "are morbidly alive to insults" (and that Europeans given to playing tricks on Malays "are likely to have their fingers cut"); that it is high treason to alter a *balai*'s [meeting hall's] shape and the fashion used to receive people; that "sitting not standing is the position of respect"; and that much significance was attached to linguistic virtuosity, most of which, as will be discussed later, is also true at present (2:83–84, 176). Newbold adds that popular traditions—including "the Malayan Undang Undang [Malayan Laws] which are orally handed down" (2:219)—are "seldom committed to writing but treasured in the memory of some of the male elders, or of some old Malay lady of rank," and that they give to the persons possessed of them "that sort of consideration which is paid to [something] containing a valuable gem" (2:134).

Even if the judicial functions and decision making of the *kadi* proceeded with some measure of autonomy vis-à-vis local rulers—and, as we shall see in due course, it seems that for the most part they did not—the judicial roles and styles of *kadi* were informed by and in many other respects encapsulated within the structure of the "more secular" political and judicial system. The more encompassing system included at its lower levels the officials Newbold referred to as *pagawayes*, *tuah-tuahs*, and village *panghulus* (officials, elders, and village headmen). Referring to such figures, Newbold makes a number of critically important points, specifically that

> should a complaint be preferred to them by any of the people under their charge, they shall without delay enquire into the case . . . [and that] they shall make themselves well acquainted with the following subjects, otherwise their functions are thrown away upon them: 1st, the Hukum Shera; 2nd, the Hukum Akl; 3rd, the Hukum Faal; and 4th, the Hukum Adat. This done, they may be termed men. (2:269, 275–76)

With reference to *hukum akl* (laws or principles of reason), Newbold says that such laws or principles are relevant in cases not provided for by (Islamic) law, where the judge must be guided by his discretion and pure principles of justice. *Hukum faal* and *hukum adat*, for their part, refer to the law of usages and old established customs, respectively (2:276). Such "laws" were among the key sources of knowledge to be mastered by *kadi*, much of which, as we shall see, is true at present as well.

On the subject of sanctions, which are central to any discussion of crime and punishment, let alone the more encompassing domain of justice and law, Newbold provides material that is valuable but also woefully incomplete and other-wise much colored by Britain's burgeoning designs on the Peninsula and its resources. Like subsequent generations of British observers, whom we shall consider in due course, Newbold focused on physical sanctions and was preoc-cupied if not mesmerized by the varieties of physical torture that he was able to catalog as well as the styles and details of the capital punishment about which he could collect information. He recounts, for example, that one Juara Magat arrogated to himself the power of inflicting capital punishment on the inhabit-ants confided to his charge; that such power was exercised by his successors until 1809, when it was rescinded by Colonel William Farquhar (the British resident of Melaka, 1803–18; resident of Singapore 1819–23); and that the last sentence of death passed by Abdul Syed (or Dholl Syed) was on a Kedah man (Sali), who carried off from Melaka two Chinese slaves, killing the man among them who resisted and selling the woman. "The present Superintendent of Nan-ing, Mr. Westerhout, who was an eyewitness described to me the ceremony of his trial and execution":

> The criminal was conducted, bound, to Bukit Penialang, or "Execution Hill," near Tabu. The Panghulu . . . [and other officials] were all seated in judgement, under a cluster of Tambuseh trees on the skirt of a hill. The witnesses were brought forward and examined by the Panghulu himself. The evidence against the prisoner being deemed conclusive, according to the forms of the Mohammedan law, he was sen-tenced, agreeably to the Adat Menangkabowe, to pay one Bhar or to suffer . . . death by the kris.

> Being unable to pay the fine, preparations were made immediately for his execution. The grave was dug on the spot and he was placed, firmly bound in a sitting posture, literally on its brink. For further security, two Panglimas sat on each side, while the Panglima Besar Sumun unsheathed the weapon that was to terminate the mortal exis-tence of the trembling wretch. On the point of the poniard, the kris panjang, the panglima carefully placed a pledget of soft cotton, which he pressed against the man's breast, a little above the right collar-bone. He then slowly passed the weapon's point through the cotton, on which he kept the fingers of his left hand firmly pressed, in a direction obliquely to the left into his body, until the projection of the hilt stopped its farther progress. The weapon was then slowly withdrawn, the panglima still retaining the cotton in its place by the pressure of his fingers, so as to staunch effectually all external effusion of blood.

> The criminal, shuddering convulsively, was immediately precipitated into the grave; but on making signs for water, was raised. He had barely time to apply his lips to the cocoa-nut-shell in which it was brought, when he fell back into the grave quite dead. The earth was then thrown over the body, and the assembly dispersed. (1:237–38)

These passages raise many issues worthy of remark, as does the fact that without even a pause, Newbold goes on to describe the responsibilities of lower-ranking political figures; for example, that the heads of *sukus* are "indi-vidually responsible . . . to the Panghulu, in fiscal matters, in levying men, and in settling disputes" (1:239). In some ways more important is that the lengthy discussion of "the ceremony of [Sali's] trial and execution" contains but a portion of a single sentence devoted to *judicial procedure* ("The evidence against the prisoner being deemed conclusive, according to the forms of the Mohammedan law"), proceeds straightaway to a brief reference to sentencing, and then fleshes out the account by devoting the better part of a full page to the precise manner of the execution in all its grisly detail. Without question, Newbold is far more interested in the lurid particulars of Sali's execution than in the more mundane aspects of judicial process that might be revealed in his trial, the more general point being that Newbold was much taken by the sensationalistic and by what he took to be exotic or bizarre.[5]

In all fairness to Newbold, I should make clear that he does not limit his accounts of physical torture, capital punishment, and judicial excess of various kinds to what he observed—or was told occurred—at the hands of Malays. He also recounts such matters at the hands of the Dutch, including their treatment around 1644 of Malays believed guilty of treason and conspiracy (for example, that one man was tortured to death and then had his body exposed on a gibbet, and that two others were decapitated and their bodies divided into four parts and exposed in several conspicuous places) (1:211). Similarly, his comments on the practical workings of British justice in this corner of the world are also highly critical, even though he shares his contemporaries' view that the British system is "armed with powers the most extensive and summary, for the administration of civil and criminal justice, that the wisdom of man could devise" (1:28). In a discussion of the pros and cons of the establishment in 1807 of British courts in Penang, he characterizes the population of the Straits Settlements as "a medley, composed of nearly half the varieties scattered over Asia . . . with wants but few and simple," and goes on to remark:

Among such a population as this, English law, . . . loaded with costly bulwarks of forms, and clogged with tedious processes, has been prematurely introduced, tending rather to embarrass than to advance the ends proposed by natural justice, good government, and common sense. . . . [I]ts inefficacy to reach the guilty . . . [and] its absolute tendency to oppress the poor and . . . further the criminal views of the wealthy litigant, are glaringly obvious to every unbiased observer. Many natives, particularly Malays, will suffer much injury and loss, rather than apply to this court; nor is it . . . much admired by the European community itself. (1:29–30)

The skepticism expressed here about the justice received in local British courts is noteworthy partly because it is also a theme articulated by many of Newbold's successors (even though, like Newbold, they were convinced that as the basis of a system, British judicial ideals were vastly superior to Malay judicial ideals). Similarly, although Newbold, like his successors, was fascinated by issues of physical torture, punishment, and judicial excess, he also presents a good deal of material suggesting a "kinder, gentler" judiciary. He comments, for example, that the "Institutes of Achin," that is, the codes of Aceh about which Reid (1988, 1993) has a fair amount to say, are *"remarkable* for the *severity* of their enactments against criminal offenses" (2:224; emphasis added). But the question that arises here is, "remarkable" in relation to what? I would suggest that what struck Newbold as "remarkable" was not so much the harshness of the Aceh codes but the *severity of the contrast* between Aceh and the Malay Peninsula, including, perhaps most notably, the prevalence in the latter area, even for serious criminal offenses such as theft, of the imposition of nonphysical sanctions such as humiliation and shaming.

Newbold does in fact describe highly conventionalized humiliation and shaming ritually imposed by central authorities for a variety of crimes (such as theft and the seduction of a married woman), and we can be sure that mechanisms of this general sort existed at the village level as well, as is true today. Such sanctions were known, at least in formal contexts, as *takzir* (a general term that refers to punishment that is "less than that prescribed by Islamic law") and were said to be prevalent not only in Johor but also in Melaka (2:278). Precedents for such sanctions exist in various legal compendia from earlier centuries, including the fifteenth-century Laws of Melaka, which contain clear admonitions that the theft of fruit, etc., shall *not* be punished with mutilation but with the fining of the thief and his being forced to march about the city. Newbold comments on the contrast with "the more extreme" punishments of the Quran and goes on to describe the former as follows:

> The thief is . . . placed upon a white buffalo, adorned with the red flower called the bungaraya, with a dish cover to shelter his head, in lieu of the umbrella of honour. His face . . . [is] daubed with charcoal, lime, and tumeric, and he . . . [is] carried in procession to the sound of the chawang (a small kind of gong), round the city, with the stolen goods about his neck. (2:239)

Other *takzir* sanctions that merit mention here include: public rebuke; "the humiliation . . . [of] Sirih Sapaminangan (offering betel to the aggrieved person)"; and in the case of seduction or attempted seduction of another's wife, humbling oneself before the husband in the presence of a large assembly of people (2: 241, 259, 287).

A final set of remarks concerning Newbold's investigations and representations bearing on indigenous polities and judicial systems especially is that his comments and perspectives on *kadi* are surprisingly "neutral" and "unmotivated," particularly in light of the extremely disparaging tone of his observations on most all other officials as well as Malays as a whole. Concerning the latter, Newbold's two-volume work is replete with references to the "resistless inundation of Mohammedan bigotry" (2:315); to "superstitious Malays" who were "passionately addicted to buffalo and cock-fighting" (1:243, 2:179–83); to "apathetic, opium-eating Malay chiefs" (2:13); to the "misgovernment and apathy of the feudal sovereign" (2:154); and to *pawang* (shamanic specialists) being "charlatans" (2:141). More generally, Newbold endorses the view given expression in the wistful remark of Colonel Farquhar that "[w]e have only to lament that a more enterprising and industrious race of inhabitants than the Malays should not have possessed this delightful region" (1:265); but nowhere does he explicitly or even implicitly criticize *kadi* or any of the judicial or other work they performed. This in and of itself is certainly not clear-cut evidence that the judicial styles of *kadi* and the types of sanctions they were inclined to impose were in keeping with European sensibilities of the day. But along with the other data and arguments presented earlier, it does suggest that Anthony Reid's assertions notwithstanding, the regular and/or systematic imposition by *kadi* or their proxies of draconian punishments (Islamic or otherwise) and *syariah* law as a whole was probably *not* a conspicuous—in the sense of widespread—feature of the judicial landscape in the Malay Peninsula either during the 1830s or earlier. To put these matters somewhat differently, we might paraphrase Gullick's previously cited (1958) assessment, endorsed by Milner (1983), Hefner (2000), and others that although references to Islamic legal doctrine appear in the Malay law codes of the historical era with which we are concerned, there is *no evidence* suggesting that such doctrine was effective law.

COLONIAL REPRESENTATIONS OF ISLAMIC MAGISTRATES AND THEIR COURTS, 1840s–1880s

Such then is what can be pieced together of the *kadi* and their courts in the Malay Peninsula through the 1830s. The material that is relevant to the next fifty or so years, which also derives primarily from European (chiefly British) sources, is in many ways more abundant but also noteworthy for its decidedly negative treatment of indigenous Malay polities and judicial systems especially. The material on judicial systems is particularly negative with respect to what the British took to be *criminal* law, less so in its treatment of what they regarded as *civil* law. Perhaps surprisingly, British accounts were in some cases rather positive and relatively charitable as regards the *kadi* and their courts.

Even so, there is lamentably little information on judicial process in these latter courts, and, as suggested by the passages from historians of nineteenth-century Malaya quoted at the beginning of the chapter, such information as does exist is exceedingly difficult to work with. There are at least two reasons for this. First, as Sadka puts it in one of the quoted passages in question (which does, however, pertain more to secular than religious justice): "The scanty, uniformly disparaging references by contemporary British observers are suspect, since they are the observations of administrators committed to the introduction of a rival system, and prejudiced in any case in favour of written codes and procedures" (1968: 249). The other factor that contributes to the difficulties at issue has to do with the nature of the colonial gaze; this in turn has at least two dimensions: the Orientalist focus on contrast and Kiplingesque divides rather than similarity, and the particular types of contrasts that were salient in colonial discourse. The British did not dwell on the real or imagined contrasts that existed either between two or more systems of *judicial ideals* (British and Malay), or between two or more systems of *judicial practice*. They focused instead on the perceived contrasts between *British judicial ideals* on the one hand and *Malay judicial practice* on the other. Such comparisons necessarily involve "apples and oranges." No small matter, moreover, as we shall see, is that when the British trained their sights on their own judicial practices in Malaya, much of the contrast disappeared, which is to say that they did not come off so well. The more general point is well put by Sadka, whom we might thus quote once again: "What little we know and understand of Malay legal and judicial systems, we owe to the reconstructions of a [subsequent] generation of colonial officers of impartial scholarship, who worked and wrote when Malay justice, as a function of government, was receding into the past" (1968: 249).

In this context we might first recall that the legal digests referred to earlier on were not composed of public enactments as such but were the hereditary possessions of chiefly families and more encompassing kin groups and were, in a good many cases, more or less "private books of reference" (Sadka 1968: 249), "copies [of which] were very rare" (Gullick 1958: 114). Moroever

> the powerful territorial chiefs who administered the law refused to be bound by inconvenient rules and regulations, and there was no one who had the power or the responsibility to interfere with their decisions. The administration of justice became, at best, assistance given by chiefs to their own followers. Litigation—in cases where the litigants did not take the law into their own hands—became a matter of diplomatic negotiation between the nobles who championed either side. (Sadka 1968: 249–50)

Some British observers had positive or at least seemingly neutral impressions of local leaders and the processes of dispute resolution they oversaw, but they tend to be the exceptions that prove the rule. Thus in an article published in 1850, Lt. Col. James Low recounts his journey through the state of Perak and describes the sultan there as "a very quiet person and very indulgent to his subjects." Low goes on to remark of the sultan's daily routine that it "admits not of much variety" and that it includes "hear[ing] complaints and settl[ing] business early in the morning" (Low 1850: 502).

Far more frequently encountered in the literature of this period are the purportedly arbitrary judgments made by chiefs, along with the use of their judicial powers to levy and derive profit from potentially burdensome fines—and in these and other ways to oppress their subjects. That such themes were much emphasized in the accounts of the first years of intervention is particularly evident in the case of Sir Hugh Clifford, who, as Sadka puts it, "spoke of [the judicial system] in the blackest terms" (1968: 250). Clifford's observations and the contours of his discourse as a whole are worth examining in some detail. Let us consider a paper titled, "Life in the Malay Peninsula; As It Was And Is," which was presented at the meetings of the Royal Colonial Institute held at the Hotel Metropole, London, on June 20, 1899.[6]

Clifford begins his address by making reference to the Malayan states' "evolution . . . from independence and misrule to protection, prosperity, and good government," noting that, as in "half-a-hundred [other] obscure localities," such evolution occurred with "the aid of . . . Our new-caught, sullen peoples, Half devil and half child."[7] Having thus invoked a key phrase from Rudyard Kipling's newly published poem, "The White Man's Burden," Clifford goes on to situate what in today's parlance we would refer to as his ethnographic authority. He does this by informing his audience that he was an agent in Pahang until a British resident was appointed to "aid" the sultan in the administration of his country during the last months of 1888, adding that he was "permitted to see native life as it exists when no white men are at hand to watch and take note of its peculiarities—native life naked and unashamed." He is perforce

> speaking of things observed at first hand; of a native system of administration—*if anything so fortuitous may be termed a system*—into the every-day working of which I have been permitted to pry; of native institutions which I have seen in actual operation for extended periods of time; and of some phases of Oriental life which went on undisturbed around me, while I myself played among them an insignificant and unconsidered part. (emphasis added)[8]

Averring throughout that he is allowing his audience a look behind the scenes, to see how "matters worked out in actual practice,"[9] Clifford has much to say about the excessive concentration of unchecked authority and power in the office of the sultan:

> The Sultan was the main pivot upon which all things in his country turned . . . the source from which all blessing flowed, . . . the person who held in his hand rewards and punishments. . . . His lightest word brought death, swift and inevitable, which most often was not preceded by any such tedious formalities as a trial or examination of the accused. He was the principal trader, the richest man, the banker and advancer of capital to his people. He was also a law to himself, and whatsoever he might elect to do, those about him would be certain to approve with loud-mouthed cordiality such as princes love.[10]

Throughout his delivery Clifford stresses as well that because of this state of affairs, a "number of little civil wars were constantly raging, and the unfortunate peasants bore the brunt of them as of all the other heavy burdens of the distracted land."[11] He goes on to comment on the judicial aspects of the sultan's role:

> Theoretically the Sultan was the supreme judge, and it was to his *balai*, or reception hall, that all complaints were made, and there that all disputes were heard, and all judgements given. Some of the more vigorous of the old Sultans actually performed this duty; but for the most part the Malayan rulers were too supine and too callous to bother themselves about such affairs. Therefore the right to judge was generally deputed to more or less incompetent persons, most often selected from among the number of the royal favourites, the upstarts of no family, hated by the hereditary chiefs, by whom the Sultan was always surrounded. These posts, naturally, were much sought after, for in the hands of Asiatics the administration of justice, so called, is always made to be a fairly lucrative business.[12]

Clifford continues with a point of similarity between the judicial systems of the Malays and the British but quickly turns to the contrasts:

All who came to the judges brought gifts—which may be taken as being roughly equivalent to our fees of court—but here the resemblance to all our methods of administration ceased, for the bringer of a handsome present could usually obtain any judgement, which he required without further question, his *ex parte* statement being accepted as sufficient grounds for immediate action, and the judgement no matter how unjust, being upheld to the last, unless the other party in the suit put in an appearance and made reconsideration worth the judges' while for the sake of their well-loved money bags.[13]

While emphasizing these themes, Clifford, like earlier observers such as Newbold, seems to have been mesmerized by issues of physical sanctions and capital punishment and by the style of executions in particular. He describes these executions in grisly detail (p. 373) and notes further that "the misdeeds of the native magistrates are carried to lamentable lengths."[14] Clifford then turns to civil matters, informing his audience that unfortunately

in civil proceedings things are no better. One half of the debt sued for is claimed by most courts of requests. . . . If the man from whom . . . [a suitor] seeks to recover money be wealthy or powerful, far worse things than that are liable to befall the imprudent creditor. . . . The *inefficiency and corruption* which is noticeable among the magistrates of a Malayan State in those parts of the country . . . *[is]* . . . *found in every department of the Government, if anything so inchoate can be described as being divided into departments*." (emphases added)[15]

It is especially important to note two points here: first, much of what Clifford rails against in the latter portion of this passage—and in other parts of his presentation to the Royal Colonial Institute—is feudalistic excess and inefficiency; second, in this regard his discourse is strongly reminiscent of the types of sentiments, interests, and overall concerns whose historical development Michel Foucault cites in *Discipline and Punish* (1977) when he seeks to account for the shift from physical torture and execution to incarceration as punishment for regicide in eighteenth-century Europe. Indeed, Clifford is not only at great pains to emphasize that "the Malays . . . had worked out for themselves . . . a theory of government on *feudal* lines which bears a startling resemblance to the European models of a long-passed epoch . . . [such that] to live in independent Malaya is to live in the Europe of the thirteenth century" (emphasis added).[16] He is also intent on underscoring the extreme "measure of misery and misrule under which the average Malayan State laboured before the cross of St. George was brought to this remote part of the world . . . [to wage] . . . yet another battle with the great dragon—the four-headed dragon of Cruelty, Ignorance, Selfishness, and Stupidity."[17] Concerning issues of excess and inefficiency, Clifford emphasizes that "*The machinery of misrule was exceedingly clumsy and inefficient, since the rulers of the land [with all their "eccentricities"] were themselves too indolent to even oppress their subjects with system and thoroughness*" (emphasis added).[18]

As regards the issue of sanctions, we have already commented on the fact that Clifford, like Newbold and others, was fascinated by torture, capital punishment, and the details of executions in particular. He notes, for example, that "a few formal executions have been carried out within my experience, . . . usually . . . accompanied by the most atrocious tortures," adding that

> [t]he laws which are administered by the native courts, and are carried out by these men, are a strange medley of the legislation of Muhammad and of the Law of Custom, the traditional code of the Malays. By the law of Muhammad many barbarities are permitted such as no European Government could countenance, but these are by no means repugnant to the Malays. Thus, for theft the prescribed punishment is the lopping off of a hand, and in Kelantan to-day the execution of this sentence is a very frequent occurrence.[19]

But the picture thus presented is immediately softened, for we are next told that "*in other parts of the Peninsula mutilation as a punishment for theft was less common, a fine being more often inflicted upon the relatives of the criminal*" (emphasis added), though "in some instances the old customary penalty for theft was resorted to." This is described much as in Newbold's account from the 1830s:

> The thief having been caught, and the stolen property having been recovered, the latter was bound about his neck. The criminal was next smeared with soot and tumeric, was placed astride upon a buffalo . . . and . . . was paraded in derision through the streets . . . by a crowd of the King's Youths, to the beating of gongs, his crime being publicly proclaimed at all the cross-roads.[20]

Most significant for our purposes is that Clifford then goes on to report: "*I have heard old men say that this punishment was far more dreaded by Malay thieves than fine or mutilation*, and I can well believe that this was the case, for *a fear of open shame and a fierce self-respect are two of the strongest feelings in the breast of the average Malay in his natural condition*" (emphasis added).[21]

It warrants remark, finally, that while Clifford saw nothing to recommend in the structure or administration of criminal justice and had little good to say about justice in civil matters, he, like Newbold, was relatively positive on the subject of the Islamic magistrates with whom he came into contact. All things considered, including in particular the pronounced antagonism of the British toward things Islamic, I find this quite remarkable. That said, Clifford presents little information on the subject.

> Throughout the State in matters connected with betrothal, marriage, and divorce, the which touch all Muhammadans very closely, *the Law of the Prophet was administered by . . . Kathis and priests; and on the whole these men did their work well*, for many of them had the fear of God before their eyes, and they hesitated to tamper with His law even for the sake of worldly profit. *They often meted out punishments with brutality; they often applied the law with a too narrow regard for its letter rather than for its spirit, but they acted for the most part, I am inclined to think, honestly*, though they stood in far too great awe of the Sultan to dare to admonish him, or even to preach against the most unholy of his practices. (emphases added)[22]

In sum, in Clifford's view, the *kadi* and presumably the village mosque officials who were reported to assist the *kadi* in making their decisions were both honest and conscientious, though inclined toward overly literal ("narrow") interpretations of the relevant Islamic legal codes as well as the imposition of overly harsh ("brutal") penalties, except when it came to the "unholy practices" of the sultan, which tended to be overlooked. Unclear, however, is the exact nature of the harsh punishments at issue, though the strong impression given by Clifford is that fines and rituals of shaming and humiliation were more common than "the lopping off of a hand" or anything comparable. The harshness is in any case relative, for Clifford reports that Malays preferred fines and mutilations to public shaming and humiliation. Such being the case, one might plausibly suggest that the exercising of the more physical "Islamic options" (such as amputation) showed greater mercy on the part of those in power than the imposition of more psychologically oriented punishments such as shaming and humiliation. Ironically, this would be consistent with Clifford's previously noted findings that physical sanctions were *less feared* than those of a more psychological sort.

Let us return to some of the broader issues broached at the outset of this discussion, one of which has to do with the types of comparisons the British drew between themselves and their colonial subjects. I noted that generally speaking, when British observers (such as Clifford) undertook such comparisons—and they frequently though often implicitly did so—they tended to focus on difference rather than similarity and in any case tended to make comparisons drawn on contrasts between British judicial *ideals* and Malay judicial *practice*. I emphasized as well that when the British trained their gaze on their own judicial procedures, they did not to come off so well. Both themes are readily apparent in the reaction Clifford received from at least one person who sat through his lengthy presentation at the Hotel Metropole that night in June 1899. I refer to W. H. Treacher, C.M.G., British resident of Perak, who offered the following remarks in response to Clifford's discourse on Malays "as they were, and as they are":

> Mr. Clifford . . . has, unavoidably of course, had to focus before you some of the worst points in Malay life, and I am trying to relieve somewhat the tension under which you must be suffering. Recollect that, not very long ago in the history of our own civilised and Christian country, women were burned for witchcraft, people were hanged for stealing sheep, Catholics burned Protestants and Protestants burned Catholics, and slavery existed under our flag, with all its horrors, to an extent unknown to the Malays.[23]

There is no way of knowing if Treacher was being ironic or satirical when he referred to his own "civilized and Christian country" and drew attention to certain of the less savory practices that had been thoroughly institutionalized there "not very long ago." What is clear is that he is offering the audience both a corrective and a palliative to Clifford's views by bringing into focus some of the similarities (and not just the differences) between Malays and British. That such was his agenda is made even more apparent by the comments that immediately followed those noted above, which focused on the civility, intelligence, and verbal skills that Treacher found to be common to (at least some) Malays and British alike: "My own Sultan [*sic*] is one of the most courteous men I have ever met. He understands both sides of a question more rapidly than many Englishmen, and he can give you a clear opinion and express his views forcibly on such vexed questions as gambling, opium-smoking, and the registration of women."[24]

Treacher is in many respects the exception that proves the rule. Far more typical were the views contained in the 1879 accounts of renowned world traveler and author Isabella Bird, which were published in five installments in a British serial, *The Leisure Hour*, in 1883. Bird was much taken with her travels in and around Melaka and Sungai Ujung; this despite her finding "The 'Golden Khersonese' as a whole 'very hot, and much infested by things which bite and sting,"[25] and despite the fact that she had very few good things to say about Malays and gave a highly mixed report of colonial judicial practice in action: "Malacca fascinates me more and more daily. There is, among other things, a *medievalism* about it. The noise of the modern world reaches out only in the faintest echoes; its sleep is almost dreamless, its sensations seem to come out of books read in childhood" (emphasis added).[26] Sungai Ujung, for its part, was even more intriguing, "regarded [as it was] as 'parts unknown', . . . a region of tigers, crocodiles, rogue elephants, and savages!" which was also home to "panther[s] . . . and other beasts, . . . large and small apes and monkeys," cobra, python, hog, deer, etc., for which reason Bird concluded that it "*must be like many parts of Western Africa*" (emphasis added).[27]

Having devoted most of the first two installments of her serialized account to descriptions of the flora, fauna, weather, and her young white traveling companions, Bird opens the third installment of her report with the admission, "It is strange that I should have written thus far and have said nothing about the people from whom this peninsula derives its name, who have cost us not a little blood and some treasure." She begins rectifying this omission as follows:

> [The Malay is] symbolised to people's minds . . . by the dagger called a *kris*, and by the peculiar form of frenzy which has given rise to the phrase "*running amuck*." . . . He shuns the town, and prefers a life of freedom in his native jungles, or on the mysterious rivers. . . . The men are not inclined to much effort except in fishing or hunting, and, where they possess rice-land, in ploughing for rice. *They are said to be quiet, temperate, jealous, suspicious, some say treacherous, and most bigoted Mussulmen. . . . [Yet] they are not savages in the ordinary sense, for they have a complete civilisation of their own, and their legal system is that of the Koran.* (emphasis added)[28]

There is much in these remarks on which we might comment, but it is arguably more productive to focus on Bird's observations concerning "governmentality" during the early days of colonial rule, especially the operations of the recently established residential system. Most of her observations on the subject are contained in her remarks concerning a certain Captain Murray, the British resident in Sungai Ujung, who was appointed when, as Bird and many of her contemporaries were wont to phrase it, the ruler presiding over the local polity (in this case, Datu Klana) "asked for" a resident, circa 1875. Noting, among other things, that Captain Murray had been "instruct[ing] the bright little daughter of the Datu Klana in lawn tennis," Bird writes that *"He devotes himself to Sungei Ujong as if it were his own property, though he has never been able to acquire the language"* (emphasis added).[29] She goes on to observe that "Murray is [not only] judge, 'sitting in equity', [but also] superintendent of police, chancellor of the exchequer, and surveyor of taxes, besides being Board of Trade, Board of Works, and I know not what besides. In fact, *he is the Government"* (emphasis in original).[30]

Obvious differences in tone aside, these latter comments, especially Bird's observation that Murray *"is* the Government," resonate with Clifford's extensive lamentations about the excessive concentration of authority and power (executive, legislative, and judicial) in the sultan and other rulers in Malaya "as it was." Indeed, Bird remarks that Murray's "Residential authority is subject only to the limitations of his own honour and good sense," though she adds that Murray's behavior was no doubt also conditioned by considerations of "possible snubs" by the governor.[31] Rather than dwell on the ironies of this situation, however, let us proceed to a consideration of what Bird had to say about Captain Murray's personal qualities, some of which, as she notes, were very much in evidence in his capacity as judge:

> He is a man about thirty-eight, a naval officer, and an enterprising African traveler, . . . bronzed, sun-browned, *restless*, almost eccentric, *never still for five minutes, disconnected in his conversation* from the habit of living without any one in or out of the house to speak to; . . . *hasty when vexed,* but thoroughly kindhearted; . . . *very blunt, very undignified,* never happy (he says) out of the wilds; thoroughly well disposed to the Chinese and Malays, but *impatient of their courtesies,* thoroughly a gentleman, but *about the last person that I should have expected to see in a position which is said to require much tact if not finesse.* (emphases added)[32]

She then describes a visit to the courthouse run by Murray, along with the hearings she observed there, one of which involved a Chinese man charged with stealing a pig. First, the courthouse: it was a

> large, whitewashed room, with a clean floor of red tiles, a tiled daïs with a desk for the judge, a table with a charge-sheet and some books upon it, and three long benches at the end for witnesses and their friends. A *punkah* is kept constantly going. There are a clerk, a Chinese intepreter who speaks six Chinese dialects, and a Malay interpreter who puts the Chinese interpreter's words into English. As the judge does not understand Malay, it will be observed that justice depends on the fidelity of this latter official. Though *I cannot say that the dignity of justice is sustained in this court,* there is not a doubt that the intentions of the judge are excellent. (emphasis added)[33]

Then what might be termed Captain Murray's "judicial style":

The Resident's restlessness, which often gives him the appearance of eccentricity, came out very strongly during the tedious business of disposing of charges. He was never still for two minutes, but was either hammering on the desk, whittling its edge, humming snatches of airs, making remarks to me, exclaiming, "Bother these fellows!" or "Do get on, and don't keep us broiling here for ever!" knowing that only the Malay interpreter understood him. Mr. Haywood, through whose hands the crime of Singapore and Malacca has filtered for twenty years, was very critical on the rough-and-ready method of proceeding here, and constantly interjected suggestions such as, "You don't ask them questions before you swear them," etc.[34]

Two themes are especially striking here. First is the seemingly unvarnished if not altogether frank account of what might charitably be termed, following Bird, Captain Murray's "rough-and-ready method of [judicial] proceeding," which comes through loud and clear if we pull together some of Bird's remarks on Murray's professional demeanor and overall judicial style: He was "restless," "disconnected in conversation," "hasty when vexed," "blunt," "undignified," and "impatient" with the "courtesies" (read "cultural sensibilities") of local litigants, witnesses, and (presumably) other relevant players such as translators, clerks, and bailiffs. And in addition to ignoring standard operating procedure by examining defendants and others without first swearing them in, he was "never still for two minutes" and was either hammering on the desk, whittling its edge, humming snatches of airs, exclaiming (in a language that was foreign to almost everyone present in the courthouse and was certainly unintelligible to the only litigants about whom we have specific information), "Bother these fellows!" and "Do get on and don't keep us broiling here for ever!"—such that he was "constantly" criticized by a visiting British magistrate. More generally, just as Bird not only admits that Murray is "about the last person I should have expected to see in a position which is said to require much tact if not finesse," she also concludes—and this is in many respects the bottom line—that justice is *not* served in Murray's court. Her precise sentiments on this key issue, recall, are: "I cannot say that the dignity of justice is sustained in this court."

The second theme that is particularly striking in all of this is the unbridled, unsupported, even blind optimism concerning the virtues of local British judicial process that Bird registers in passing, despite the volume of observations and conclusions concerning Murray's glaring incompetence or at least his inappropriateness for the job of local judge. Indeed, Bird concludes the paragraph recounting how, when court is in session, Captain (here Judge) Murray is given to hammering on his desk, whittling its edge, humming, talking to visitors, blurting out his frustrations in English, and being "constantly" castigated by a more experienced colonial magistrate with the jarringly dissonant remark, "*Informal as its administration is, I have no doubt that justice is substantially done.*" The "evidence" proffered for what is in the given context a most peculiar conclusion is quite straightforward but would also have to be judged thoroughly circumstantial and largely irrelevant. It consists of the "fact" that in

Bird's view "*the Resident is conscientious, . . . truly honourable, . . . very lovable, [and] . . . is evidently much beloved, . . .* [for he] . . . is able to go about in unguarded security" (emphasis added).[35]

I have dwelt on Isabella Bird's observations concerning judicial practice in Captain Murray's court partly to underscore that British observers were well aware of the chaos in their courts but preferred their own brand of judicial chaos to the Malay variants they encountered or imagined, and partly to emphasize that the British did in any case turn a blind eye to the irregularities and excesses of colonial judicial practice. Phrased in more abstract terms, the irregularities and excesses of colonial judicial practice that the British observed did not disrupt their hegemonic view that British judicial practice was just, honorable, and altogether superior to its indigenous counterparts.

It remains to consider, finally, what Bird has to say about Malays in general and *kadi* in particular:

> [Malay] "honour" is so sensitive that blood alone can wipe out some insults to it. . . . [They] are bigoted, and for the most part ignorant and fanatical Mohammedans. . . . They are . . . ruled by the law of the Koran, and except where the Kali [*kadi*], who interprets the law, decides (which is very rarely the case) contrary to equity, the British magistrate confirms his decision. In fact Mohammedan law and custom rule in civil causes, and the Imaum of the mosque assists the judge with his advice.[36]

What I find both remarkable and ironic about this passage is that while it contains more or less blanket condemnation of Malays as "bigoted," "ignorant," and "fanatical Mohammedans," it also grants that *kadi*'s interpretations of the law are almost always equitable (only "very rarely" "contrary to equity"). More generally, Bird's grudging praise of *kadi* resonates with the deeply ambivalent views of Newbold, Clifford, and other British observers who express intense antipathy toward many aspects of Malay life and customs, including religion and the handling of criminal matters by local rulers, but were nonetheless relatively charitable in their assessments of the work performed by Islamic magistrates.

The Reorganization and Rationalization of the Courts, 1890s—1980s

> Malay judicial responsibility appears to have been regarded as an administrative imperfection, unavoidable in the early stages of intervention, but to be superseded by European authority as soon as possible, or circumscribed by limited jurisdiction and, in the more important cases, by the presence of a British magistrate who would be the effective dispenser of justice. . . . [Key concerns] in their administration of justice as in other branches of government . . . [were] . . . recognizing the petty jurisdiction of *penghulus* [village leaders], and allowing it to function as informally as possible within a general system of British courts, governed by British rules of procedure and administering state law or the law of the parties, according to the nature of the

case. . . . *But it was essentially a single system.* (Sadka 1968: 263, 273; emphasis added)

The reorganization, standardization, and rationalization of Malaya's Islamic legal institutions that occurred at the hands of British colonial authorities began in earnest in what might be termed the "long decade" of the 1890s (the fifteen or so year period extending from the final years of the 1880s through the first few years of the twentieth century). This was, not coincidentally, a period marked by the rapid consolidation of British colonial power through the residential system and the pronounced though highly uneven constriction of indigenous authority entailed in the imposition and subsequent development of that system. Because indigenous institutions and traditions of all kinds, especially those bearing on what the British took to be matters of politics, were increasingly subject to the ever more systematic colonial gaze during this period and the decades that followed, we know a good deal more about *kadi* and the judicial procedures in which they were involved during this time. Still, as the epigraph for this section suggests, indigenous authorities were effectively shunted aside or severely constrained by colonial fiat, which heavily circumscribed their judicial responsibilities and jurisdictions on the whole. This fact, coupled with the British imperial bias toward written codes and substantive law as opposed to, say, more informal, unwritten modes of operation, including, especially, those bearing on procedure and the cultural logic of judicial process, means that we do not know much about actual judicial process in the *kadi*'s courts during any period of colonial rule. That said, the larger context in which *kadi* and their courts operated is fairly clear.

Toward the beginning of this period, the colonial rule of thumb seemed to be that in judicial matters, British magistrates were to rely on "The law prevalent in Mahomedan States supplemented when necessary by the laws of Great Britain."[37] Instructions prepared in 1882 by the assistant resident of Perak (George Maxwell) prescribed "the Straits Penal Code as the guide in criminal jurisdiction," specifying in addition that "procedural details should be as in the English Court of Petty Sessions, a manual on which was to be furnished to every court, and [that] the English law of evidence was to be followed."[38] The instructions continued: "Native laws and customs should be allowed due rights, but as no uniform body of native law is in the hands of Magistrates for enforcement, reference should be made to head-quarters in cases of difficulty turning entirely on native custom." Instructions along these same lines were reissued in Selangor and Sungai Ujung in 1890 and 1894, respectively.[39]

Many such codes and procedures were borrowed wholesale from the Indian Penal Code and the Straits Settlement Law (much of which was modeled on the Indian Penal Code). Speaking of the administration of law generally, Sadka notes that "magistrates in the early years administered the law according to their own ideas of equity, modified by what they knew of Malay and Chinese custom and the Indian or the Straits Penal Code."[40] Not surprisingly, Isabella Bird, who witnessed the operation of the system, concluded that it was "a most queerly muddled system of law, . . . Muhammadan law existing alongside of fragments of English criminal law, the Resident's notions of equity overriding all else."[41]

Bird was by no means the only observer to reach such conclusions. Others, including those with a much greater stake in the management of local affairs, were also alarmed by the relative messiness and chaos they encountered in local British judicial domains. Among them was Frank Swettenham, who argued in 1891 that "lawyers should be kept out of the courts, not only for reasons of principle but also because 'they [the state governments] do so many things for which they would be puzzled to produce any legal warrant that the advent of educated and intelligent lawyers would be disastrous to the Native States system at the present time'."[42]

As mentioned earlier, however, irregularities in local British judicial processes were much preferred, or at least more inclined to be tolerated, than real or imagined irregularities in Malay judicial systems. The former, in any case, did not undermine the hegemonic views of British judicial superiority; the latter, in contrast, were absolutely central to imperial hegemony concerning Malay judicial process. In some ways more important, they provided grist for the ideological mill that helped churn out and sustain what proved to be widespread and enduring British (and eventually broadly diffused Western) ideologies that were either subsumed under the relatively specific rubric of "*kadi*-justice" or keyed to more general and diffuse assumptions as to the inequities, backwardness, and overall irrationalities of Islam.

We shall return to the themes bearing on "*kadi*-justice" and related matters in due course (chapter 2). In the meantime it bears emphasizing that unfortunately, the precise role "played by Malay authorities in the administration of justice [during this period] is not easy to determine."[43] That said, it is clear that with respect to numerous categories of cases that the British deemed serious, such as homicide, burglary, rape, arson, forgery, and coining, Malay "judgement was not altogether trusted" and Malays tended to be excluded from all substantive participation in judicial process. This was partly because "it was a rare thing for a Malay to appear as an offender in a criminal court, . . . the accused [being] mainly Chinese with a percentage of Indians, . . . [typically up on charges of] . . . drunkenness, breaches of the peace, vagrancy, petty thefts, and similar minor offenses."[44] Despite being drawn out of the loop in such cases and despite being fairly closely supervised by British officials in others, "[Malay authorities] had had some judicial responsibility from the very beginning of the Residential system, and it was in this sphere of government perhaps that they participated most actively."[45] When British courts were established, local Malay rulers met regularly with residents and district magistrates, though, as noted above, serious offenses were handled by British officials in accordance with British notions of justice, propriety, due process, and the like.

We need to exercise caution in interpreting such circumscription for at least two reasons. First, the judicial functions of the chiefs extended beyond the courts: in Negeri Sembilan, for example, "it was customary for the 'chief' (by which, presumably, was meant the lineage headman) to attempt to settle civil cases in the first instance by arbitration."[46] (Criminal cases were the responsibility of the police, but even in these cases the chiefs of persons charged were required to be present and presumably played some role as well, via mediation, negotiation, etc.) Second, senior chiefs and *rajas* assisted European magistrates, "not only by hearing and considering the evidence with [them], but by advising [them] as to Malay custom in civil cases."[47] This was of considerable importance not only with respect to the specific cases at hand but also with regard to the shaping and future relevance of authoritative texts and state-defined spheres of *adat* and Islam (see Peletz 1993a).

According to Sadka, "for the most part, the Malays who held court independently were the *kathis* and *penghulus* with minor jurisdiction."[48] In 1891, *kadi* and *penghulu* in Perak were empowered "to charge twenty cents for every summons, postponement, service and judgement ticket, and ten cents for every subpeona."[49] (But this varied; in Selangor, for example, *penghulu* did not charge any fees.) Such fees were "a fraction of those prevailing in the ordinary courts, but they must still have made litigation in the villages unnecessarily complicated and expensive."[50] Even so, in 1890 *penghulu* and native chiefs in Lower Perak were reported to have disposed of more cases than the district courts.[51]

"In Pahang where (according to Clifford) the only justice to speak of in pre-British days was administered by *kathis*, the Resident's initiative appears not to have been necessary," and by 1890 a *kadi*, "probably a pre-Residential appointment, was sitting with the Pekan magistrate."[52] In Negeri Sembilan around the same time, a *kadi* was "hearing cases in open court once a week." In the latter state, however, the jurisdiction of *kadi* seems to have been limited to religious offenses, narrowly defined. The British resident of Negeri Sembilan, for example, "noted that the chiefs of that state adhered to the customary law [*adat*] in property and inheritance cases, and failing a settlement in their courts, the cases were brought into the civil courts." By contrast, in Sungai Ujung and Jelebu the chiefs apparently had adopted the *syariah* in such cases, which were thus referred to the *kadi*'s court.[53]

Colonial records from this era refer to chief *kadi* and assistant *kadi* being "salaried officers of the state." They also note that such "'Muhammadan priests' were required to keep a register of all marriages and divorces"; and that while they had powers to fine, they were required to report matrimonial offenses, including "enticement" and remarriage within the *edah* period[54] to the (British) district magistrate.[55] Cases of the latter sort were beyond the jurisdiction of *kadi*, but *kadi* did sit as assessors, just as their assistants (*naib*), though without jurisdiction per se, might "settle small disputes with the consent of the parties" involved.[56] Interestingly, some areas, such as Lower Perak, had been treating adultery as a penal offense since 1881. As the district magistrate of Batang Padang wrote in 1892:

> When I first came to the State [prior to 1881] these cases were dealt with by the Malay *Imams* etc and were punished by shaving the head, flogging in public etc.

[T]his was abolished and for some time there was no recognized punishment but afterwards at the suggestion, I believe of the late Sultan (then Regent) it was ordered that cases of adultery should be tried by a Magistrate sitting with an Asst. Kathi or native Magistrate and the maximum punishment was fixed at six months imprisonment of either description and (or) fine not exceeding $60/. . . . This was the custom in Kinta when I left and I introduced it here. It is also in force in lower Perak.[57]

In 1894 these sanctions were institutionalized in states such as Perak and Selangor through legislation that defined adultery by Muslims as a criminal act punishable by fine or imprisonment: "Prompt arrest and punishment of offenders was not merely an authoritarian exercise; as the Sultan of Perak explained when he argued the need for such legislation before Council, most of the serious crimes by Malays were crimes of jealousy, and some action was needed to prevent people taking the law into their own hands."[58]

One of the reasons that the very existence of *kadi* was particularly troublesome from the point of view of the British is that they were key symbols of Islam generally and of Islamic law specifically, the administration of which "was a source of considerable embarrassment to British officers."[59] "The existence of a dual judicial responsibility disturbed" British officers, "as it has disturbed other temporal authorities faced with the claims and pretensions of religious courts," partly because "they had an individualist and secular repugnance to a code which punished neglect of religious duties with fines, and adultery with heavy prison sentences."[60] The dilemma was ameliorated in part by limiting the jurisdiction of *kadi* (for example, by bringing the more serious cases before secular magistrates) and by overseeing their work in various ways. Thus, "in Perak, reports of cases and petitions for appeal were channeled through the European officers to the Chief *Kathi* and the Sultan." Even so, it remained "difficult for some European officers to reconcile themselves to the temporal punishment of sin."[61]

Despite but also partly because of their ambivalence, the British forged ahead with judicial reforms of various kinds, many of which made provision for the establishment of new "mixed courts."[62] But problems persisted and complaints were manifold: in some of the new courts, Malay judges were reported to dispense with witnesses and to levy fines without trial.[63] More generally, "various judicial personnel lacked the due modicum of judicial knowledge; judges had no lawyers to help them, they got no publicity and were subject to no public opinion."[64] In Negeri Sembilan, moreover, because of the British view that *kadi* "were not versed in the procedures of examination of witnesses and the admission or rejection of evidence, the help of a European magistrate" was deemed "beneficial," though "not so much to interpret the *shari'a* as to oversee rules of evidence and procedure."[65] Such "mixed courts" are among the more important legacies of the colonial era, as we shall discuss in more detail in due course.

We have concentrated thus far on the reorganization and rationalization of Islamic courts but have said little about the effects of these and related processes on preexisting courts, on the authority of traditional leaders in the form of district chiefs and their subordinates, and on the sensibilities of the rural Malay majority. To address these latter issues, I shall focus for the moment on the district of Rembau and the state of Negeri Sembilan generally. As early as 1889, by which time Rembau boasted a state-appointed *kadi*, the district had three somewhat separate court systems, each with its own realm of jurisdiction and distinct traditions governing procedure, justice, and retribution, though as noted in Sadka's epigraph to this section, they were all encompassed within and ultimately subject to the constraints of a single system of British and over-whelmingly secular design.[66] From the very beginning, of course, Rembau's Islamic court and its cadre of officialdom came under the de jure authority of the *undang* (though the latter was ultimately beholden to the British). The *undang* therefore retained his traditional supreme position as chief arbiter in re-ligious affairs and as Allah's vice-regent (*khalifah*) within the district. None-theless, events of 1889 engendered a separation of powers and legitimacy analogous to that between church and state, which had not existed in Rem-bau—or anywhere else in the Peninsula—prior to colonial rule.

With the creation of an Islamic court in Rembau, many of the prerogatives, responsibilities, and symbols of *adat* leaders became vested in Islamic magis-trates and their official representatives. As a direct consequence, in 1889 Rem-bau's *undang* virtually ceased to participate in the civil aspects of villagers' marriages and divorces (Parr and Mackray 1910: 52, 57); these duties were thenceforth assigned to Rembau's *kadi*. The following decade saw the passage of legislation requiring Friday mosque attendance by males residing in the vi-cinity of a mosque; it also made village-level Islamic functionaries directly responsible to the *kadi* for enforcing the payment of small fines by those irregu-larly present at Friday services.[67] These developments effectively extended cen-tralized political control into an area where it had never before penetrated, creating in addition new loci and linkages of authority both in villages and in the district as a whole. All such legislation impinged on the duties and stature of clan leaders, who had previously regulated all local affairs including the observance of religious obligations. Even though the processes in question were fairly gradual, clan spokesmen were clearly victims.

It is notable that much of the impetus behind religious hierarchical expansion and more consistent enforcement of Islamic law emanated from the highest echelons of the indigenous polity itself—including the *undang* and *yang diper-tuan besar*. This was partly because Islamic administration and reform was one of the few areas in which elite initiative received the formal approval and en-couragement of British authorities (Roff 1967; Milner 1995). We need to bear in mind that the British introduced legislation bearing on virtually all domains of Malay life, thereby severely restricting indigenous rulers' involvement in substantive political activities. These circumstances prompted indigenous elites throughout the Peninsula to seek expression in progressively more elaborate displays of their traditional power and status, and further encouraged them to play an ever greater role both in the administration of religious affairs and in the more formal implementation of Islamic law.[68] That their activities in this latter area often worked to erode the stature of clan chiefs and their subordinates was, it seems, of little direct concern and occasionally was even to their advantage. One need only recall that status rivalries and political antagonisms rather than common interests seem always to have been characteristic of vertical (and structurally complementary) relationships in the indigenous polity (see Peletz 1988b, 1996).

No less important here were the challenges posed to the traditional political elite (the Kaum Tua or "Old Group") by Sumatrans and other, mostly foreign-born Muslims whose activities in Singapore, Melaka, and elsewhere in the Peninsula from about 1900 threatened both the elites' positions of privilege and their supremacy in the eyes of Islamic subjects. Criticizing the old guard as reactionary and feudalistic, and spearheading a modernist movement that came to be known as the Kaum Muda (Young Group), these activists sought sweeping religious and educational reform as a means of improving the lot of Malays, their Indonesian brethren, and Muslims the world over. Among other things, they endeavored to rid Malayan Islam of local accretions emanating from *adat* and to persuade influential Islamic men of learning (*ulama*) to rectify past errors associated with their conveyance of "false doctrine" and religious impurities more generally (Roff 1967: 58). This involved encouraging individual Muslims to exercise rationality (*akal*) and informed judgment (*ijtihad*) so as to eradicate the uncritical acceptance of intermediate religious authority (*taklid buta*), which was said to prevail throughout village society and to ensure a perpetuation of the status quo.

Modern education and greater contact between local elites and (mostly foreign-born) Muslims in Singapore, Melaka, and other parts of the Malay-Indonesian archipelago also enhanced Malay awareness of and dialogue with developments in Egypt, Saudi Arabia, and other regions of the Islamic heartlands. This had the effect, in the Malay world, of galvanizing diverse currents of Islamic nationalism and reform and of promoting nationalist discourse on the virtues of Islamic rationalization and the necessity of eradicating the "backward," pre-Islamic (animist/Hindu-Buddhist) elements of Malay culture to help in bringing Malays and Malayan Islam into the modern era.

One of the better-known nationalist leaders to emerge from the Malay community in the early part of the twentieth century was Dato Sedia Raja Abdullah bin Haji Dahan, Rembau's eighteenth *undang* (r. 1922–38). Dato Abdullah was among the Malays of royal birth (a member of a gentry clan) chosen to receive the benefits of an English-style education. Educated in Singapore and elsewhere, he campaigned vigorously for modern education for the Malay populace and for the development of numerous voluntary (especially self-help) organizations that would help improve the social and economic standing of the Malay community. Hailed by some British officials as "the ablest Malay in the country,"[69] Dato Abdullah also broke with longstanding tradition by publicly discouraging rituals of pre-Islamic origin, such as *berpuar*, which were conducted every three years in accordance with the dictates of venerated and feared *pawang* (shamanic specialists). These rituals entailed mock battles, blood sacrifice, and other activities geared toward securing the blessings of local guardian spirits, driving evil downstream toward the Straits of Melaka, and otherwise ensuring bountiful harvests.

Some sense of the reasons why Dato Abdullah sought to discourage such rituals and the beliefs undergirding them can be discerned from his comments on beliefs in the efficacy of *berpuar* and the local spirits associated with them.

> It is idle to hope for the economic progress of the Malays so long as this and similar beliefs prevail among them. Where those beliefs are deep rooted, science cannot make much headway, for superstitions and scientific truths cannot exist side by side. It is difficult, if not impossible, to deal scientifically with pests if damage to crops is believed to be due to the ravages of evil spirits.[70]

In much the same fashion, Dato Abdullah's brief overview of the more revered *keramat* beings (which he translates as "saints") held to exist in Rembau during the 1920s concludes on the following note:

> Such is the influence of these saints on the overwhelming majority of the Malays and it is needless to add that this influence is a lamentable obstacle to their economic, spiritual and moral advancement. Though Islam recognizes no intercessors between man and Allah, the relics of the pre-Islamic "Days of Ignorance" survive and will continue to exercise a disastrous influence so long as Malays are ignorant of the fundamental teachings of their religion and remain indifferent to the benefits of secular education.[71]

It is significant that reformist arguments such as those of Dato Abdullah were not only couched in appeals made in the name of secular education, science, and progress, but also contained few if any references to the philosophical or existential "quests for meaning" frequently cited by "intellectualist" theorists (Geertz [1964] 1973; Horton 1971; cf. Parsons 1963: xlvii–xlviii) as stimuli for religious conversion ("internal" or otherwise) or cultural rationalization generally.[72] More broadly, the symbols and idioms associated with terms such as "education," "science," and "progress" were of central importance in nationalist and transnational discourse, especially as they helped provide a new basis for translocal (pan-Malay and pan-Islamic) community identification.

In sum, Kaum Muda spokesmen and early nationalist leaders like Dato Abdullah launched an explicit attack on the spiritual and other evils stemming from a blind adherence to the religious figures who throughout the Peninsula bolstered and sanctified the positions of traditional rulers, including the most senior. The latter, for their part, reacted rather swiftly to this challenge. But they did so primarily through legislative channels, for by the turn of the century they enjoyed virtually no other legitimate options, the more general and salient point being that since the very beginning of early modern times in Southeast Asia *"the good ruler was always concerned with 'modernity'*," including, not least, acquiring *"the most modern spiritual doctrines and techniques"* (Milner 1983:

45; emphasis added). Thus the year 1904 saw the passage of an act forbidding the teaching or preaching of any religious doctrines outside one's home without the prior written permission of Negeri Sembilan's *yang dipertuan besar*.[73] This legislation also provided for the penalization of persons involved in "deviationism" through the propagation of "false doctrine," which could conceivably occur even in the case of duly authorized religious instructors despite the fact that "'deviationism' as such is unknown to any orthodox formulation of *Shari'a*" (Abdullahi A. An-Na'im 1999: 163).[74]

One other sphere of activity over which Islamic magistrates and their representatives attained jurisdiction during the early decades of colonial rule involved villagers' behavior during the fasting month, Ramadan. *Kadi* throughout Negeri Sembilan were charged with overseeing conformity to prohibitions on eating, drinking, smoking, and the like during the daylight hours of Ramadan, and by 1915 they could also fine local shopkeepers engaged in the daytime sale to Muslims of any food fit for immediate consumption.[75] These developments further confirm the larger process whereby outside authorities backed by the state intruded on the realm of village religion, clearly at the expense of clan leaders.[76]

Negeri Sembilan's *kadi* had encroached on the authority of local clan spokesmen even earlier, however. In 1888, to cite one example, the State Council of Sungai Ujung gave the district *kadi* and village-level mosque heads (*imam*) the power to prevent parents from demanding extortionate marriage payments from their daughters' suitors.[77] Local people undoubtedly saw this act as an infringement on both the prerogatives of clan officials and the autonomy of those with marriageable daughters. Of greater historical import is the previously noted Muhammadan Laws Enactment of 1904. This legislation did not simply embrace offenses associated with "deviationism" and the propagation of "false doctrine"; it also covered heterosexual impropriety (but not homosexual activities of any kind, despite their prohibition by the Quran) including adultery and incest as defined in Islam.[78] The fact that the enactment construed incest in exceedingly narrow terms (sexual relations between persons forbidden by Islamic law to marry), is extremely revealing since the British by this time no longer supported prohibitions within the far broader category of incestuous behaviors glossed *sumbang*.[79] These constitutional biases engendered by British policy thus increased the cultural distinction between *adat* and Islam.

One can easily imagine that the *kadi*'s jural sphere was of great concern not only to indigenous rulers but also to the architects of colonial policy. The creation of the *kadi*'s office did in fact result in highly charged disputes within Malay and British official circles concerning both the types of penalties Islamic magistrates could impose on transgressors of religious law and the precise limits of their jurisdiction on the whole. Villagers obviously held opinions on such matters too, as suggested (although perhaps overstated) by the comments of Negeri Sembilan's first British resident: "Nothing is more distasteful to the people than that Muhammadan law should be applied where custom provides the remedy, and as the Kathi is generally anxious to exercise Muhammadan law only, great care has to be taken to prevent him from interfering in cases of custom" (Lister 1890: 319).

Overall, issues relating to the *kadi*'s authority proved quite problematic in terms of British policy and villagers' relationships with clan leaders and representatives of the state. This was particularly true within the area of property and inheritance. Indeed, as discussed elsewhere (Peletz 1988b), many of the major legal, political, and cultural quandaries that emerged as early as 1890 centered on the devolution of rights over certain categories of property, especially land, and the extent to which village-level inheritance affairs ought to be directed by religious authorities and Islamic property codes more generally.

The appointment to Rembau of an Islamic magistrate in conjunction with the progressive empowering of religious hierarchies precipitated numerous dilemmas within the village—as well as profound legal and administrative problems for the British—owing also to the Malay people's varying knowledge of Islamic doctrine. The rural majority's understanding of Islamic doctrine has always been far less sophisticated than that of indigenous elites at the highest levels of the traditional polity or religious bureaucracy. Until recently, villagers' familiarity with the specifics of Islamic texts was at best rudimentary; typically, it was confined to what could be gleaned from the preachings of itinerant *ulama*, local mosque officials, and clan spokesmen.[80] Through religious instruction in the village, males gained the skills required to recite Quranic verse; this recitation proceeded in Arabic, however, not Malay, and the Quran was never widely available in the vernacular. This situation holds true even at present; extremely few rural or urban Malays are able to read (as opposed to recite) or speak Arabic. (In the late 1980s, for instance, the village of Bogang boasted no one with such skills, although it contained a mosque and a prayer house, three Islamic functionaries, a few certified religious instructors, and more than a dozen *haji*.) In the nineteenth century, then, the village majority undoubtedly lacked sufficient knowledge of Islamic legal theory to perceive any disjunction between *adat* and Islam within the domain of property and inheritance.

Representatives of the highest levels of the indigenous hierarchy, in contrast, have long enjoyed a relatively sophisticated understanding of Islamic doctrine, as well as an awareness of how *adat* and Islam diverge with respect to certain aspects of property and inheritance. It would be difficult to overestimate the extent to which colonial administrators and their policies contributed to the cultural realization of such divergences as contradictions; nevertheless, elite perceptions along these lines can be documented for the 1890s and probably originated much earlier. To cite one example, by 1893, the Sungai Ujung leader with the title of Dato Klana had petitioned the district's British resident to clarify official policy concerning rights over intestate property. More precisely, he had requested the British resident to ask the State Council whether the *kadi*'s adjudications in such cases should proceed in accordance with Islamic law or "the ancient custom . . . by which the property always remains with or descends to relations on the female side." The outcome of this inquiry appeared in a decree of April 27, 1893, which stated that "the Muhammadan law should be the one to be followed in a Muhammadan state and [that] the other could not be recognized in a Kathi's Court."[81]

Historical sources concerning late nineteenth-century Rembau testify to a similar situation as regards elite perspectives toward *adat* and Islamic inheritance codes, including their favoring of Islamic conventions, at least in certain contexts (see Lister 1890). In Rembau, however, the changes advocated by indigenous rulers were far less extreme than those proposed in Sungai Ujung, for they did not urge the elimination of the system grounded in matrilineal rights and divided title (as the Sungai Ujung measures definitely did). This divergence may be attributed to the greater commercial development in the tin-rich territories of Sungai Ujung as compared with Rembau at the time and the resultant premium placed on the autonomy of proprietors at all levels of that region's indigenous hierarchy. It is highly instructive in any event that Malay leaders in Rembau focused on a dimension of property relations that seems always to have been characterized by structural contradictions and that would undoubtedly have caused controversy even without an Islamic emphasis on patrifiliation at the expense of collateral links through women. I refer to the fact that rights to a full half-share of a deceased man's conjugally acquired movable property (cash, weapons, livestock, and the like) could go to his mother or sisters—for the benefit of the latters' progeny—rather than his own offspring, particularly if he had failed to bequeath such rights to his children through "paternal provisioning" (*tentukan*). Specifically, by 1890 the leaders of Rembau's indigenous polity had tentatively decided that all such items "became unconditionally the property of the children and could not in any case return to the man's [matrilineal] relations," since the alternative "made a great deal of difficulty, as it [was] not in accordance with Muhammadan law" (Lister 1890: 317).

The implications of these perspectives are taken up elsewhere (Peletz 1988b; esp. chaps. 4 and 8). Here I would only reiterate generally that elite awareness of areas in which *adat* and Islam diverge with respect to the distribution of intestate property rights existed as early as 1890 and clearly predated similar perceptions among the populace at large. This should come as no surprise given the wealth of the indigenous elite and the far greater likelihood, as compared with the village majority, that they could afford the pilgrimage to Mecca and fraternize with coreligionists of disparate cultural backgrounds, among whom were many of a strong reformist and modernist bent.

Much of the emphasis in the development of Islamic law, Islamic courts, and the jurisdiction of *kadi* during the first few decades of colonial rule was realized in legislation that focused on a relatively limited number of issues. These included adultery, incest, irregular mosque attendance, failure to fast during Ramadan, teachings deemed to be out of keeping with locally acceptable versions of Islam, and, last not but not least, whether appeals from the *kadi*'s courts should be heard by Malays (as Malay leaders preferred) or by Europeans (the British preference). There was in all of this considerable discussion and controversy surrounding *kadi* and their mandates, but our knowledge of such matters is highly skewed. Most of what we know on the subject involves debates that took place among British officials who held contrasting views on the issues at hand, relating in some cases to one of the central conflicts underlying British colonialism—whether to "keep the natives native," "make them better Muslims," and/or "bring them into the modern world." Some material bearing on policy discussions between British and Malays does exist, but unfortunately there is very little information concerning the debates pertaining to such matters that occurred among Malays themselves. According to some sources, however, enactments of subsequent decades, such as those passed in 1938 which standardized and gave more bite to provisions concerning offenses against Islam, generated "interest [that] was so keen" that "in every *mukim* [parish] in the Federated States [Perak, Selangor, Negeri Sembilan, and Pahang], people were meeting at the mosques to discuss . . . [them], as a rule with a *penghulu* or *kathi* as chairman."[82] We have no information on whether such discussions included all members of the community (for example, women). But we do know that at least in the case of Rembau's 1951 "*adat* crisis," women actively voiced their opinions and made clear to their husbands and male kin that they would not tolerate further legislative infringement on their inheritance rights or other "customary" prerogatives.

Rembau's "*adat* controversy" of 1951 merits brief consideration for a number of reasons. The Religious Affairs Section of the Rembau branch of UMNO (the United Malays National Organization) precipitated the crisis by launching an extremely pointed and public attack on women's privileges in proprietorship and inheritance. UMNO spokesmen claimed that from the perspective of Islam, continued adherence to these constitutionally upheld conventions specifying women's monopolistic proprietorship over houses and land was illicit (*haram*) and that adherents to *adat* incurred grave sin and would thus encounter unspeakable horrors in the Afterlife. UMNO's public attack on these long-enshrined features of matrilineal inheritance was broadly advertised in the local press and the national media and clearly forced people to take a long hard look at—and attempt a more systematic and comprehensive formulation of—the relationship between their matrilineally oriented *adat* on the one side and patricentric Islam on the other. It also succeeded in polarizing various segments of the Malay community, particularly "old" and "new" leadership (clan spokesmen and modern-day political leaders, respectively) and women and men. This is especially ironic in light of UMNO's mandate to transcend regional differences and parochial loyalties so as to unite the Malay community and thus not only protect it from the menaces and machinations of non-Malays but also facilitate both its economic development and the creation of a more pronounced and sustaining national consciousness based largely on the teachings of Islam.

Rather than taking up the resolution of Rembau's *adat* controversy (for such matters, see de Josselin de Jong 1960; Peletz 1988b: 120–27), I would emphasize two more general points. First, controversies and crises such as these, along with the attacks on local tradition that precipitated them, were engendered by colonial-era processes that not only eviscerated traditional institutions and radically diffused the functions, sanctions, and authorities once concentrated among clan spokesmen but also politicized *adat* and Islam and polarized their respective institutional expressions. Stated differently, crises such as these are best seen in light of the shifting political fortunes of distinct groups of Malay leadership, the development of new forms of education and expertise that contributed to the highly uneven distribution of knowledge pertaining to Islam, as well as heightened geographic and social mobility, occupational specialization, and social stratification—all of which chipped away at the cultural like-mindedness long characteristic of rural Rembau. The second point is a higher level and more abstract reformulation of the first. These types of crises were part of the price Malays in Rembau and elsewhere paid for their incorporation into national-level political organizations and for their encapsulation more generally within the broadly encompassing political and moral orders of what Benedict Anderson (1983) has referred to as an "imagined (national) community."

Reorganization and Rationalization in the Postwar Era

Malaya's occupation by Japanese military forces during World War II helped engender nationalist and anti-British sentiments of various kinds and also contributed to heightened polarization of ethnic relations, especially those involving Malays and Chinese. The accounts of local elders suggest that Malays emerged from the occupation beset by deep-rooted fears that their very existence was threatened by the predominantly Chinese Malayan Communist Party. These same accounts indicate that Malays felt menaced by Chinese and Indians as a whole, who by this time outnumbered Malays in Negeri Sembilan and other western Malay states. Some of the more cosmopolitan villagers still living also point to British policies just after the war as contributing to these feelings of insecurity and impending doom—for, as occurred also in Indonesia with the Dutch and among other colonial powers in Southeast Asia, the British resumed control in Malaya showing little concern for the past. It was as if they felt they should be able simply to pick up where they left off when they effectively abandoned their colony to the Japanese. By and large the Malay elite found this attitude unacceptable, particularly since British plans for the immediate future of the Malays involved a serious curtailment of their positions of power and prestige vis-à-vis the Chinese and Indians. These three groups were in fact accorded more or less equal treatment under the constitution embodied in the Malayan Union, which was rushed into existence in 1946.

The foundation of the Malayan Union met with immediate opposition from Malay leadership and led in the same year to the formation of UMNO.[83] UMNO was neither the first nor the only Malay political party on the scene, and it was viewed by many of its Malay detractors as aristocratic, feudal, and "insufficiently Islamic," the latter partly because it did not advocate the creation of an Islamic state, as did those who formally inaugurated the Hizbul Muslimin (Is-

lamic Party) in 1948.[84] But UMNO proved to be the dominant force in mobiliz-
ing Malay sentiment against the Malayan Union; indeed it has received much of
the credit for the union's replacement in 1948 by the Federation of Malaya.
With the birth of the federation, the residential system was dismantled in favor
of a constitutional arrangement whereby Malays regained some of their prewar
ethnic privileges and acquired greater autonomy in administering their own affairs. Among other changes, the status of resident was downgraded to British
advisor, who served primarily in an adjunct capacity to a Malay executive
styled chief minister (*menteri besar*). Henceforth the principal organs of government within the state were essentially twofold: a legislative assembly in the
form of a unicameral parliament referred to as the Council of State (Majlis
Mesyuarat Negeri), whose president was the Chief Minister; and a cabinet
known as the State Executive Council (Majlis Mesyuarat Kerajaan), the members of which were both to aid and advise the *yang dipertuan besar* in the
conduct of his executive functions as council head and titular head of state, and
to appoint the chief minister (albeit with the approval of Negeri Sembilan's
ruling chiefs).[85]

With regard to religious administration, the state constitution empowered the
yang dipertuan besar and ruling chiefs to enact laws regulating both Islamic
affairs and *adat*. In consequence, the year 1949 saw the creation of a proposal
to establish a Council of Islamic Religion and Malay Custom (Majlis Agama
Islam dan Adat Istiadat Melayu).[86] Given the thrust of state encroachments on
the realms and interrelationship of *adat* and Islam, it was decided that an Islamic juriconsult (*mufti*) should sit at the head of such a body. More important,
within a few years of the Federation of Malaya's independence in 1957, the
state created a powerful administrative hierarchy known as the Department of
Islamic Religion (Jabatan Agama Islam).[87] All dimensions of *adat* were theoretically excluded from the department's sphere of jurisdiction; moreover, and
of broader historical relevance, *adat* received no institutional supports in any
way comparable to those underwriting Islam. Perhaps most significant, the creation of Negeri Sembilan's Department of Islamic Religion furthered a process
set in motion at the outset of colonial rule: the institutional differentiation of
functions and authority associated with state-defined realms of *adat* and Islam.

It remains to consider some other important developments of the mid-
twentieth century, including certain implications of the creation in Negeri Sembilan of the office of *mufti*. To reiterate, this office, though common elsewhere
in the Muslim world during the first half of the twentieth century and long
before, did not exist in Negeri Sembilan before 1950. Up until then or, rather,
since 1889 (or perhaps the 1830s), the state's district-level Islamic magistrates
stood as the highest-ranking authorities of a "purely religious" nature. These
magistrates were in theory free of the political influences of persons and agencies whose esteem and expertise derived from knowledge and explication of
Islamic texts (even though their activities were regulated by British officialdom
and to some extent by the district *undang*). When Negeri Sembilan received its
first *mufti*, however, things changed, for these officials have always been

charged with issuing authoritative interpretations concerning Islamic doctrine, including all points of Muslim law.

All such trends undermined the autonomy of district-level Islamic functionaries and their village subordinates. They also further eroded the ritual prerogatives vested in the *undang*, clan leaders, and local matrilineal groups. In the interest of standardizing and otherwise tidying up the administration of Islamic affairs, for example, the *undang*'s role in declaring the opening and close of the fasting month of Ramadan was given over to a national committee. Their involvement in selecting Islamic magistrates was also greatly reduced. At the village level, moreover, localized clans were stripped of their sanctified privilege to provide mosque officials from among their members, and clan leaders were rendered superfluous in the collection and distribution of religious tithes and taxes (*zakat* and *fitrah*). In some areas of the state, such shifts provoked militant reaction from villagers, who had long construed such responsibilities as falling squarely within the dominion of clan leaders and *adat* (Swift 1965: 93–96). These historic developments illuminate colonial-era trends marked by the tremendously enhanced jurisdiction of Islamic officials in regulating the domestic, property, and other affairs of villagers, all at the clan leaders' expense. In short, the institutional differentiation and segregation of *adat* and Islam contributed immeasurably to undermining the integrity of *adat* spokesmen and the *adat* concept itself.

No small matter is that at present the scope of the *adat* concept is quite narrow and attenuated and far more secular than ever before. It is also more in keeping with Islam than ever before, for many previously sacrosanct dimensions of *adat*—for example, essentially pre-Islamic rituals associated with shamanism and various types of local spirit cults—have been relegated, by some villagers at least, to the dustbins of history and culture by being reclassified as *kepercayaan*, which is best translated in this context as "mere belief" or "superstition" (though it can also convey the less perjorative "belief"). This paring down and rationalization of the *adat* concept on the part of the more educated, cosmopolitan, and politically active villagers has helped maintain the integrity of the relationship between *adat* and Islam that is posited in the locally well-known aphorism, "*Adat* hinges on law, law hinges on the book of God" (*Adat bersendi hukum, hukum bersendi Kitab Allah*). The long sacred postulate embodied in this aphorism is still of central value to many if not most adult villagers, including the more educated, cosmopolitan, and politically knowledgeable activists among them. But it is increasingly meaningless to village youth, who see the *adat* concept as referring primarily to a congeries of beliefs and practices that is both out of keeping with Islam and especially inimical to religious development and modernity.[88] Circumstances such as these attest to the importance of analyzing the *adat* concept historically and in relation to forces of political and economic change in particular (Abdul Rahman bin Haji Mohammad 1964: 67–68).[89] This type of analysis yields insights that both complement and serve as a corrective to Geertz's approach to *adat* (1983a), which is mainly concerned with abstracting the "essential," "universal" features (symbols and meanings) of *adat*, irrespective of time and place, to illustrate that like law everywhere, *adat* is "part of a distinctive manner of imagining the real," "a species of social imagination" (Geertz 1983a: 184, 232). Geertz's perspective is fascinating, though ultimately rather disappointing because it is essentializing and static.

Another extremely significant development in the mid-twentieth century was the introduction in the late 1950s and early 1960s of various Administration of Muslim Law Enactments, such as those passed in 1960 for the state of Negeri Sembilan. Gazetted both in Malay and in English, these were in many respects *the* summary documents and points of reference for Islamic magistrates and their staff through the mid- to late 1980s. Especially relevant for what follows is that they were the key texts at hand in the Islamic court of Rembau and its counterparts elsewhere in the state of Negeri Sembilan and in various other states during my second period of fieldwork (1987–88).

The enactments of the late 1950s and early 1960s were amended in mostly minor ways in the years following their introduction. More important in the long term is that in each state in Peninsular Malaysia these enactments were superseded by the passage of comprehensive legislation bearing on Islamic law and its administration that took effect during the period 1983–91.[90] As will be discussed in chapter 2, this legislation, which was introduced as law in Negeri Sembilan and certain other states *after* I completed my second period of fieldwork, made provision for stiffer fines and other "beefed-up" punishments for violations of Islamic law as well as secular laws bearing on Islam. We will also see that such legislation effected a further standardization and centralization of Islamic administrative hierarchies within each state by introducing another administrative tier into the upper echelons of the state bureaucracy dealing with matters before the Islamic courts.

Despite the references to Islamic law that exist in fifteenth-century texts such as the *Undang-Undang Melaka*, there is little if any solid evidence to indicate widespread knowledge or implementation of such laws in the Malay Peninsula prior to the nineteenth century. The mere existence of individuals referred to as *kadi* does not mean that Islamic magistrates presided over formal courts or advised "secular" leaders as to the proper implementation of Islamic law, and Acehnese data bearing on crime and punishment during the seventeenth century are not representative of Indonesia, Malaysia, or Southeast Asia as a whole during that century, or before or after. The more general points are as follows. There is far more to justice and law than crime and punishment, and if we seek to understand how people manage disputes or resolve conflicts, we need to bear in mind that "lumping it," exiting, negotiation, mediation, and arbitration are far more commonly pursued than adjudication. Even when formal adjudication did occur in the precolonial Malay context, it did not typically involve the draconian physical punishments (maiming, amputation, capital punishment) that so fascinated British observers; more informal sanctions such as shaming and shunning were both more widespread and more dreaded.

We also saw that British representations of Malay courts in the nineteenth century tended to focus on the real and imagined contrasts between the judicial *practices* of the Malays and the judicial *ideals* of the British and that such comparisons helped motivate the reorganization and rationalization of Islamic legal institutions that were instigated by British authorities during the long decade of the 1880s and have continued to the present. Much of the reorganization and rationalization at issue occurred in the context of competing visions of the "true nature," "essence," and place of Islam, and of *syariah* in particular, in the lives of Malays and in Malaysian society at large. The visions that prevailed were both "moderate" and oriented toward modernity. To flesh out these and related arguments bearing on the ways in which the reorganization and rationalization of the courts have been realized in local practice, we shall proceed to a detailed consideration of the work of the courts as I observed them during my second period of fieldwork.

The Work of the Courts

In the last instance the proper understanding of Islam is not to be sought in either formal doctrine or village studies alone but in the substantive analysis of particular social formations.
  —*M. B. Hooker, "Introduction," Islam in South-east Asia*

Now that the law for the non-Muslims has been made clear and brought into line with *modern* thinking it is time that the Muslims have a look at the Islamic laws of marriage and divorce. . . . It is time that the Muslims in Malaysia show that the Muslim law is as concerned with the welfare and interest of the parties of the marriage, including the wives and the children, as any other *modern* system of law.
  —*Ahmad Ibrahim, "The Law Reform (Marriage and Divorce) Bill, 1972"*
  (emphases added)

THIS CHAPTER DEALS with the roles, jurisdictions, and operations of Malaysia's Islamic courts and is especially concerned with the cultural logic of judicial process in the Islamic court of Rembau. The first parts of the chapter provide background and context on the state-defined roles and operations of the courts, including their domains and jurisdictions; the nature of the criminal and civil cases that come before them; and various aspects of criminality and transgression in local society and culture and in Malaysia generally in the late twentieth century. Subsequent sections of the chapter are concerned primarily with judicial process; they focus on the ways that Rembau's Islamic magistrate and his staff deal with the cases brought before them, both in the sense of interpreting these cases and in terms of constructing and deploying strategies to effect outcomes consonant with their interpretations and objectives.

One goal of this chapter is to present detailed descriptive and interpretive material on some of the localized offices, institutions, and quotidian practices through which the state is instantiated. A second is to draw on this material, which includes data bearing on twelve cases I observed in the Islamic courts, to speak to a central theme in Max Weber's ([1925] 1968) work on Islamic law. Weber argues that judicial process in Islamic courts appears capricious, ad hoc, and irrational, and bereft of the concern with procedural regularities and doctrinal consistency said to be characteristic of Western-style courts. The material presented in this chapter confirms Weber's assertion that there are some striking contrasts between Islamic and Western-style courts. But it also illustrates that Weber and others exaggerate and misconstrue such differences and that there are pronounced regularities in the workings of Islamic courts in Malaysia and elsewhere, which reflect broadly shared cultural understandings bearing on consensus, negotiation, social relatedness, human nature, gender, and the like. A central objective of this chapter, then, is to show how, in the case of Malaysia, these local cultural concepts inform the ways in which officials of the Islamic courts deal with issues of legal liability, moral responsibility, and guilt. A related objective is to suggest that many of these concepts are contextually variable and contradictory and that the anthropology of law thus needs to be attuned to contrasting cultural representations and their contextually variable realization, and to the political economy of contested symbols and meanings.

A final set of introductory comments concerns methodology and the manner in which I render courtroom narratives presented in this and subsequent chapters. As noted earlier (see also Peletz 1988b, 1996), I have interviewed rural and urban Malays at great length about kinship, gender, and related matters, including the ways in which they, their close kin, and other Malays experience, understand, and represent myriad aspects of marriage and divorce. For the most part, however, I did not interview the litigants whose narratives are presented in the following pages. There are various reasons for this, the most compelling one being that since many of the litigants were palpably distressed by having to narrate and in some instances relive extremely negative experiences in court, I decided early on in the research that it would be inhumane and otherwise inappropriate to add to that distress by traipsing after them as they left the court or tracking them down later to try to arrange "follow-up" interviews. This decision had both disadvantages and advantages. One obvious disadvantage is that it precluded gathering firsthand data on these particular litigants' understandings of the hearings and their emotional reactions to them; one advantage is that it allowed for immediate discussions with staff of the *kadi*'s office concerning how they viewed and attempted to negotiate the most salient dynamics of each case. As for the manner in which I render the narratives in the pages below, I employ two different styles. One involves presenting more or less verbatim accounts of who said and did what when. (This was the style most commonly adopted by my research assistant when he attended and took notes on the hearings.) The other involves presenting some verbatim dialogue but doing so in a way that is more oriented toward providing summary overviews of the conversations and interactions at issue. While there are benefits and drawbacks to each of these styles, each of them should provide the reader with a clear and relatively nuanced sense of the ways in which litigants and court personnel alike construe and articulate the issues at hand.[1]

BACKGROUND AND SETTING

The progressive expansion and empowering of state-controlled Islamic administrative hierarchies that began under colonial rule continued after Independence in 1957 and have clearly led to the more centralized and standardized implementation of Islamic religious law. We need to bear in mind, however, that Islamic magistrates and their courts have long been constrained by their position within a pluralistic legal system, which, in turn, is embedded within and very much controlled by a powerful state that has to contend with a great deal of ethnic and religious diversity. The state not only confines the jurisdiction of the Islamic legal system to Malaysia's Muslim population, which includes all Malays but is nonetheless just over half of the country's total population, it also limits the jurisdiction of Islamic law to a rather narrow range of Muslims' affairs. In terms of civil matters, Islamic law is largely restricted to what is sometimes referred to as "family law": marriage, divorce, and their registration; issues of conjugal maintenance; the adoption, custody, and support of children; aspects of inheritance and other types of property relations, etc. In criminal matters, Islamic law tends to be confined in practice to various types of sexual offenses ("illicit proximity" [*khalwat*], adultery, rape), failure to fast during the month of Ramadan, nonpayment of religious tithes and taxes, and the like, though Islamic magistrates also have the authority to deal with matters of potentially broader scope, such as "the propagation of false doctrine."

Matters of this latter sort are sometimes dealt with by the national (statutory) courts, which is, to overstate the case, where most of the real power in the system lies. The national (statutory) courts also deal with theft, assault, homicide, sedition, treason, and countless other matters ranging from minor traffic and firearms violations to drug offenses and stock market fraud. Some sense of the power of these (national) courts can be seen in the fact that they can, and occasionally do, impose capital punishment—death by hanging. As for the "flavor" or "complexion" of the national courts and the more encompassing secular legal system of which they are a part, I would emphasize that the system is thoroughly grounded in the traditions of English common law. Reliable estimates from the 1980s suggest that at least 90 percent—some would say fully 99 percent—of Malaysia's laws come directly from England or are based on English precedents (Mead 1988: 49, 85n. 9). The laws are not only borrowed from England but also implemented within what many members of the Malaysian Bar Council and others view as "an essentially English system," especially in terms of the creation and passage of legislation, the importance of precedent, evidentiary and procedural standards, the nature of appeals, and so on, including even the attire of judges and the near universal use of English as the language of the courts, at least through the 1980s. There are of course differences between the Malaysian and the English systems; for instance, in Malaysia the jury system has always had very restricted application, and the ideal of a judiciary independent of the executive branch is frequently honored in the breach. But, as one observer put it not too long ago, "by and large, an English barrister licensed to practice in Malaysia [i]s immediately at home" (Mead 1988: 5; see also Mohammad Hashim Kamali 2000: 25, 57).

In contrast to the situation in the national courts, the formal sanctions at the disposal of *kadi* are extremely limited and infrequently invoked. *Kadi* can and do issue summons—mostly to recalcitrant husbands who have deserted their wives and children. But these are often ignored by the parties to whom they are delivered. *Kadi* can also impose (typically nominal) fines on offenders, though this is relatively uncommon. In terms of physical sanctions, *kadi* can incarcerate offenders who have engaged in particularly serious offenses or are unable or unwilling to pay court-ordered fines. This too, however, is a relatively rare occurrence, as is the corporal punishment *kadi* are entitled to authorize in some contexts. It merits note, in any event, that when *kadi* order incarceration or caning, they rely on the national police to implement their orders; they do not have their own police or jails (though they do have their own criminal investigators).

Before proceeding any further in my description of Islamic courts in late twentieth-century Malaysia, it will be useful to comment briefly on perceptions of Islamic law that have been dominant in the West since the nineteenth century (and long before). Particularly relevant here are the early twentieth-century views of sociologist Max Weber ([1925] 1968). Weber's views are both a reflection and a scholarly elaboration and codification of Orientalist biases of the Victorian era (some of which we examined in chapter 1), though they are also much more than that. More important is that these views have had a strong and enduring impact on Western scholarly discourses concerning Islamic legal systems and Islamic societies in general. Weber argues that judicial process in Islamic courts is relatively unsystematic and irrational and that it bespeaks a relatively unelaborated concern with procedural orderliness and doctrinal consistencies of the sort inshrined in Western-style courts. Seizing on and popularizing the phrase "*kadi*-justice" that was coined by one of his colleagues to refer to such patterns,[2] Weber averred that unlike their counterparts in feudal Europe, Islamic legal institutions failed to provide security of person and property and were thus among the key factors that hindered the development of rational capitalism in the Muslim world. Still much debated in the literature is whether, in Weber's view, these features of Islamic legal institutions derive from the actual content and allegedly indeterminate nature of Islamic law, which is held to be divinely inspired and was codified many centuries ago, and is thus (in an overdetermined sense) held to be immutable, or from the fact that historically (or at least in later Islamic dynasties), Islamic legal systems were often under the control of oppressive patrimonial bureaucracies.[3] It merits note in any case that Weber's interest in "*kadi*-justice" and "the Islamic ethos" was part of his larger concern to lay the groundwork for a comparative historical sociology of domination (and the roles played by different types of bureaucracies therein). The more general point is that unlike some of his disciples (most notably Geertz), Weber had an abiding interest not simply in distilling the "cultural essence(s)" of different legal and religious systems but also and more important, in elucidating the varied ways in which such essences were shaped by—and in turn helped inform—the vicissitudes of local, regional, and transnational histories and political economies.

Much of what Weber wrote on the subject of Islam is extremely insightful and, not surprisingly, there are some striking differences between Islamic and Western-style courts. But as Bryan Turner (1974), Lawrence Rosen (1980–81, 1989b), and others have demonstrated with reference to Middle Eastern and North African material, there are serious shortcomings in Weber's analyses of the decision-making processes of Islamic judges. Many of the problems reflect Weber's failure to adhere to the methodological and theoretical guidelines that he himself set forth in his outline of interpretive (*verstehende*) sociology, which emphasizes the building up of interpretations of social action based (at least in part) on the actor's subjective definitions and categories of lived experience, his or her implicit motives, explicit intentions, etc., that is, what Geertz (1983b) has referred to as "the natives' point of view." My data from Malaysia, along with studies of Islamic courts in Morocco (Rosen 1980–81, 1989b) and other parts of the Islamic world, indicate that there are indeed pronounced cultural regularities in the judicial behavior of Islamic judges. These regularities vary in important ways from one Islamic society to the next, but they also reflect certain cultural understandings bearing on notions of negotiation, consensus, harmony, social relatedness, human nature, gender, and the like that are broadly shared within the societies in question and, in some cases, among them.

As a step toward understanding the cultural logic of judicial process in Malaysia's Islamic courts, we will first consider the setting and atmosphere of the courthouse that I began studying intensively in August 1987. We shall then proceed to a consideration of the domains, jurisdictions, and operations of Islamic courts in Rembau and elsewhere in Malaysia.

The Setting

The relatively quiet district capital of Rembau is an ethnically heterogeneous town of about two thousand residents which has grown up along the railroad line linking Kuala Lumpur and Singapore. Toward the edge of the town, near a school, a health clinic, and various abandoned buildings, are the physically unimposing offices of the local Islamic magistrate and his court. The buildings and the surrounding grounds are standard fare for late twentieth-century Malaysia: the compound is encircled by a chain-link fence and barbed wire, which serves the dual purpose of keeping out wandering cattle and stray water buffalo and increasing the likelihood that groups of young boys do not deface or enter the building when it is formally closed. The building itself is a single-story affair, covered in stucco of faded yellow and sporting a tiled roof. A sign toward the front entrance of the compound identifies the offices as the Pejabat Kadzi Daerah (the District *Kadi*'s Office), using a form of spelling that was once common but is out of keeping with standard Malay as currently defined by the government and its retinue of official linguists and policymakers.

August 21, 1987, is my first visit to the Islamic court during my second period of fieldwork and I am accompanied by Haji Adam, a local luminary in his late fifties who became a close friend during my first fieldwork from 1978 to 1980. I had asked Haji Adam to accompany me to the court partly because of our friendship but also because he had worked as a clerk in the Islamic court-house for some twenty-five years and was well acquainted with both the place and the personnel. The fact that he had a car and could drive us to the court-house was an added plus, especially since visiting the court entailed a seven- or eight-mile journey and also presupposed introductions from some sort of offi-cial or intermediary.

We drove off from Haji Adam's house in his shiny new Nissan, which, as he told me for the second time in as many days, had cost him M$22,000 (about US$10,000). It is a luxurious car, complete with tape deck and many other extras, and he drives it very smoothly and quite slowly. In response to my comments on his good driving, he remarked that Malaysia has the highest auto-mobile accident rate in the world. He emphasized his disgust—adding that people "do not follow the laws" or "drive like they should." He framed his comments in a way that became very familiar to me as we talked about diffi-culties in marriage and in social relations generally.

After going to the District Office, we stopped at one of Haji Adam's favorite watering holes for tea and snacks. I thought it would be a fitting gesture if I paid, but Haji Adam seemed embarrassed by my attempt to take care of the bill. The proprietor explained that Haji Adam likes to treat people, partly because of his generosity but also because he knows he has a good fate (*nasib*) and can afford it. We then headed over to the part of town where the Islamic court is located.

The Building

One of the first things a visitor is likely to notice on approaching the structure in which the *kadi*'s offices are housed is the sign posted over the arch of the main entrance, which admonishes all who enter to be properly attired. Most Malays with business in the building come from at least a few miles away and would not think of traveling even a short distance without wearing clean clothes and otherwise dressing appropriately. As such, the sign may seem unnecessary or redundant, at least (or especially) for men. For women, however, the issue is not as straightforward, for the criteria of proper attire for women are very much in flux, partly because of the Islamic resurgence, which has encouraged the veiling of women and has otherwise endeavored to impose new definitions of femininity. The message probably seems more clear once one enters the offices and sees that the two women on the nine-person staff are dressed in the head-gear and long gowns donned by Malaysian women who self-identify with the Islamic resurgence.

The building is new and nondescript, with seven desks in the main room. Most of the men working there are dressed rather formally (all but one with long sleeves), and both women have *dakwah*-style hoods. The room is lit with neon lights that buzz loudly enough to be noticed whenever there is silence, and two of the three overhead fans whir slowly.

Outside the *kadi*'s chambers and over the doorways and elsewhere are signs emblazoned with the message, "Leadership Follows Example" (*Kepimpinan Melalui Teladan*). There are other slogans and decorations as well and information of various kinds. The wall behind the four desks that includes the desk of the chief clerk for the court is adorned with a number of official charts and notices. One provides the names of individuals authorized to teach in mosques in the district of Rembau; another gives the names of mosque officials in the district. In addition, there is a large chart which reads "Organizational Chart of the Kadi's Office in the District of Rembau, Negeri Sembilan" (*Carta Organisasi Pejabat Kadi Daerah Rembau, Negeri Sembilan*). There are also a few commercial calendars on the wall, as well as pictures of the king and queen, and in the counselor's office a poster resembling a film advertisement, which pictures a woman and includes the large caption, "The Heart of a Mother" (*Hati Seorang Ibu*).

The *kadi* is not in but I meet various members of the office staff, including the chief clerk, Zaki, and the chief clerk for the court, Araffin, who would later become one of my key informants concerning the workings of the court and most everything else that was pertinent to my study. After I explained my purpose in coming to the office, they offered to help and said that I could come back the next morning (Saturday), as the *kadi* would be in then. He is not there every day, they explained, partly because of a recent vacancy in the *kadi*'s office in the neighboring district of Tampin, which requires that the *kadi* for Rembau divide his time between the two locales.

The *kadi*'s current workload necessitates that he be in the Rembau office on Monday, Thursday, and Saturday, and in the Tampin office on Tuesday, Wednesday, and Friday. The Rembau *kadi*'s office is busiest on Mondays, I am told, because Sunday is a day when people are especially likely to get together and, as such, especially likely to experience frustration and anger of the sort that "boils over." Since the *kadi*'s office is closed on Sundays, the first chance that people have to go to the *kadi*'s office is thus on Monday morning. Not surprisingly, mornings are also busier than afternoons. Most of the cases they handle, in any event, are civil cases (bearing on marriage, divorce, reconciliation, maintenance, etc.) rather than cases involving criminal offenses (such as "illicit proximity," adultery/fornication, and failure to fast during Ramadan).

The Kadi and His Staff: An Introduction

When I went back the next morning, I was introduced to the *kadi*, Haji Musa (aka Harun) bin Haji Ibrahim, and spoke with him for about three-quarters of an hour. At least one of the clerks had informed him that I had stopped by and was interested in meeting him and obtaining his permission to observe court proceedings and examine the courts' written records, so he had some sense of the purpose of my visit. On first meeting I found him to be a rather gracious and commanding figure, with a quick mind and rapid speech to match. In terms of physical appearance, he is short and rather plump and sports a thick mustache as well as a white skullcap signifying his having made the pilgrimage to Mecca.

During our initial conversation I learned that he was about forty-four years of age and had been born and raised in an eastern district of Negeri Sembilan. I later found out that he attended the prestigious al-Azhar University in Cairo, focusing his studies on *usuluddin* (knowledge of the tenets of Islam) and ultimately earned a bachelor's degree there. Overall, he spent some seven years in the Middle East, which helps account for his fluency in Arabic. He also speaks a bit of English, much of which he picked up from trying to follow English-language films, especially Westerns, which he enjoys a great deal. He told me that he has been serving as the *kadi* for Rembau for about six years, adding that he hopes to take courses in Islamic law at the International Islamic University of Malaysia (located in Kuala Lumpur) beginning in the next couple of months.

One of the *kadi*'s initial reactions after I explained what I was doing in Malaysia was to tell me that I would be better off talking to the circuit *kadi* (*kadi litar*), who are based in Seremban, the state capital. "They are far more knowledgeable than I am," he maintained. This is a very common reaction: "I do not know all that much, really. Better to meet with someone who really knows about such things. The experts have a wider, deeper understanding of what you are after." After I wrote down the names of the circuit *kadi* and said yes, indeed, it would be a good idea if I met with them, I explained that I was interested in more than the books and published views of experts. I also wanted to see how the proceedings actually work.

He clarified that the cases that come to his desk for deliberation are only the ones that have not been worked out earlier by the (female) counselor, who is like an assistant (*penolong*) to him. The counselor tries to resolve differences between husband and wife so that they need not get to the point of no return. One clear advantage of having a counselor is that women are not reluctant (*segan*) to approach the *kadi*'s office. Also worthy of note is that men are not reluctant to talk with her either. Indeed, she successfully counsels women and men alike on all variety of family and household matters.

On the *kadi*'s wall, to the left as one faces his desk, is a large map of the world that is color-coded to show the percentage of the population of each country that is Muslim. Similar maps adorn some of the offices of the Department of Islamic Religion in Seremban, and the clear impression one gets from talking to officials about these maps is that the percentage of the world that is Muslim is rapidly increasing. The assumption is that such increase derives not merely from relatively high birth rates but also, and more important, from acts of conversion on the part of Christians and others.

Near the map, in back of the *kadi*'s desk, is a coat rack that supports large, dark brown judicial robes. I never saw the *kadi* wear these or any other robes. For that matter, most of the hearings in the courthouse are held in the *kadi*'s chambers, not in the actual courtroom. The *kadi* prefers to hold hearings in his chambers because those who appear before him are more comfortable and relaxed in that setting.

The *kadi*'s concern to help make people feel relatively comfortable in his courthouse is shared by other members of his staff and is particularly evident in the comportment of his chief assistant, Kamariah bte. Haji Ismail, aka the counselor, who was born in the state of Kelantan around 1964 and was thus about twenty-three years old when we first met in 1987. Kamariah began working at the *kadi*'s office in January 1986 after a short stint teaching Islam in elementary and secondary school, and she is a key player in the affairs of the court. This is partly because of her dual role as assistant for Islamic religious affairs (*penolong hal ehwal agama Islam*) and assistant official for the welfare of women (*penolong pegawai kebajikan wanita*). In these roles she performs various official functions, such as providing counseling and advice, taking down statements, signing forms, and sending out letters from the court. Partly because she is in every day the office is open, she takes care of a good deal of the routine work that might otherwise come to the desk of the *kadi*, who as noted earlier, is usually in the office roughly three days per week.

Though born in Kelantan, Kamariah moved to Seremban with her family before she started school. Because she has lived most of her life in Negeri Sembilan, she is well aware of—and compassionately attuned to—local customs and dialects. In terms of formal education, she sat for and passed the nationwide (STPM) exams that students are expected to take upon completion of their secondary schooling, but she did not enroll in any special courses to aid her in her present job, though she said that she will be doing so in the future. One of her major tasks is to counsel couples that are having problems. On the wall behind her desk is a large slate with a list of the people she is scheduled to meet over the next two weeks or so. She tends to schedule the meetings with them on days that the *kadi* is in the office so that if there is anything that she cannot resolve, they will be able to meet the *kadi* himself. She said that she *kasihan* (pities) them since they sometimes come from far away, and she does not want them to have to waste their time by having to come twice, when they could as easily come once. She also made the point that if she succeeds in her work, the cases will not have to go to the *kadi* since she tries to effect reconciliations and encourage people to resolve their differences rather than go through with a divorce. If she fails (she used the English word "fail"), then the cases are referred to the *kadi*. It merits note, in any event, that her position has only been in existence in Rembau and elsewhere in Negeri Sembilan since 1986.

One other member of the staff who merits mention here is Araffin (age thirty-one), who, as noted earlier, is the chief clerk for the court. Like Kamariah, he assists the *kadi* in numerous areas and has extensive dealings with litigants and others who come to the court seeking assistance of one sort or another. Also like Kamariah, Araffin plays a key role in the initial framing and subsequent construction of complaints. Other members of the staff have more specific roles: delivering notices and summonses; assisting in the arrest of those charged with criminal offenses; typing up letters and documents of various kinds; and overseeing the collection and recording of *zakat* and *fitrah*. Although I interacted with all of them, I spent most of my time with the *kadi*, Kamariah, and Ariffin.

The Atmosphere of the Courthouse

The *kadi*'s son, who appears to be three or four years old, is frequently at the *kadi*'s office and is often running around in the room where the hearings occur, making noise, banging on the walls and chairs with whatever he happens to have in his hand (ping-pong paddle, lunchbox, juice container). He is constantly opening and slamming the door that connects the *kadi*'s office with the room that is used to prepare and drink tea and other snacks; he often tugs at the remainder of the plastic wrap that was once used to cover up the chairs used by husbands and wives when they sit at the *kadi*'s desk; and he frequently walks behind the *kadi* and picks up the phone to dial and talk. The *kadi* is very tolerant of his behavior but often threatens him with scowls, raised voice ("Hey, be quiet!"), and sometimes a tweak of the sort used to flick a bug off one's arm. There is a constant undertone of babble and noise from the boy, most of which goes unheeded. It is quite distracting, however (at least to me), and does at times make it very hard to hear the proceedings. Partly for this reason, the *kadi* is sometimes forced to summon one of his clerks to take the little boy out of the room.

The room where tea and other food is prepared, to the left of the formal hearing room where my research assistant and I often pored over records of past cases, is just big enough to hold a full-sized ping-pong table. The staff sit around the table during tea breaks and presumably during midday meals. On some occasions the table is used for intense, fiercely fought ping-pong matches between the *kadi* and one or another of his (male) staff. The games typically take place around lunch, but before the official lunch break, and are usually hotly contested affairs that go on for a good fifteen to twenty minutes.

Under the glass that covers the whole of Araffin's desk is a large cardboard or paper checkerboard. He frequently has checkers piled up toward the front of his desk when I arrive there in the morning, although they are sometimes on the table I used in the back room. The clerk to the left of Araffin (as you face them from the center of the room) has inserted beneath the glass covering his desk what appears to be gift-wrapping paper with floral patterns and the (English) words "Wedding," "Wedding," "Wedding" every few inches. Also under the glass on the desk are snapshots of friends or family and pictures of motorcycles.

The various decorations adorning the desks and work spaces of the staff help render the courts more familiar to litigants and others who visit the building, as does the previously noted fact that one or another of the *kadi*'s children is frequently running around the *kadi*'s chambers, making much noise and ruckus. The presence of the *kadi*'s children contributes to the informal atmosphere within the courthouse and helps convey the impression that the *kadi* is a father and, by implication, a husband. Because he is a "family man," the *kadi* certainly knows something of the challenges of maintaining relationships, of what is involved in supporting a wife and children, and of what his familial duties and responsibilities are. And if only on this account, he is, in theory at least, someone people can relate to. Bolstering this image is the fact that the *kadi* endeavors to perpetuate marriages if there is even a glimmer of hope that they can be saved (and sometimes sighs with exasperation, "So much divorce around here; divorce, divorce, divorce!"). This clearly works to the disadvantage of some women who come to the court. But he is not always in favor of maintaining marriages, as numerous cases presented below make clear.

Among the other factors contributing to the relative informality of the atmosphere in the district-level *kadi*'s office are the absence of lawyers and the infrequency of oaths or swearing of any sort. Personnel in Rembau told me that they had never heard of lawyers being used in the Rembau *kadi*'s office, but the staff do have a list of seven or eight (Muslim) lawyers that they will provide to litigants who request a lawyer's services. Lawyers are more likely to be involved in cases that are heard by the chief *kadi* (*kadi besar*). This is because cases involving relatively large amounts of property are referred to the chief *kadi* for disposition, and the relatively large amounts of money involved help motivate litigants to seek out lawyer's services. Reliance on lawyers in such contexts has been reported for Kedah (Sharifah Zaleha Syed Hassan 1985) and areas around Kuala Lumpur (Azizah Kassim 1984; Horowitz 1994). More generally, the use of lawyers in Islamic courts is on the rise, due partly to the growth of a Malay middle class and partly to the establishment of various women's groups and NGOs, such as Sisters in Islam, which facilitate the publication of handbooks that help safeguard women's interests. Significantly, the increased use of lawyers in Islamic courts was cited during 1998 interviews with Islamic magistrates and other knowledgeable experts as one of the major changes that has occurred in the courts in recent years.

As for oaths and the like, there are two relevant terms to consider: *ikrar* and *sumpah*. Dictionary definitions of *ikrar* include "promise," "pledge," "legalize," "acknowledge," and "allow"; definitions of *sumpah* include "swear," "vow," "promise," "say solemnly or emphatically," "take an oath," "curse," "revile," and "use vulgar language against." Some five months into my research on the courts I interviewed Araffin on a host of matters including the differences, if any, between the two types of oaths. He explained that *ikrar* is not as heavy (*berat*) as *sumpah*, and that *sumpah*, if done properly, involves putting a Quran on one's head, utilizing "holy water" (*air sembahyang*), and swearing in the name of God. "Such formal *sumpah* are rarely done here," he maintained; indeed, I never saw a *sumpah* of this nature. On some (relatively rare) occasions, though, a less formal *sumpah* is done, by raising one's right hand. One can also put one's hand on the Quran when making a *sumpah*, Araffin said. (If one person takes this oath, both must; that is, it is not something done only by one party [cf. Rosen 1989b].) Such *sumpah* are not undertaken lightly.

When I asked Araffin what would happen if someone lied after having taken a *sumpah*, he replied, "Well, we really do not know, but I heard about someone in Seremban who undertook an oath [in the *kadi*'s office?], went outside, and was run over by a bicycle, which broke his leg." The implication was that the individual had lied and that God quickly punished him. Partly by way of elaboration on the general theme, Araffin added, "Some people go crazy [*gila*] after taking oaths."

On the subject of oaths and swearing, which occurred during a *fasakh* case involving insanity (discussed below), Araffin said that such oaths are not usually made but that in this instance there were some "areas of confusion," and they wanted to underscore to everyone the importance of speaking the truth. In theory everyone is always bound to tell the truth, "but sometimes you just can't tell." A case in point cited by Araffin was that of the old *haji* who had been in twice in recent days, claiming that he had repudiated his wife with two—as opposed to three—*talak* (pronouncement[s] of a divorce formula) and that, as such, he had not irrevocably terminated their marriage.[4] His wife contested his claim, insisting that he had repudiated her with three *talak*, such that they were irrevocably divorced. It seemed to all present that the old man was "waffling." The larger issue is that swearing does not so much prevent lying as render it less likely.

I also asked Araffin's opinion on whether, in the case of lying, it is usually men or women who lie. After some hemming and hawing, he responded, "Men." On the related question of who is typically at fault in divorce cases, he said that "much is men." "About one-third of all cases involve men not being responsible financially; another third involve "'misunderstandings','" he added, giving as an example "a man striking or beating his wife, and then her going home to her parents. But there are other things involved as well."

During this same interview Araffin also expressed concern that I might think the *kadi*'s style is too informal or lacking in some of the trappings of "real" law. He said that the proceedings in the *kadi*'s office were much less formal and the air much more relaxed than in "the magistrates' courts" (the secular courts). He added that he sometimes looks over at me and sees me with a "certain expression" on my face, which he takes to mean puzzlement or disapproval concerning the way the *kadi* makes decisions. I responded that this was not at all the case and that any puzzlement or frustration on my face had more to do with the difficulties of following the proceedings in all their detail, especially when people speak very quickly in the local dialect (as opposed to standard Malay).

Some of what I see is simply the *kadi*'s "personal style," Araffin explained. I acknowledged this as probably true and in any event certainly acceptable, adding (as seemed more or less necessary at the moment) that I thought the proceedings were valid and quite just in terms of the sentences handed down. I did not elaborate on my view that in some instances the *kadi* could perhaps press harder on men when they contend they cannot afford to pay child support (*nafkah anak*) to their wives. My sense was that Araffin was trying to get at something along these lines, trying to acknowledge that he would handle some of these cases differently, but he was not explicit and there were others present, so it was difficult to know exactly what he might have said if he had felt less constrained by the setting of our conversation.

Araffin brought up the subject of the larger room that is the more official, more formal chambers for holding hearings, reiterating that in some instances these chambers are used, though usually not. "The *kadi* wants to provide a more relaxed, less formal atmosphere"; hence he uses his chambers and not the more imposing context. A somewhat related matter had to do with Araffin's point that the *kadi* has the power to pursue criminal proceedings against those who refuse to abide by his (civil) decisions; that is, he can bring criminal charges and, if need be, have the defendant fined or thrown in jail if his orders or decisions have been ignored or flaunted. But this is rarely done, for, according to Araffin, it would rarely serve anyone's purpose. "What good is it to have a delinquent husband in jail, if it isn't going to make his wife's life any better?" Nor would it result in her getting money that was her due, he said. I did not pursue the argument about "making an example" of such a husband and thus perhaps deterring future delinquency of this sort. Araffin was apparently thinking of the relative short run, and the relevant argument(s) did not occur to me anyway.

Araffin also spoke of the relative weakness of the sanctions at the disposal of the *kadi*, underscoring that they were not sufficient to allow him to do the work that he is charged to do. This same point was made by the counselor and others, including the registrar of marriage and divorce in Seremban (discussed below).

DOMAINS AND JURISDICTIONS

A few themes bearing on crime and criminality merit brief note before turning to a discussion of the types of criminal and civil cases handled by Malaysia's Islamic courts. The first is that many cases involving criminal (*jenayah*) offenses that fall under the jurisdiction of the Islamic courts never reach the courthouse because they are dealt with informally at the community level. There is, as we have seen, a clear preference for handling most transgressions and disputes informally—through negotiation, mediation, or arbitration—within the community in which they occur. There is, moreover, a disinclination both to talk explicitly about others' transgressions and to level charges at others believed guilty of one or another offense. For example, those who believe themselves—or are thought by others—to be victims of poisoning or sorcery do not usually seek to identify (through divination or otherwise) those who may be responsible for their afflictions; and they do not usually refer to the physical and other ailments that afflict them as being the result of poisoning, or sorcery, or human malevolence of any kind, but tend instead to state that they have "miseaten" (*salah makan*; see Peletz 1988a, 1993b, 1996). One result is that narratives and more encompassing discourses bearing on transgression are heavily euphemized. This means, among other things, that court records bearing on criminal matters are not necessarily a reliable indicator of the frequency of transgressions of a criminal nature.

Criminality defined as an "emergency case" should, in any event, be handled within twenty-four hours of its occurrence. In fact, according to court personnel, this is not merely a "should" but a "must." Such cases include sexual offenses, most notably *khalwat* (illicit proximity), as well as the consumption of alcohol and failure to fast during the month of Ramadan.

Most of the criminal cases before the Islamic court of Rembau during my second period of fieldwork fell into one of two categories: "marriage without the permission of the *kadi*,"[5] or "failure to pay *zakat* and *fitrah*." The case involving *rogol* (rape) that I discuss below (case 5) was not classified or handled as an instance of rape by the Islamic court but was dealt with instead as a crime of *zina* (fornication/adultery). While the partial "resolution" of this case (such as it was) involved pressuring the guilty man to marry his victim as his second wife, there are two issues of more immediate relevance here. First, this case provides a particularly clear example of the euphemization of transgression; second, the specifics of the original charges (rape) were such that a formal complaint was lodged with the police, as representatives of the secular component of the legal system (who set in motion their own investigation). The secular system, to repeat a key theme emphasized earlier, is the locus of most of the power in the judicial system as a whole. This is a very sore point not only with individuals who work in or are involved in the administration of the Islamic courts but also with those who seek to expand the jurisdiction of the Islamic legal system and the relevance of Islam generally.

Issues bearing on the (limited) jurisdiction of Islamic courts emerged repeatedly in my interview with the registrar of marriage and divorce in Seremban. The registrar, Zul, is a very articulate young man about thirty years old. He talked of his frustrations that the *kadi*'s office, and the Islamic courts overall, are relatively powerless in the face of the secular courts and gave as an example of this the fact that litigants can appeal the decisions of religious courts by taking them to the secular courts, where they can be overturned.[6] One such case involved the issue of child custody. "They don't go back to religious courts, don't even necessarily try to work with them," he complained. "So where does that leave the *kadi*'s courts and the Department of Islamic Religion more generally?" The religious courts do not have the authority to overturn the secular courts, he added, and often the secular authorities only consult the religious authorities *after* they have reached decisions that should have been made by the religious authorities in the first place (or they consult them but go ahead and make the decisions they want to make anyway). This is definitely a problem with land subject to Islamic laws of inheritance (*tanah faraidh*), he pointed out, claiming that while the religious (law) specialists are sometimes called in to tell secular officials what fractions to divide the land into, the secular officials often go ahead and divide it however they wish.

The interview with Zul raised various thorny issues of a jurisdictional nature, some of which have plagued the courts since the late 1880s. There are of course others, some of which stem from the fact that the jurisdictions of the Islamic courts are not always clear to litigants or others who approach court personnel either to obtain information or clarification or to resolve problems of one sort or another. This is partly because those who are not legal specialists are not always cognizant of the shifting boundaries of state-defined bureaucratic domains. Relevant as well, as the interview with Zul makes clear, is that the boundaries demarcating certain domains are contested. The following cases help illustrate some of these points.

Case 1: *A Broken Engagement:* "'Adat,' *Hence Outside the Kadi's Jurisdiction.*" This hearing was initiated by a woman who appeared to be in her mid- to late fifties or early sixties. The petitioner and the *kadi* were present throughout the hearing; Araffin joined them when the *kadi* called him in for assistance.

The petitioner began by recounting that for some eight months her son had been engaged to a young woman who then proceeded to terminate the engagement. One of the first things the *kadi* said is that he had recently met with the headman of the petitioner's village when he was there for a prayer recital (*baca doa*). He quickly added, before many of the details were recounted: "This is *adat*, so I can't deal with it," and then went on to advise the petitioner that she had to "find *adat* people to work through this."

Even so, the *kadi* proceeded to ask the petitioner what her clan was. She replied (Payah Kumbuh, Empat Ibu) and then went into the specifics of her complaint, explaining, among other things, that "If the guy goes ahead and breaks off the engagement, that's one thing. But if the girl does it, there's a quarrel. The clan officials [(*orang*) *besar*] in my village don't want to refer this matter 'above' [*atas*], so who should I get in touch with?" The *kadi*'s response: "Who is the clan sub-chief [*buapak*] there, who received the betel [*tepak sirih*]?"

A bit later the petitioner stated, in response to the *kadi*'s questions, that her son and his former fiancée had met in Rembau and had gotten engaged on the basis of mutual attraction (*suka sama suka*). She noted that she had already met with the girl's mother about all of this; the girl's mother also thinks they should get married, but the girl refuses. The petitioner had visited the girl's mother to get things straight, and vice versa, but to no avail.

The *kadi* called Araffin in to help out and continued to gather information from the petitioner, who informed the *kadi* (in response to a question or two on the subject) that "the girl's father isn't involved in any of this" and that she (the petitioner) had already asked the relevant clan officials to discuss the matter. The petitioner made reference to the engagement ring (purchased at a cost of M$600) and said something to the effect that according to "custom" (*adat*), two rings should be returned, not just one. (It was not clear from anything anyone said whether or not the ring, or anything else that had been exchanged, had been returned.)

The *kadi* then told the petitioner that if she is not happy with the way things are going, she should take it up with the *undang* in a formal request (made through his clerk) for his intervention. The petitioner replied: "I'm female, and sort of weak, and afraid to meet higher-ups" (*betina, lemah sedikit, takut jumpa orang atas*). A bit later, however, at the advice of either the *kadi* or Araffin, she said that she would "first try the clan chief [*lembaga*], then the *undang*; this is more appropriate."

Comment: Throughout most of this hearing, the *kadi* was sorting through wedding invitations that had been accumulating in his desk drawer. He would glance over an invitation, squint a bit so as to bring it into better focus, and then hand it over to his daughter, who was playing in his chambers through the session. Of broader interest is that the *kadi* allowed the petitioner to give her (informal) deposition even though it was clear to him from the very beginning that the disputed issues are outside his jurisdiction, since, as he put it, "This is *adat*, so I can't deal with it." In local Malay culture and in Malay culture generally, the ritual exchanges associated with formal engagement are not seen as all that distinct from the exchanges keyed to marriage. But they are entirely separate matters in terms of more formal legal jurisdiction, in the sense that the former fall within the realm of *adat*, the latter within the domain of Islam. In earlier times (for example, the nineteenth century), jurisdictional divisions such as these did not exist, for the indigenous polity headed by the *undang* handled all aspects of marriage, including engagement and divorce alike.

In some ways more important is that this is the *only* hearing I sat in on in any Islamic court in which the *kadi* requested information about any litigant's (or anyone else's) clan or lineage affiliation. The Islamic courts attach considerable importance to the concept of "origin-point" (*asal-usul*), which is of central importance in Malay culture as a whole, but the notion of origin-point emphasized by the courts is a far more attenuated one than found in the culture at large. In the culture at large, at least for those over fifty, one's clan and lineage affiliation is a key component of one's origin-point. In the state-sanctioned discourses of the court, however, such components of identity are of marginal significance at best. More generally, this hearing may be considered as the exception that proves the rule with respect to the role of the state in the attenuation and overall redefinition of notions of relationality, personhood, and identity. On the other hand, by making explicit the dichotomy between Islam and *adat*, the state is centrally involved in underscoring what is central and what is not.

Many other jurisdictional dilemmas beset the Islamic courts and those who are involved in their activities. Some of these emerge from the following (1988) interview with a Tamil man by the name of Shaiful, who serves as clerk and Tamil interpreter at the secular (Magistrate's) court located across the way from the *kadi*'s offices.

Shaiful and the Secular (Magistrate's) Court

Shaiful is an extremely interesting and articulate man, born in 1955, thus about thirty-three years old when we first met. He speaks perfect English and has worked both in the statistics division of the prime minister's department and for the first woman to serve in Malaysia as a High Court judge. Shaiful was born a Catholic, baptized, and given First Holy Communion, but he lost interest in Catholicism, perhaps because of his father's atheism. He began studying other religions—Hinduism, (Mahayana) Buddhism, and Hare Krishna—and eventually came to Islam. He is married to a Malay woman, whom he met and fell in love with, but he explained that he would have converted to Islam even if he had not been interested in marrying her.

There were signs that he would eventually embrace Islam; for example, when he was involved in Hinduism, he always wanted "to pray with a mat under [his] feet, like Muslims do." He later went to an astrologer who read his horoscope and told him that he would marry someone of a different race and religion, to which he replied incredulously, "Hey, me? How could that be?" I do not know how long he has been a Muslim, but he did make clear that Islam is "certainly for him." When he prays now he is "much more successful," and his "prayers are answered ten times faster."

Shaiful's comments about religion came up largely in response to my question about the likelihood of an Islamic state being established in Malaysia. He pondered my query for a while and replied that he thought this might well occur, but only if most non-Muslims first converted to Islam. He felt that this could well happen. From his personal experience, the prospect of other "races" converting to Islam is not all that unusual or unlikely.

Shaiful felt that the legal and procedural differences between the Islamic legal system and the secular system could be overcome; he did not see this as a major sticking point. But there are problems with the current relationship between Islamic law and non-Muslims. In most states, Islamic law does not apply to non-Muslims. In Johor, however, there are provisions for Islamic law to pertain to non-Muslims, such that if a non-Muslim man and a Muslim woman are guilty of *khalwat*, both—not just the Muslim woman—can be punished according to Islamic law. This may be unconstitutional, according to Shaiful, and so far as he knows, no one has raised the constitutionality of the law by challenging it in court. The constitution of Malaysia protects freedom of religion, and it also guarantees that if there are conflicts between religious law and the constitution, then the constitution shall prevail. The freedom could possibly be infringed upon if the non-Muslim man in question were subject to Islamic laws bearing on *khalwat*.

Another problem: What happens when a Muslim man or woman is guilty of *khalwat* and then renounces Islam to avoid the legal consequences of his or her actions? According to Shaiful, there have been instances of this, and there is really nothing the courts can do. This is why Shaiful thinks that Muslims should be liable for all their offenses under Muslim law, so long as the offenses took place while they were Muslims. Thus, even if someone converts to another religion to try to avoid legal action, he or she would still be held responsible since the offense occurred while he or she was still a Muslim. Shaiful went on to say that in keeping with the Quran, those who renounce Islam are to be "sent to the guillotine."[7] But in contemporary Malaysia, there is no punishment for this, as it would conflict with constitutional guarantees of freedom of religion. There are efforts underway in some states, however, to make this a serious offense. And PAS, among others, is quite upset with the provisions that allow Muslims to renounce Islam, particularly to avoid offenses committed while they were Muslims.

Shaiful also mentioned an incident involving charges of "deviationism" or "deviationist teaching" under Islamic law. The case occurred in Kedah, and the man thus charged followed a variant of Islam that developed in India; among other things, he prayed in the direction of the sun rather than toward Mecca (*kiblat*), as is the usual Muslim custom. In his defense he claimed that according to the state's interpretation of Islam, he was studying a false version of Islam, not "true Islam," and thus was not a "real Muslim." As such, he could not be charged under Islamic law. The outcome of the case, unfortunately, was not altogether clear from our conversation.

Shaiful reiterated that he had previously worked for Malaysia's first female High Court judge, Puan Siti Normah bte. Yaacob, and that there was a good deal of opposition from some Muslims to her being on the court, since, according to Islam, or at least certain interpretations of Islam, women cannot preside over or adjudicate at the trials of men. And, "to make matters worse," it was within her powers as a High Court judge to pass the death sentence. Because of all the ruckus she was put in the family division, where there was little if any likelihood of her being involved in cases entailing the death penalty and where, to use Shaiful's words, she may have "natural affinities" since the cases deal with "emotional," "family" issues.

Some Muslims, moreover, do not like bowing to the judge in the Magistrate's court in which Shaiful is currently employed. They only bow to Allah; hence they will only nod their head a bit in the courthouse. This came up in connection with Shaiful's telling me that it is expected that everyone will bow whenever they enter or leave the court if the judge is present or whenever the judge enters or leaves. "But do not bow like Japanese," he cautioned, demonstrating a bow involving lowering the head a few feet. Another dilemma at present is that some Muslims resent having sentences passed on them or even being tried by a non-Muslim. The presiding judge, Frederick Indran Nicholas, is of "Indian" (perhaps Sri Lankan) ancestry and a Christian to boot.

Shaiful explained that there is much disagreement among Muslims on some of these issues. He was told, for example, that he should not mention non-Muslims in his prayers because it is wrong to pray for non-Muslims. "This is ridiculous," he said. "I can't even pray for my own mother, who isn't a Muslim? How can this be?" Shaiful also brought up the donation of blood. In the course of a "blood drive" at an office in which Shaiful once worked, he was ready to give blood when some of his Muslim coworkers informed him that he "couldn't, since some of the blood might go to non-Muslims." He did not agree with this and had never come across anything that said he should not donate blood simply because some of it might go to non-Muslims. So he asked a *kadi* about it. The *kadi* told him, "There is nothing wrong with donating blood; do whatever you feel like doing."

Other jurisdictional issues that emerged in the interview with Shaiful had to do with the fact that the *kadi*'s decisions may be enforced in the secular courts. Thus, if the *kadi* seeks to recover money that a delinquent husband is supposed to pay to his wife, he may turn the case over to the maintenance division of one of the secular (sessions) courts. As for appeals, someone can appeal the decision of a *kadi* in the court of the chief *kadi* or in the High Court, and a decision can be overturned in either of these forums. The High Court in particular will overturn a *kadi*'s decision if it feels that the ruling of the *kadi* is against "natural justice," as defined by the High Court. Decisions of the secular courts, on the other hand, cannot be appealed in the religious courts.

Shaiful also explained that the (secular) judge for whom he works has little occasion to interact with officials of the Islamic courts. Shaiful depicted the two legal systems as "totally separate," adding that much of his knowledge of the Islamic courts and of Islamic law as a whole comes from serving as the interpreter for Tamils (Hindus) who have converted to Islam and have to go before the *kadi*'s courts, whose proceedings are invariably in Malay. Interestingly, and of broad significance for the arguments in this chapter and the book as a whole, Shaiful also assumed that the Islamic courts do not have any precedents that they rely on and that procedure in such courts is of minimal concern as compared to what one finds in their secular counterparts.

To better appreciate some of the differences (and similarities) between the two legal systems, we might consider various aspects of the proceedings in the secular (magistrate's) courthouse in which Shaiful currently works.

Rembau's (Secular) Magistrate's Court. The building housing this court is located within a few hundred yards of the *kadi*'s court. Most of the cases brought before it involve traffic offenses (reckless driving, driving without a license, etc.), although there are also cases of failure to pay income tax, gambling, "misbehavior" (a euphemism for drunk and disorderly conduct), and theft. Cases of sorcery do not come before this or any other court because there is no provision for such cases under "evidence" (that is, there usually is not any acceptable evidence that sorcery has occurred).

In terms of its physical appearance, the courtroom is very large and imposing, with high ceilings and an enormous desk, behind which sits the judge. All officers of the court, with the exception of police officers, are clad in outfits that include black sports coats. The judge wears a black business suit, as does Shaiful, who in this case serves both as clerk of court and Tamil interpreter. The Malay woman who is clerk of court and Malay interpreter also wears a black jacket (of the same style as the others) over her *dakwah*-style outfit (*baju kurung* and mini-*telekung*).

Those present on the occasion of my visit include: the judge, an Indian Christian; the clerk of court and Tamil interpreter (Shaiful, a Tamil [Hindu] convert to Islam); the clerk of court and Malay interpreter, a Malay woman; the court orderly, a large Sikh officer; a prosecuting officer (of undetermined ethnicity); and the defendant, a thirty-nine-year-old Malay man by the name of Yusof bin R., who works as a laborer with the Drainage and Irrigation Department and is charged with the theft of about eight kilos of scrap rubber (valued at roughly M$7) from an estate. There were an additional ten to twelve people seated in the part of the courtroom reserved for public seating.

It was extremely difficult to hear what was being said, partly because of the size of the room but also because there were large—and very old—air conditioning units in some of the windows, which made a tremendous amount of noise. I sat in the very front of the court, but I had great difficulty hearing the judge, let alone anyone else.

The judge spoke to the other officers of the court in English, not in Malay (although on occasion he threw in a few Malay words). The court officers, including the Malay and Tamil interpreters, likewise conversed with the judge in English. When the judge wanted a question or comment conveyed to the defendant, he stated it to the Malay interpreter, who then translated it into Malay, got the defendant's reaction, and then restated it to the judge in English. Needless to say, such procedures make the hearing and the overall experience of appearing in this type of court all the more foreign, imposing, and incomprehensible to the defendants and the plaintiffs (except where one or the other of these is in the government, as where the government prosecutes for failure to pay income tax). The defendant, for his part, stood up for most of the hearing and looked quite nervous, uncomfortable, and seemingly oblivious to most of what was said.

As the hearing unfolded, Shaiful was kind enough to make fairly detailed notes of what was going on. What follows is a slightly shortened version of the notes he gave me at the end of the hearing.

> What you have just seen . . . [is] a typical case for sentencing.
>
> 1. Case was called out (R)AC 92-2-88; Yusof bin R. (age thirty-nine years).
>
> 2. Accused appears. Charge read over and explained to him: "Sek 329 P.Code, theft of scrap rubber."
>
> 3. Accused pleads guilty. He says he understands the nature and consequences of his plea of guilt: "that no witnesses will be called, but he will be given the opportunity to be heard in mitigation."
>
> 4. Prosecuting officer gives a brief statement of facts pertaining to the case. (In practice, a typewritten fact sheet is given, P1. Also read out. This saves the court time.) Also tenders the exhibit. The recovered rubber is tendered. Marked P2.
>
> 5. Accused is asked if he admits the facts. He says, "Yes."
>
> 6. Court finds him guilty as charged. Asks him to [speak] in mitigation before deciding sentence.
>
> 7. Accused mitigates. (He has sent in a written mitigation.)
>
> 8. Court convicts the accused. Sentence: Bound over under Sek 173A CPC in the sum of M$500 with one surety for a period of one year. Order as to exhibit: Scrap rubber to be returned to rightful owner through prosecution. The accused will be required to sign a bond for good behavior and released. (All the above procedures adopted are provided for in the Criminal Procedure Code, chap. 6).

He signed the bond, put up the money, and was released (but he may also face charges from his superiors, for he is an employee of a government department).

Comment: After the hearing was over, Shaiful showed me the written statement that the defendant had submitted in order to be treated leniently. It was about twelve typed pages, and mentioned, among other things, that the defendant's mother had died shortly before the theft occurred, that he was very upset and not thinking clearly, and that he had many children and relatives to support. Shaiful said that his pleas for leniency resulted in a lighter sentence than he would have otherwise received.

The party who brought the case to court is the manager of a rubber estate, not simply a smallholder who has an acre or so of rubber. Chances are pretty good that the estate manager is non-Malay and that the estate owner is non-Malay as well. Cases of theft involving rubber taken from a smallholder do not usually reach court, Shaiful said, partly because as Muslims, Malays are supposed to forgive (*ampun*) those who commit wrongs. As for the sentence in this case, "Being bound over in the sum of M$500 for one year" means that the accused puts up a bond of M$500 and is required to be on good behavior for one year. If he is convicted of any serious offense during the one-year period dating from the sentencing, he loses the M$500 and has to deal with the charges for the new offense.

There is clearly much to say about this hearing and the (secular) court system in which it occurs. In the present context, however, I will simply draw attention to a few themes that the reader should bear in mind throughout the ensuing discussion. The most important of these themes are: the language (English) in which the case was heard; the overwhelmingly non-Malay staff of the court and their predominantly Western attire; the presence of police; the extreme formality of both the hearing itself and the courtroom as a physical/cultural space; the relatively severe sanctions that were imposed on the defendant; and last but not least, Shaiful's comments that Islamic courts do not rely on precedents and, compared to the secular courts, display little if any concern with judicial procedure of any sort.

OPERATIONS

I have emphasized that one of the most striking features of the atmosphere within the Islamic courthouse is its relative informality. We have seen that one or another of the *kadi*'s young children is frequently running through the building, creating much noise and distraction; that most of the cases that come to the magistrate's attention are aired in his private chambers, rather than in the actual courtroom, which is used primarily to store official records and for games of checkers among court staff; and that litigants are not usually sworn in or administered oaths of any sort. To this I would add that the *kadi* rarely makes reference to religious or legal texts or to specific points of Islamic law. In these respects—and many others—the Islamic court of Rembau and its counterparts elsewhere in Malaysia diverge not only from the courts found in the West but also from Western-style courts in Malaysia (such as the secular [Magistrate's] court).

Islamic judges in Malaysia are generally expected to work within the guidelines of the Shafi'i legal school of Islam,[8] many of which were fixed in legal text by the end of the tenth century. But this does not mean that Islamic magistrates are bound by centuries-old legal conventions or interpretations. First of all, magistrates are enjoined by Islam to render evaluations and judgments based on reasoning by analogy (*kias*), consensus with fellow legal specialists (*ijma*), and/or "local custom" (*adat*). They are, moreover, equipped with various pamphlets and booklets published by the state that provide compilations of relevant enactments and other guidance. Most important, though, Islamic magistrates have broad powers of discretion, which they use to help make sure that the cases before them are dealt with in a manner in keeping with their notions of "justice," "equity," and "due process" (*keadilan*). These notions are of course cultural, as are their understandings of "fact," "truth" (*hal, kebenaran*), and the like. All of this would have been clear to Weber if his commentaries on Islamic courts had been consistent with the methodological and theoretical guidelines that he established for interpretive sociology.

In Malaysia, for example, the Islamic court has a pronounced concern with consensus, reconciliation, and compromise (*muafakat, persesuaian, persetujuan*), rather than zero-sum outcomes of the sort characteristic both of Malaysia's national (statutory) courts and of many venues within court systems like our own. The Islamic magistrate does, of course, adjudicate the cases brought before him, but before doing so the magistrate and members of his staff try to settle cases through the less formal and less binding processes of mediation and arbitration. In seeking to attain this goal, the court relies heavily on the court counselor, who interviews most litigants before they have a chance to discuss their case with the *kadi*. Like *kadi*, counselors are enjoined by Islamic doctrine and state directives alike to provide *nasihat*, an Arabic-origin term which refers to "advice" but is also "a concept of central importance in Islamic moral theology" that conveys the sense of "moral advice" or "morally corrective" advice (T. Asad 1993: 214). The counselor told me on numerous occasions that if she succeeds in the (morally corrective) work that she is mandated to carry out, the cases that come before her will never reach the *kadi*, for her explicit objective is to see that couples resolve their differences rather than divorce.

The counselor's comments highlight what the *kadi* and his staff see as their principal objectives in regard to matrimonial matters. The most compelling of these objectives is to keep marriages intact, regardless of the stated wishes— and to some extent the behavior—of the husband and wife. The critical assumptions here are that it is in the God-given, natural state of things for adults to be married (see Sharifah Zaeha Syed Hassan 1986: 184–85 passim; Peletz 1988b, 1996); that those who are already married are typically better off remaining so than experiencing divorce and life without a spouse; and that the high divorce rates long characteristic of the Malay population are both cause and consequence of various kinds of social and cultural backwardness.[9] In short, as with Islamic judges in Singapore, Indonesia, and elsewhere in the Muslim world, the *kadi*'s central goals are to get people back into a situation where they can successfully (re)negotiate their relationships (Sharifah Zaleha

Syed Hassan 1986: 195; Djamour 1966: 177 passim; Lev 1972: 125–27; Rosen 1989b). This means, among other things, providing a forum—such as the *kadi*'s chambers or the office of the counselor—in which people can air many of their differences in a productive fashion.

Since providing such a forum is among the main objectives of hearings in Islamic courts, it should come as no great surprise to find that officials of Malaysia's Islamic courts rarely make reference to religious or legal texts or to specific points of Islamic law and do not usually place great emphasis on formal swearing or oaths of any sort. More broadly, officials of the courts appear to have relatively unelaborated concerns with discovery and evidentiary procedures, with establishing "fact" and "truth." Indeed, in many court hearings I observed, the phenomenal reality of "what actually occurred," though very much contested, seemed largely irrelevant both to the judge's and the counselor's line of questioning and to their subsequent allocation of responsibility as well as their ultimate disposition of the case.

I hasten to add, however, that the *kadi* and his staff do display a strong interest in ascertaining the social background (including, especially, the genealogical and geographic "origins" or origin-points) of the litigants and others who come before them, as well as their general temperaments, personalities, etc., if only to help them better determine what "might have" happened in the circumstances under investigation. More generally, as in the case of the Dou Donggo of Eastern Indonesia described by Peter Just (1986, 1990)—as well as most civil proceedings in the West—concerns with what "might have" happened typically take precedence over attempts to establish "fact" and "truth" in the narrow sense. Many of these points are illustrated in the following cases, the first few of which were handled by the counselor, the others by the *kadi*.

Case 2: *The Husband Who Had His Wife Called in So That They Could Discuss Their Problems*. This case was heard in the counselor's chambers. Present, in addition to the counselor, were the husband, Salim bin B., age thirty-four; his wife, Rokiah bte. N., age thirty-three; and one of their three daughters, who appeared to be about five years old.

The husband, who is from Kuala Pilah, first approached the court, seeking to have his wife, who is from Rembau, called in so that they could discuss their problems. One of these is that she left him; he wants her to come back and live with him in Seremban, where he works in a supermarket (with a wage somewhat over M$200 a month).

When they were first married they lived with the wife's family in Rembau, but, according to the husband, his mother-in-law complained a lot about him, presumably because of his limited earning capacity. At some point they moved to Seremban and lived in a house with his mother. The wife testified that he drove her from their home (this occurred a few months before the hearing), although she later indicated that she had returned to Rembau to give birth to their child, since she had to have a caesarian and wanted to be near her mother.

The wife, who taps rubber, complained that the husband rarely comes back, sends very little money, and is irresponsible in not supporting them and in not even coming to see his children, one of whom is deformed or disabled (*cacat*). She said he does not even send M$50 a month. She also spoke at length about his being late for and missing work, claiming not only that he has "no thoughts of work" but also that he does not think about *fitrah* (alms), that he does not pray on Fridays, and that in six years of marriage he has never fasted for the entire month of Ramadan. They live very near the mosque, and she is embarrassed about his poor mosque attendance. He has also refused to work in a factory and has apparently turned down other work as well; this (his irresponsible behavior) seemed to be the major issue as far as the wife was concerned.

She added that he has never come back after work and found that she had failed to cook rice. He has not come to visit the sick child either; the husband does not even know or care whether or not she has a fever. The husband's reply was that he has too much work and does not have time to come back to Rembau.

Following the wife's narrative, the counselor lectured the husband on his responsibilities, on the nature of his proper role as husband/father: "You are no longer a bachelor; think of the example you are setting; think of what your children feel when they are hungry." The counselor then asked the husband if he smoked. After he replied, "Yes," she continued: "Think of how you feel after an hour without a cigarette; that is how your child feels when it does not get enough milk. . . . You must be diligent and find a way." The counselor then emphasized that the *kadi*'s office was not going to make a decision for them, thus underscoring that she wanted them to reach an agreement on their own.

The wife agreed to follow him back to Seremban but warned that she could not take his attitude much longer. He needs to give more *nafkah*, she said, claiming as well that he "does not see any of his own faults." The husband reiterated that he still loves (*sayang*) his wife.

The counselor drew up a written agreement specifying that the wife would follow the husband by the end of the year if he changed his role/behavior. If he does not change, she has every right to come back to the office and petition. The wife responded that she is tired of coming here and does not want to have to come again. The husband, for his part, agreed to try to find a different house for himself and his wife and children so that they would not have to live with his mother. The latter condition was important because the husband's mother has interfered in the marriage and has apparently told her son that he should divorce his wife.

Comment: In this case there is not much that is contested. The husband does not deny any of the wife's allegations, and he does not take issue with the counselor's characterization of the proper roles and responsibilities of husband and father. More important for present purposes is that the counselor is less interested in—as we might put it—"righting past wrongs" than in "getting things back on track." She draws up a written agreement with this latter goal in mind, though the document also serves as a reminder to the husband that his behavior is not acceptable and that it may be sanctioned in the future, if only in the sense that the wife's future petition might be granted. Note, in any event, that the counselor endeavors to provide them with a time frame and experimental period to reestablish proper relations. She has succeeded in her defined role, even though it is not at all clear to the counselor that the marriage will endure in the long run or even the relatively short term.

Other cases like this indicate that concerns with reconciliation and compromise are usually more important than "fact-finding" in the narrow sense and, more generally, that there are methods and procedures here, as well as clear goals. Consider the following.

Case 3: *The Husband Who Claims His Wife Is Having an Affair with Their Son-in-Law*. This case involved Mohd. Yusof (bin S.), who is sixty-one or sixty-two years old, and his wife, Siti Rohani, fifty-one years old, who first approached the *kadi*'s office in Seremban with the complaint that her husband did not trust her. They have been married for thirty-six years, have seven grown children (all married), and are currently living together in Chengkau. The husband has no work; he is old and sickly looking; his right hand trembled uncontrollably throughout the hearing; and his voice was frail and hoarse. In response to the counselor's opening questions about his health—this case was heard in her office—he explained that he had "sickness in his bones" (*sakit dalam tulang*).

The hearing began with the counselor's taking the husband's I.C. (identity card) and particulars, eliciting his statement, and filling out the relevant form in her file. A short while into this, the counselor addressed the husband, saying that the problem is jealousy ([*perasaan*] *cemburu*). She lectured the husband, though not in a condescending fashion, saying, "This is a common problem, one I see all the time. You are jealous of your wife's relationship with your son-in-law; this is the central issue."

When the husband is asked to list his objections to his wife's behavior, he responds by saying: "She goes out without telling me; she waits on and treats the son-in-law in a way that's not nice (*tak elok*); and she will not listen to what I say." He adds that his wife and son-in-law are always walking around together, which the wife proceeds to deny. A bit earlier, the counselor had said something to the effect that interactions involving casual contact with a son-in-law do not invalidate ablutions (*batal air sembahyang*); but it was very difficult to hear exactly what was said since there was constant hammering on the wall next to where I was sitting. (Chinese workmen were installing an air conditioning unit in the *kadi*'s chambers.)

The husband indicates that he is extremely upset (*sakit hati*), relating as well that his wife had once asked for a divorce. After hearing what the husband has to say, the counselor responds, "We should try to overcome this problem; let's try to prevent it." She then left the room to answer a phone call and returned about five minutes later.

The husband went on to explain that he is not satisfied (*puas hati*) with his wife, to which the counselor replied, "There is no one in the world who is 100 percent right or true all of the time." The husband then elaborated on his chief complaint about his wife's selling cloth, which is that it involves her going out of the house without his permission. The wife replied that she sells cloth to help cover household expenses. A moment later the husband claimed that he has seen his son-in-law with his hand on her thigh. The wife's response: "This was in passing, touching in passing, an accident." The counselor then said: "Pakcik ["Uncle"], don't misunderstand." He interrupted by insisting, "But she always lies to me," at which point the counselor asked how long they had been married. One or the other answered "thirty-six years." The wife was crying silently, wiping her eyes with the washcloth she dug out of her purse.

The counselor then remarked to the husband: "I can't believe that your wife would have an affair with her own son-in-law. People just don't do that." "Pakcik," she continued, "maybe you have been especially sensitive or emotional because you have been sick. . . . You need to accept or receive (*terima*) your son-in-law as your own child. Selling cloth is to get money for kitchen expenses. It is for Pakcik's benefit, too, right? Don't you like that?" The husband replied, "It's not that I don't like it, but I don't see any capital (*modal*) from selling cloth." The counselor responded, "I think that if your wife didn't sell cloth, there wouldn't be enough money." The husband went on to underscore that he does not want his wife to sell cloth in other villages, after which the wife reiterated to the counselor, "My husband doesn't trust me."

The counselor then said to the husband, "Don't you trust your own wife? You must trust your wife. You have to accept her. I don't want to hear any more that Pakcik is jealous of Makcik and the son-in-law. It's not nice. You must look at your in-law as your own child. Your wife knows the laws of Islam, the laws of the Afterlife." She continued to clarify to the husband what is involved in selling cloth, saying that most people pay in installments, telling him how profits are made, that the money is for kitchen expenses, etc.

The counselor then instructed the husband to sign the statement she wrote out on his behalf, which constitutes his promise not to get jealous anymore and to refrain from the specific behaviors the wife finds objectionable. He responds that he cannot sign because he cannot read or write, so the counselor gave him an ink pad on which to stick his thumb; thereafter he thumbprints the page, just below the statement containing his agreement. The counselor also reminds him that he is fortunate to have children who come home and visit, adding that there are many children who never return home to see their parents. As the counselor stands up, thereby indicating that the session is over, she asks for forgiveness, mainly, it seems, from the husband, in case she spoke roughly or said anything harsh or coarse (*keras*).

Comment: Especially significant here are the counselor's reactions to the unfolding of the depositions and her overall strategy and objectives in the hearing. Bear in mind that she made no real effort to get at "the facts." For example, the counselor never said to the wife, "So, are you having—or did you have—

an affair with your son-in-law?" Nor did she address the more specific issue of the son-in-law allegedly touching the wife's thigh. And she never asked the husband to give a precise account of "the evidence" of such an affair. The more general point is that the counselor made no attempt to resolve the inconsistencies in their testimonies. This may be because the counselor had had one or more previous sessions with the wife and had already decided, on the basis of what came out then—if only in the sense of what kind of person the wife was—what "might have" happened between wife and husband (and son-in-law).

"The facts" and "the evidence," as generally understood in Western court systems, were thus largely irrelevant in the hearing. This situation exists not because the counselor is a relative novice or has few real sanctions that she can deploy to help establish the phenomenal reality of "what really occurred," for the same pattern obtains in the hearings the *kadi* oversees (as we will see in due course), and he (the *kadi*) is neither a novice nor lacking in sanctions. Such patterns prevail because the main objective of hearings from the court's point of view is to promote reconciliation, through a cathartic airing of differences, if necessary, and thus to prevent divorce, which the court generally regards as an unfortunate (though in some cases unavoidable) occurrence.

Clearly guiding the counselor are implicit but nonetheless widely shared notions bearing on human nature, on how, for example, a "reasonable man (or woman)" behaves toward a son- or daughter-in-law. Having established for herself that the wife is a reasonable person, the counselor finds it inconceivable that she would engage in sexual relations with her son-in-law. The son-in-law is, after all, "like her own child," and sexual transgressions with one's own children or those "like them" are clearly abhorrent in Islamic law and the Afterlife, as is well known locally. At the same time, however, the counselor acknowledges that (reasonable) people do get jealous "all the time," can get emotional when ill, and sometimes fall short in honoring filial obligations to their parents. Interesting as well, the counselor discounts the husband's feelings not by considering them "rational but unimportant, . . . [but] by considering them irrational and hence dismissable."[10]

Note also the counselor's positive sanctioning of the wife's right to earn a cash income by selling cloth, which involves, among other things, going from village to village and interacting with a relatively broad range of people, women and men alike. Her argument to the husband is that the wife's selling of cloth is for their collective good (for kitchen expenses) and that without the money derived from this activity, they probably would not have enough to eat. The counselor thus reframes and glosses over, even ignores, some of the issues the husband raises, like that of his wife leaving without his permission, which is an instance of legally salient recalcitrance (*nusus*) that commonly comes up in hearings. She does this partly by pointing out that domestic survival and well-being need to be accorded a high priority, higher, indeed, than the issue of permission to leave the house, especially in light of the husband's poor health.

The court's concerns with reconciliation, compromise, and "saving face" are dominant themes in Malay culture, which is to say that many of the basic objectives and values of the court make good cultural sense to those who, for whatever reason, find themselves interacting with an Islamic magistrate or one of his staff. This enhances the legitimacy of the Islamic legal system in the eyes of local Muslims and contributes to the Islamic courts being relatively accessible to most people (men and women alike).

Other examples of broadly shared cultural assumptions informing the judicial behavior of Islamic judges can be seen in the sanctions imposed on husbands who are delinquent either in supporting their wives and children or in coming forth with support payments after a divorce. Though this is a recurrent dilemma in the courts—and in Malay society as a whole (Jones 1994; Peletz 1996; Mohammad Hashim Kamali 2000)—the *kadi* rarely invokes the full weight of the sanctions at his disposal and commonly refrains from imposing even relatively minor sanctions. His reasoning is that many of the men involved are simply "village folk" (*orang kampung*) and, by implication, relatively poor and thus will not be able to meet court-ordered payments. So what good will it do to fine them or have them incarcerated for failing to support their wives and children? Who will benefit from such a course of action? Here we see the judge avoiding a course of action—the imposition of court-ordered fines and/or incarceration—which is legally justified but nonetheless socially and morally inappropriate both in his own eyes and in the eyes of local society at large. What we have, in short, are broadly shared cultural notions of the public good taking precedence over what are construed as ultimately narrow concerns with legal liability, moral responsibility, and guilt.

Officials of the court are well aware that there are some unfortunate social consequences of this latter type of reasoning and of the judicial decisions that sometimes follow from it. Official awareness of these dilemmas informed judicial handling of one of the relatively rare cases involving a criminal offense (case 5, below) that came before the Islamic court in Rembau during my second period of fieldwork. Before turning to the latter case, we might consider an instance in which the *kadi* ignored the stated wishes of husband and wife alike so as to help ensure that the wife received the monthly financial support from her husband to which she was legally entitled.

Case 4: *A Husband Seeking a Divorce from a Second Wife That the Kadi Will Not Allow (Even Though the Second Wife Consents to It) Because the Husband Owes Her Back Support*. Present were the (second) wife, the *kadi*, and the counselor.

The outlines of the case were these: the husband requested a divorce and the wife was here to testify that she was willing to go along with it. She claimed that the husband had deserted her; that she rarely sees him since he hardly ever comes home; and that she has not seen him at all for nine or ten months. The husband has no work, or at least insists that such is the case. The wife maintains that he lies about this as an excuse for not supporting her and their child.

The *kadi* made it clear from the outset that he was not going to grant the husband a divorce even though both parties wanted one. He would only authorize a divorce on the condition that the husband come up with M$600 (M$60 a month for the roughly ten months that have passed since he last saw his wife). If the husband agrees to this condition, he will also be expected to make additional maintenance payments so as to help support his wife during her *edah* period and provide for their child (that is, *nafkah edah* and *nafkah anak*, respectively).

When the wife indicated that she did not know the husband's whereabouts, the *kadi* asked her where his mother lived, the response to which was that she (the husband's mother) lived with or near the husband's sister. The wife could not produce her mother-in-law's full name; when asked where the husband's father was, she replied that he was dead. The *kadi* suggested to the wife that they would probably be able to contact the husband through his mother or sister, or through mosque officials in his natal village.

Comment: After the session was over, the counselor explained to me that the wife present at the hearing was the second wife and that the husband is still married to his first wife. When I asked why a woman would wed a man who is already married, she explained that the second wife was pregnant at the time of their wedding and that they were forced to get married. The first wife apparently consented to her husband's taking a second wife, presumably so that he would avoid other more serious sanctions. The counselor does not think the husband will go through with the divorce since he probably will not be able to come up with the money.

The problem, though, is that this leaves the (second) wife in the lurch since she is not getting any support from the husband at this point and has not been maintained by him for a good portion of their marriage. She is thus forced to remain married to him, one consequence of which is that she will not be able to marry anyone else (assuming she might be inclined to do so).

Somewhat similar dilemmas obtain in the next case, which involved three hearings to which I was privy (and a good many others prior to my fieldwork), and is the most complex of all the local cases about which I have information.

Case 5: *(Mohd.) Said bin K. Seeking a Divorce from Hasmah, the Woman He Raped and Was Forced to Marry*. Present at the first hearing of this case that I observed were the petitioner, (Mohd.) Said, age forty, and a man serving as his spokesman, who appeared to be in his fifties. This case initially entailed a charge of *rogol* (rape) but had been (re)classified as *zina* (illicit intercourse, fornication, adultery). The petitioner was married and had sex with another woman (Hasmah) without her consent. Hasmah, a divorcée with six children by her first husband, is *gila* (crazy) according to the counselor and others. More relevant to the case is that she became pregnant and eventually explained what had happened to her uncle, who was also a mosque official (*imam*). The uncle took the matter to the police, the petitioner was either formally charged with rape or threatened that he would be so charged, and a police investigation was initiated.

In the meantime, other "village-level solutions" to the problem were pursued, including having the petitioner marry and support Hasmah. The petitioner consented to this arrangement and went to the *kadi*'s office to obtain permission to take a second wife. The *kadi* did not know about the *rogol/zina* when he approved the petitioner's request. The petitioner and Hasmah got married and within the month their child was born. Now, some five months later, the petitioner is seeking to divorce Hasmah.

The petitioner opened the hearing by explaining to the *kadi* that he is in court to divorce Hasmah. The *kadi* is clearly reluctant to allow a divorce without first talking to Hasmah. He tells the petitioner that he cannot *lafazkan* (pronounce a divorce) without her and proceeds to call the local police to find out the status of the case so far as they are concerned—as if to impress upon him the severity of the overall situation. It is apparently still an open case, but this may be because the police have not had time to do the paperwork necessary to close it. One of the reasons the *kadi* does not want to go ahead and allow the petitioner to divorce Hasmah is that "after all that has happened," her family might be extremely upset if the *kadi* grants a divorce; they might think a travesty of justice has occurred.

At one point in the hearing the spokesman for the petitioner proclaimed that if the *kadi* would not allow the divorce to occur then perhaps they "would take the case elsewhere," by which he presumably meant the office of the chief *kadi* or simply another *kadi*'s jurisdiction. This clearly irritated the *kadi*, who replied angrily, "Okay, take it wherever you want, whatever you like," but he then calmed down and proceeded to comment on various issues, including the importance of getting in touch with Inspector A. of the police department. The hearing was concluded with talk of the next hearing.

Two months later I observed a second hearing in this case. The petitioner was accompanied by a young man in his twenties or thirties (his son by his first wife?), and he was once again submitting a request for a divorce from Hasmah, though on this occasion he was discussing the case with the counselor, presumably because the *kadi* was not in that day. The counselor took down the particulars, including the fact that the marriage was "forced" and that the wife was "pregnant at the time of the wedding."

During this hearing it came out that the petitioner does not reside with Hasmah. There was also talk of a "letter of agreement" (*surat perjanjian*), referring (I believe) to the letter of support the petitioner intended to write for Hasmah and/or their child. He made reference to having put some money aside, adding, though, that he had not yet given the money to Hasmah. The counselor lectured him on his responsibilities as a husband and clarified some of the procedural matters and other details relevant to his request. The petitioner clearly wanted a divorce immediately but was told by the Counselor that this was not possible since "the *kadi* will have to weigh the case." Having said that, the counselor implied that he would probably not encounter any problems in obtaining the requisite approval.

Throughout the hearing the petitioner spoke very softly and appeared to be acutely embarrassed. It took him a fair amount of time to answer the questions the counselor put to him, and he looked pained as he responded to her queries. Some of his apparent embarrassment and discomfort could, of course, have been feigned. He was, after all, very eager to divorce Hasmah and put the whole thing behind him, and he might have been especially eager to please court staff, who clearly have much discretion in disposing of the case.

The third hearing about which I have information occurred five days later. The petitioner was present, as was Hasmah. My research assistant, Kamaruddin, attended the hearing and took detailed notes, which he later recopied and discussed with me. The relevant dialogue is as follows.

Kadi: What is your claim?

Wife: I am claiming *nafkah* and I want him to divorce me; the support I want for the child should [cover the period] . . . from his birth until the present.

Kadi: Okay. I'm going to give a decision concerning *nafkah edah* [three months, ten days] and *nafkah* for the time you were married [eight months].

Husband: How much would be appropriate for me to give?

Wife: I'm asking for M$150 a month.

Kadi: What kind of work does he do?

[Wife's response, if any, is unclear.]

Kadi: We must look at his work or job and take that into consideration.

Wife: I was three months in Chenggang without *nafkah*. I gave birth there. . . .

Kadi: I understand you spent three months staying with other people. And I know it's not the same as being at one's own place. . . . Staying there, your expenses were certainly more. . . . Okay, I agree to your request for *nafkah* for the three months you were there, for M$150 a month, so M$450. Now let's discuss *nafkah* at your own house [for five months]. I ask you to reduce it a bit.

Wife: I'll ask M$100 a month.

Husband: If it's that much, I cannot (*tak mampu*), Tuan Kadi.

Kadi: You can pay in installments.

Husband: I request that you reduce it some more.

Kadi: Okay, M$700 for eight months, plus *nafkah edah* . . . M$100.

Wife: I want him to pay it all now. . . .

Kadi: Do not worry. The payments will go through this office. [To husband:] How much do you want to pay a month?

Husband: I can manage M$25 a month. . . . I [only] do village work (*kerja kampung*).

Wife: M$25 a month, how is that possible, after all you've done to me?

Kadi: Pay as much as you can. If it's less, then the time you pay will be longer.
Husband: If I get more, I'll pay more. But if I cannot, how am I gonna pay more?

The husband pays M$250 and the *kadi* presents him with a divorce agreement, instructing him to "recite it and sign it. But only once, not twice or three times." The husband then proceeds to read the agreement, but with three *talak*. The *kadi* is shocked, demanding of him, "Why did you read it with three *talak*? Didn't I instruct you [to do it with] one *talak*?" The husband answers, "I don't want to hassle anymore," at which point the wife says (sarcastically?), "Nice, let him free me completely," and walks out of the room.

Kadi [to husband]: You pay M$30 a month; a dollar a day until you finish off the M$100.
The husband agrees, pays, and exits.

Comment: There are a number of issues of interest here. Consider first the highly sanitized way in which the case is framed in the official, written records of the court, one indication of which is that it appears under the heading, "Request to have two wives." Included in the relevant file is a statement from the first wife (aged forty-nine), which reads: "I permit my husband to marry again, with the condition that he behave with justice [*adil*] and responsibly toward me and my child[ren]. I hope the second wife will become kin [*saudara*] and that there will be closeness or intimacy [*kemesraan*] among us." Court records also include a written statement from the husband: "I am married and . . . have five children [by my first wife]. I have discussed with my wife [that I am] marrying another woman. She agreed, with conditions [as above]. Today I'm here with my wife to petition to take another wife." The official records also indicate the husband wants to divorce his wife (but they do not specify which one).

As to the actual hearing, it should be emphasized that very little is contested in this case, the partial exception of course being Said's right to procure a divorce. Hasmah did not contest this right, nor did the counselor. The *kadi*, however, did—his position was that Hasmah's family or relatives would be extremely upset if he (the *kadi*) allowed a (unilateral) divorce "after all that has happened" and might think a travesty of justice had occurred.

In the latter connection the counselor explained to me that it would not be appropriate to let the petitioner off so easily, the more general point being that in the eyes of the court, there should be some checks and restraints on men who divorce their wives "at the drop of a hat." The counselor also lamented, as did many other court officials, that the laws currently in place are in many instances ineffective because the fines and other sanctions at the disposal of the *kadi*'s office are negligible. "What good is a fine of M$25 nowadays," she asked rhetorically, referring to the penalty for false marriage declarations, "when people can just pay it with a M$50 bill and say, 'Hey, keep the change. No big deal'."

The exercise of judicial discretion in this case, along with the counselor's comments on the issues involved, reflect the court's concern to reallocate some of the responsibility and liability that inhere in Islamic law. According to Islamic law, a man may divorce his wife for any reason he chooses, even if she has been an unreproachably responsible wife and mother and a paragon of virtue in all respects. A woman, on the other hand, is normally entitled to divorce her husband only if she proves to the court's satisfaction that her husband has been thoroughly irresponsible or that he has a serious illness or other impairment that precludes fulfillment of his conjugal duties or other features of the marriage contract. This legal asymmetry *is* recognized by local Islamic courts; and although the courts are not really in the business of eradicating or even minimizing social inequality or of bringing about other social (or even narrowly legal) change, they frequently endeavor to temper legal asymmetries through the use of judicial discretion. They do so in accordance with broadly shared cultural notions about human nature, gender, and the like, including the idea that most of the problems in marriage stem from the inappropriate behavior of husbands who, as one man put it, "are basically lazy" and "expect to eat for free."

With regard to issues of the latter sort it is interesting to consider why the *kadi* instructed the husband to pronounce a single *talak*, as opposed to two or three *talak*.[11] When asked about this the *kadi* explained that he prefers that men seeking divorce recite a single *talak*. This is so they will not succumb to a temporary affliction known as "*talak* craziness" (*gila talak*), which refers to a man becoming emotionally unbalanced after a divorce and, more specifically, to his going into a fit or frenzy once he has divorced his wife. The *kadi* has observed "*talak* craziness" on numerous occasions, for example, when husbands come into the office in a rage, trying to find and destroy the relevant files, wreaking havoc in the process.

The idea that men sometimes become unbalanced and irrational might seem out of keeping with the constructions of gender often associated with Muslim societies. I should thus underscore that there are contextually variable constructions of gender, some of which are contradictory in the sense that they entail mutually incompatible representations of the similarities, and especially the differences, between men and women. These representations are keyed to contrasting views of kinship, marriage, and affinal exchange that I have discussed elsewhere (Peletz 1996). One of the context-specific constructions of gender encountered among Malays in Negeri Sembilan and elsewhere in the Peninsula may be referred to, following Pierre Bourdieu (1977), as the "official"—and "more Islamic"—view of gender. This view is inextricably linked with local understandings of biology, sexuality, and reproduction; it focuses on the idea that compared to men, women have less "reason" (*akal*) and more "passion" (*nafsu*) and are, among other things, more lustful, more difficult to satisfy sexually, and otherwise more "animalistic" in Ortner's (1974) sense.[12] This view is produced not only by official representations of kinship and various Islamic institutions (such as the mosque) but also by spirit possession (*kena hantu*), which predominates among women and is interpreted by men and women alike as evidence of women's greater animality and spiritual weakness.

The most prevalent of the other context-specific constructions of gender encountered among Malays in Negeri Sembilan and elsewhere promotes a "practical"—because more thoroughly grounded in everyday practice—view of men and women. Keyed to practical views of kinship, it focuses on the culturally elaborated belief that men are less responsible and less trustworthy than women, both with regard to managing household resources and in terms of honoring basic social obligations associated with marriage, parenting, and kinship generally. This latter construction of gender, which depicts women as more deserving and more in need of subsistence guarantees than men, is reinforced by the structure of affinal relations; especially in the case of Negeri Sembilan Malays, this includes the heavy expectation that married men will produce property rights, wealth, and prestige for their wives and their wives' kin. These expectations, along with the affinal demands with which they are associated, frequently exceed the productive capacities of married men, particularly men at the lower end of the social class hierarchy. For these and other reasons they exacerbate tensions in marriage and affinal relations and commonly lead men—especially relatively poor men—to divorce or simply desert their wives and any children they might have. This course of action, in turn, feeds into local views that men are far less responsible than women, which is a dominant, indeed hegemonic theme in practical views of gender. As numerous cases discussed here make clear, we need to make analytic provision for all such constructions of gender, even—or especially—when they are mutually contradictory.

Case 6: *The Wife Who Seeks a Divorce Because Her Husband Doesn't Like Working ("Only Wants to Fish").* Present at this hearing were the wife, age thirty-one, and the husband, age thirty-seven, who sported a wild, Malay-style "Afro" and was rather unkempt, especially when compared to others who come to the *kadi*'s office.

Both husband and wife are from Rembau, and they have one child. The wife, who works in a factory in Seremban, approached the *kadi*'s office seeking a divorce because she was upset that her husband *tak ada kerja* (doesn't work; has no work). (They divorced earlier, but they reconciled; according to the counselor, the problem then was also that the husband did not work [or did not have any work].) The two of them were thus called in to discuss the matter, which they did in the counselor's office. There was a good deal of heated arguing in the office for about fifteen minutes, the wife insisting, among other things, that her husband "doesn't like working. He only likes fishing [and selling what he catches]. He doesn't like other kinds of work, and certainly doesn't like factory work."

When the case moved into the *kadi*'s chambers, the husband reiterated that he wanted to be "given a chance to find work," adding specifically that he wanted "six months." The *kadi* responded, "I will give you four months, not six; this follows the *taklik* clause," and went on to explain that if the husband had not found work by the end of four months, then the wife had the *kadi*'s permission to come back to the office and ask for a divorce.

Comment: In most Malaysian states (Perlis is an exception), the *taklik* clause appears on the forms that (Muslim) husbands sign when they marry. Normally recited by a husband at the time of the solemnization of the union (*akad nikah*), it gives a wife the right to petition for divorce in the event that a husband fails to provide adequate material support (*nafkah [zahir]*) for a period of four months (three months in some states) or is absent without news for a comparable period (up to six months in some states). In this hearing, the *kadi*'s reference to the *taklik* clause may be seen as an effort on the part of the court to put the husband on notice that the court takes seriously issues of nonsupport. Put differently, the court reaffirms the husband's responsibility to provide support, along with the wife's right(s) to receive such support and if such support is not forthcoming to petition for a divorce.

Also of interest in this hearing is the de facto discursive exclusion of fishing from the category of "work" as well as the sharp discursive contrast drawn between fishing and factory work. Note also that in this hearing, as in some of the others discussed earlier, the *kadi* is less concerned with "the facts"—Does the husband prefer fishing to all other kinds of work? Is he willing to do factory work? Has he looked for or been offered factory work or employment other than fishing?—than with "what might have happened." Similar concerns are evident in the next case and many others considered further along.

Case 7: *The Wife Who Wants a* Fasakh *Divorce Because Her Husband Is Crazy*. Present at the outset of this hearing were the *kadi* (and his son, playing in the background), Araffin, and the wife (Kalsom), who looked to be in her thirties. Two witnesses waited outside and were called to testify during the latter part of the proceedings.

The hearing began with Araffin swearing in Kalsom, who was instructed to stand and to repeat words to the following effect: "I, Kalsom bte. . . . do solemnly swear or vow (*berikrar*) in the court that my petition/statement is given with information that is truthful." The main issue was the husband's "abnormal behavior": "Sometimes he doesn't wear clothes" (she later referred specifically to shirts, not pants or *sarung*). "He left . . . [about a year ago] and hasn't been back since. . . . He went back to his mother's house," and in response to the *kadi*'s question on the subject, "No, he wasn't driven away. . . . And he does not work now." As it turns out, he is too disturbed to work.

The *kadi* asked, "Is he *miring, otak miring, gila* (crazy, mad, insane)? Does it follow the moon, like when the moon rises [gets full]? Does it arise or get worse then?" The wife replied, "No, he's always like this." She added, in response to questions from the *kadi*, that she does not love (*sayang*) him. She tried to visit him a couple of times at his (mother's) house. She got as far as the *rambutan* tree in the garden, but his mother would not let her in.

The *kadi* then asked about his *keturunan* (descent, ancestry), revealing among other things a concern with origin-point and classification: "Is his

brother okay? Didn't you know about his *keturunan* before you got married?"
And then, "Well, do you want him anymore, or not?" "No," she replied, to
which the *kadi* said, "According to the law, it is better if you wait until he gets
treated. Can he be treated or not?" (I didn't hear what, if anything, she answered to this question.)

At this juncture the first witness, an *imam* who appeared to be in his fifties,
was called in and administered the oath. The *imam* began his comments with
references to the husband's clothes, testifying that he dresses like a "hero"
(tough guy), "is always like this and doesn't really bother people, though he
laughs to himself, walks around talking to himself and grinning, and dresses
like a cowboy . . . like Hang Tuah" (perhaps the best known of all Malay
legendary figures). The *imam* added that as far as he knew, the husband had
been this way for at least three or four months. It was around this point in the
conversation that the *imam*, or someone else present, used the term *sakit jiwa*
(sick soul or spirit; mental illness) to refer to the husband's condition. The *kadi*
interjected that it was fortunate that there were no children born of the marriage. The witness was then thanked and shown the door.

The second witness, a man who appeared to be in his fifties, was then called
in. "He's not *siuman*," said the witness, which means, more or less, that he is
"not right in the head." "He wears things around his head, like scarves or
bandanas; sometimes he walks around with no shirt, though . . . [in response to
the *kadi*'s question] he always wears pants. . . . He has been like this for about
two years. Before he was married he was like this; that's why he had to quit
work."

The *kadi* then asked, as he had before, "What kind of *gila*?" "*Gila miring*, or
gila babi?" "*Miring*," said the witness; and in response to the *kadi*'s question on
this point, "it doesn't follow the month[s] (*bulan*)."

Kadi [to wife]: Why didn't you go visit your husband?
Wife: I did, but his father drove me away.
[The witness then turned to the wife and said in an accusatory voice, "Hey,
    don't lie; don't bring your lies in here."]
Wife: I'm not lying. . . .

The *kadi* took notes throughout the session, repeating back what the parties
told him and rewording their testimony for the sake of clarity. After obtaining
all of their statements, he read them aloud, seeking their confirmation that this
was what they said. He then had each of them sign his or her statement.

The second witness left, at which point the *kadi* instructed the wife, who had
been sitting in the chair to the left of the *kadi*'s desk (where the counselor
usually sits) to go back to the chair in front of his desk. He told her to rise and
proceeded to announce: "The decision (*keputusan*) is that a *fasakh* divorce is
granted with one *talak*." He asked the wife if she accepted the decision; she
said yes. The *kadi* then informed the wife and Araffin about the difference
between a *taklik* and *fasakh* divorce and proceeded to explain the *edah* issue to
the wife: "The period is three months and ten days from today." He then asked
her, "Pardon me, have you menstruated already?" The wife replied that she had,

and he directed her to "come here after three more menstruations, after you've bathed; even if it's before that date, and tell me and the period will be up." He went on to make clear that there is no *nafkah edah* since it was the wife who asked for the divorce.

Comment: This is one of the few cases I observed in which there was any formal swearing in of litigants or witnesses. The reason for such formality in this instance is that it was a request for a *fasakh*, which is a type of divorce or judicial rescission or voiding of the marriage contract (sometimes referred to in the literature as an annulment) available to women under certain conditions. As explained by Araffin, such conditions exist if the husband is crazy or insane (*gila*); disabled or deformed (*cacat*) and "can't give sex"; and/or unable to maintain his wife. The most common of these conditions, according to Araffin, is *gila*. Hence the importance of having witnesses from the husband's side, for as Araffin pointed out, "if the husband is *gila*, he might not be able to . . . give evidence." As for the second condition (*cacat*), Araffin said that the wife must give the husband time (one year) to be treated; presumably this would apply to cases of *gila* as well.

Kadi enjoy considerable discretion with respect to *fasakh* divorce. They are reluctant to grant *fasakh* (and other kinds of) divorces to women for numerous reasons, some of which are related to the fact that divorce is generally seen as a male prerogative, one that could be eroded by approving women's petitions for termination of marriage. At the same time, given the specific legal provisions for *fasakh*, *kadi* are obliged to grant them to women if they are more or less convinced that the relevant conditions have been fulfilled. The swearing in of witnesses helps assure the court that the conditions alleged by the wife do in fact exist, though as Araffin's earlier commentary makes clear, these measures provide no guarantee that such is the case; oaths serve mainly to enhance the likelihood of the testimony's being true.

Araffin also explained that *fasakh* divorces are not all that common for various reasons, one of which is that even if a woman is—or feels—entitled to a *fasakh* divorce, she will often ask that her husband grant her an amicable divorce or "divorce on good terms" (*cerai cara baik*), which, in effect, leaves the final decision up to him. This enables the husband to divorce his wife in a manner that causes him less embarrassment and allows him to save face. If the husband denies such a request or refuses to deal with the wife's request to proceed in this way, she can go ahead and seek a termination of the marriage via *fasakh*.

There are a few other issues to bear in mind here. One has to do with the *kadi*'s concern to discern the particular type and origin (*asal-usul*) of the husband's mental illness. This is a recurrent theme in the hearing, partly because the *kadi* needs to know if the condition is treatable, hence perhaps a temporary problem that need not result in judicial termination of the marriage. A second is that matters bearing on the wife's reproductive capacities and menstrual cycles are part of the judicial record here, as when the *kadi* asks the wife if she has recently menstruated so as to calculate more precisely the *edah* period. A third issue to bear in mind in the ensuing discussion is that the *kadi* uses his judicial discretion to deprive the wife of the *nafkah edah* that she might successfully claim from another *kadi*, his reasoning being that she forfeited her claims to it by bringing divorce proceedings against her husband. The *kadi* is thus treating a woman's legitimate request for a divorce as a form of *nusus* (recalcitrance); in Islamic law, a wife's *nusus* effectively invalidates many of the financial claims she might normally make at divorce (for example, for *nafkah edah* and *muta'ah*). The more general dynamic is that Islamic courts throughout Malaysia sometimes punish women for exercising their legitimate legal options (see Mohammad Hashim Kamali 2000: 93 passim). This is but one manifestation of the courts' tendency to support husbands over wives and men over women generally, which we see in the next case and many others.

Case 8: *The Wife Who Requests a Divorce Because Her Husband Does Not Support Their Children and Rarely Comes Home.* The proceeding was initiated by the wife, who first approached the *kadi*'s office about a year before this hearing. She and her husband have been married for some thirteen years and have four children. The wife petitioned for a divorce on the grounds that the husband does not support the children and rarely comes home. About a year ago the husband had been ordered to pay M$200 per month and to buy kitchen supplies (*barang dapur*). He has been delinquent in these payments, to the tune of M$960. The wife initially claimed that the husband was delinquent in the amount of M$1,080, but this was later corrected when the *kadi* ordered Araffin to check the files and ascertain the amount of money that the husband had sent her.

Among the most salient issues as far as the *kadi* is concerned was that the husband claimed to love (*sayang*) the wife and did not want a divorce. Early in the proceedings he made clear, in response to the *kadi*'s questions about what he was seeking, that the *kadi* could go ahead and grant a divorce if he (the *kadi*) so desired. The *kadi*'s response was that "this isn't the way it works," and he proceeded to clarify that he needed to know what the husband wanted. The husband admitted that he had been at fault with respect to late payments (*nafkah*). He insisted that he wanted his wife back, though he also acknowledged that she would not have him. The wife spoke up a number of times, indicating that there was no point in talking any more about any of this since she was fed up.

Neither the wife nor the husband works, according to the counselor, but the husband has a truck that he utilizes in some sort of business. The counselor also told me (after the hearing) that the husband had married another woman as well, but that the first wife had not given her approval to that marriage. Not only did he marry the second wife under false pretenses (by telling her that he was single), he also drinks, gambles, and is "jolly" (as the counselor put it). The counselor explained that "this is a big problem," "this" referring to men who are dishonest when they fill out the marriage form, take a second wife without following the prescribed procedures, etc.

The *kadi* was not at all taken by the husband's tale of his woes, and he impressed upon him time and again that his word was somewhat in doubt and that if he wanted to keep his wife he had to "put up or shut up" (my expression, not his). The *kadi* decreed that the outstanding M$960 had to be paid within ten days; if not, the wife's request for a divorce would be granted or, as the *kadi* expressed it, "one *talak* will fall."

Earlier in the hearing the husband had offered to pay the sum in question whenever the *kadi* wanted, so the *kadi* took him up on it by saying, "Okay, how about in a week?" The husband appeared to say "Okay," but then paused for a moment, seemed to have second thoughts, and suggested that he might need a bit longer. The *kadi* chided him about his earlier statement to the effect that he would come up with the money whenever necessary. The husband also offered to transfer ownership of the truck to his wife whenever she wanted it, as evidence of his sincere intention to change his ways. The *kadi* asked the wife if she wanted this. Her reaction was, "I don't want . . . anything to do with any of this; no more stories." It was at about this point that the wife started crying and walked out of the proceedings.

The *kadi* was clearly displeased by the lack of consensus between husband and wife on the key issue of whether or not they should stay together. He would have been more satisfied if the wife had agreed to take the husband back or if the husband had consented to a divorce. Be that as it may, he proceeded to announce that since he could not resolve the matter, he would refer it to the chief *kadi*, who also serves as a circuit *kadi*, making rounds to the various districts on a regular basis.

Shortly thereafter the husband signed a statement prepared by the counselor, which specified that he would pay the outstanding money in ten days. It was clear that this document was to become part of the evidentiary record that would be reviewed in any future proceedings. There was also a reference to another M$1,000, but I did not hear the specifics. More important were the *kadi*'s repeated comments to the husband to the effect that, "If you really want her, really love her, then pay up." It was either at this point in the hearing or perhaps a bit earlier that the husband made a reference to women and men having different kinds of "skin" (*kulit*), apparently in an effort to help the court make sense of some of the difficulties he was experiencing with his wife.

The husband's prior marital history did not come up in the hearing. It may have helped inform the *kadi*'s position, although this is hard to say. In point of fact, it is doubtful if very much of the husband's behavior figured into the decision of the *kadi*, for the *kadi* essentially upheld the husband's right to keep the marriage formally intact, even though the wife wanted a divorce.

Comment: After the hearing I discussed the case with the counselor. She made clear that at this point the ball is in the husband's court and that if he does not pay the outstanding M$960 in ten days, his wife's request will probably be granted. According to the counselor, the husband will most likely get the money from his father, who accompanied him to the hearings but sat outside talking with Araffin.

When I asked the counselor about the *kadi*'s disinclination to grant the wife the divorce she sought and whether this judicial stance might impose continued hardship on her, the counselor explained that the *kadi* really tries to do what he can to take into account the feelings and wishes of the husband (though, as the following case illustrates, such efforts are ultimately situational). The counselor did not come right out and say that the husband has more rights or prerogatives or a higher priority in terms of Islamic law, though that seemed to be her point. She also acknowledged as true my comment that the wife was possibly burdened by the *kadi*'s decision.

Case 9: *Hasnah Who Seeks a Divorce Because Her Husband Hits Her.* The case involves Hasnah (age nineteen) and her husband, Jafri (age twenty-two).

Kadi: Where are you people from (*Orang mana*)?

Husband: Bahau, but originally Pahang.

Wife: Formerly from Sepri; we were "caught wet" (*tangkap basah*; guilty of "illicit proximity") in Bahau.

Kadi: Okay, you want to speak frankly. What kind of work do you do?

Husband: Factory work in Chembong. I've been living in Pedas, at the house of my adoptive father for about a year.

Kadi: Why did you come here?

Husband: My wife seeks a divorce.

Kadi: You were "caught wet" in Bahau, so why do you come here seeking a divorce?

Wife: He hits me frequently [or all the time] (*Dia selalu pukul saya*).

Kadi [to husband]: Why do you hit her frequently [or all the time]?

Husband: I work as a guard. I get off work at 10:30 in the evening and my wife is always "noisy" (*bising*). . . .

Kadi: How many times have you hit her?

Husband: I just recently hit her.

Kadi: How long have you been married?

Husband: About a year, more or less.

Kadi: How many times have you been struck?

Wife: Lots of times.

Husband: She doesn't wait on me enough, and she always goes out of the house without permission.

Kadi: Do you pray frequently [or all the time] or not?

Husband: Rarely.

Wife: Rarely.

Kadi: This marriage, you know, it involves lots of responsibility. But you always neglect your prayers. You really do not take your religion seriously. . . . Do you have children?

Wife: The child died about a week after it was born. . . . the funeral was in
   Pedas. I was there but my husband wasn't.
Kadi: Your child dies and you don't even go to the funeral? You, as father,
   should know your responsibility. Both of you really do not take religion
   seriously. . . . So, is it correct that you're requesting a divorce?
Wife: Yeah.
Husband: I'm not ready or willing (*sanggup*) to divorce. I still love her.
Wife: I want a divorce.
Husband: There's a guy who frequently comes to the house while I'm off at
   work. . . .
Wife: He's one of my mother's relatives (*saudara*).
Kadi: You already have a husband; you can't do that. It's like you do not
   know the law.
Wife: He always drinks beer.
Husband: When I was a bachelor. Not now.
Kadi: And you want to request a divorce?
Wife: Yeah.
Kadi: This means that you can't seek *nafkah edah*. You were the one who
   petitioned first, right?
Wife: Yeah.
Kadi: Over the course of the marriage, what has your husband given you?
Wife: A bicycle and kitchenware.
Husband: She is always talking about my shortcomings with other people.
Kadi: Cik Hasnah, you should understand your [husband's?] responsibilities
   and your husband's point of view. Just ask for what you need. Don't ask
   for what he can't provide. . . . Okay, I'm giving you three months and ten
   days to decide if you want to reconcile or not.

The *kadi* then gives the husband the divorce certificate (*surat cerai*), instructing
him to read it aloud; he does so, thus effecting a divorce with one *talak*.

Comment: This narrative begins, as do many others in Islamic courts in
Malaysia and elsewhere, with the *kadi* eliciting information on the litigants'
origins or origin-points (*asal-usul*). In responding to the question as to origins,
the wife volunteers the information that they were forced to get married due to
having been "caught wet." The phrasing of this admission signals the *kadi* that
they want to "speak frankly," which he notes as a prelude to frankness on his
part. Issues of origins are intertwined with questions of jurisdiction inasmuch as
they were "caught wet" in Bahau, which is in a different district, and were
presumably "processed" by officials in that district, but they have come to Rembau for assistance with their marital problems, partly, it seems, because they
live in the district of Rembau and were born there as well. Also relevant to their
origins in the sense of "where they are coming from" are their jobs and occupa-
tions, which in this case involve the husband's employment in a factory.
   It is significant that the husband does not deny hitting his wife, though he

contests her claim concerning the frequency with which she was struck, insisting it was only once and implying it was justified on the grounds that she does not fulfill the responsibilities entailed in the gendered division of labor and the marriage contract generally (does not "wait on him enough" and "always goes out of the house without his permission"). It is notable that the *kadi* does not pursue this point any further but attempts to gather more information on "what kind of people they are" by asking them one at a time if they pray on a regular basis. The *kadi* is quite distressed by their response (that they "rarely" pray), telling them that marriage involves lots of responsibility, yet they do not take their religion seriously.

The issue of divorce is the major area of contestation so far as the *kadi* is concerned, but in many ways the bottom line for the *kadi* appears to be the profound incompatability between husband and wife, which is exacerbated by their moral laxity. The husband's basic position is that he still loves his wife and is not ready to give her up. Interestingly, when the wife responds to remarks along these lines by reiterating that she wants a divorce, the husband mentions "another man" who frequently visits his wife while he is at work, at which point the the *kadi* tells her, ". . . you can't do that. It's like you don't know the law." The wife's denial of wrongdoing is coupled with the accusation that her husband always drinks beer, the partial truth of which he acknowledges ("When I was a bachelor. Not now").

After the *kadi* reconfirms the wife's desire for a divorce and makes clear to her that since she is the one seeking termination of the marriage there is no *nafkah edah*, he forges ahead and instructs the husband to pronounce the *talak*, even though the husband has just registered his opposition to the idea of divorce. The *kadi*'s use of judicial discretion in this case is noteworthy in light of the fact that he could have just as easily sent the couple away for an unspecified period to try to work through their problems. That he chose instead to terminate the marriage is but one indication of the increased legal and overall cultural salience of emotional compatability between husband and wife as a prerequisite for the continuation of marriage (Horowitz 1994; cf. Jones 1994). Somewhat similar indications of the heightened salience of "companionate marriage" can be seen in the following case.

Case 10: *The Wife Who Seeks a* Fasakh *Divorce Because Her Husband Sent Her Away. (The Husband Claims She "Drove Him Away Like a Dog.")* Present at the outset of the first hearing of these proceedings were the twenty-three-year-old wife (Rohaiyah), her thirty-year-old husband, and the *kadi*; they were later joined by the woman's (maternal?) grandfather and the counselor.

The wife approached the *kadi*'s office about nine months earlier, indicating that she wanted a *fasakh* divorce because the husband had driven her away, that she had moved out and was currently living with her grandfather, and that she had not had any contact with her husband for quite some time. The husband was thus called to appear before the *kadi* and he did so, insisting that he would *not* grant the wife a divorce. He was summoned on subsequent occasions, presumably on account of his tardiness or refusal to pay the prescribed support, and many times failed to appear. I suspect it was on account of this poor showing that Araffin had warned me that this particular hearing might not take place.

The *kadi* opened the hearing with remarks about the husband's responsibilities, how it was expected that he provide for his wife and child, and so on. He used the example of the problems created by men who take second wives, dwelling on it to such a degree that I thought there might be another woman involved; I was wrong.

The husband responded by citing his major complaint, which is that he was not allowed to see his child and that when he appeared at his wife's grandfather's house he was "driven away like a dog" (*halau macam anjing*). In describing these facts and his view of the problem(s), he was extremely emotional and "hot" (as Malays say); the wife was less so, but she appeared to be fighting back tears throughout much of the hearing.

The husband claimed that he has tried to give the wife money, but she will not accept it. This was contested by the wife, who maintained that although he had given her money on at least one occasion, he proceeded to ask for or demand it back. She added that she was afraid to let him see their daughter because she feared that he would take her and harm her. In this regard she recounted that the husband had once returned and said something to the effect that he was going to take the child, that the child was better off with him no matter what happened, even if the child "died in his arms." The husband did not deny saying this when questioned on the topic by the *kadi*. Instead, he insisted that the treatment he was receiving from his wife was altogether unacceptable; the child was, after all, his own flesh and blood (*darah daging*; literally, blood and flesh/meat).

The *kadi* stated repeatedly that the child's proper home from birth until seven years of age is with the mother, and in this connection he cited the Administration of Muslim Law Enactment, 1960, and the schedule of preferences listed therein. Only after this could arrangements be made to have custody of the child transferred to the father (or someone else). But the proceedings did not seem to be getting anywhere, so the *kadi* called as a witness the wife's grandfather (a *haji*), who substantiated the wife's version of the difficulties. The grandfather testified that the husband had come around rarely, thus also contradicting the husband's statements on this matter.

It was about this time that the *kadi* invited the counselor in to have her write up a statement to be signed by the husband. It was agreed that the husband had a right to see the child, and it was further agreed that the husband would be able to meet the child at the *kadi*'s office. Once a month he would phone the *kadi*'s office indicating when he would like to see the child; the *kadi*'s office would then contact the grandfather, who would either arrange for the child to be brought to the office or bring her himself. Here, as in many cases, we see the *kadi* and his staff serving as go-betweens for husbands and wives who can no longer communicate effectively.

This problem resolved, the next issue was support. The husband was informed that he had to send money once a month to the *kadi*'s office, and the *kadi*'s office would see that the wife received the money. This, they said, is how it is always done to reduce problems of people saying the money was sent when it was not, or was not received when it was.

The husband then insisted that he wanted the monthly payments contingent on his being allowed to see his daughter. The *kadi* said absolutely not; these were separate issues and the support of children was obligatory (*wajib*) according to the Quran. Then came the issue of how much the husband was going to give the wife and daughter. Thus began a long and stalemated part of the proceedings.

The husband testified that his monthly wage was M$520, "M$470 clean [after deductions]." It was agreed that the *nafkah anak* should be M$60 a month, plus clothes and books for school until the child marries or begins working. There followed a lengthy discussion of how this money would be taken out each month. The husband did not like the idea of his employer docking his monthly wages and making arrangements for sending the money to the *kadi*'s office.

It was about this time that the counselor was asked to go out and get the *nafkah* forms, which she did. The *kadi* then helped her prepare a statement that read something like, "If I don't appear at the *kadi*'s court in three weeks, then one *talak* will fall on my wife." This was to be signed by the husband and witnessed by two people (the *kadi* and the wife's grandfather), but first the husband was supposed to recite it. The idea was that he would come in with a final decision about whether he was going to grant the wife the divorce she requested. The husband was then instructed to sign the document, but he hesitated and waited for quite a long time. All the while the others, especially the *kadi*, were getting very impatient. Finally, the *kadi* said: "Look, you *must* sign this, and you have to read it out loud. This is called *lafaz*."

The husband would not read it aloud or sign it, so the *kadi* ordered that a new agreement be drawn up. This one, drawn up in the husband's hand, said, "I will appear in the *kadi*'s court . . . [in three weeks] with information for my wife." The *kadi* read this and argued that "information" was not sufficient; he wanted a *decision* concerning their marital status. The *kadi* thus made a slight editorial change to this effect and let the matter lie.

A second hearing occurred exactly three weeks later. Present at this hearing, in addition to the *kadi*, were the counselor and the *kadi*'s young daughter, who ran around creating much noise (though not as much as the *kadi*'s son typically makes). The hearing began with the *kadi* asking the couple, "So, where are things?" and proceeding to offer comments to the effect that he was interested in seeing justice served in this matter.

He then turned to the husband and said quite frankly, "Look, your wife doesn't want you." The husband acknowledged his responsibility in supporting his child but also claimed that he was not sure he could support her. But this had nothing to do with whether he was going to agree to divorce his wife. (Recall that this was the day he was supposed to come with a final decision on this matter.) The *kadi* grew impatient. It was clear to the *kadi* and everyone else, except the husband, that there was no marriage to be saved, and the *kadi* thus told him to read the statement on the form that included the phrase, "with clear mind and without force . . . I divorce my wife."

The husband protested that some other way could be found to resolve their problems, but this seemed unlikely and the court seemed uninterested in what he had to say. The tone of the husband throughout the hearing had been one of rather lame self-defense and rationalization, trying to "make up the law as he went along," with little understanding of his obligations or his legal options and a great deal of whining and self-serving talk, which clearly irritated the *kadi*. As the *kadi* grew more and more angry, he read aloud the statement that the husband had signed a few weeks back (which said that he would come to the court with a final decision) and ordered him to do the same and sign a declaration of divorce, adding that the issue of child support would be decided later. At the *kadi*'s insistence, the husband read aloud and signed the following statement: "I divorce my wife and the *nafkah* of the child falls on my wife until the child *berakal* [has reason; reaches maturity] at which point I will support the child and give it whatever it wants."

After a brief lecture on his responsibilities as a husband, what would happen later if his daughter met him on the street and did not even know him, who would take care of her in the event that something happened to her mother, etc., the *kadi* thanked the husband and shook his hand partly, it seemed, as a gesture to get him to leave the room. Shortly thereafter, the wife attempted to shake the *kadi*'s hand, but the *kadi* abruptly withdrew his hand before she got a chance to shake it, saying that "it wasn't necessary."

The wife's grandfather was then called in, and the *kadi* asked him for his cooperation and help in locating the child's father in the future, in the event the wife needed to find him. The *kadi* told the grandfather that if need be, she could sue the father later to get support from him.

About five months later I sat in on a third hearing in this case. The grandfather, who was involved in the other hearings, came in, accompanied by his now divorced granddaughter and her young daughter. The *kadi*'s first move was to send the divorced woman and her daughter back into the main office. At issue is *nafkah anak* and conjugal property (*harta sepencarian*), distribution of which had not been decided during the hearing a few months back because the *kadi* felt that he "could only go a few steps at a time." The wife wanted to receive *nafkah anak* at the rate of M$60 a month and was claiming what she referred to as *harta sepencarian*: television, refrigerator, kitchenware, and so forth.

The *kadi* spent much of the time explaining to the grandfather why he chose not to deal with the *nafkah anak* and *harta sepencarian* issues during the previous hearing, reiterating how much time and effort it took to get as far as they got (to force the husband to let his wife go). The *kadi* indicated that the issue could not be resolved at present and would be postponed until next month. The grandfather's response included a comment to the effect that, "If the husband isn't present at the first summons, he'll be forgiven. If he's not present at the second summons, he'll be forgiven as well. But if he's not present the third time around, jail."

The *kadi* then said, with reference to the *sepencarian* property, that some of this is not even *sepencarian*, that it belongs straightaway to the wife and thus need not be divided up because the wife is raising the child. Araffin interjected, "Yes, usually this is true, but if the husband won't give it to her?" The *kadi*'s rejoinder: "Okay, we'll make a letter about this later."

Comment: Initially this case involved an attempt on the part of the wife to have the marriage annulled based on the provisions of *fasakh*. But the husband was not away long enough (according to the counselor), and a *fasakh* divorce was thus ruled out.

It merits remark as well that the husband had struck/beat (*pukul*) the wife. This did not come up in the hearing itself, but it was apparently among the allegations made by the wife at an earlier hearing with the counselor (or the counselor and the *kadi*), and apparently it was accepted as fact by the court. Circumstances such as these may help explain why the *kadi* used his judicial discretion to effectively insist that the husband let the wife go.

With respect to the second hearing, the arrangement that was worked out struck me as rather inequitable, since it deprived the wife of child support for at least a few years. Part of the reason for this decision was that it was the wife who pressed for divorce. The *kadi* also wanted to get the divorce through as painlessly as possible, and given the stubbornness of the husband coupled with the wife's deep-seated antipathy toward him, this seemed like a good opportunity to end the marriage as a first step toward resolving the problems in their entirety.

Note also that throughout this hearing and the others we have considered in this chapter, the discourses of the court focus on spousal duties and responsibilities (*tugas, tanggungjawab*), such as those entailed in the locally defined gendered division of labor and in the marriage contract specifically. The flip side of the coin of duties and responsibilities are, of course, "rights" (*hak*), and while rights as such make up a component of local culture (and the culture of law in particular) that is clearly cognized, they are not culturally *elaborated* to any significant degree or comparable extent and are not given extensive expression in the courts. This is to say (among other things) that while the courts tend to elaborate a discourse of the responsibilities of men, they do not articulate a discourse focusing on the rights of women.[13] A more general point to which we will return later is that these features of local legal discourse fit exceptionally well with the current political climate and with state narratives bearing on citizenship. The latter narratives focus on citizens' responsibilities as Muslims, as Malays, and as Malaysians, not on their rights with respect to these or other culturally or politically salient categories.

Similar themes appear in the next case, which, like all of the others examined thus far, was aired in the district of Rembau. A key difference, however, is that this case was overseen by the chief *kadi*, *Kadi Besar* Ustaz Baharom, who came down from the state capital, Seremban, to adjudicate the issues involved. That this case came under the jurisdiction of the chief *kadi* rather than the "regular (district) *kadi*" had to do mainly with the greater sums of money at stake (and contested). Especially important to note, particularly since they are harbingers of the changes that occurred in subsequent years due to the gradual implementation of the 1984 Islamic Family Law Act, which "by the end of 1991 had finally been enacted in all states" in Peninsular Malaysia,[14] are: the greater formality of the hearing; the more direct, challenging style of investigation, which was at times somewhat inquisition-like; and the greater stress on "proof," particularly in written form.

Case 11 (Heard by the chief *kadi*): *Wife Seeking Past and Ongoing* Nafkah *and Repayment of Debt from Former Husband.* I arrived at the courthouse shortly after 9:30 A.M. and immediately noticed a fair number of people waiting outside. Most were women, but there were two men of roughly the same age standing off by themselves in a corner of the parking area whose interactions led me to assume that they came together or were friends. As it turned out, they were the respective defendants in the two cases and probably did not know each other ahead of time. The husband involved in the second case was wearing a smart blue *songkok* and an aquamarine *baju melayu* (Malay shirt), khaki-colored pants, and shoes with socks. He carried a file full of papers relating to the case, including letters from the bank attesting to his debts and the mortgaging of his house.

The chief *kadi* arrived shortly before the cases were to begin at 10 A.M. and was formally attired in a black business suit, long-sleeved white shirt, black *songkok,* and black leather shoes. He went into the *kadi*'s chambers to look over papers relating to the cases and to talk to Araffin, and was served tea or coffee and given some cakes as well. Before the first case began the chief *kadi* needed to confer with Rembau's *kadi*, who was home for a day or so (on vacation), so Araffin rang him up. The way the case unfolded, it would have been beneficial if Rembau's *kadi* had been there in person.

In terms of the setting inside the courthouse, where the hearings occurred, I need to emphasize first that these cases were heard in the official *courtroom,* not in the *kadi*'s chambers, which is where *all* hearings involving the Rembau *kadi* take place. In court there were nine adults and two children, although another adult man came later. Of the nine adults mentioned, all were women except the two husbands. The chief *kadi* sat in the chair behind the huge imposing desk at the front of the courtroom, whose top is a good five and a half or six feet off the ground. Toward the front left corner of the courtroom was a raised "witness box," in which husband and wife stood when they were called on to approach the chief *kadi* and make their statements. Toward the back of the courtroom were two tables pushed together at right angles; Araffin sat at one of them. In the far back of the room were four rows of wooden benches with upright backs. This is where the husbands and wives sat, along with family members and others who attended the hearings.

Araffin came into the courtroom at about 10:15 with a large grin on his face as a result of opening the door and seeing that everyone was staring at him. He put a stack of papers on the desk and sat down. About two minutes later the chief *kadi* entered and Araffin instructed everyone to rise. The chief *kadi* greeted those present with *Assalam alaikum* (Peace be with you); those present gave the appropriate rejoinder.

The first case involved Natra and Osman. Araffin informed the chief *kadi* that the case was heard last year but was not fully resolved. Natra was told to take the stand and was sworn in by Araffin, who instructed her to raise her right hand and say, "I swear [*berikrar*] that everything I say is the truth," etc. There were no references to Allah or God (*Tuhan*).

The chief *kadi* asked the wife her name and address, which she proceeded to supply, and then said, "This case has been heard before, right?" to which the wife replied, "Yes, but my husband didn't come." The chief *kadi* requested that the wife tell him her husband's name as well as the court's previous decision. The wife supplied this information (I did not hear it all), adding, "But my husband didn't pay *nafkah anak*."

The chief *kadi* then asked about the amount of the *nafkah anak* (I could not make out her response) and the rest of the decision.

Wife: To pay my brother back the M$300 that he [the husband] owes him.
Chief Kadi: Brother's name, age?
[The wife supplies this information.]
Chief Kadi: Why isn't your brother here?
Wife: He's not *berani* [he's not courageous; he doesn't have the guts].
Chief Kadi: But you're courageous, you have guts?
Wife: Yes. But my brother is young; he isn't *berani*. He doesn't know about things here. But he told me to claim the M$300.
Chief Kadi: Where's the letter that says you're representing him?
Wife: I do not have one.
Chief Kadi: Does your husband work now?
Wife: Yes, but he didn't used to. He also lied about not working; he claimed he didn't work when he really did have work.
Chief Kadi: Where does he work?
Wife: I don't know the exact address. . . . And he's married again.
Chief Kadi: Do you have any proof that he's working? . . .

The wife then accuses the husband of lying and says, "He thinks he can run away." She adds something to the effect that they have been divorced for about three years and that he has never paid *nafkah* and has never even seen his children. They have a three-year-old boy and a six- or seven-year-old girl.

Chief Kadi: So, no proof that your husband is or was working, huh? Just what people said [hearsay]?
Wife: No [proof].

The wife concludes her statement and leaves the witness box. The husband is instructed by the chief *kadi* to take the stand and is sworn in by Araffin. The chief *kadi* then asks the husband his name, if he is Natra's former husband, if he has children with her, how old they are, where he originates ("a village in Bahau"), where he lives now ("Kuala Lumpur"), what his address is, and what kind of work he does ("I'm a temporary clerk" [at a large corporation]), his income ("M$300 a month"), how long he has been working there ("just a month"), and so on.

Chief Kadi: M$40 a month [per child] was the order; M$80 total. Have you ever paid that?
Husband: Yes [for about eight months].
Chief Kadi: Do you have receipts for this, proof of this?
Husband: No. The other *kadi* has some of them. [But] I haven't paid [for over a year and a half].

The chief *kadi* then asks about his current (as opposed to former) wife: what her name is; when they were married; whether she had been married before (she had); and about the nature of the marriage payments. The husband replied that there were no *hantaran* and that he just gave M$200. There was no specific indication of exactly what this payment was or how it was defined (for example, it was not *hantaran*, according to the husband).

The husband goes on to say, in response to the chief *kadi*'s questions, that after marrying he lived in Klang; when he worked there he was making M$650 a month, but he had stopped working about seven months ago. After that he tapped rubber and helped his mother-in-law at the evening market. "I did village work [*kerja kampung*] and the work is not certain [*tak tentu*]," he explained in response to the chief *kadi*'s question concerning how much he has made over the past few months. He lives in Kuala Lumpur now because "there is no work in the village."

"How much do you pay for the place you live?" the chief *kadi* asks him. The husband's answer, which struck me as relatively reasonable for Kuala Lumpur, was followed by the chief *kadi*'s somewhat rhetorical question, "Why do you pay so much?" In his defense the husband explains that "it is only a room . . . if I could find something cheaper, I would."

Chief Kadi [to the wife]: Do you have any questions you want to ask your husband [about the information he gave]?
Wife: Yes. [She then goes off on a tangent about the *nafkah* she wants.]
Chief Kadi: That's my job [to decide about that]. Address your husband, not me. Otherwise the court will accept what he says as true. Do you agree with what he says about when he worked and when he didn't?
Wife: So, how much did you get at the night market? [She continues with comments about his responsibilities, for example, to pay *nafkah anak*.]
Chief Kadi: So how much do you get?

Husband: It isn't certain [*tak tentu*]; it's *buku* [joints, for example, of sugar cane?], ninety cents a kilo.

Various people sitting in the back of the courtroom are talking, and the chief *kadi* expresses his anger at them for making noise. He then asks the husband if he received the warrant that was sent to him. The husband replies in the affirmative, and the chief *kadi* informs him that according to the warrant, if he did not show up in court he would be arrested. He proceeds with: "So, why shouldn't you be jailed? You know the court has the power to arrest and jail you."

Husband: Because I can't [*tak mampu*]; no fixed income.
Chief Kadi: Do you agree that you should pay?
Husband: Yes, but not at the rates previously worked out [by the local *kadi*].
Chief Kadi: Then how much?
Husband: M$20 a month.
Chief Kadi: What sort of food can you get for M$20 a month?
Husband: My wife said that even if I get M$10 I should give [her] half of it.
Chief Kadi: If you are ordered to pay *nafkah anak*, how are you going to pay?
Husband: Through the *kadi*'s office.
Chief Kadi: And the outstanding debt?
Husband: When I'm able to pay it, I will.

The chief *kadi* is silent for awhile, pondering the case; he then proceeds to announce that after discussing and conferring about the matter, the court's decision is: the husband will pay M$40 a month, beginning at the end of this month, and if he does not pay, his wages will be garnished; the back *nafkah* charge is dropped because the husband did not (or does not) have work, and the wife did not prove that he had (has) work; and the debt (to the wife's younger brother) will be paid.

The chief *kadi* then announces, "That's it," Araffin instructs all present to rise, people stand up, and the chief *kadi* leaves the room.

Comment: Noteworthy in this case are three things, roughly in order of their appearance in the text. First, is the much greater formality and impersonal nature of the hearing, especially in terms of its physical setting in the official courtroom (for example, the necessity of standing up when the chief *kadi* enters, the raised witness box, the considerable physical and status distance between the chief *kadi* and the litigants), and the attire of the chief *kadi*, particularly the smart white dress shirt and the black business suit—which represents a sharp contrast to the attire of the "regular" (district) *kadi* and is more or less identical to the attire of Judge Nicholas Indran of the secular courts and, of course, corporate businessmen worldwide. Second is the more direct, challenging style of questioning and investigation, which seemed at times geared toward making the parties feel embarrassed and was in any event somewhat inquisition-like and on occasion intentionally threatening ("You know the court has the power to arrest and jail you"; "Why shouldn't you be jailed?"; "Address your husband not me. Otherwise the court will accept what he says as true"). Third is the greater stress on proof, especially in written form—such as letters, receipts, and the like—coupled with the greater reliance on standards of the secular, common-law based courts, including (but not limited to) the inadmissibility of hearsay and the importance attached to clarifying what is and is not admissible as evidence. Note, finally, that in these and other respects, this hearing instantiates ongoing processes involving the centralization, standardization, and rationalization of the Islamic courts, the ways in which such processes entail convergence with the secular legal system, and what various observers (Lawrence 1998; Ong 1999b) have referred to as the increasingly "corporate" inflection of contemporary Malaysian Islam.

Case 12 (Heard by the chief *kadi*): *Wife Seeking* Nafkah, Harta Sepencarian, *and Continued Custody of Adopted Child* (Anak Angkat). This case involved a woman named Hasnah and a man named Tajul. The wife was the first called to the stand and was sworn in by Araffin as in the previous case.

Chief Kadi: What is your name?
Wife: Hasnah bte. B. . . .
Chief Kadi: Village?
Wife: Penajis, Rembau.
Chief Kadi: I.C. [Identity Card]?
Wife: Yes. [She gets up and gives it to Araffin, who gives it to the chief *kadi*.]
Chief Kadi: Former husband's name?
[Wife gives answer.]
Chief Kadi: How long were you married to him?
Wife: Eleven years.
Chief Kadi: Any children?
Wife: Yes. An adopted child [*anak angkat*].
Chief Kadi: Name?
[Wife gives child's name.]
Chief Kadi: Married what month?
[Wife answers.]
Chief Kadi: When were you divorced?
Wife: [About two and a half years ago.]
Chief Kadi: What was the agreement then?
Wife: My husband was to provide *nafkah anak*, M$100/month; *edah*, M$200/month. He paid the *edah* for one month. He never paid the *nafkah anak*. He only gave money once at Raya [Hari Raya; celebrations following the end of Ramadan].

The chief *kadi* then reads out the wife's request: *nafkah anak*, M$1,800; *nafkah edah*, a total of M$400; and *harta sepencarian*, which includes one or two houses, some land, and two water buffalo. The value of the *harta sepen-*

carian was listed by the chief *kadi*, but it was not altogether clear to me what was said. (One house was apparently valued at M$38,000, according to the wife, the other at M$68,000.) The chief *kadi* concludes this portion of the hearing by asking the wife about some of these items of property.

The husband is then called and sworn in. He tells the chief *kadi*, in response to his question, when he got divorced. The chief *kadi* says something to the effect that, "This case was heard already, right?" The husband confirms this and goes on to corroborate, again in response to the chief *kadi*'s questions, that their adopted child is about five years old, is in his former wife's care, and was born to his younger sister. The husband adds that it was his wife who asked for the divorce, not him. He also acknowledges that he owes the *edah* money the wife is claiming but insists that he paid more than M$100 (a reference to *nafkah anak*?). As for the wife's claim that he is seriously delinquent in paying *nafkah anak*, this is not true.

As the chief *kadi* starts going through the *harta sepencarian* claims, the husband proceeds to dispute most of the wife's contentions about ownership— who has rights to what, the value of the property, etc. He goes on to clarify that he and his wife raised the child on a temporary basis, that there was no written agreement, and that in any case his wife was the one who wanted the child. His agreement with his younger sister and her husband was that they (he and his wife) would take the child until he grew up. When he split up with his wife, he (or someone else?) told his younger sister and mother to take the child back, but his wife drove them away. (I could not catch all of the discussion about this.)

The chief *kadi* then asked, "Where is the child's *real* mother?" "She is not here today," the husband replied, at which point the chief *kadi* inquired of the wife if she would like to question her husband about anything. Her response: "He already said in front of the [district] *kadi* that I should raise the child," but it was "stated orally" (*cakap mulut saja*).

At the chief *kadi*'s request, Araffin was then brought into the discussion to help clarify matters. He indicated that to the best of his knowledge, the "real mother" did not claim anything after the divorce. But he also made clear that there was no official, written record of any of this, at which point the chief *kadi* instructed him to locate "the earlier decision." Araffin left the room to find it.

At about this stage in the hearing an old woman in the back row yelled something out; a young woman sitting next to her hit her on the leg to silence her. The chief *kadi* got upset with them and told them to be quiet, adding, "I am only allowing these two to talk." He then turned to the husband, demanding to know why he had not paid the money he was supposed to. The husband responded: "I couldn't; I didn't have any work; I was sick." The chief *kadi* then asked: "Do you have a letter from a clinic indicating you were sick?" The husband replied in the negative and went on to testify that he had given his wife some milk, rice, and other cooking supplies to help feed their child, about M$100 worth. The wife sneered at this, interjecting, "He disappeared for some time and then came back with the food, [but] that was . . . [before] we divorced."

Chief Kadi [to husband]: Do you have any proof that you gave her this?

Just after the husband stated that he had no proof for the chief *kadi*, Araffin came back into the courtroom with the (Rembau) *kadi*'s notebook, clarifying that the amount specified for *nafkah anak* was M$1,800. The husband said he paid about M$200, hence there is about M$1,600 left. Both husband and wife agree on this sum and on the M$400 *edah*; the outstanding payments amount to M$2,000. The husband, in response to further questions from the chief *kadi*, insists that he does not have any means, that he is sick and staying with relatives, and that he did not bring his card from the health clinic. He has no fixed work and makes a mere M$1,200 a month. It also appears from his testimony that he has a second wife, to whom he has been married for about a year.

The wife counters with information that her husband owns trucks and factory buses that he leases out for about M$1,250 a month: "This is what he told me himself before we divorced." But in response to the chief *kadi*'s question, she has no proof of any of this.

The husband denies owning any trucks, saying that he only has a permit. He claims that he does not own the house, that it is mortgaged and owned by the bank. In this connection there is a reference to M$44,000. The value of the house may be around M$70,000. The husband maintains that the house is wrapped up in court action with the banks. The Senalang house is also mortgaged, he says, at which point the wife interjects that she does not want the house, just her share of the money. In response to the chief *kadi*'s questions, the husband testifies that the M$8,000 deposit on the house was money that he acquired while they were married, but they did not earn it together.

As for the two acres of land, valued around M$10,000, the husband maintains that he bought the land with a bank loan. Concerning the water buffalo, the husband insists that the wife only has rights to one of them. (They are valued at M$900 each, and the husband apparently sold them to pay off debts or handed them over to creditors.) At this point, the wife interjects angrily and with a good deal of venom, "In the Afterlife [*akhirat*] you will have to account for all of this," adding something else to the effect of "You'll get yours."

Shortly thereafter the husband launches into an argument that the wife cannot claim *nafkah edah* or *nafkah anak* because she was the one who asked for the divorce, "because of a relationship with someone else. . . . I accused her of this and she refused to listen to what I had to say. . . . I have witnesses, but, no [in response to the chief *kadi*'s question], I did not bring them . . . because I figured this could all be worked out. . . . This happened while we were married and while she was still in *edah*. If I'm lying, let my finger or hand/arm be cut off. [Or: "If I'm lying, I will cut them off"; the way he expressed it wasn't altogether clear.] . . . I will swear this with the Quran. . . . That's why I won't pay."

Wife: These are all lies. He's just saying this because he doesn't want to pay. I met with the *kadi* about this. . . .

The chief *kadi* then concludes the proceedings by announcing that the hearing will be adjourned because the contested issues need to be studied more and that the husband and wife will be informed of the date for the continuance.

Comment: The proceedings were adjourned partly because the chief *kadi* wanted to "talk things over with the husband and wife before they met again in court." Araffin mentioned this to me in a subsequent conversation, during which time he ackowledged his feeling that the husband was, as we might put it in English, a "rather slippery" individual—one indication of which is that he had ignored summonses and had laid low for some time, which he probably would not have done if he had been reliable. Araffin also acknowledged that when the husband had come in at one point, he (Araffin) or another employee of the court had made a serious mistake by showing him the wife's petition; Araffin later realized that this could well have hindered her case.

Much of the reason the case got bogged down and had to be postponed was because of the absence of clear, unambiguous records of earlier proceedings. For example, when Araffin went to find the records bearing on the previous hearing(s), he seems not to have found anything conclusive, such as a written agreement about the custody of the child. Also, while Araffin's records (or those kept by the *kadi*) seem to indicate that it was the husband who divorced the wife, they apparently contain little if any relevant information about who first requested the divorce and thus do not help clarify the husband's claim that his wife does not deserve *nafkah* because it was her idea to terminate the marriage. If the wife really requested the divorce in the first place, then presumably the *kadi* would have made a note of this and would have made a decision about *nafkah edah* with this in mind. Why did not the husband bring this up at the previous hearing? There are many holes and contradictions in the husband's testimony and, in my view, a great deal of self-serving rationalization. The case does, in any event, bring to light some of the procedural and other problems that face the courts and impact litigants in major ways.

As in the other case involving the chief *kadi*, we see here the greater emphasis on proof, especially proof in the form of written records (letters, receipts, etc.). It is interesting in this connection that when the husband claimed he was sick, the chief *kadi* immediately asked him for hospital records of his illness, implicitly according greater legitimacy to cosmopolitan medicine as opposed to traditional village medicine, as practiced by *dukun*, for example, who, needless to say, do not provide their clientele with receipts acknowledging payment for services rendered. In these and other ways (for example, by disallowing evidence in the form of hearsay), the chief *kadi*'s mode of adjudication reveals a major departure from customary Islamic legal practice, which distrusted writings as susceptible to tampering and forgery and preferred oral testimony. Western courts on the whole construe such things differently and so (albeit variably so) do contemporary Malaysian authorities, including *kadi*, who generally prefer written documents to potentially unreliable witnesses. More directly relevant to dynamics in contemporary Malaysia is that the hearings overseen by chief *kadi* valorize written records and the culture of writing and literacy even more than the hearings of district *kadi*. Put differently, chief *kadi* are even more centrally implicated in encouraging rural and other Malay involvement in the modern world.

THE CULTURAL LOGIC OF JUDICIAL PROCESS

Having examined material drawn from twelve cases brought to the Islamic courts, we are now in a position to return to some of the broader issues raised at the outset of this chapter. Some of these concern Weber's baldly stated contention that judicial process in Islamic courts is relatively arbitrary, ad hoc, and irrational, particularly inasmuch as there is little if any emphasis on procedural regularities and consistencies of the sort valorized in Western courts. The data presented in this chapter, along with the findings of research on Islamic courts in the Kuala Lumpur area and in the states of Kedah, Selangor, and other parts of Malaysia,[15] corroborate Weber's view that there are some striking differences between Islamic and Western or Western-style courts, including the secular (national statutory) courts established in Malaysia by the British, which do, of course, continue to operate in the postcolonial context. But the material in this chapter and in other relevant studies also illustrates that there are rather pronounced procedural regularities and consistencies in Malaysia's Islamic courts and that these patterns are keyed to broadly shared cultural understandings bearing on the contractual responsibilities (though not so much the rights) entailed in marriage, the importance of reconciliation and compromise, and, more generally, the nature of social relatedness, personhood, human nature, gender similarities and differences, and the like. However, I am not suggesting that all Islamic courts in Malaysia or elsewhere are identical, in the sense of operating with the same, invariant set of procedures and in terms of the exact same underlying cultural grid. Islamic courts in the Kuala Lumpur area and other urban settings, including state capitals, tend to be more formal ("lawyerly"), bureaucratic, and imposing than their rural counterparts, some of which, not surprisingly, is signaled by the contrasts in Rembau between the hearings overseen by chief *kadi* on the one hand and those overseen by district *kadi* on the other.[16] And the specific constellations and valences of values and interests at play in the narratives, operations, and overall social and cultural standing of Islamic courts in Malaysia are by no means identical to those characteristic of Islamic courts in Singapore, Indonesia, Yemen, Morocco, Kenya, or Ottoman Syria and Palestine, to cite but a few well-documented examples—all of which is to say that we clearly need more work of a "theme and variation" sort.[17]

Rembau's *kadi*, as we have seen, rarely makes explicit reference to legal or religious texts or to specific points of Islamic law or doctrine. In these and many others respects the Islamic court of Rembau and its counterparts elsewhere in Malaysia differ not only from the courts found in the West but also from Western-style courts in Malaysia, such as the secular (Magistrate's) court considered earlier. Coupled with the relatively informal atmosphere of the court is what appears at first glance to be a relative lack of concern with bureaucratic record keeping and procedure regarding, for example, how to establish "facts" and "truth," "guilt" and "innocence." We see this in sharp relief in the marriage forms the state requires prospective brides and grooms to fill out prior to their weddings, which ask for information concerning the age, marital status, etc., of the bride- and groom-to-be, as well as the amount of the marriage payments agreed upon by the various parties contracting the marriage, which are impor- tant indicators of the status and prestige of the principal parties involved in the proposed union. As discussed in more detail in chapter 4, the forms I examined were quite complete with respect to information concerning age and marital status, but typically lacked complete data concerning the size of marriage pay- ments. This despite the fact that these forms provide the only written, notarized record of these payments and are thus essential for negotiations and financial settlements associated with the dissolution of marriage through certain forms of divorce (such as *tebus talak*, where the wife compensates the husband for "mar- ital release"). One of the staff told me that in many cases the marriage pay- ments are not recorded on the forms because the families are embarrassed and ashamed (*malu*) about the payments being "small" and because public knowl- edge of such small payments is much more likely if the size of the payments is written down on the forms, which must be signed by two witnesses and a local mosque official. The handling of marriage forms indicates that employees of the *kadi*'s office (as well as local mosque officials) are both attuned and sympa- thetic to villagers' sensitivities concerning status and prestige and are willing to dispense with some of the formalities and red tape if it seems that too much concern with "bureaucratic issues" would embarrass people. More generally, officials of the court tend to orient their own behavior—and to interpret the behavior of others—in terms of the same cultural assumptions that inform the actions and understandings of the people whose interests they are enjoined to serve.

The Islamic judge in Rembau, like Islamic judges elsewhere in Malaysia, is generally expected to work within the framework of the Shafi'i legal school of Islam, much of which was fixed in theoretically immutable text many centuries ago. But this is not to suggest that Islamic magistrates are bound by centuries- old legal conventions or interpretations. Inter alia, the judges have broad powers of discretion, which they use to help make sure the cases before them are dealt with in a manner in keeping with their notions of "justice," "equity," and "due process" (*keadilan*). Their notions are of course culturally and histori- cally specific, as are their understandings of "fact," "truth" (*hal, kebenaran*), and the like. This point was largely lost on Weber, who popularized the phrase "*kadi*-justice" to refer to this phenomenon and similar cases in which judicial decision making appears to be relatively unsystematic and irrational. Some of Weber's perspectives on the subject of Islamic justice are extremely incisive. But as Lawrence Rosen (1980–81, 1989a) and others have illustrated with material drawn from the Middle East and North Africa, Weber's critiques of the decision-making processes of Islamic judges are problematic because of his inconsistencies in adhering to the methodological and theoretical guidelines that he developed in his justly famous outline of interpretive sociology.

In Malaysia, Islamic courts display a pronounced concern with consensus, reconciliation, and compromise, as opposed to zero-sum outcomes of the sort favored both in Malaysia's national (statutory) courts and in many venues of Western legal systems. In their efforts to resolve disputes in informal ways, Islamic courts place a great deal of emphasis on the work of counselors, who converse with most litigants before they have a chance to air their grievances in the presence of a *kadi*. As noted earlier, the counselor in Rembau remarked to me on various occasions that successful work on her part means that the cases that come before her will never reach the *kadi*, for she wants people to resolve or set aside their differences rather than go through a divorce or even set up an appointment with the *kadi*.

The counselor's remarks provide clear testimony of what the *kadi* and his staff see as their most compelling objectives with regard to matrimonial matters: to keep marriages "alive" or at least intact, regardless of the explicitly articulated desires—and to some extent, the behavior—of the husband and wife. We have seen that the key cultural assumptions here include the implicit belief that it is in the God-given, natural design of things for adults to be married; that individuals who are already wed are normally better off to remain so than to experience divorce and its aftermath (such as life without a spouse); and that the high rates of divorce long characteristic of the Malay community are simultaneously cause and consequence of their "agrarian backwardness" and their attendant inability to hold their own in economic terms with local communities of Chinese and Indians. In sum, as is also true elsewhere in the Muslim world, the central goals of the *kadi* and his staff are to get people back into a situation where they can successfully (re)negotiate their relationships. Hence the importance of providing a forum, such as the *kadi*'s chambers or the office of the counselor, in which people can ideally thrash out and resolve their differences.

Inasmuch as providing such a forum is arguably the main goal of the officials who run the courts' day-to-day operations, it should not be all that surprising to find that these officials do not display all that much concern with discovery and evidentiary procedures, with establishing "fact" and "truth." Indeed, in many of the proceedings I observed, the phenomenal reality of "what really occurred," though strongly contested, appeared to be largely irrelevant not only to the *kadi*'s and the counselor's lines of questioning but also to their subsequent allocation of responsibility and the ultimate disposition of the case. Similarly, in most instances (cases of *fasakh* and *taklik* are the main exceptions) witnesses were not called on to help establish "fact" or "truth," and there was little reliance on formal oaths (either *sumpah* or *berikrar*). Some of the factors that may help explain these patterns include the widespread Malay belief, which is shared by the *kadi* and his staff, that there is no necessary correspondence either between words and deeds (for example, between what people say in the court-house and how they have actually behaved in the past) or between words and deeds on the one hand, and intentions, motivations, and the like on the other. Rural and urban Malays believe that fellow Malays are frequently motivated by greed, envy, and malice and are forever trying to get the better of one another through displays of status and prestige and by attempting to gain control over one another's resources, loyalties, and affections. These suspicions are not usu-ally expressed openly, however, nor are personal desires or individual inten-tions. The formal rules of social interaction prohibit such behavior just as they proscribe many forms of direct speech that could possibly enable people to better read what is on the minds of others. Villagers are quick to point out that one's inner spirit or soul (*batin, roh*) is invisible, concealed beneath the physi-cal body (*badan*), and that one's real intentions, motivations, likes, and dislikes are similarly shielded from view and typically unknown. Outward behavior is no indication of what is on someone's mind or *dalam hati* (in one's liver), for outward behavior is not only constrained by generally restricted speech codes, in which most utterances are "pressed into service to affirm the social order" (Douglas 1970: 22), it also intentionally disguises inner realities. These themes are highlighted in numerous local expressions, such as *ya mogun*, which refers to a "yes" that really means "no"; *janji melayu* (a Malay promise), which is sometimes used to convey similar meaning; *cakap manis, tapi hati lain*, which can be translated as "sweet words or talk, but a different (not-so-sweet) liver"; and *mulut manis, tapi hati busuk*, which refers to a "sweet mouth but a stinking, rotten liver" (see Peletz 1988a, 1993b, 1996). In sum, just as cultural beliefs such as these are clearly shared by the *kadi* and his staff, so too do they inform judicial process in the Islamic courts.

It is notable, in any event, that the *kadi* and his staff do display a marked interest in ascertaining the general dispositions and personalities of the litigants and others who come before them, if only to help them better discern what "might have" happened in the case at hand. Here, too, however, we see strong evidence of the court's reliance on (and reaffirmation of) local cultural beliefs concerning origin-point, personhood, the contractual responsibilities (though not so much the rights) entailed in marriage, the importance of reconciliation and compromise, as well as the nature of social relatedness, gender similarities and differences, human nature and all its frailties, the patterning of faults in marriage, the main causes of divorce, and so forth.

I agree with Rosen (1980–81, 1989b) then, that in light of Weber's legacy, it is both necessary and worthwhile to emphasize, or at least be especially atten-tive to, regularity and predictability in the ways officials of Islamic courts inter-pret cases and construct and deploy strategies to effect outcomes consonant with their interpretations and objectives. I do not want to spend too much time or energy on the issue of difference—or similarity—with Western-style courts, however. Although they constitute the ultimate (and frequently unmarked) stan-dard in Weber's (but not Rosen's) work on Islamic law—and by dint of We-ber's influential writings, need to be addressed—they need not occupy this position of singularity or preeminenence for us. By the same token, I do not want to place too much stress on the consistency of the courts and the principles informing judicial process and decision making in particular. The latter point is significant since there is a strong temptation, in responding to Weber's emphasis on the relatively arbitrary and irrational nature of Islamic jurisprudence, to overvalorize consistency both among the objectives, strategies, and decisions of Islamic courts, and among the broadly shared cultural concepts that inform them. There is, put differently, a danger of erring in the opposite direction by *overemphasizing* consistency both in the cultural logic of law and in the distribution of local knowledge pertaining to law. The specific dangers here include giving short shrift to the existence of paradox and contradiction, to the differential (for example, gendered) distribution of cultural knowledge (pertaining to Islam and to dealings with bureaucrats and state institutions generally, for instance), and to the political economy of contested symbols and meanings.

The importance of making analytic provision for such matters becomes clear when Rosen's arguments and overall positions on culture and law, which derive from research in Morocco, are viewed in light of Daisy Dwyer's (1978, 1979) data and arguments, which are based on research conducted in Morocco at about the same time. Although Dwyer's empirical foci and comparative and theoretical objectives are in many ways less ambitious and otherwise more narrowly construed than Rosen's, she deals explicitly with gender inequities in Moroccan Islamic law; with Moroccan women's knowledge of the law, which is quite limited compared to that of men; and with women's experiences in their dealings with officials of the Islamic courts and other representatives of the state, which tend to be very negative. She illustrates among other things that women's restricted legal knowledge is used by male litigants and by the predominantly male personnel of the courts and the police forces to silence them and "keep them in their place." In Malaysia, the gendered legal asymmetries are not as pronounced as what one finds in Morocco or in other regions of North Africa or the Middle East. But like the "downside(s)" of the cultural logic of judicial process generally, they merit descriptive and analytic attention (see chapter 3; see also Peletz 1996).

The main way in which the analysis presented here differs from that of Rosen has to do with certain aspects of the central problematic, which, for Rosen, is essentially a dialogue between Weber's position on the cultural core of "*kadi*-justice" on the one hand and data bearing on the ways in which the symbols and meanings that obtain in Morocco's Islamic courts resonate with those in Moroccan society at large on the other. Rosen's extremely incisive exploration of these issues displays a dizzying erudition and brilliance that has inspired and otherwise helped shape the anthropological study of law (including the present volume) and has also put all scholars of Islam in his debt. But the Geertzian problematic that orients much of Rosen's work on law also strikes me as rather narrowly cast, especially with respect to dynamics of power, domination, and change. In addition to glossing over issues of the sort noted above, it tends to ignore relations of power that link and/or differentiate the producers and consumers of legal knowledge and various types of legally binding decisions, just as it smooths over critical differences between low-level office functionaries on the one hand and exceedingly powerful agents of secular and religious bureaucracies on the other.[18] Put differently, it effectively jettisons Weber's lifelong professional project to establish the framework for a comparative historical sociology of domination, which was the larger context in which Weber pursued his interest in "*kadi*-justice."

If we take the dialogue noted above as our central problematic, it is also easy to lose sight of key sources, trajectories, and other dynamics of change within systems of Islamic law in Malaysia and elsewhere. Indeed, I would be greatly oversimplifying if I implied that it is only *Western* scholars and legal experts who invoke standards that are derived from or generally isomorphic with the sensibilities of Western legal traditions in evaluating the work of Islamic judges. In Malaysia, as in most of the forty countries that have Muslim-majority populations or significant Muslim minorities,[19] the system of Islamic law does not make up the entire legal system; it is but one component of a pluralistic legal system, the various elements and interrelationships of which are defined largely by national (statutory) law and ultimately by the state. In Malaysia, Indonesia, and many other Muslim countries, including Morocco, *local* legal experts and scholars of various kinds, particularly those trained in the West or in Western-style institutions, espouse some of the same types of critiques of Islamic jurisprudence that one finds in Weber's writings on "*kadi*-justice." A case in point is provided by comments made to me in the course of my (1988) interview with Shaiful. As we saw earlier in this chapter, Shaiful was of the opinion that procedure is of minimal concern in the Islamic courts. Similarly, clerks at the *kadi*'s court in Rembau mentioned to me on more than one occasion that they were quite concerned about "lax procedure." During the latter part of my second period of research, moreover, they introduced new forms and procedural guidelines with the explicit objective of ameliorating some aspects of this situation.

Interviews I conducted in 1998 and 2001 are particularly germane here, especially since they occurred well *after* the implementation (during the period 1983–91) of various nationwide reforms geared toward resolving these types of problems. Some of the critiques I heard articulated in these interviews, which involved Muslim and non-Muslim lawyers involved in the secular legal system as well as Muslim and non-Muslim journalists and feminist activists who have extensive familiarity with the inner workings of Islamic courts, include the following: there is no procedural regularity or consistency in the Islamic courts; the *kadi* and their staff, including court counselors, are poorly trained (in Islamic jurisprudence and professional counseling) and otherwise ill equipped to deal with the cases that come before them; and, more generally, that the Islamic judiciary in its entirety constitutes a sort of "legal backwater" compared to the far more prestigious secular legal system. There is, in addition, a widespread perception that the courts invariably favor men and are hostile to women and "their concerns" (children, domestic maintenance) or at least are far less sup-

124

portive than they might be. Charges of the latter sort are broadly congruent with Weber's point that judicial process in Islamic courts is vulnerable to entrenched political interests. More relevant to the issues at hand is that they have been voiced not only by Muslim feminists and others active in furthering women's rights but also by Malaysian Prime Minister Mahathir and many other national politicians. In 1996, for example, then Deputy Prime Minister Anwar remarked (with some hyperbole) that "under the jurisdiction of [Malaysia's] Islamic courts 'women are tortured, abused, tormented, and abandoned without alimony.'"[20]

Also highly germane in this connection are the myriad state-sponsored (and typically mandatory) seminars, conferences, and workshops geared toward improving the qualifications and education of personnel of the Islamic courts, which are part and parcel of recent state efforts to further centralize, standardize, rationalize, and otherwise modernize Malaysia's Islamic legal system in its entirety. Various local organizations formed to improve Muslim women's living standards, as well as their legal and other options in marriage and divorce, such as the well-known Sisters in Islam, also merit mention here. These (largely Western-educated) Muslim feminists have campaigned vigorously to ensure greater legal safeguards for women in the courts and have effectively forced the government to respond with various legislative and policy measures (for example, a 1995 national law against domestic violence) that have begun to inform judicial process in local-level Islamic courts.

A good number of the legal reforms that have been proposed and implemented in Malaysia in recent years have been motivated by concerns on the part of government officials, Muslim lawyers, Muslim feminist organizations, and of course Muslim resurgents (*orang dakwah*) of various stripes to strengthen and expand the administration of Islamic law, including the Islamic court system in its entirety, and to otherwise effect a more Islamic way of life. The legal changes in question are often phrased in terms of efforts to make the system of Islamic law "more Islamic," and not surprisingly they often entail looking beyond the local Islamic courts and religious bureaucracies (for example, to other countries) for specific models and general guidance that will be of use in the in-situ development of Islamic legal and administrative machinery. The sources of such models and guidance are instructive. They include the models of Islamic law and administration prevailing in the former British colonies of India, Pakistan, and Singapore, but *not* those from formerly Dutch Indonesia (now the largest Muslim nation in the world), from the formerly Spanish/American region of the southern/Muslim Philippines, or from most other areas of the Islamic world. More significantly, the models and guidance that are sought to centralize, strengthen, rationalize, and otherwise modernize the Islamic legal system tend to be adopted from Malaysia's *secular* courts and the more encompassing system of national (statutory) law, which, as noted earlier, is based largely on British common law, and from Britain itself.[21] Phrased differently, Malaysian political and religious leaders' much-vaunted objectives and accomplishments with respect to the twofold goal of making the extant Islamic legal system "more Islamic" and simultaneously effecting a merging of Islamic and secular law have involved less of a movement from the traditions of British common law to those of Islamic law than one in the opposite direction (from Islamic to common law). This is perhaps most clearly symbolized in the dramatic contrasts between the "traditional" Malay-Muslim garb of the district-level *kadi* (long, loose-fitting shirt, baggy/flowing trousers, sandals, etc.) and the "corporate" attire of his superiors at both the state and federal levels (impeccably tailored black business suits, starched, button-down white shirts, Western-style neckties, black leather shoes, etc.).

Many technical examples of this shift in legal sensibilities—bearing on, for example, the increasingly restricted legality of men's prerogative to enter into polygynous unions and to effect extrajudicial divorce; the more liberal division at divorce of conjugal earnings; and the expanded grounds for divorce initiated by women (such as *fasakh*)—have been delineated with great insight and clarity by Horowitz (1994), Jones (1994), and Mohammad Hashim Kamali (2000). I shall thus limit my immediate remarks to a few points bearing on some of the widely ramifying changes that occurred in the courts in Negeri Sembilan and various other parts of the Peninsula after I completed the fieldwork from which much of the material in this chapter (and chapters 3 and 4) is drawn. One such change involved the introduction of another administrative tier into the upper echelon of the state bureaucracy dealing with matters before the Islamic courts, such that *kadi* in the capitals of each state are now charged with adjudicating matters that were formerly dealt with by district-level *kadi*. This means that the more formal, inquisition-like hearings outlined in cases 11 and 12 have become increasingly common (if not the norm) throughout the Peninsula; it also means that district-level *kadi* have been stripped of much of their authority to resolve matrimonial disputes and have thus seen serious erosion of their power and prestige. Another innovation, alluded to above and discussed in more detail in chapter 4, has involved the prohibition and penalization of extrajudicial divorce, such that men are no longer legally entitled to pronounce the *talak* outside of the *kadi*'s offices, though many of them still do with impunity.

A third change that merits mention here has to do with the founding and publication, beginning in 1980, of a new legal journal titled *Jernal Hukum* (The Journal of Law). One of the main functions of this journal and of the other similarly oriented publications that have sprung up in the intervening years is to collect and disseminate the judgments of Malaysia's Islamic courts (much as colonial-era law journals and their successors have done for the judgments of Malaysia's secular courts for many decades now). The precise role that these judgments have played in recent years is still unclear, as is the particular status they will be accorded in future cases. Hooker observes that such judgments are intended "to form a set of precedents for the future," contending that since, "strictly speaking, precedent has no place in *syari'a*, what we see is an English law form being imposed" (1989: 228). This may be an overly literal interpretation of the future uses of these decisions; it is possible that the decisions will be used more like *general* guidelines rather than more or less binding precedents.

The overall trend, however, is clear, as is the impetus for such developments. In the latter connection it warrants remark that a good number of the new journals and other publications concerning Islamic law in Malaysia—along with various conferences on the role of Islamic law in Malaysia, Singapore, Indonesia, and the Philippines—have been sponsored by the U.S.–financed Asia Foundation, which has taken initiative in these areas to help ensure that there is a forum for "moderate voices" in the Muslim world. It may or may not be coincidental that the initial (1980) publication date of this journal came right after the fall of the Shah of Iran and the rise to power of Ayatollah Khomeini, coupled with the seizing of American hostages by revolutionary students. What is beyond question is that transnational, indeed, thoroughly (though unevenly) global strategies geared toward the containment of "the Islamic revolution" have contributed to the particular ways in which Islamic legal discourses circulate within Malaysia and well beyond.

The circumstances described here pose a multitude of deeply interesting, ironic, and paradoxical challenges to Muslim political machineries in Malaysia and elsewhere. Some of the challenges have to do with the fact that Islamic courts are central to government claims to authenticity, legitimacy, and authority both in the Malaysian context and in many other countries with large Muslim populations. Spokesmen for Muslim governments in Southeast Asia, South Asia, and far beyond frequently point to the Islamic courts and the values enshrined in their proceedings to justify their claims to represent and further the interests of their Muslim constituencies. Ironically, "more Islamic" opposition political parties (such as PAS) also frequently point to the same Islamic courts (for example, to their typically limited jurisdictions, to the relatively weak sanctions at their disposal) to challenge the authenticity, legitimacy, and authority of those in power. So, too, do Muslim feminists, local NGOs, foreign (especially Western) powers, and international human rights organizations, all of whom draw on cases from these courts to temper or otherwise challenge the claims and agendas of national governments and the various institutionalized interests they serve. This situation presents governments with the unique challenge of representing the legal changes at issue as simultaneously acceptable to "conservative" Islamic resurgents (some of whom, like PAS, seek the creation of Islamic states) on the one hand, and those in favor of more "liberal" and "cosmopolitan" legal orders on the other. Either way, governments find themselves committed to utilizing court cases and related material from Islamic legal systems to validate their claims to authenticity, legitimacy, and sovereignty and, in the process, to silence all of those who contest government claims in these areas.

The more general analytic points may be stated as follows: In Islamic societies in which processes of religious and legal rationalization are underway, which is, I suspect, most everywhere in the Muslim world, the cultural logics of Islamic jurisprudence are subject to the transforming gaze of the state apparatuses in which they are embedded. And despite the ideologically laden pronouncements of political and religious leaders to the contrary, such apparatuses are almost always strongly secular in terms of their modern origins and contemporary institutional design (Roy 1994). If only on this account, the cultural logics of Islamic courts are invariably under assault from within "the system" (broadly defined) as well. Moreover, while in one sense "the system" is that of the modern nation-state, the discourses circulating within nation-states are inevitably both nationalist and (always in the case of Islam) transnational, hence "the system" at issue always extends far beyond the boundaries of any nation-state.[22] The bottom line in all of this is one that Weber took great pains to emphasize: the more encompassing systems at issue make up the larger context we must analyze if we are to understand the dynamics of judicial process, and of law generally, even if we aim primarily to understand law as a system of symbols and meanings.

Litigant Strategies and Patterns of Resistance

> Every schoolboy knows that there are more dishonest criminals among men than among women.
> —*Tun Mohamed Suffian, former Lord President of Malaysia,* An Introduction to the Legal System of Malaysia

> Men, they all lie; that's what you see all the time at the *kadi*'s office.
> —*Female elder in Bogang, 1988*

> Among the [Malay] poor, poverty itself appears to dissolve marriages.
> —*David J. Banks,* Malay Kinship

IN THE PREVIOUS chapter we analyzed the roles and jurisdictions of Malaysia's Islamic courts, with particular reference to the Islamic court of Rembau. We also examined the basic ethos and worldview of the courts and the variable ways in which these latter phenomena, along with the state structures and nationalist and transnationalist discourses that help shape them, inform the structure and operation of the courts, especially judicial process. This chapter approaches the courts from a different set of perspectives inasmuch as the main concern here lies with the men and women who use the courts to help them resolve disputes rather than with those who help run the courts or oversee their operations. The first part of the chapter presents nine case studies and other material illustrating how and why women use the courts. The second provides eight cases and other data bearing on how and why men utilize the courts. I then examine gendered similarities and differences with respect to the initiation of legal discourses and proceedings, and various aspects of the strategies and tactics deployed by men and women in their roles as plaintiffs and defendants. A recurrent theme, as we shall see, is that men have more readily at their disposal and can otherwise far more easily exploit the deeply ambiguous and frequently contested symbols and meanings of time, space, language, law, and "custom" (*adat*); a corollary is that this greater access to and easier manipulability of these symbols both flows from and further enhances powers available to men that women do not have.[1]

The third section of the chapter, which incorporates material drawn from two cases, deals with issues of resistance, though the theme necessarily emerges earlier as well. We begin by asking exactly what men and women may be said to resist not only in the courthouse but also with regard to the institutions of marriage, divorce, and (Islamic) law, as well as other features of their social and cultural landscape(s). We then proceed to a consideration of how they do so and what the discursive and other effects of such resistance might be—"what [if anything] does it change, limit, suspend, rework, empower, etc.?" (Sholle 1990: 99). The remainder of the chapter is devoted to a discussion of broader topics bearing on oppositional discourses. Our primary concerns here are the scope and force of these discourses, including, in particular, the various constraints on their elaboration and some of the comparative and theoretical implications of the data bearing on these (and related) issues.

With regard to time frame, I should perhaps reiterate that as in the preceeding chapter, most of the Rembau hearings that I describe and analyze took place during the period August 1987 through February 1988, which was (just) *before* the Islamic Family Law Enactment of 1983 began to be enforced in Rembau and elsewhere in Negeri Sembilan. (Recall that "in many states, the date of enforcement was much later than the date of enactment" [Jones 1994: 266n. 14]). As in the previous chapter as well, my commentary on certain cases includes discussion of changes that have occurred in legal and other arenas since the time of the hearings. I also examine various patterns in Islamic courts in the states of Kedah, Selangor, and elsewhere in Malaysia during the early 1990s *after* the enforcement of the Islamic Family Law Enactments in question. The latter discussions also incorporate material relevant to continuity and change from the early 1990s through the present (2001).

Litigant strategies are informed by reluctances and other constraints as well as various types of incentives. For these and other reasons they are profitably viewed in light of litigants' experiences in the world and in marriage in particular; their specific objectives in going to court; and their understandings of both the legal resources available to them and the operations and likely decisions of the court. It should thus be noted at the outset that culturally defined interests in saving or maintaining face tend both to discourage involvement with the courts and, if such an involvement seems necessary, to make it an option that is reluctantly embraced. This is partly because going to court entails airing private matters publicly, which is embarrassing and stigmatizing and can also be time-consuming, troublesome, and costly. In many cases, litigants' strategies and goals change over time, from their initial decision to pursue a case in court, to their behavior in the session with the counselor and/or the *kadi*. One reason for this is that their initial inquiries concerning how to proceed, as well as their informal statements and formal depositions, are shaped by court personnel such as Araffin, who dispense vital knowledge concerning the workings of the court and how best to proceed.

The narratives of dispute presented in the cases below are usefully viewed in this larger context, for they are framed at least in part in such a way as to elicit favorable responses from the court. We need to bear in mind, though, that men and women approach the court with dissimilar experiences in the world, and in marriage in particular, and with different objectives. Women, who turn to the courts far more often than men, have often been abandoned by their husbands and usually seek either financial support for their children (and in some instances limited support for themselves) or termination of marriage on the grounds specified in the *taklik* clause recited during the solemnization of marriage (for example, failure to provide news or material support for a period of four months) or in the laws pertaining to *fasakh* (insanity, impotence, etc.), or both. Clarification of marital status is also something women seek through the courts, often in combination with the goals of obtaining financial support and, if necessary, effecting a divorce. More generally, women typically turn to the courts to deal with issues of abandonment and/or ambiguity.

Men, in contrast, do not utilize the courts to obtain support for their children (or themselves) and usually have no need to turn to the courts to effect termination of marriage, unless they are involved in polygynous unions, in which case there is a felt (though not necessarily clear legal) need to work with the *kadi* or at least secure his de facto recognition or approval of their actions. Nor do men usually seek clarification of ambiguous marital status. Instead, they use the courts in hopes of encouraging or forcing their wives to return home after they have run away, or to curb other behavior deemed inappropriate in the context of marriage (for instance, to "stop having affairs," or to "serve them better").

Women's Strategies and Experiences

I begin this section with a relatively extended discussion of a case involving a woman named Suzaini, whom I knew relatively well during the second period of fieldwork since she lived in the fieldwork site of Bogang, resided in a house near my own, had young children who enjoyed playing with my son Zachary, and helped us out with cooking and other chores. The relatively extended treatment of this case includes the presentation of "background" material of the sort missing from my presentation of data bearing on other cases, which are in many respects mere "snapshots" of what are usually long, drawn-out domestic dramas and crises. The discussion also raises many points that resonate deeply with the experiences of women and their strategies as litigants, though it is by no means typical in all statistical senses. The case is of additional interest in that it illustrates how the courts as well as local coffee shops operate as sites for the production of counterhegemonic discourses on gender, especially those focusing on kinship-based critiques of masculinity that are animated by disjunctions in husband/father and brother roles brought about by the historic restructuring of social and economic relations of all varieties.

Case 13: *Suzaini Seeking Back Support.* Suzaini is a thirty-seven-year-old woman with four children who was born and raised in the fieldwork site of Bogang. She is of mixed Malay-Javanese ancestry (her locally born mother is Malay; her deceased Javanese father immigrated to Malaysia from Java [in the 1940s?]) and is a member of a low-status clan (Biduanda Dagang) whose members include people of heterogeneous ancestry, many with tainted origin-points and pedigrees (for example, persons of Javanese parentage, like herself, people descended from slaves purchased in Mecca in the nineteenth century, and so on). Suzaini heads up one of the very poorest households in the community and lives in what is probably the most dilapidated house in the entire village. She once worked in a lumber factory in a nearby town (about which more below), but during the second period of fieldwork her income derived primarily from the rearing of livestock (mostly goats but also cattle and chickens), public assistance (from the federal government), and the money she received from us for the help she provided with cooking and laundry. She was supposed to receive M$80 a month from one of her former husbands for the support of her two youngest children, but did not.

Our relationship with Suzaini proved to be one of the highlights of our second period of research, particularly since we thoroughly enjoyed her company and her acerbic sense of humor especially, and learned much from her perspectives on village life and the world at large. She was exceptionally warm, upbeat, and funny, and her young children were very fond of our son Zachary, and vice versa. Partly because of her marginal position in the community social structure, she was unusually outspoken on many topics of direct interest to me (such as local views of men as husbands). Suzaini also provided a perspective on village life that differed radically from the ones we encountered in the course of our interactions with our adoptive parents and other members of the local elite, which thus helped impress upon me that with respect to a good many issues, villagers neither speak in a single voice nor passively accept the ways in which they and their worlds are defined by the powers that be (see Scott 1985, 1990).

In the course of an interview focusing on gender (see Peletz 1996: chap. 6), Suzaini spoke at length about her delinquent husbands—she has been married and divorced three times—especially the third one, Noryazid bin M., who fathered her two youngest children. She recounted how they met, and how he had deceived her prior to their (forced) marriage. He had presented himself to her as a widower and had even showed her what he claimed was his wife's death certificate. The latter document, alas, turned out to be his mother's death certificate! When she discovered he had lied to her about his marital status, Suzaini secretly followed him. She later confronted him about the situation. He was eventually forced to admit the truth to her in the face of incontrovertible evidence.

During the interview on gender, Suzaini's desire to go to the *kadi*'s office in Rembau came up, as it had on numerous other occasions when we had spoken. She wants to go there to lodge another complaint against Noryazid, but she is embarrassed to do so because she has been there various times in the past and would have to see all of the clerks once again. She said something about going instead to the *kadi*'s office in Seremban, because this way she would not have to interact with the staff at the Rembau office. It merits note, in any case, that Suzaini frequently plied me with questions about whether she should go to the *kadi*'s office again, how things worked, and so forth. I answered her questions as forthrightly as I could and also encouraged her to go to court. However, I stopped short of actually accompanying her to court because I thought that such action would be inappropriate.

When Suzaini finally went to the *kadi*'s office, she was accompanied by my wife, Ellen, and Zachary. Her purpose in going was to have Noryazid brought in to pay the outstanding *nafkah anak* and the other money he owed her according to the agreement that was worked out after (or as part of) their divorce about two years earlier. When Suzaini entered the building, she was directed by a female clerk to Araffin. While Araffin looked for the relevant files, the *kadi*, who was sitting at one of the desks in the front of the office, soon got involved in the discussion. The *kadi* and Araffin alike made clear that they were appalled that Noryazid—a former policeman, now nicely pensioned, who had recently made the pilgrimage to Mecca—had been so delinquent, the *kadi* adding, "Hey, I know him, we are from the same village." One of them, Araffin I believe, got on the phone with the police to find out "if he was still alive." The police confirmed that Noryazid was indeed alive, informing Araffin in addition that he had recently purchased a new house. They gave Araffin his proper address (he had given Suzaini a false one). Suzaini was told to come back in two weeks, and Noryazid was sent written notification that he was to appear then as well.

One week later when I was at the *kadi*'s office, Suzaini showed up with one of her daughters. I don't know why they came; perhaps Suzaini got the dates mixed up. When I arrived, she and her daughter were sitting at the desk usually occupied by Araffin, talking to the counselor, and seemingly inquiring about the payments that would be necessary to have her former husband summoned. Apparently the court had not yet issued a summons but just a letter telling him to come to the courthouse. If he ignores the letter, then they issue a summons. Suzaini seemed surprised and frustrated by this two-step approach. They were trying to calculate the cost of the summons, the crucial issue being the distance between the nearest *kadi*'s office and the residence or workplace of the person being summoned.

As it happened, Noryazid did not show up at the *kadi*'s office when instructed to do so. Shortly thereafter a summons was sent out. When Araffin told Suzaini that the summons had been issued, he also informed her that Noryazid would undoubtedly try to contact her within a few days of receiving it. In addition, he advised her not to accept anything he (Noryazid) might try to give her before their next appearance in court.

Sure enough, Noryazid then showed up in the village looking for Suzaini. Among the comments he made to her after he found her were: "Look, let's not let this thing go to the *kadi* and have everyone see our affairs. We don't need to go to the *kadi*'s. Here is M$400. Take this and tell the *kadi*, and tell them we don't need to have a hearing. I promise I will give you more on the tenth or twelfth of next month."

Suzaini replied that she did not want his M$400, adding, "Hey, let the *kadi* settle it." Noryazid told her she was hardhearted (*hati keras*; literally, "hardlivered"), that his pension is only a little more than M$200 a month (in fact, it is over M$500). He gave one of his daughters and one of Suzaini's other daughters M$2 each and left, apparently very upset.

Comment: Suzaini's case was then scheduled to be heard by the chief *kadi* in Rembau, but I left the field before the hearing (and received no news of the case in letters I later received from Suzaini) so I never found out what happened. I do know, however, that the case was turned over to the chief *kadi* because the sum of money involved was more than double the M$1,000 limit of the local *kadi*'s jurisdiction. (Noryazid had previously promised Suzaini M$1,500 as *muta'ah* [an obligatory consolatory gift payable to a wife divorced without fault] as soon as he started getting his pension, but he had not delivered any of this. There is also about eight months of back *nafkah* at M$80 per month, that is, M$640, thus a total of at least M$2,140.)

Experiences of the sort that Suzaini has had with her delinquent ex-husband are exceedingly widespread; most cases that reach the courts, after all, are brought by women who have been abandoned by their husbands (or ex-husbands). Similarly, we see in this encounter with the courts the no-shows and attendant delays that women commonly experience when they attempt to deal with issues of abandonment and ambiguity in their marital status (see Mohammad Hashim Kamali 2000: chaps. 4 and 5). Highlighted as well are women's concerns with court fees (in this instance the costs of having an ex-husband served a summons), which tend to be reallocated to husbands and ex-husbands by court staff who, as mentioned earlier, often "cook the books."

An important set of issues to note here has to do with the court's clear willingness to move quickly—indeed, immediately—in this case (recall that as soon as Suzaini began recounting some of the particulars of the case, Araffin was on the phone to the police to obtain relevant information on the ex-husband). This despite not only Suzaini's dubious morality but also her ex-husband's considerable wealth and the high status he enjoys by virtue of being a former (now pensioned) police officer and someone who has made the pilgrimage to Mecca. To elaborate on the issue of Suzini's morality, I need first emphasize a point only partly alluded to in the preceding text, which is that in terms of local community standards (shared in this instance by court personnel), Suzaini has had a highly checkered marital history. She had been married and divorced three times. At least two of her marriages were a result of her having been caught in compromising circumstances with married men; she was guilty (minimally) of the criminal offense of *khalwat* in one instance and *zina*, which led to her pregnancy in another. Not surprisingly, other women (and presumably men as well) viewed her as a "husband stealer" and a troublemaker in general.

Two other factors contributed to her dubious morality so far as many villagers were concerned. First, Suzaini had worked for a spell at a local (lumber) factory and, like all female factory workers, was widely assumed to have questionable sexual standards (see Ong 1987; Peletz 1996). Second, she was frequently seen flirting, hence assumed to be "involved," with a young Javanese man who had been adopted by our mother's brother-in-law and had taken up residence in Bogang but was nonetheless assumed, like all local Javanese, to be shiftless and transient.

In light of Suzaini's past history, which involved multiple transgressions of a serious moral and criminal nature, I attach considerable signficance to the fact that the courts came to Suzaini's aid, especially since doing so involved taking on a high-status man who was in many respects a repository of order and meaning. As this case shows, the courts are intent on making available to even the poorest of women a forum where they both voice their legitimate grievances and seek justice as defined by local agreements entailed in the marriage contract and the institution of marriage generally, or, as is perhaps more accurate to say in this instance, justice as defined by divorce agreements engineered with the help of the courts.

A second issue to which I attach significance in this case has to do with the fact that even though Suzaini had the most checkered marital history in the entire village of Bogang and was widely regarded as something of a floozy, she received strong, heartfelt support from the many village women who knew of her former husband's pattern of lying, delinquency, and overall poor showing. As might be expected, Suzaini's situation was the subject of much local gossip, and much of the gossip focused squarely on the delinquency of her ex-husband. Shortly after her ex-husband visited her and attempted to persuade her to drop the proceedings at the *kadi*'s office, Suzaini appeared at the *kedai* (coffee shop; store) nearest the mosque and the railroad tracks cutting through the village and proceeded to hold court on what had just occurred, recounting how her ex-husband had come to her house, and what he had said and done. Those present at the *kedai* included her mother, her Javanese friend, a highly respected woman married to the caretaker of the mosque, as well as two of the wealthiest women in the entire village, both of whom have been to Mecca, and, visiting from Singapore, one of the latter women's daughters and her husband. The women present, who were clearly in the majority, reassured Suzaini in the strongest possible terms that she did the right thing and roundly condemned her former husband's behavior, also in the strongest terms ("yeahlah, don't just cut [garnish] his wages, cut his neck!"). Conversation of this general sort was by no means unusual, for this particular *kedai* had become a meeting place for women, now that one of the proprietors had died, leaving his wife to run it on her own.

A third issue of note in this case bears on the fact that a strongly male-defined domain—the local *kedai*—emerges as a key site in the production and circulation of experiences, understandings, and representations of gender that are not only different from those of the official, hegemonic line emphasizing male "reason" and female "passion" but are in fact explicitly counterhegemonic inasmuch as they focus on the view that men (especially in their roles as husbands and fathers) are neither reasonable nor responsible. More to the point is that the Islamic court—another predominantly male-defined domain—is another such site. We will discuss this theme and its implications in greater detail in due course. In the meantime, suffice it to recall the pithy remark of my adoptive aunt that serves as one of the epigraphs for this chapter: "Men, they all lie; that's what you see all the time at the *kadi*'s office."

A final set of issues worthy of brief mention in this case has to do with its illustration of women's experiences as regards not only abandonment but also ambiguity concerning, for example, whether an ex-husband is still alive, where he might be, etc. This case also shows how women use local courts to resolve both sets of dilemmas, albeit with embarrassment and other forms of reluctance that sometimes lead them to consider "forum shopping" (for instance, taking their grievances to another court to avoid having to deal with local court personnel they may know). Variations on these themes run throughout a great many other cases initiated by women. Consider the following.

Case 14: *Robaiyah Who Wants a* Fasakh *Divorce.* This case involved a twenty-five-year-old woman, Robaiyah, who came to the office with her two children (both boys; one two and a half years old, the other around three and a half) and her older sister. She was seeking a *fasakh* on the grounds that she had not heard anything from her husband, Abdul Rahman bin U., for about nineteen months.

Robaiyah, who is from Lubuk Cina, began by stating that she had not received any news from her husband for a very long time. I don't think she actually said that the husband might be in jail, but the counselor assumed that this might be so and responded with something like, "Maybe he's in jail," to which she added, "I'll have to check with all of the jails in the country." In response to the counselor's questions about whether she had ever been to the *kadi*'s office before, Robaiyah replied no.

It was at this point in the questioning that the counselor obtained the husband's name and ascertained (from Robaiyah?) that he had indeed been in prison. The counselor then took Robaiyah's particulars and asked her who the other woman in the office was. Robaiyah replied that it was her older sister, to which the counselor responded that she noticed some resemblance. The smallest child, meanwhile, was sitting on Robaiyah's lap, making lots of noise.

"Who's the *imam* there [in your village]?" asked the counselor after being told the name of Robaiyah's village. The counselor then obtained information on the husband. "Drugs were involved," Robaiyah told her, "he takes drugs" (*hisap dadah*). Robaiyah restated her husband's name, said that he is twenty-seven years old, used to work in a factory, and has never even seen his youngest son. They were married a little over four years ago on the basis of mutual attraction (*suka sama suka*), she tells the counselor, in response to questions about their marriage. Concerning how they met, Robaiyah stated that she had also worked in a factory at the time they met, but at a different factory. She then told the counselor the ages of the children and their gender, in response to questions on the issue, adding that she and her husband lived with her family when they were first married. The husband stopped factory work when he was arrested for taking drugs, but she did not know he was involved with drugs until *after* he was arrested.

"So, what are you seeking?" the counselor asks her, such being the first time in the hearing that the counselor mentions anything along these lines. The reply: "I'm requesting a *fasakh*." Robaiyah then explains that her husband was thrown out of Rembau some eighteen months earlier and that since that time she has not heard from him.

The counselor made a few comments about the difference between *fasakh* and *taklik*, saying that *fasakh* depends [more?] on the *kadi*, that "he will weigh it, and will look at the husband's behavior." These, along with good-byes, were her final remarks.

Comment: It is quite common for women to turn to the courts to help them resolve issues of abandonment and/or ambiguity. In this case, the wife was abandoned and received no news of her husband for nineteen months, not even knowing if he was living as a "free man" somewhere or was in jail, though she seems to have had a strong suspicion that he had been incarcerated due to his drug and other problems. (It turns out that the husband had been in jail for approximately two years and that shortly after he was released from jail he was thrown out of Rembau.) Unlike the next case, the wife was not seeking clarification of her marital status. Rather, she sought clarification of her husband's whereabouts and a termination of the relationship on the grounds that he had violated the provisions of the *fasakh* laws.

Case 15: *A Woman Who Hasn't Received Any Support Seeking Clarification of Her Marital Status.* This hearing involved a thirty-three-year-old husband, his twenty-eight-year-old wife (Maimunah bte. J.), and the wife's younger brother. The counselor was present throughout much of the hearing, and the *kadi*'s daughter was in and out of the office throughout the entire session, causing considerable distraction and noise.

The couple has two children. They were married seven years ago, were divorced (at the *kadi*'s office) two years ago, and were remarried that same year. They are here again, this time at the request of the wife, who seeks clarification of her marital status.

The story is as follows. The husband used to work on an estate but now has no work. They had a minor misunderstanding and the wife left without the husband's permission, taking their two children with her. It has now been four months that she has not received any support.

The husband was or is living with his elder sister in her house in Kuala Lumpur. The wife has a job in Seremban and lives there in a rented house with many others. At one point the wife's brother approached the husband and said, "So what's happening between you and my sister?" The husband replied, "Kira-kira dah cerai" ("It's like [we've] divorced"). The brother-in-law took this to mean that the two were in fact divorced, and apparently rather than pursue it any further, he reported what the husband had said to his sister.

It is not clear exactly what words he used, but apparently he did *not* say, "Saya ceraikan kakak awak" ("I [have] divorce[d] your older sister"). If he had said this, even if the wife was not within earshot, it would be a legally binding divorce. The *kadi* was very explicit on this point and was quite irritated when the husband hemmed and hawed about the precise words he used when he conveyed the *kira-kira dah cerai* news to the brother-in-law. In fact, as the *kadi* was explaining all of this, he emphasized the necessity of utilizing names other than those of the people involved, thus underscoring the power of the word.

The *kadi* made it very clear that the husband's saying *kira-kira dah cerai* does *not* constitute a legal divorce (*tak jutah* ["it doesn't fall"] was the way he put it). He had the husband write down exactly what he had said to the brother-in-law. The *kadi* also underscored to all present that a wife leaving without getting her husband's permission is a sin in Islam.

A bit later the *kadi* moved the discussion to the subject of what to do next. "Do you want your wife or not?" he asked the husband. "If you want her, then we will seek out one path; if you don't, we'll seek another." The husband's response was that he still *suka* (likes) the wife, but she does not like him and may not love him anymore; he does not want to have to keep coming to the *kadi*'s office. It was about this time I noticed the husband was crying, dabbing his eyes and nose with his handkerchief. He was not actually sobbing or making any noticeable sounds, but neither was he really trying to hide the fact that he was in tears.

The *kadi* asked the wife what she wanted, if she still liked her husband. She said it is "up to the husband to decide what should be done." The *kadi* then instructed her to go back with her husband. But the problem of what to do about their work and housing situations was not entirely resolved. Recall that the wife works and lives in Seremban; the husband is unemployed and residing in Kuala Lumpur. The children, for their part, are staying with the wife's mother in Kota.

On more than a few occasions the husband exhorted his wife to speak up about why she is dissatisfied, but she said nothing on this score. The hearing ended with the *kadi* telling them he would give them until the end of the month (three weeks' time) to reach a decision.

Comment: In this case, the court's handling of the wife's concern to obtain clarification of her marital status overshadowed many other legally salient and practical issues, including the fact that neither she nor her children had received support (*nafkah*) for a period of four months. Indeed, most of the hearing was given over to what exactly the husband had said to his brother-in-law—whether it was more along the lines of, "It's like we've divorced," or "I have divorced your sister"; and the court made no attempt to resolve the matter of the back *nafkah* that the wife claimed the husband owed, even though the husband tacitly acknowledged being delinquent in supporting his family by failing to contest the wife's claims on this matter. Nor did the court raise issues having to do with the latter delinquency's constituting legitimate grounds for the wife's seeking a divorce, even though the husband also acknowledged that his wife might not love him anymore and does not seem to like him anymore either. The court's failure to raise these issues may be attributable to a combination of factors, including the wife's stated willingness to abide by the husband's wishes as to what they should do in the future, coupled with her deafening silences when asked about her dissatisfaction in the marriage. Whether or not we regard the wife's strategy of silence as a form of resistance or as effective in any way, the fact remains that—aside from instructing her to go back with her husband, informing her earlier in the hearing that leaving without the husband's permission is a sin in Islam, and telling them that he would give them until the end of the month to make a decision—the *kadi* made no effort to mediate, arbitrate, or adjudicate the maintenance (*nafkah*) issue at hand. In this instance, then, the court's attempts to resolve the ambiguity as to what exactly the husband said to his brother-in-law overrode all other considerations, clearly leaving the wife in the lurch with respect to maintenance for an indeterminate period into the future. Put differently, while the court effectively resolved one set of ambiguities, it simultaneously allowed for the reproduction of others (such as whether the husband can or will support his wife and children). Similar dynamics obtain in the next case.

Case 16: *A Woman Seeking Clarification of Her Marital Status and Back Nafkah.* This case involved a twenty-nine-year-old woman and her thirty-year-old husband; they were married six years ago and have three children. The petition/request came from the wife, who was unclear about her marital status due partly to her husband's motorcycle accident, which occurred about four years ago. It was not entirely clear if the wife was actually petitioning for a divorce.

The wife was present but the husband was not; he was represented by his elder brother, since he has apparently not yet recovered from the accident and seems to have recurrent emotional problems, which are aggravated when he sees his wife.

The husband is in the army (or another branch of the military), stationed at Port Dickson; apparently this is where the accident occurred. The wife's major complaint at this point is that the husband has given no *nafkah* for about ten months, except for M$100 given during the last Ramadan. The *kadi* calculated that at the (previously agreed upon [?]) rate of M$119 per month, the husband owes M$1,190 minus the M$100, for a total of M$1,090. I am not sure where the figure of M$119/month came from, but this must be for the wife and three children (the oldest of whom is five years old).

Through his brother, the husband claimed that after his accident the wife did not want to care for him and ran away. The wife testifed that this was not true; she did not have much opportunity to visit him in Port Dickson because she was busy with their children. She also testified that she and her husband always argue; that he does not care about her and the children anymore; and that when he has money, he sends it to his mother, not to her.

Much of the rest of the discussion had to do with property and the wife's claim that she is not getting her due share. On the subject of *harta sepencarian*, the *kadi* asked her if the husband had a house or a car (the answer to which was no) or a bank account, which would also fall under the heading of *harta sepencarian*. It seemed that the husband did have some sort of bank or savings account, but the *kadi* felt that the issue could not be resolved at the moment due to lack of proper documents and precise information. Such property would be counted as *harta sepencarian*, however, and would thus be divided more or less equally between husband and wife.

It was agreed that the brother of the husband, that is, the husband's representative (*wakil*), would pay the money owed in *nafkah* payments so as not to disturb the husband anymore. Shortly thereafter the *kadi* asked the wife to leave his chambers so that he could clear up a few things with the husband's brother, after which the hearing ended.

Comment: A major issue in this case is that no one seems to know whether or not the husband already pronounced a divorce (*lafazkan talak*) on his wife. The wife was not sure about this; the counselor didn't know either, although she checked with officials at Port Dickson and was informed that they had no information or official record of anything along these lines. Nor, it seems, had the husband registered a divorce anywhere else. Hence the ambiguity that the wife approached the court to help resolve.

The ambiguity at issue is all the more significant because the husband wants to marry another woman and can only do so if he has the first wife's permission, or if he has already divorced the first wife, in which case he should have registered the divorce. Most of this information was explained to me afterward by the counselor; it did not come up in the hearing itself. The wife does agree "to be let go," but this is only relevant if the husband wants (or is willing) to divorce her. His *wakil* cannot pronounce a divorce on his behalf. This was made quite clear by the *kadi*, so the case was not resolved.

Among the unusual features of this case is the active participation in the hearings of an individual designated to represent one of the litigants (the husband's elder brother). Siblings almost never participate in hearings in any capacity (case 15 is another exception to the rule); in this instance the only reason the husband's brother was involved was because the husband was too *gila* to appear in person. That siblings—and for that matter parents and other close kin—are so rarely included in hearings is but another indication of the highly atomized and individualized nature of contemporary marriage and social relations generally, including negotiations bearing on the dissolution of conjugal bonds.

The fact that the representative here is an elder brother (*abang*) is highly ironic, inasmuch as it could not help but underscore the disjunction between the elder sibling's role on the one hand, and the elder sibling aspect of the husband's role on the other, which, as noted earlier, provides grist for the mill of counterhegemonic representations of masculinity emphasizing how much men fall short in their roles as husbands and fathers. It is significant in the latter regard that when the wife was running through her husband's shortcomings, she emphasized that "when he gets money he sends it to his mother," which is a sign of a good son. So the wife's claim is not that he is a bad person overall, or even that he fails to honor all of his kinship obligations, for he is at least in some respects a good son, but rather that he falls short in the roles of husband and father.

One further point to note about this case concerns the wife's explicit contention that she is not getting "her due share." Claims articulated in such terms are highly unusual, the more general point being that women do not usually stress their rights but focus instead on their husband's responsibilities (how they have not met them). Such responsibilities are those that men have to their wives and children, needless to say, but this is a very different discursive strategy and indeed a very different way of conceptualizing marriage and social relations on the whole.

The next few cases illustrate additional approaches to some of these matters. More specifically, they reveal some of the alternative strategies women pursue to help them resolve issues of ambiguity that are understandably of great concern to them and their households.

Case 17: *Wife Seeking Clarification of Martial Status, Eventuating in Reconciliation.* This hearing took place in the *kadi*'s chambers. The *kadi* was present throughout, and Araffin was called in toward the end of the hearing for assistance. The elderly husband, who was a *haji*, had a nervous tick which made him squinch up his face every few seconds, and his dentures did not fit very well either; all in all he looked rather uncomfortable. The wife seems to have initiated the petition, ostensibly to have her marital status clarified.

The *kadi*'s first question was whether or not the husband had divorced her. About the time the husband said, "No," the wife made reference to a divorce that occurred some twenty years earlier, the husband claiming, "That is another, long story."

In connection with the more recent divorce to which the wife referred, the *kadi* asked the wife to clarify exactly what the husband said. She did this and the husband acknowledged that he had said something that in the court's opinion amounted to a *talak*. The *kadi* then asked the husband about the current situation: "How are things now between you and your wife?" The husband mentioned the problem of *saudara* (relatives), and it became clear that the husband did not like living with the wife's younger sibling (*adik*). The wife responded that she did not want to hear any more about the *adik*, that the *adik* is "part of the arrangement."

There seemed to be a modicum of good feeling between husband and wife but the wife wanted to know where the "divorce ticket" was. This raised the question of whether or not the husband's *talak* had been pronounced a full three months ago. The *kadi* and Araffin made brief calculations and decreed that a full three months had passed since the husband's pronouncement and that they were therefore divorced.

The *kadi* then said, "Okay, then, we'll arrange a reconciliation." The wife, who was more forceful and spoke much more loudly than the husband throughout the hearing, responded with, "Okay, but who is going to pay [the relevant registration fees]?" The husband appeared embarrassed by his wife's loud responses and questions and told her to be patient. She, in turn, enjoined him "not to get a big head about all of this [the reconciliation]." The *kadi* ushered them out of his chambers, thanking me in the process as a way of saying, "That's it now, time to go," apparently eager to have his morning tea.

Comment: Along with the previous two cases (15 and 16), this hearing raises a number of important points concerning the sociolinguistic and legal prerogatives that are vested in men and denied to women and the ways that men can exploit the ambiguities of such prerogatives in ways that simultaneously work to their advantage and to the detriment of women. The proceeding outlined here illustrates, for example, that when husbands threaten their wives with divorce, they sometimes invoke specific words or phrases that are not necessarily intended to be—but at least from the court's point of view are in fact—performative utterances, inasmuch as they actually bring about the referenced state of affairs. Complicating the picture is the absence in the Malay language of verb tense (in the sense of different forms of a verb for different tenses) and the tendency to signify or imply tense by context, such that a declarative statement like "I will divorce you" does not necessarily differ in a narrow linguistic sense from one such as "I [hereby] divorce you." Other issues surface in this proceeding as well: for example, the problems of *saudara*, this being primarily a complaint of men; concerns or anxieties about paying the relevant legal fees, which, as in this instance, tend to be more pronounced among women than among men; and last but not least, concerns to avoid causing and experiencing loss of face and other forms of embarrassment, which are shared by male and female litigants alike but are obviously accorded reduced priority when, as in the following case, there is a serious deterioration of marital relations.

Case 18: *Wife Petitions for Divorce ("on Good Terms") Because Husband Is Crass, Irresponsible, and Hits Her.* This case involves a man by the name of Shaharuddin Md. S., who appears to be in his mid-twenties or thirties, and his wife, Khatijah bte. F., age twenty-six. The *kadi* begins by reading the wife's petition aloud.

Husband: All of that is false, Tuan Kadi.
Wife: Get a Quran, make an oath; it's so hard to make a statement. . . .
Kadi: What proof or witnesses do you have?
[Wife expresses exasperation.]

Kadi [to husband]: She petitioned in Seremban and she is asking you to acknowledge that you divorced her. Did you or not?

Husband: No.

Kadi: In this petition your wife says that you divorced her by saying, "I divorce, I divorce you."

Husband: None of that is true, Tuan.

Kadi [to wife]: When did this occur?

Wife: This occurred a week after I left the house. In addition, I was still sick; he hit/beat me.

Kadi: Give me the doctor's letter.

Counselor: [Concerning] the result of the doctor's exam, here is the decision. . . .

Kadi: The information [in this letter] from the doctor indicates: (1) normal injuries or wounds; (2) the bones are in good condition; (3) no injuries to the senses; and (4) some evidence or suspicion that she was struck or beaten. [To husband:] You went to the hospital with her, yeah?

Husband: She fell on the cement. She gave a false statement.

Kadi [to husband]: What kind of fate do you have? It was me who married you. . . . Okay, both of you say that there is a M$200 ring. Which ring are you claiming?

Wife: The marriage ring cost M$200.

Husband: I married her as a divorcée, Tuan Kadi. I don't understand all of this.

Kadi: Has the M$500 *hantaran* [cash marriage payment due under *adat*] been taken care of?

Husband: At the time we married, there were none of these issues, Tuan.

Kadi: In the marriage form here [it's written that] there is *hantaran*, . . . etc. At the time you married, who made the agreement?

Husband: This thing was just between me and her. If [you] want to divorce, just divorce. Don't make false claims.

Kadi: Who is serving here as a mediator for you two?

Wife: His aunt [*makcik*].

Kadi: Call her in.

[*Makcik* enters.]

Kadi: You arranged the marriage of these two?

Makcik: I did.

Kadi: What can you [clarify]?

Makcik: Shaharuddin said he didn't want to marry because he didn't have any money, but Khatijah wanted to get married anyway. She was a divorcée, so just *adat* money M$25. Khatijah's older sister said just do a "cowboy marriage" [*kawin koboi*].

Kadi: Where did the money you're claiming come from? According to the wife's petition, you claim: *hantaran*, M$500; ring(s), M$200; a [debt], M$60; and *kenduri* expenses, M$40.

Wife: All I received was M$45 *mas kawin*. . . . I was still sick. It wasn't me who asked for it.

Kadi: Who did this accounting? Now Khatijah is asking M$500. Where did this all come from?

Wife: I conferred with my older sister. He still owes on the ring. . . .

Husband: Let's not talk a lot. If you want to divorce, I will divorce.

Wife: I want child support.

Husband: The child that was born, I didn't even know about it. She didn't even tell me.

Kadi: This M$60 debt?

Wife: [It] . . . hasn't been paid yet. . . .

Kadi: The M$40 debt?

Wife: He borrowed from my elder sister to have a feast [*kenduri*].

Kadi: Where was the marriage feast?

Wife: At Rasah.

Husband: If it's at her house, she's the one who puts out the money.

Kadi: If the *kenduri* is at your house, then it's appropriate that you put up for the expenses. If a divorcée's marriage, how much *hantaran*?

Makcik: If you marry a divorcée, it's not necessary to have *hantaran*.

Kadi: Okay, I'm going to resolve this matter. Where did the M$500 *hantaran* come from?

Counselor: We want to know who made an agreement about the *hantaran*?

Kadi: You live in Rasah?

Wife: Yeah. . . .

. . . .

Kadi: When did she run away from the house?

Husband: I don't remember. I don't want to concern myself with her anymore.

Kadi: According to the information on this form, she left [over nine months ago].

Counselor: *Hantaran* wasn't noted on the marriage form.

Wife: But it is noted on the form at Kedah.

Kadi: Give me the marriage form. Where's the form for marrying outside the district? Okay, on this form . . . it's noted *belanja* [expenses] M$300 and a ring.

Husband: That I don't know; she's the one who filled it out in Kedah.

Kadi: So, which form are we gonna use? As they say, if you're in a cow's pen, moo; if you're in a goat's pen, bleat. So, we'll use the form here.

Wife: It doesn't matter. I can't force [him]. I seek an amicable divorce [*cerai baik*].

Kadi: Puan Khatijah, no matter where you go to court, you can't win. Concerning your relationship here, what?

Husband: She claims she missed her period.

Wife: I gave birth [two and a half months ago]. . . .

Kadi: Where was the child born?

Wife: At the Main Hospital in Seremban.

Kadi: Who's the father of the child?

Husband: I didn't register it. I don't know anything about it.

Wife: Let him not acknowledge it then. After, . . . in the Afterlife, he won't be able to run.

Kadi: There's much *keraguan* [suspicion, doubt, perplexity]. It's appropriate that the father should be involved in the birth of his child. But how were you able to register your child when the father wasn't there at the time? How is it that you got the child's [birth] certificate?

Wife: Someone [or people] helped.

Kadi: I don't want to be harsh. . . . I want to resolve this nicely.

Husband: I am not satisfied with this whole claim.

Kadi: The information is not complete. . . . The decision of this hearing isn't *putus* [final].

Wife: He doesn't acknowledge that he's the father of the child. He punched my stomach and accused me of being pregnant before marrying him.

Kadi: At the time you gave birth, why didn't you tell your husband?. . . . I'm forced to refer this case up [to the chief *kadi*].

Wife: It's not necessary, Tuan. I don't want to hassle anymore. He doesn't acknowledge. . . .

Kadi: I am going to pass this case up [to the chief *kadi*].

Wife: It's not necessary, Tuan. I'm going to work and make a living for my child.

Kadi: What about this M$200?

Husband: I don't know, Tuan.

Kadi: Who else is a witness?

Wife: My Makcik [*Makcik #2*].

[*Makcik #2* enters.]

Kadi: So what's with this M$200 ring; is it true or not?

Makcik #2: Is it true Khatijah? Yeah, I guess so. I didn't hear all that they agreed upon.

Kadi: Give me the divorce form. The issue now is the M$500. The child is really Shaharuddin's because he knew [or knows] that Khatijah didn't get her period. The child support must be discussed.

Husband: So what about the child, Tuan? I can raise it.

Kadi: If anyone wants to claim the child, [they] make a request to the chief *kadi*. But I feel you can't win, Shaharuddin.

Wife: I don't want to give the child to him. I was the one who was . . . pregnant. . . .

Kadi: So now, about the *nafkah edah* and the *nafkah anak*. . . .

Husband: Tuan, you make a decision.

Kadi: How much do you want to give? There isn't any *nafkah edah* because Khatijah doesn't want it. *Nafkah anak*, M$25 a month.

Husband: I can't, Tuan.

Kadi: The *nafkah anak* is set at M$25 a month. Okay, that's resolved. The
wife isn't claiming anything because she asked for the divorce.
Shaharuddin, you read the divorce certificate with one *talak*.

Shaharuddin pronounces a divorce with one *talak* and it is decided that the
nafkah anak will proceed via garnishing his wages.

Comment: There is clearly a great deal that is contested in this hearing, but
what sets it apart from others we have considered thus far is that it is one of the
very few cases that came before the Rembau court in which one of the litigants
(here the wife) suggested that the court rely on an oath to help establish what
might have happened between the litigants. Perhaps because the suggestion
came from one of the litigants, as opposed to the *kadi* himself or one of his
assistants, this strategy is not pursued.

The wife's strategy also includes painting her husband's behavior in very
broad strokes: "He hits me, is irresponsible, and crass," and he "doesn't even
know that I gave birth to our child." By way of substantiating the claims concerning the injuries allegedly inflicted on her by her husband, she comes
equipped with (or arranged to have sent to the court) written evidence in the
form of a letter from a doctor testifying to the nature of her injuries. The letter,
however, is inconclusive as to how exactly the injuries were sustained, one
consequence of which is that much of the rest of the hearing is given over to a
discussion of marriage gifts, the costs incurred in hosting the wedding, etc. This
in turn founders because the marriage forms were not filled out in sufficient
specificity and, to further complicate matters, were filed in two different
jurisdictions.

The *kadi* feels that there is too much at stake for him to resolve, so he
remarks that he will have to refer it to the chief *kadi*, to which the wife responds that "it isn't necessary," that she can work and make a living for her
child. The *kadi* takes this an indication that the wife does not want any
nafkah edah, and although he awards her M$25 a month for *nafkah anak*, he
decrees that she is not claiming anything (else), "because she asked for the
divorce."

A more general issue here is that the wife wants a divorce "on good terms"
(*cerai cara baik*) but will settle for a divorce that is less than amicable. As
mentioned earlier, she is relatively well equipped with proof (a letter from the
doctor verifying her injuries), and she brings witnesses, but they cannot confirm
other elements of her narrative concerning, for example, the marriage payments—rights to which she effectively forfeited both by requesting the divorce
and by suggesting that she would work and make a living for the child.

Note, too, the wife's comments that while her husband may refuse to acknowledge their child and admit to his other transgressions, "he won't be able
to run" in the Afterlife, coupled with her suggestion that the court rely on oath-
taking to help establish what really happened, both of which entail references to

God and mystical sanctions. The husband, in contrast, simply contests the wife's claims, stating that they are false, that he would raise the child, etc.

Bear in mind, finally, that various problems arise in this hearing because the marriage forms were not filled out completely; that the two witnesses in this case were women; and that the testimony each one provided seems to have been accorded more credibility than the husband's. Given the stipulation in classical Islamic law that the testimony of a female witness be accorded only half as much weight as that of a male, it is noteworthy that neither the *kadi* nor anyone else present raised this issue or commented on the fact that the evidence codes in force at the time of the hearing emphasized the equal weight of male and female testimony.

Case 19: *Eliciting a Divorce from Constable Zainuddin*. The case was recorded by my research assistant (Kamaruddin), who joined the hearing while it was in progress. It involved a police constable (age thirty-seven) from Rembau and his wife Maimon (age forty-four), who is from Melaka. They were married via family arrangements and have four children (ages eight, ten, twelve, and fourteen).

Kamaruddin characterized the husband as a patient man but noted that when there are household problems, he is inclined to quarrel with his in-laws and other kin. Kamaruddin described the wife as a person who is *kasar* (coarse, crass) and always hitting her husband.

The problem began at the police barracks. They always quarrel. The wife kicked and hit the husband with a broom and has accused him of having a relationship with someone else. The wife has often petitioned for divorce but the husband would not divorce her. Some five or six weeks ago the wife returned to her village. The wife's older sister accused the husband of having an adulterous relationship with another woman, and they will not accept the husband anymore. The husband is [was?] always patient but finally petitioned for divorce about ten days before the hearing.

The decision of the court: *nafkah edah*, M$60 a month (M$200 total); *nafkah anak*, M$200 a month, in addition to school expenses, payments to be made by garnishing the husband's wages. There is not any *harta sepencarian*; the household items go to the wife. *Muta'ah*: M$1,000 by garnishing the husband's wages at the rate of M$100 a month for ten months.

Comment: Unfortunately the notes on this hearing are not as complete as I would like. Various features of the case are nonetheless noteworthy, including the wife's strategy for dealing with the problems she experienced in her marriage. From what we know, these initially involved arguments, which escalated to crude language and physical assaults on the husband. She sought divorce from her husband, which (along with striking or beating a husband) is widely construed as a grave sin in Islam, but the husband would not consent to letting her go. She then fled their home, returning to her village. In and of itself this action, also construed as sinful, would have caused the husband considerable embarrassment and shame. To make matters worse for the husband, his wife's elder sister then accused him of having an affair with another woman. This accusation may have occurred when the husband tried to approach his wife in her village; in any case, it seems to have coincided in a general way with their refusal to receive him.

Of broader relevance here is that since the wife could not secure her husband's consent to a divorce, she effectively elicited his repudiation by actions (running away, refusing to receive him, etc.) that were geared toward angering or humiliating him or, in any event, that had that effect. The value of such a strategy is, first, that she was granted the divorce that she sought, and second, that she obtained a divorce that was construed by the authorities as technically initiated by her husband and, in doing so, retained her rights to *nafkah edah* totaling M$200 as well as *muta'ah* in the sum of M$1,000.

It is not clear to me how widespread such practices or strategies are (though I suspect they are common), or how broadly distributed is the knowledge of what women stand to gain if they effectively elicit their husband's divorce instead of seeking divorce from the court. What is obvious, though, is that in this case the wife had enough information at her disposal to effect a strategy consonant with her objectives of getting out of the marriage and doing so in a way that would result in her incurring minimal financial loss. The wife's strategy in the following case is in some ways similar to what we have just seen, though the case is far more complicated and the wife is far more cosmopolitan and refined—and of a decidedly higher social class—than Maimon.

Case 20: *The Wife Who Seeks to Divorce Her Husband Because He Wants to Marry His Mistress as His Second Wife.* This case involved a woman (Nasariah bte. Haji U.) who wanted a divorce from her husband (Ismail bin B.), with whom she has two teenage children. The first portion of the hearing was held in the counselor's office, the latter part in the *kadi*'s office (where the wife was joined by the husband, who, like the wife, appeared to be in his late thirties or early forties). The wife was accompanied by a woman some five to ten years her senior. Both were dressed in the same fashion, with attractive, similarly cut Malay outfits (*baju kurung*), high heels, expensive-looking Western-style purses, lipstick, etc., and both spoke a fair amount of English, which they mixed with Malay every now and then, as educated Malays often do. The woman who accompanied the wife to the courthouse did not sit in on the hearings, but she did come into the *kadi*'s chambers at the end of the case after the *kadi* had left, at which point the wife and the counselor were having a lengthy discussion about the wife's options and strategies.

The basic problem is that Ismail has a mistress (Dalia) he wants to marry, and according to various local interpretations of state law (though not the laws of Islam) he needs the consent of his wife, Nasariah, to marry her. The wife refuses to agree to this and wants to divorce him, but he is unwilling to consent to a divorce. Thus there is a stalemate.

Nasariah narrated the following story. Ismail had been working in Johor Baru and while he was there (some three years ago) had an affair with a secretary or typist. At some point he was transferred to Seremban (though he resigned his job just last week). Ismail's current mistress, Dalia, was recently divorced from her husband (with whom she has three children). Ismail and Dalia want to get married after Dalia's *edah* period is up.

As Nasariah elaborated, she related how she came to learn of the affair, saying that she and her husband and children had been in an accident and that while her head was still bandaged, Dalia's mother contacted her, informing her that her daughter was involved in a relationship with her (Nasariah's) husband. Nasariah called her husband Ismail home from work and confronted him, but he denied the whole thing. Dalia even came to their house on Hari Raya, telling Nasariah that she wanted to discuss it all. At this point in Nasariah's narrative, Ismail, who had been sitting in the waiting area outside, stuck his head into the counselor's office, saying that it was already 10:30 and that he had an appointment. The counselor politely instructed him to be patient and wait outside, which he did.

Nasariah drove Dalia out when she appeared at the house, repeating to the counselor (in English) what she had warned her at the time, "You get out before I lose my head," at which point Dalia grabbed onto the husband, lamenting, "But you said your wife is understanding." Nasariah then turned to the counselor and stated rhetorically, "But what wife would understand this?" Dalia then left, and Ismail followed. Shortly after this Dalia got back together with her former husband but continued to have an affair with Ismail. "They went all around together, . . . even drove in the car together in front of my friends."

Nasariah then switched gears, turning to a discussion of how she had been forced to vacate their house in Seremban. I do not know how this came up in the discussion, but it became clear that the bank was going to repossess the house and sell it off, so the family was forced to get everything out immediately. Nasariah testified that the husband told her to return to Rembau; apparently she hired a truck to take the household possessions back to her (mother's) natal village.

"My husband is still involved with this woman. I have *proof* of their relationship. Do you want to see it?" Then as an aside, partly in my direction, she said, "I'm embarrassed," at which point she dug in her purse to find a picture, which she produced and handed over to the counselor, who assured her that there was no cause for embarrassment. After she looked at the picture, which showed the husband with another woman (presumably Dalia) in a posed shot, the counselor asked her how she got it. Nasariah was evasive and turned to a brief discussion of how the husband had ordered her to go to the Seremban *kadi*'s office to give her consent to his taking the mistress as his second wife. She replied, "You must be mad." To the counselor she said, "What wife would allow her husband to marry again?" She told him, "If you want her, let me go." He refused. She went on to say that Ismail left home almost two years earlier, lives with Dalia and her three children, but continues to come home on weekends.

Nasariah then indicated that she is willing to grant a divorce but with certain conditions, mainly that the children be supported. Throughout much of the hearing, the counselor was making notes in Jawi on an official form that was to become part of the file. When it appeared that most of what Nasariah had to say had in fact been said, she asked the counselor to read back the petition. The counselor then said, "Can you read this?" (meaning Jawi), but there was no intelligible answer so far as I could tell and it was upside down anyway, so the counselor went ahead and read back the statement, a few details of which the wife corrected.

At this juncture in the hearing, if not before, the counselor realized that Nasariah was very intent on pursuing a divorce and began asking about their *harta sepencarian*. "Is there any?" she asked. "Well, there is a car, in my name, that I bought; [but] no land, no house." The counselor then went into consider-able detail explaining a woman's rights with respect to *nafkah edah*, *muta'ah*, and *harta sepencarian*. Nasariah replied that she wants M$1,000 a month for the children. For *edah*, she wants M$300. The counselor then asked her, M$300 for the entire *edah* or M$300 a month? "M$300 a month" was the answer. The counselor smiled at some of this, perhaps especially the M$1,000 a month, which indicated to me that these were very large demands. She also said some-thing about this having to be weighed or decided by the *kadi*. Nasariah added that the husband can afford M$1,000 a month, especially if he can afford a place in Kuala Lumpur for himself for M$750 a month.

Nasariah and the counselor then left the room and went into the *kadi*'s cham-bers where the hearing continued, albeit with Ismail as well. This portion of the hearing began with the *kadi* looking very briefly over the forms the counselor had prepared, asking where the husband and wife were from, how many chil-dren they had, what their ages were, whether they (the children) were male or female, where they worked, where the children were living, etc. Either the husband or the wife said that they had had "misunderstanding[s]" for the past six or so years. They had lived in Seremban, but the house was torn down. The *kadi* then read out the statement that Nasariah had given to the counselor. Is-mail kept interrupting him and was told by the *kadi* that he would have his turn.

When Ismail was given the opportunity to state his version of things, he inquired of his wife (very politely but also with definite emotion), "Why do you want a divorce?" to which she replied that if she "didn't get a divorce, there would be no justice." The reference to the possibility that justice might not be served seemed to irritate the *kadi*, for he began intimidating Nasariah by raising his voice and repeating, "So you want a divorce, do you?"

The hearing moved along and it became clear from Ismail's testimony that he is from Melaka and is now involved in trading (importing biscuits from Den-mark, lichees from Taiwan, and so on); that the house that they (he and Na-sariah?) had been living in costs M$1,800 a month; and that he does in fact come back to see his wife. When Nasariah was asked about her line of work she indicated that she is a nurse, adding, "I don't want my husband to be with the other woman; I can live without him." The *kadi* responded to the latter remark by asking her, "Can he marry the other one?" She replied no and the *kadi* proceeded to tell her, "According to Islam, it is wrong for the wife to ask for a divorce. . . . I'm not here supporting the husband, but according to Islam. . . ." This went on for a while; Nasariah held firmly to her position.

The *kadi* offered to give them "some more time." Perhaps because Nasariah quickly made clear that she did not want more time, the *kadi* began going through the *harta sepencarian*. The property included a house (the proprietary status of which was unclear), listed in the husband's name and valued at M$180,000, as well as a car in the wife's name (valued, when new, at M$16,800). The husband stressed that he bought everything for the house that his wife could possibly need and added, very sincerely, "She can have it all."

Kadi: People don't know the laws of the Afterlife [*hukum akhirat*]. . . .
Wife: I don't care; I don't want to stay married to him. . . . Adultery is a
  serious sin.
Husband: Show me the man who's going to take care of you, then I'll divorce
  you.
Wife: I don't want to argue anymore with him. It's a sin. I want to resolve all
  of this today.
Kadi [to husband]: It depends on you. [To wife:] The court upholds the
  husband. I'll give you until [the end of the month], because you've never
  been here before. I do this with first-timers. . . . [To husband:] By the
  thirtieth [of the month], 10 A.M. I want a decision from you on what you
  are going to do.

As the husband went out of the *kadi*'s chambers, he asked the *kadi* to forgive him for anything "rough" that he may have said and shook hands with him. He was clearly flustered and frustrated by the way things went, but he retained his composure. As the wife and the other woman who accompanied her put it later, "Dia memang pandai cakap" ("He's really clever when it comes to talking").

After the *kadi* left the room, the other woman came in so that the counselor was there alone with the wife and the other woman (and me). The counselor informed Nasariah of her rights, of how the courts proceed, and helped her devise a viable strategy. The counselor thus advised her: "Why don't you let him marry the other woman first? Then you can see if he lives up to the conditions that will be imposed on him [to treat both wives equally]." But Nasariah was obviously not interested; in making this clear she stated that she could have them caught for *tangkap basah* (illicit proximity; literally, a "wet catch"), "but I don't want it that way."

The counselor emphasized that the *kadi* cannot force Ismail to divorce her, reiterating that the *kadi*'s office merely gives views and opinions and does not really make decisions. This point, which had been made earlier, is only partially true. Nasariah's response in any event was: "What if I order an investigation of my husband's affair?" The counselor proceeded to explain the types of conditions that would be imposed on the husband and to speak of polygyny in general. She said Ismail would have to provide *nafkah anak*, would have to spend roughly half of his time with each wife, would have to support both wives, etc. If he broke these conditions, Nasariah would have a better case (for divorce).

A lengthy discussion ensued, involving the counselor, Nasariah, and Nasariah's friend/elder sister. The latter two queried the counselor on Nasariah's options and most viable strategies. It was here that the counselor underscored that divorce is not *elok* (pretty, appropriate), which is of course a dominant view underlying much of the *kadi*'s refusal to facilitate the divorce in the first place. It is the duty of the office to discourage divorce, partly because of the consequences for children, as suggested by the posters on the wall of some of the offices in the Department of Religion in Seremban, which portray abandoned children, emphasizing that they are the victims of divorce and that Allah regards divorce as wrong and evil.

At this point in the discussion Nasariah also talked of her husband's taking her to the *kadi*'s office in Seremban to get her to consent to his proposed marriage. "What about that petition?" she asked, mentioning as well that the husband had told her more than once that if she refused, he could still divorce her. "We depend on talk, not the written complaint [*aduan*]," the counselor responded, a very important point about the nature of evidence.

Comment: Both Nasariah and the woman she brought with her to court seemed very forgiving of the husband; the counselor was struck by this as well as she made clear to me after the hearing. The counselor felt that if Ismail broke off his affair with Dalia, Nasariah would be glad to have him back. Nasariah never came right out and said this, however, and in fact she indicated that she was tired of having him break his word. In the latter connection Nasariah brought up the previous affair that he had had and how he had promised never to do anything like that again, after which she forgave him. Both the wife and the other woman said, "Hey, where are people who have never done anything wrong? We forgave him."

Note also that in this case, as in many others considered here and in the previous chapter, the *kadi* does not spend much time or energy trying to work out the inconsistencies and contradictions in the testimonies, trying to establish "fact" and "truth." Although the same is true of the counselor, she provides far more advice on strategy and how to cope with difficult situations and is ultimately far more supportive and helpful in an informational sense. She does not resort to intimidation or browbeating. This in contrast to the *kadi*, who, as in this proceeding, resorts to such tactics, especially if he feels that his authority or judgment is being questioned—as when Nasariah made the unequivocal claim that it would be unjust if she was not granted a divorce.

Recall, finally, that the wife threatened to bring legal action against her husband on the uncontested grounds of his adultery and that this did not become a legally salient issue, though the husband's prerogatives in marriage and divorce clearly did as when the *kadi*, in a rather uncharacteristic comment, said quite clearly and without any qualifying caveats that in contested matters the courts uphold the husband.

This latter hearing, like all of the others discussed thus far in this chapter, was initiated by a woman and was chosen for discussion in this section of the chapter because the focus here is on women's strategies and experiences. In the final case I consider in this section of the chapter, the hearing was initiated by the husband but shaped in significant ways by the wife's successful manipulation of her husband's apparent ignorance of the law.

Case 21: *The Husband Who Wants to Divorce His Wife (They Call Each Other Animals, Etc.).* This hearing, which was held in the counselor's office, involved a man who appeared to be in his fifties and his wife, who may have been in her forties. The husband approached the *kadi*'s office because he wanted to divorce the wife. The wife will consent to a divorce on two conditions: that she be given *nafkah edah* and that her husband return the money she had saved for the pilgrimage to Mecca that she insisted he took from her. She went on to complain that her husband is irresponsible and is like an animal (*haiwan*), which, thus baldly stated, is an extremely offensive accusation in any context of Malay society. To add insult to injury, in the course of the hearing she made repeated reference to her husband's being *haiwan*, forgetting he was a human being, etc. The husband responded in kind: *she* was like an animal, not him.

The husband maintained that he should not pay any *nafkah edah* because his wife does not merit it. She does not assume responsibility (*tanggungjawab*); in fact, he cooks and does other work around the house; she is delinquent in this regard. The wife replied that she cannot do all of this because she works at night and does not have time.

The counselor made clear that *nafkah edah* is obligatory (though she did not add that especially in this particular court, a wife who initiates divorce effectively forefeits her claims to such money) as is the back support the husband owes. The husband was not persuaded by the counselor's remarks and continued to insist that he did not touch the money earmarked for the pilgrimage or *haj* (the "*tabung haji* money"). The wife responded that the husband took the money from her [to build a house?] and has to return it. But unfortunately for the wife, there is no proof or evidence (*bukti*) of the husband's having absconded with the money, so, as the counselor repeatedly underscored, "This is between [your] husband and God." The husband's response to this was to say to the wife: "You can take me to court on this if you want," referring (I assume) to the secular Magistrate's court.

The back support the husband owes extends over a period of some eighteen months. After the husband reiterated that he could not pay it all, the counselor told him he could pay in installments and that it was not her job to make things difficult for him. She then asked the husband for documents relating to his pension, which he produced, insisting that he does not work and has only the pension to depend on. At about this time the counselor asked about the *harta sepencarian*, if any, that the couple had, the answer to which was: "There isn't any." The counselor then indicated that the *kadi* would make the final decision about the monthly payments, and the matter was referred to him.

After the husband left the room, the counselor asked the wife if she was "less than satisfied" with the way things had worked out. The wife replied that she was not very pleased and went on to talk about the husband's shortcomings. Later in the morning I observed the husband giving a statement to Araffin; shortly thereafter he went ahead and divorced his wife by pronouncing one *talak* in the presence of the *kadi*.

Comment: Among the reasons this case is of interest is that it illustrates, first, a lack of familiarity with the relevant laws pertaining to marriage and divorce on the part of husband and wife alike and second, a woman's successful manipulation of her husband's relative ignorance of the law to achieve (some of) her own objectives. As regards the latter issue, note that the wife plays on her husband's apparent ignorance of the fact that her consent is not necessary to his obtaining a divorce from her and that she forces him to appear before the court both for the purpose of discussing and hopefully resolving contested financial issues and (it seems) to humiliate him in public and otherwise "get even." Having said that she plays on her husband's ignorance of the law, it also appears that she is lacking in knowledge in this area (on the issue of consent) or is at least successful in bluffing him as to his options. On the other hand, she appears not to know that she is entitled to *nafkah edah* in this court so long as she is without fault and the husband initiates the divorce, just as she seems unaware that mere verbal assertions concerning her beliefs (as opposed to facts) that her husband took her *tabung haji* money are insufficient as evidence in a court of law.

The wife's heaping of verbal abuse on the husband (calling him an animal and so on) is a noteworthy feature of this hearing in that most proceedings do not involve such explicit and demeaning insults. So, too, is the husband's responding in kind and his raising the issue of his wife's not assuming responsibility for cooking and other work around the house as a way of claiming that she does not merit any *nafkah edah* since she has not lived up to the reciprocal arrangements entailed in the contract of marriage. Another theme to consider here is the husband's sidestepping the issue of whether or not he should or will pay back support, with the simple and straightforward remark, "I can't." In a great many cases, strategies of the latter sort are effective because there is no way for the *kadi*'s office to obtain precise information about men's (especially rural men's) incomes. In this instance, however, there is a fixed pension about which the *kadi* can inquire, and he can arrange for it to be garnished.

As for the wife's *tabung haji* money, the counselor explained to me that such funds are not regarded by the court as *harta sepencarian* because a wife's money (in the form of income/wages, bank savings, and the like) is considered to be hers alone, regardless of its origin, even if the money in her savings account was given to her by her husband. Furthermore, although the wife may do so, she need not share her wages or income from tapping rubber or other sources with her husband.

The situation is quite different in the case of a husband's money (in the form of income/wages, bank accounts, etc.). All such money is considered *harta sepencarian* and thus subject to more or less equal division at the termination of marriage for the simple reason that "it is the husband's duty to support his wife." The relatively recent codifications of legal distinctions between "wife's money/property" and "husband's money/property" and of their respective fates in consequence of the dissolution of marriage are exceedingly important both in the Malaysian context and in Indonesia and various other parts of the Islamic world (see Peletz 1988b; Horowitz 1994). The more encompassing dynamics at issue involve increasingly widespread legal and more general cultural recognition of women's rights both to maintain property and to work for cash remuneration outside the home unencumbered by male claims. Involved as well, though this is a less recent development, are "liberal" innovations in Islamic traditions bearing on conjugal property or, put differently, a rephrasing in Islamic idioms of longstanding Malay (*adat*) traditions that favor equality in the division of conjugal earnings and happen to accord nicely with common-law practice relevant to non-Malays in Malaysia (and beyond).

Commentary on Women's Strategies and Experiences

The nine cases I have discussed thus far in this chapter have focused on women's strategies and experiences in Rembau's Islamic court, particularly as plaintiffs. Eight of the nine cases were initiated by women. (In case 19, a woman forced her husband's hand by engaging in behavior that had the desired effect of eliciting her husband's divorce through repudiation. I thus "credited" her with initiating the discourse that resulted in her obtaining a divorce.) In case 21, a woman did not so much initiate the legal discourse as play a central role in shaping it by manipulating her husband's ignorance of the relevant laws concerning consent and the like. The more general point is that in Rembau, elsewhere in Negeri Sembilan, in other areas of Malaysia such as Kedah, Selangor, and Kuala Lumpur, and in various other parts of the Muslim world, such as Kenya (Hirsch 1998), the vast majority of the cases that come before the Islamic courts are initiated by women. Equally important is that even when women do not actually initiate or effectively generate the proceedings, they often play a central role in shaping key features of the discourse(s) at the heart of the hearings.

The factors that motivate women to turn to the courts to help them manage or resolve marital disputes clearly vary, as do the specific grievances and goals highlighted in the narratives they articulate in the presence of the *kadi*, the counselor, and other members of the staff (Araffin, for example). As indicated by the data summarized in table 1, which pertains to the district of Rembau and is organized in terms of the theme(s) most strongly emphasized in the narratives of the litigants involved in the proceedings I observed, the most commonly articulated objectives include obtaining current and/or back maintenance (*nafkah*) and/or one or another type of divorce. What the summary tabulation of data presented in the table does not illustrate is that many of these cases are also motivated by concerns to resolve ambiguity—as is particularly apparent from the contours of the narratives in question. The ambiguity at issue typically relates to: whether or not a husband or ex-husband is still alive; whether or not a husband or ex-husband is in jail; and/or whether or not the relationship between a woman and the man she married still has the legally binding status of marriage. This is to say, among other things, that women's understandable concerns to resolve such ambiguities are much more pronounced than is suggested by the figures given in the table for cases categorized under the heading, "Clarification of Relationship/Marital Status."

The patterns described for Rembau are in many respects similar to what one finds elsewhere in Malaysia. This is clear from a comparison of the material summarized in table 1 with the data summarized in table 2 and table 3, which were gathered at the District Religious Offices in Kempas, Selangor, and Kota Jati, Kedah, respectively. The findings presented in the latter two tables derive from the study conducted by Sharifah Zaleha Syed Hassan and Sven Cederroth (1997). The authors of the study categorized their data based on information presented in the official complaint forms (*borang aduan*) they examined, which were prepared by clerks, mediators, and other officials, who grouped and distinguished cases based on their understandings of the most salient legal issue(s) at the heart of each dispute. The authors underscore that there is much overlap in their categories, as is also true of those I employ. I might point out as well that the categories they use differ from those I utilize, partly in being more numerous and specific. That said, the commonalities in our data are pronounced and clearly outweigh the differences with regard to tabular presentation and other, more substantive themes. The most striking of the similarities is the overwhelming preponderance in all three venues of female plaintiffs as a percent of total plaintiffs, the relevant figures being 66.7 percent for Rembau, 79.3 percent for Kempas, and 92.2 percent for Kota Jati.

It remains to add that at the time of the Selangor and Kedah study (the early 1990s), many of the cases that had previously been handled by the district-level *kadi*'s office (now known as the District Religious Office) came under the jurisdiction of the newly designated Syariah Court and that the preponderance of female plaintiffs in the latter venues is as striking as what one finds in the other venues noted earlier (see tables 4 and 5). The authors of the study do not provide a gendered breakdown of plaintiffs in the Syariah Courts, but it is clear from the types of cases they handle—the vast majority of which are classified under the headings of *taklik* divorce, *fasakh* divorce, wife maintenance, and child maintenance—that the overwhelming majority of the plaintiffs are female.

What is not readily apparent from any of the tables presented here but is strikingly evident from the proceedings summarized in the foregoing pages and from other relevant studies (including Azizah Kassim [1984]; Sharifah Zaleha Syed Hassan [1989]; Sharifah Zaleha Syed Hassan and Sven Cederroth [1997]; Horowitz [1994]; and Mohammad Hashim Kamali [2000]) is that women are buffeted about by the courts in ways that men are not. Such are among the gendered differences and similarities in court use and experience that we shall address in more detail later on. In the meantime, let us turn to men's strategies and experiences in the courts.

Table 1

Types and Number of Cases Handled by the District Kadi's Office in Rembau, Negeri Sembilan, by Gender of Plaintiff, 1987 and 1988[a]

Female Plaintiffs	*Number of Cases*	*Number of Cases as Percentage of Female Total*
Mediated discussion	–	–
Broken engagement	1	4.51
Current and/or back maintenance	7[b]	31.82
Clarification of relationship/marital status	3[c]	13.64
Divorce/Monogamous union	5[d]	22.73
Divorce/Polygynous union	–	–
Fasakh divorce	3	13.64
Tebus Talak divorce	1	4.51
Registration of divorce	–	–
Reconciliation	–	–
Matters related to conversion	2	9.09
Total	22	99.94

Male Plaintiffs	*Number of Cases*	*Number of Cases as Percentage of Male Total*
Mediated discussion	2	18.18
Broken engagement	–	–
Current and/or back maintenance	–	–
Clarification of relationship/marital status	1	9.09
Divorce/Monogamous union	4	36.36
Divorce/Polygynous union	3	27.27
Fasakh divorce	–	–
Tebus Talak divorce	–	–
Registration of divorce	1	9.09
Reconciliation	–	–
Matters related to conversion	–	–
Total	11	99.99

Female Plaintiffs as percentage of total plaintiffs: 66.7% (22/33).

Male Plaintiffs as percentage of total plaintiffs: 33.3% (11/33).

Notes: [a]Includes only cases involving proceedings that I or my research assistant observed; excludes three cases discussed in text (cases 25, 30, 31) in which it is not clear which party to the marriage initiated the proceedings.

[b]Four of these cases also involve other financial claims; one of them also involves custody issues.

[c]Two of these cases also involve claims for current and/or back maintenance; one of them also involves other financial claims.

[d]Two of these cases also involve claims for current and/or back maintenance; one of them involves maintenance and other financial claims.

TABLE 2

Types and Number of Cases Handled by the District Religious Office in Kempas, Selangor, by Gender of Plaintiff, 1990 and 1991

Female Plaintiffs	*Number of Cases*	*Number of Cases as Percentage of Female Total*
Maintenance	96	28.83
Negligence	25	7.51
Estrangement	45	13.51
Illicit affair(s)	8	2.40
Desertion	56	16.82
Assault	8	2.40
Child abuse	4	1.20
Divorce	27	8.11
Polygyny	20	6.01
Endorsement of Talak	33	9.91
Disregard of court order	6	1.80
Consent for marriage of offspring	5	1.50
Total	333	100

Male Plaintiffs	*Number of Cases*	*Number of Cases as Percentage of Male Total*
Maintenance	–	–
Negligence[a]	26	29.89
Estrangement	9	10.34
Illicit affair(s)	5	5.75
Desertion	22	25.29
Assault	2	2.30
Child abuse	6	6.90
Divorce	–	–
Polygyny	12	13.80
Endorsement of Talak	–	–
Disregard of court order	–	–
Consent for marriage of offspring	5	5.75
Total	87	100.02

Female plaintiffs as percentage of total plaintiffs: 79.29% (333/420).

Male plaintiffs as percentage of total plaintiffs: 20.71% (87/420).

Note: [a]Eleven of the cases included here were classified by court officials in Kempas as cases involving men's claims that, among other things, their wives neglected or failed to provide them their "conjugal rights" (*nafkah batin*). Partly because *nafkah batin* is a type of *nafkah* (maintenance or support), these cases appear under the general heading of "Maintenance (*nafkah*)" in the original table on which this table is based, even though the men lodged no claims for the material support (*nafkah zahir*) that is usually referred to by the shortand *nafkah*. I am indebted to Sharifah Zaleha Syed Hassan (personal communication, February 22, 2001) for clarifying these matters and for underscoring that in light of their overall "content," the eleven cases at issue could have just as easily—and probably should have—been grouped together by court officials under the heading "Negligence."

Source: Sharifah Zaleha Syed Hassan and Cederroth (1997: 62).

158

TABLE 3

Types and Number of Cases Handled by the District Religious Office in Kota Jati, Kedah, by Gender of Plaintiff, 1990 and 1991

Female Plaintiffs	*Number of Cases*	*Number of Cases as Percentage of Female Total*
Maintenance	97	22.93
Negligence	56	13.24
Estrangement	72	17.02
Illicit affair(s)	15	3.55
Desertion	46	10.87
Assault	20	4.73
Child abuse	3	0.71
Divorce	30	7.09
Polygyny	29	6.86
Endorsement of Talak	37	8.75
Disregard of court order	4	0.95
Consent for marriage of offspring	14	3.31
Total	423	100.01

Male Plaintiffs	*Number of Cases*	*Number of Cases as Percentage of Male Total*
Maintenance	–	–
Negligence	3	8.33
Estrangement	6	16.67
Illicit affair(s)	4	11.11
Desertion	17	47.22
Assault	0	–
Child abuse	2	5.56
Divorce	–	–
Polygyny	2	5.56
Endorsement of Talak	–	–
Disregard of court order	2	5.56
Consent for marriage of offspring	–	–
Total	36	100.01

Female plaintiffs as percentage of total plaintiffs: 92.16% (423/459).
Male plaintiffs as percentage of total plaintiffs: 7.84% (36/459).
Source: Sharifah Zaleha Syed Hassan and Cederroth (1997: 63).

TABLE 4

Types and Number of Cases Handled by the Syariah Court of Kempas, Selangor, 1990 and 1991

Types of Cases	Number of Cases	Number of Cases as Percentage of Total
Validity of marriage	12	9.09
Marriage guardian	–	–
Taklik divorce	63	47.73
Fasakh divorce	2	1.52
Khuluk [Tebus Talak] divorce	3	2.27
Wife maintenance	16	12.12
Child maintenance	26	19.70
Custody of children	5	3.79
Shared property	5	3.79
Total	132	100.01

Source: Sharifah Zaleha Syed Hassan and Cederroth (1997: 74).

TABLE 5

Types and Number of Cases Handled by the Syariah Court of Kota Jati, Kedah, 1990 and 1991

Types of Cases	Number of Cases	Number of Cases as Percentage of Total
Validity of marriage	14	9.27
Marriage guardian	3	1.99
Taklik divorce	68	45.03
Fasakh divorce	5	3.31
Khuluk [Tebus Talak] divorce	2	1.32
Wife maintenance	31	20.53
Child maintenance	18	11.92
Custody of children	5	3.31
Shared property	5	3.31
Total	151	99.99

Source: Sharifah Zaleha Syed Hassan and Cederroth (1997: 75).

Men's Strategies and Experiences

The cases discussed in the previous section highlight the experiences and strategies of female litigants, especially as plaintiffs, though they also shed important light on the experiences and strategies of male litigants, particularly as defendants. The cases outlined in this section round out the picture by providing material that focuses more heavily (though not exclusively) on men as plaintiffs—and women as defendants. The more general objective of this section is to present data conducive to a focused discussion not only of similarities and differences in the legal experiences and strategies of women and men, but also of oppositional discourses and strategies of resistance.

Case 22: *The Elderly Security Guard Who Wants News from His Wife*. This hearing occurred in the counselor's chambers and involved Othman bin I., a seventy-six-year-old man who married Saodah bte. Y. some forty-five years ago and works as a security guard in Singapore. Saodah lives in Rembau, but Othman returns home regularly (and presumably provides support). Othman petitioned the *kadi*'s office to have Saodah called in so that they would be able to discuss their problems. He appeared on the specified date, but Saodah did not. The reason, according to the counselor, is that Saodah knows the *kadi* and would be embarrassed to have to interact with him.

Saodah told Othman to inform the *kadi*'s office that they have settled their differences. But Othman is not satisfied with this arrangement or with his wife's behavior in general. In fact, he is very irritated with the way things have gone, which is why he petitioned the *kadi*'s office. He "wants to know," "wants to hear from the wife herself . . . why she won't receive" him, "why she wouldn't treat or serve [him] on his recent trip home from Singapore." He comes home regularly (four times a month) and obviously considers himself a good husband. "Does Saodah have another man?" "Doesn't she like me anymore, or what?" This is what he wants to know and why he wants Saodah to file a report at the *kadi*'s office.

Comment: After the hearing was over, the counselor explained to me that she intended to call Saodah in and obtain a statement from her. She would then send the statement to Othman in Singapore. Whether this will appease Othman is uncertain. What is clear is that it is highly unusual for men to use the court to ascertain the status of their marriages. This is, in fact, the only case of this sort that I observed, though there are two other, somewhat similar cases (cases 2 and 3) that involve men who sought to have their wives called in so that they could work out their differences. In all three cases the men are quite old and appear to have relatively little clout with their wives, as evidenced by the fact that they must turn to the courts to initiate or sustain the kind of dialogue with them that they assume will eventuate in changes in their wives' behavior. Most men have enough standing with their wives to initiate such dialogue without the help of third parties.

Cases of this sort (aimed at obtaining clarification of marital status) involving female plaintiffs, on the other hand, are relatively common (see, for example, cases 15, 16, and 17). There are two reasons for this commonality and the gendered skewing thus entailed. First, as we have seen, at the time of my fieldwork in the courts it was still altogether legally acceptable for men to unilaterally divorce their wives on any grounds, anywhere they chose, whether or not their wives were present, and women, who have never had any comparable rights or prerogatives, were sometimes uncertain if such unilateral declarations of divorce had been effected. The Islamic Family Law Enactments of 1983–91 were meant to ameliorate this situation by making it an offense, punishable by a fine up to M$1,000 or imprisonment up to six months, for a man to pronounce the *talak* outside the courthouse (without the permission of the court). But the enactments have been largely ineffective, partly because the formal prohibition and (extremely sporadic) punishment of extrajudicial *talak* does not necessarily invalidate the pronunciation of *talak* or the divorce. Amendments passed in Kuala Lumpur and various states in 1994 at the urging of Muslim clerics and others opposed to key provisions of the 1983–91 laws further diluted the reformist intent of the enactments. Thus a 1996 survey conducted by the Women's Crisis Center in the state of Penang "found that the number of men who pronounced the *talak outside the court and in contravention of the law* is more than *three times* [the number of] those who applied for divorce through the court" (Mohammad Hashim Kamali 2000: 86–89; emphasis added). The more general problems were highlighted in a joint memorandum submitted to the federal government in 1997 by the National Council for Women's Organizations, the Association of Women Lawyers, and Sisters in Islam: "[F]ew other provisions in law are violated with such impunity and regularity as the divorce provisions under the Islamic Family Law statutes"; put differently, *"We are back where we started"* (cited in ibid.; emphasis added).

A second reason for the commonality at issue is that there is a centuries-old tradition of out-migration involving males, generally referred to as *merantau*— but no such tradition involving females (though this is beginning to change, especially with the establishment of Free Trade Zones and, more recently, the Multi-Media Super Corridor and the predominance there of high-tech industries seeking female labor for work in assembly lines)—and this can entail male absences of many weeks or months at a stretch. Such absences may involve men fulfilling the role of husband/father in an exemplary fashion. On the other hand, such absences may result in the complete abandonment of the role and, by definition, the abandonment of a wife and any children a couple may have. This profound ambiguity as to the meaning of husbands' absences, coupled with inequitable distribution of legal prerogatives enabling individuals to effect termination of marriage through unilateral renunciation, are largely responsible for women not always knowing their marital status and being forced to turn to the courts for clarification of this all-important issue.

If we turn to the second most common reason that men appear before the (Rembau) court as plaintiffs, we see that these are cases that involve men who seek to divorce women they have taken as their second wives after they have gotten caught in compromising circumstances involving "illicit proximity" (*khalwat*), or after they have been found guilty of adultery or rape (*zina* or *rogol*). In such cases, the *kadi* is more likely than not to discourage divorce as forcefully as possible (as we saw in cases 4 and 5). The following case is unusual in that the *kadi* is relatively supportive of the husband who petitions the court to divorce his second wife. This is, I suspect, because he approached the court in a very straightforward manner, with the complaint that he simply could not support her. The narrative is, in any event, instructive.

Case 23: *The Husband Who Seeks to Divorce His Second Wife Because He Can't Support Her.* Present at this hearing were the husband, Shaharuddin K., who is twenty-six years old, and his second wife, Zainab bte. A., also in her twenties. They were married about a year ago and have one child.

Kadi: Where do you live?
Husband: Palong 8, Jempul.
Kadi: What's there, oil palm or rubber?
Husband: Rubber.
Kadi: At Jempol how many children do you have with your *first* wife?
[The husband's answer is unclear.]
Kadi: So now what? Where is there a wife who doesn't want her husband? If her husband doesn't return for a long time, certainly the wife will be concerned or anxious.
Husband: I live there, but it's really difficult. I can't afford two wives.
Kadi: So what can be done?
Husband: I'm forced to drop one *talak*. If/when [she has good] fortune, she'll get a new one.
Wife: It's not easy for me to get a new one. . . .
Kadi: This case has been going on for a long time. We have to resolve it now. Where is your marriage certificate?
Husband: It's lost.
Wife: He's not honest [or trustworthy]. He doesn't even know when his own child was born.
Kadi: It's not that he's not honest; he just can't take all the responsibility.
Husband: I work with FELDA people.[2] The money/capital [*modal*] is other people's.
Kadi: So what about the *nafkah*?
Husband: I can't pay it all at once.
Kadi: First you pay the *nafkah edah*. How much do you want to pay monthly?
Husband: I can pay M$50 for *nafkah edah*.
Kadi: How is that gonna be enough if it's M$50 for three months and ten days? How much do you get a month?
Husband: I can pay M$75.
Kadi [to wife]: Can you do this, or not?
Wife: It's up to him. But M$75 for three months really isn't reasonable.

Husband: If she wants M$100, I can pay in installments each month.

Kadi: Okay; now let's talk about *nafkah anak*.

Husband: Can I raise the child or not?

Kadi: That's up to the chief *kadi*. At present you can't. When the child is seven, then you can petition. *Nafkah* for the child, how much are you gonna give?

Husband: The rubber [trees] can't be tapped yet. For two more years I [have to rely on] money from assistance. If M$30 a month, I can do that.

Kadi: You are going to give M$30 a month until she is married.

Wife: If it's M$30, how is that gonna be enough for food and clothes? Moreover, when the child gets bigger, M$30 won't be enough.

Husband: Give me the child; I'll raise her.

Kadi: Our requests follow what's possible. When the child is bigger, that's another story. [To wife:] If he can't afford it, how can we petition?

Wife: He trades at FELDA. He opened a coffee shop.

Kadi: Don't worry. Our side will investigate.

Wife: He's trying to run from his responsibilities.

Husband: Is it obligatory that I support this child, because she was born a month after we got married?

Wife: He wants to upset me.

Kadi: Whose child is it?

Husband: We had relations before marriage, but she also had lots of "friends." If she wants to claim, then it's fair/appropriate enough.

Kadi: We don't want you to be *tindas* [oppressed, dominated, ruled unjustly or cruelly], Shaharuddin. How much are your installments going to be from the time the child is born until now?

Husband: How much is appropriate for me to pay, Tuan?

Kadi: The child is eleven months old. If M$30 a month, then you've got to pay M$330. That's if you are able to. Make the payments through this office.

Husband: If M$30 a month, then I can't.

Kadi: It's up to you. The sum you need to pay is M$100 *nafkah edah*, M$330 *nafkah anak* for the eleven months, and M$30 *nafkah anak* for this month, i.e., M$460. You can pay however much you can afford each month, but you must clear the entire sum, regardless of how long it's outstanding. Now read this divorce certificate. But not [with] two or three [*talak*].

[The husband reads/recites the divorce formula with one *talak*.]

Kadi: How much are you gonna pay today?

Husband: M$50 for *nafkah edah*.

Kadi: That means there is another M$50, plus M$330, plus M$30, that's M$410. . . .

Comment: As noted earlier, this case is unusual in relation to others involving men seeking to sever ties with women they were forced to take as their second wives due to sexual transgressions in that the *kadi* is relatively supportive of the husband and places no obstacles in the way of his pursuing a divorce.

This may be because the husband approached the court in a seemingly sincere way, claiming that financial hardship prevented him from supporting the second wife, thus effectively acknowledging the financial responsibilities that husbands have toward their wives. Indeed, I suspect that it was largely for this reason that the *kadi* did not lecture him on his responsibilities as a husband or father and made no reference to other people being upset if he (the *kadi*) allowed a divorce (as he did in case 5). The *kadi* also appeared to accept the husband's account of his financial and other difficulties and did so in an unqualified fashion, even teaming up with him in response to challenges from the wife concerning his being irresponsible and not even knowing when his child was born. This despite the fact that the husband as much as admitted that he had been delinquent in supporting their child since the day of its birth nearly a year earlier, and was, like the wife, guilty of criminal sexual misconduct prior to (indeed, necessitating) marriage.

The husband's narrative strategy is one that we see in many earlier cases and will encounter in many others below: "I don't have the means to support my wife and child; I only do village work." But then, "Do I really need to support them? Is this obligatory, in light of the fact that the child was conceived out of wedlock [and might not even be mine]?" Also, although less common, "I will raise the child," followed by, "Can I do that?" As also in the next case, the husband's experiences in the courthouse appear to be relatively painless.

Case 24: *Rosli Registering a Divorce.* The husband, Rosli L., is about thirty-two years old; his wife, Sharifah J., is about twenty-eight.

Kadi: When did you write this letter seeking a divorce?
Husband: [About five and a half weeks ago], at home in Melaka.
Kadi: At the time you wrote it, did you either say it or state it in your heart?
Husband: In my heart I vowed that I was going to [wanted to] divorce my wife.
Kadi: Is this really true?
Husband: Yeah.
Kadi: Okay, that is the date of the pronouncement of the divorce [the *talak*] and the beginning of *edah* too.
Kadi: Fill out this divorce form.
Kadi [to wife]: Do you accept this? Gonna make a petition?
Wife: Yeah, I accept it.
Kadi: Do you have children or not?
Wife: No.
Kadi: *Nafkah edah*, what about it? [To the husband:] How much are you going to give? What is your monthly wage?
Husband: My wage is M$990 a month.
Kadi: How much does he usually give you each month?
Wife: M$100.
Kadi: *Nafkah edah* for three months and ten days. If M$100 a month, then

M$330 for the *edah*. *Muta'ah*, how much are you going to give? You've been married a year. It's up to the husband.

Husband: I am going to give M$1,000.

Kadi: When are you going to pay it?

Husband: In two or three days.

Kadi: You better think this through carefully. It's not easy to come up with M$1,000.

Husband: Yeah, I am going to give her M$1,000.

Kadi: *Nafkah edah*, when are you going to pay that?

Husband: Within the week.

Kadi: When are you coming back to this office?

Husband: Thursday.

. . . .

[The *kadi* gives the husband the divorce certificate, which he reads with one *talak*.]

Comment: As this case indicates, men's strategies and experiences effecting divorce are often quite straightforward and seemingly painless insofar as they are relatively unencumbered by formally codified legal constraints, by the inertia and frequently byzantine logic of bureaucracies, and by moral pressures and/or threats of supernatural sanctions mobilized by the *kadi* in the name of propriety, "family values," and/or Islam. This is especially so if a wife does not contest any of the key particulars of a husband's narrative and if there are no children. Note, for instance, that in the unfolding of the narrative, the first legally salient issue is whether or not, in composing his letter, the husband effectively divorced his wife and that virtually all other issues taken up by the *kadi* were phrased as relatively polite, emotionally neutral, and more or less purely informational questions addressed to the husband in such a way as to suggest that everything was at his prerogative (for example, How much *nafakh edah* are you going to give your wife? How much *muta'ah* are you going to give her? When are you going to pay it?—followed by comments to the effect, Are you sure you want to pay it so quickly?). The *kadi* also treated the *muta'ah* as a purely voluntary "gift" from husband to wife when, in fact, it is obligatory in Islamic law if the wife is divorced without fault (Ahmad Ibrahim [1965] 1975: 223–24; see also Mohammad Hashim Kamali 2000: 92–93, 226). The more general point is that it was not until I had almost completed my fieldwork in the courts that the *kadi ever* mentioned *muta'ah* as one of the forms of payment to which a Malay or other Muslim woman in Malaysia may be entitled upon divorce.[3] What's more, the *kadi* never asked the husband if he was absolutely sure that he wanted to divorce the wife or what, if anything, "was wrong with her" (or their marriage).

The husband's smooth sailing in this case is by no means uncommon, and of course the asymmetrical legal prerogatives that he enjoys vis-à-vis his wife are extended to all men in their roles as husbands. Women's experiences in the courts, in contrast, could hardly be described as smooth sailing. All of this was meant to be changed by the Islamic Family Law Enactments of 1983–91, but developments since that time, including, not least, the dilution of these enactments through amendments passed in 1994, indicate that as Horowitz has put it,[4] the equalizing thrust of the enactments may be so dissonant with respect to preexisting practice that they are perhaps most commonly honored in the breach (see also Mohammad Hashim Kamali 2000: chaps. 4 and 5).

Case 25: *The Couple Who Claimed That the Husband's* Talak *Was Not Valid Because He Was Crazy When He Pronounced It*. Present were the husband and wife, and the counselor. The basics were these: The couple had been married for about seventeen years, and the husband had pronounced a *talak* four months earlier. About a month ago, he was called to appear before the *kadi*'s office (or simply appeared) perhaps for purposes of reconciliation. (This was not clear.) More than one hundred days had passed and he had not renounced the *talak* he had pronounced. The divorce was thus in effect. He and his wife appeared now to make a case (or at least the husband's argument was) that he was "crazy" or "insane" (*gila*) when he pronounced the *talak* and that it should therefore be invalidated.

Throughout the very brief hearing the husband kept saying that he was *gila* at the time he recited the *talak*. The counselor's file was full of letters from doctors and employers (and apparently copies of prescriptions) indicating that he had indeed been ill for some time. The catch, though, was that there was no clear indication that he was *gila* at the time he pronounced the *talak*. The counselor, acting on behalf of the *kadi*, said that the *talak* was valid, as was the divorce.

Did they now want to get remarried? There seemed to be no interest in this, and there wasn't much emotion displayed at any point in the hearing, though both parties seemed embarrassed and nervous about the whole thing. The wife in particular was wringing her hands, and the husband said a few times that it was hard to talk about some of the issues the counselor raised with him. Most of the discussion, and certainly the most animated part of the hearings, concerned the settlement, for example, how much *nafkah* should be set aside for the two children (the decision was M$60). Unfortunately I did not catch all of the discussion concerning the amount of the *nafkah edah*, but I believe it was M$100.

Comment: This is one of the relatively rare instances in which a man appears before the court as part of an effort on his part to sort out potential ambiguities with respect to his marital status. We have seen that women, in contrast, routinely turn to the courts in efforts to resolve ambiguities in their marital status and, more specifically, to find out if the reason they have not heard from their husbands or received money from them is because they have been divorced. Such cases are quite different from the one considered here, for in this instance the husband knows full well that he repudiated his wife (whereas women seeking clarification often do no know whether a repudiation has occurred), and he is not financially dependent on his partner in the marriage. The legally salient issue here was simply whether the husband's being sick around the time of the pronouncement (which was never revoked) invalidated it. It did not, which is to say that it was legally binding. In the next case, too, we see some of the ways in which the arguably shortsighted utterances of men bring into being states of affairs that cannot necessarily be undone.

Case 26: *The Man Who Divorced His Pregnant Wife*. Present were the *kadi*, Araffin, and husband and wife, who were married during the previous year. Both seemed to be in their twenties; at least one of them is from Istana Raja.

The beginning of the session suggests that at least from the *kadi*'s point of view, it was the wife who initiated the hearing, for the *kadi*'s initial comments take the form of questions to the wife concerning the circumstances and wording of the divorce that her husband has pronounced, which she proceeds to relate. Her remarks include statements to the effect that a fair number of people heard her husband's pronouncement. The *kadi* then asked the husband if he agreed with or accepted her rendition of the events. He did.

Kadi: Any children?
Husband: No.
Araffin: But pregnant, right?
Husband or Wife: Ya.
Wife: A month and a half.
Kadi: Then the *edah* is ten months. . . . It is forbidden [*haram*] to divorce
    your wife while she is pregnant, but it is valid [*sah*]; and you've already
    done it. If it is already done, we try to advise, counsel. *Nafkah* [for the
    wife] through the delivery. [To husband:] What's your work?
[The husband's response is inaudible.]
Kadi: Wages?
Husband: M$400 clean [after deductions].
Kadi: *Nafkah edah*?
Husband: M$50.
[The *kadi* says something about this being quite low, followed by, "Do you
    smoke?"]
Husband: Ya.
Kadi: How much a day . . . do you spend on cigarettes?
[With the *kadi*'s help the husband calculates that he spends M$60 monthly on
    cigarettes.]
Kadi: I feel that M$50 a month [for *nafkah*] isn't enough.
Wife: Hey, that's okay. . . .
Kadi: Hey, shhh. Wait first; we'll come back to what you have to say. [Then,
    to husband:] You can't marry within this period [referring to the *edah*
    period, which extends until shortly after the birth of the child]. But you can
    reconcile during this period, at any time.

[These remarks are followed by mumblings from the husband, wife, or both,
    to the effect that they do not seek to get back together.]

Kadi [to Araffin]: So, what shall we do, Araffin?

Araffin: Add some.

Kadi: M$50 for the wife, M$50 for the child. . . . [To wife:] We'll discuss the *nafkah anak* in greater detail later, when the child is born.

The husband protests the payments. The *kadi*, in response to something the wife says (which was inaudible to me), refers to the custody of the child, indicating that he will deal with the custody issue after the child is born.

The *kadi* states that the M$100 will be garnished from the husband's wages. The wife responds by claiming that the husband also has an "outside allowance" and that his total monthly compensation may be closer to M$1,000. The husband denies this, at which point the *kadi* brings up the issue of *muta'ah*, asks the husband how much he is going to give, and goes on to explain what this payment is, using the expression *sagu hati* (money given as reparation or consolation), indicating also that it is not obligatory. The husband responds after thinking for a moment: "None."

The *kadi* proceeds to the issue of *harta sepencarian* and begins going through a list of likely possibilities: House? Land? Car? Motorcycle? Other things? The husband replies "no" to each. The *kadi* then asks if there are shares (in stock). The husband answers "no," adding something about such being forbidden (*haram*).

Kadi [in response to someone having brought up the issue of household furnishings]: Furniture, that's different; that belongs to the wife.

[The husband protests that he owned or purchased the furniture before they got married.]

Kadi: If there is no agreement on this, it will go to the chief *kadi*.

Araffin [to *kadi*]: Decide it all now, including the *nafkah anak*, then they won't have to be called again and come back.

Wife: What's important is the *nafkah edah* and the *nafkah anak*. The rest doesn't matter.

Kadi: If the child is a girl, then the *nafkah anak* is until she gets married; if it is a boy, it's until he begins working.

The conversation shifts to how soon the wife will be getting the money that will be cut from the husband's wages. It seems that it will take a while (six to ten weeks) for the order to go into effect. The husband indicates that he will take care of the intervening period and proceeds to produce M$200 for *nafkah edah* for the rest of this month and the next. The husband and wife then leave, after thanking the *kadi*. As they go out of the main room of the *kadi*'s office, the large number of relatives who accompanied them to court begin to disperse.

Comment: This case bears some similarity to case 25 in that here, too, we see the court faced with courses of action initiated by men that have consequences that cannot necessarily be undone or reversed. In this instance, the husband's actions (repudiating a pregnant wife) are forbidden by Islam but legally acceptable, as the *kadi* made clear at the outset, and the *kadi* thus tries to make the best of a bad situation. Legislation pending in Negeri Sembilan and various other states in Malaysia at the time of this hearing, which has since been brought into effect, was intended to render cases of this sort (and the one previously discussed) much less likely, insofar as the legislation forbids men from divorcing their wives outside of a *kadi*'s office (without the permission of the court). Men who fail to observe the new strictures are liable to fines and imprisonment, but obviously much depends on the enforcement of the provisions at issue. Interviews conducted in 1998 and 2001, along with previously cited surveys and other studies undertaken in the past few years (see Mohammad Hashim Kamali 2000: 86–89) indicate that the enforcement of such provisions is sporadic at best and, as noted earlier, that the formal prohibition of extrajudicial *talak* does not necessarily invalidate the *talak* or the divorce. Bear in mind also that the *kadi*'s admonition that failure to settle the case in his office will lead to his referring it to the chief *kadi* might be said to work to the husband's advantage, at least in the short term. Note in any event the husband's strategy of insisting that the payments suggested by the *kadi* are "beyond his means." This is an exceedingly common strategy, as indicated by the following cases, the first three of which involve men as defendants.

Case 27: *Woman Seeking Back* Nafkah *and Resolution of* Sepencarian *Dispute, Sent Out for Not Having Her Head Covered.* This case involved a thirty-six-year-old man and a twenty-nine-year-old woman who had gotten married twelve years earlier and had divorced four months ago. The husband remarried about a month after his divorce; the wife has apparently remarried as well. One of their four children sat on the husband's lap throughout the hearing.

When they walked into the *kadi*'s chambers, the *kadi* snapped at the wife, "Where is your scarf/head covering [*kain tudung*]?" This relatively abrupt and harsh "greeting" appeared not to phase the wife, who turned on her heels and went out to fetch a scarf, which she then wore casually across the top of her head but not with all that much attention either to how it appeared or to whether she had offended the *kadi* by coming into his chambers without proper attire.

The husband had originally approached the *kadi*'s office for a divorce on the grounds that his wife talked back and ran away from their home. Then his mother-in-law interfered, which made things worse as far as he was concerned. Some of the disagreement between husband and wife had to do with the husband's expectation that his wife help him sell *nasi lemak* (a rice dish), which involved a good deal of extra work on her part and also required her to get up very early in the morning.

The hearing at hand, however, turned on the fact that the husband had been delinquent in *nafkah* payments and owes his former wife about M$400 (which would indicate that he has not paid anything to date, since he is required to pay M$100 a month). He is in court, presumably at the wife's request, to explain his actions and "to get with the program." The *kadi* told him to pay "whatever you can each month," adding that "if you can't come up with the whole M$100, then just pay something." The husband protested that he "never goes to night clubs" and was not in a position to provide M$100 each month since he does not have any work right now and therefore has no money.

Most of the rest of the discussion focused on disputed *sepencarian* property. At issue is a house that the husband apparently bought from his former father-in-law for about M$6,000. The father-in-law seems to live there now with his daughter (and the daughter's new spouse and children?), and they claim that they have rights to the house which have not been acknowledged by the husband. The house is considered *sepencarian*; thus, half of it should go to the wife and half to the husband, but the husband does not accept this because he does not get to see his children.

The *kadi* informed him that these are altogether separate matters, adding that the value of the contested property exceeds his (M$1,000) jurisdiction and that since there is still contention on the issue, the case has to be referred to the chief *kadi* in Seremban. The husband and the wife each signed a document to the effect that no decision had been reached on the house.

Comment: This is one of a number of cases I observed in which a woman was sent out of the *kadi*'s chambers for not being appropriately attired, in the sense of not having her head properly covered. (I did not encounter any instances in which men were sent out of the *kadi*'s office for being improperly attired, even though men sometimes appeared at the courthouse in very dirty clothes and looking extremely unkempt.) Cases such as these, along with those in which the *kadi* asks women if they are pregnant, whether they are currently menstruating, when they had their last period, etc.—to say nothing of the chief rationales for the *edah* period—help illustrate that whatever else they are "about" in either a narrow, technical, or more encompassing legal or cultural sense, the discourses of the court always devote more attention to the bodies, reproductive capacities, and sexualities of women than to those of men. This is not surprising given the proliferation throughout Malaysia of competing discourses bearing on the emotionally laden and highly politicized subject of women's *aurat* (body part[s] that should not be seen or exposed according to Islamic law),[5] but it is worth emphasizing nonetheless.

Of more immediate concern here is the husband's discursive strategy in this session. Note that it does not involve refusing to acknowledge his financial, legal, or moral responsibility toward his (former) wife and their children. There is no such denial in this session—or in most of the other cases discussed in this or other chapters. His strategy is, rather, to make the by now familiar claim that he simply cannot pay the entire (M$400) sum since he has no work and thus has no money. The husband highlights these facts as well as points about his character ("I never go to night clubs") in an attempt to reframe the legally salient issues at hand and, more specifically, to suggest that it is his alleged joblessness and resultant poverty, rather than his personal character, vices, or poor showing as a husband and father, that are the real source of the financial hardships experienced by his wife and their children.

His efforts to reframe the issues before the court also involve claims concerning his wife's alleged refusal to allow him to see their children. Recall that this claim is invoked both in connection with the disputed *harta sepencarian* in the form of the house that had been purchased from his father-in-law and as part of the grounds for his refusal to recognize that his wife is entitled to half the value of the house. To appreciate the frequency of the husband's strategy in this instance, consider the following two cases.

Case 28: *Woman Seeking* Nafkah *from a Former Husband*. Present were the *kadi*, another member of his staff, the husband and wife (both of whom appeared to be in their forties), and a child about three years of age. This hearing was initiated by the wife, on the grounds that the former husband had not paid all of the *nafkah edah* and was delinquent in providing the *nafkah anak*, insisting that he had not paid any since the festivities following the end of Ramadan (Hari Raya Puasa). He was supposed to pay M$105 a month for his six children, but this sum was later reduced to M$80 a month or, if he could not afford that, "however much he could manage." The husband acknowledged that he had been delinquent, claiming in his defense that if he paid all that, then how much would there be left for him to live on?

"That isn't the point," countered the *kadi*, adding that the agreement that the husband had signed simply said, "M$80 a month or as much as you can afford to pay." "Now, you haven't honored this agreement? Why not?" In response, the husband went on and on about being broke and on the verge of declaring bankruptcy in the (secular) courts and not being able to afford the M$80. The *kadi* was extremely frustrated, indeed, exasperated, with the husband's failure to understand that if he could not come up with the entire M$80, then he could pay "as much as he could manage—that's all." But by the end of the hearing none of the issues had been resolved.

Comment: The husband's strategy in this case is much like that of the husband in the previous hearing (case 27), albeit more straightforward or streamlined in the sense that it does not involve invocation of issues bearing on his upstanding character (such as references to the fact that he "doesn't go to night clubs"); nor does it entail allegations that his wife had not allowed him to see his children or that she violated any of his other rights or otherwise behaved in a morally or legally inappropriate fashion. His strategy boils down to the simple claim that due to his poverty and impending bankruptcy, he cannot afford to pay the *nafkah edah* or the *nafkah anak* in its entirety. Though not explicitly stated as such, the other key component of his strategy involves refusing to pay anything on the grounds that he cannot pay the entire sum.

Case 29: *Claim against Yusuf P., for M$6,000 in Back* Nafkah *and* Sepencarian. This hearing occurred in the *kadi*'s chambers and involved a man named Yusuf, the *kadi*, and Araffin. Some eighteen years ago Yusuf sent his wife (who, according to court officials, was not "right in the head") back to her parents' house, but apparently he did so in such a way that it was not clear whether this was meant to be a permanent arrangement or not. Fourteen years later, Yusuf and his wife divorced. Their *harta sepencarian* included four acres of rubber land that the court decided should be split in half, with each getting two acres. The court also decreed that Yusuf owed his (former) wife about M$6,000 in back support for all the years he had not supported her.

This latter figure was arrived at with the assistance of the wife's younger brother, who helped the wife press her claim and has been to the courthouse on numerous occasions in the past few years to represent the wife's interests by insisting that Yusuf honor his part of the agreement. Apparently it is only (or primarily) because of the pressure maintained by the brother that the court has tried to get Yusuf "on the ball." The problem, in any event, is that to this day Yusuf has not divided up the land in question and has paid only a few hundred *ringgit* of the M$6,000 he owes his wife.

The hearing began with Yusuf claiming his wife wants more than he is able to pay. The *kadi*'s response was: "But you have a pension," which turned out to be around M$500 a month, "and you are engaged in trade/commerce." Yusuf replied that he has lots of debts and made oblique reference to having a child or children to support as well. The wife wants around M$200 monthly as installments on the M$5–6,000 that is owed. Yusuf testified that he cannot afford this. The *kadi* pressed the point that Yusuf should give her M$200 a month, at least until he finds someone to buy his land. This was in response to Yusuf's comment that since he does not have sufficient cash to pay his wife "the money she wants," he would sell his share of the *harta sepencarian* and give her the cash or just let her have the land. The *kadi* was not taken with this offer, partly because Yusuf has yet to actually transfer to the wife the two acres that is due her, even though, as mentioned earlier, they divorced about four years ago.

Yusuf wants to pay only M$100 a month until he can find someone to buy his land; then he will pay the balance (roughly M$5,000). But, as noted, the *kadi* was not very receptive to this, as suggested by his comment, "Look Pak-cik, it's not that I don't believe you, but you made an agreement previously, right? You promised, and what about that?"

Much of the argument before and after this turned on whether the monthly installments to the wife were going to be M$100 or M$200. At one point Yusuf claimed in his defense that he has children (not simply one child) to support and is not involved in trade/business anymore. "Please help us," implored the *kadi*, who proceeded to reiterate the previous agreement, about which nothing had been done. It merits emphasis that in the original agreement between Yusuf and the *kadi*, Yusuf agreed to pay M$5,000 cash.

The compromise, such as it was, was to give Yusuf three weeks' time to have the names changed on his four-acre rubber grant. He promised to bring in the updated grant within that period, and the new deal worked out was that he would transfer three acres to his wife and the remaining one acre would go to his child (presumably the child from their marriage). This meant that the wife would get one acre more than what the original agreement called for, this being in lieu of the large sum of cash Yusuf owes her. Araffin offered to help Yusuf with some of the red tape at the District Land Office since Yusuf does not want to have anything to do with the wife.

At the end of the hearing the *kadi* asked forgiveness (*maaf*) from Yusuf for speaking rather roughly at times, this type of apology (to men) being quite common. Yusuf did the same and each of them assured the other that nothing the other had said was offensive or in any way out of line.

Comment: Araffin later told me that this case may go to the secular court, apparently because of the value of the property at issue. Two themes of additional interest merit brief comment. The first is the involvement of a sibling (the wife's younger brother) in the proceedings; such involvement is an exception proving the rule, but only a partial exception since the wife "isn't right in the head" and presumably cannot represent herself. The second is the very common male strategy that involves claiming, "I can't pay" and stalling for time. To view such matters in broader perspective, let us turn to summary comments on men's strategies and experiences, particularly in relation to those of women.

Commentary on Men's Strategies and Experiences

In Rembau and elsewhere in Malaysia most male litigants who deal with the Islamic courts do so as *defendants*. They are called in or formally summoned to the courts on the basis of formal requests or complaints made by their current or former wives, usually on the grounds that they have failed to support their wives and children in a fashion consistent with the entailments of the marriage contract (*akad nikah*). In some cases, wives' petitions seek only financial support; in others, wives seek both support and divorce. Another category of cases involving men as defendants centers on wives' requests to have their marital status clarified. In some of these cases, the ambiguity of a woman's marital status is deepened by the passage of a period of months in which husbands have had no physical, visual, or other contact with their wives and children and have failed to provide them with financial support. As one might expect, this liminality leads women to wonder if they have been divorced (or simply abandoned), and it sometimes results in women taking their concerns to the *kadi*'s office for resolution of the ambiguity at issue.

One of the most common strategies that male defendants deploy involves stalling and waiting out their (current or former) wives and the courts. Men invoke this strategy partly because as defendants, they usually have no strong incentive or desire to participate in, let alone expedite, proceedings and partly because they seem to know (from their own prior experience, that of friends or relatives, or hearsay) that there are typically few if any sanctions deployed by the courts to discourage such behavior.[6] Indeed, they can—and frequently do—miss the hearings that they are asked or formally instructed (via summons) to attend, doing so with little fear that serious sanctions will be imposed on them as a consequence of their behavior. It should be added that in cases such as

these, the informal sanctions of community gossip and censure are not necessarily all that effective either, especially since many male defendants no longer
reside with their wives, nor even necessarily in their wives' communities or
their natal villages.

Another strategy deployed by men to stay out of court and/or to get their
(current or former) wives to discontinue proceedings involves paying them
"drop-in visits," during which time they ply them with what they hope will be
persuasive arguments and "gifts" (of some of the money they owe them) geared
toward "softening them up." This is what happened in case 13 and would appear to be a common strategy, given that Araffin warned Suzaini that this would
occur, admonished her not to accept any money from her ex-husband if he did
show up, and otherwise informed her precisely how to deal with an eventuality
of this sort.

When men are unsuccessful in avoiding court appearances and are ordered
by the *kadi* to pay back support or to provide their (current or former) wives
with other money, they can and in many cases do respond with "I can't; I do
village work." Such responses entail at least tacit recognition on the part of the
men that they *do* have responsibilities to their wives and children and that they
have been delinquent in fulfilling them, just as their wives claim. There is, in
other words, no contesting the nature of such responsibilities. Be that as it may,
such references to "village work"—which is a catchall term for tapping rubber,
digging trenches or graves, cutting down trees, fetching coconuts, selling fish,
and other types of casual or intermittent labor—are something of a deal breaker
for the *kadi*. This is because there is really no way of knowing how much
money a man (or woman) makes if they are involved in such labor. This kind of
work is often seasonal and in any event highly uneven and unreliable; and,
needless to say, it is not necessarily all that remunerative. The *kadi*'s option to
garnish wages, which he sometimes exercises if the husband has a wage that
can be garnished, is simply not available for most of the men who appear
before the court. Men know this and often behave accordingly.

Other strategies of male litigants involve efforts to reframe what is at issue,
as when a husband contends that his wife "doesn't pray regularly," "doesn't fast
regularly," "drinks beer," or "goes out without permission" (for example, cases
2, 3, 9, 31). Such allegations are grave as far as the courts are concerned (far
more so than contentions along the lines of, "My wife won't let me see our
children"), for they suggest an individual who is in some sense beyond the pale.
Charges concerning the consumption of alcohol, failure to pray on a regular
basis, or failure to fast during Ramadan are taken as all the more serious and
threatening in the multiethnic, extremely "race conscious" context of Malaysia,
where Islam is a key symbol of Malayness and where any failure to uphold
Islam is liable to be viewed as "letting down the side." In this setting it is
especially significant that a Malay (or other Muslim) divorcée's failure to maintain a proper Muslim home environment, as evidenced, for instance, by her
marrying a non-Muslim, is clear grounds for her losing custody of her children.

When male litigants (especially defendants) feel that hearings are not going as they wish, they sometimes threaten—or otherwise make explicit reference to the possibility—that they may take their case elsewhere (to a *kadi* in another district) to effect a more favorable outcome (for example, case 5). This strategy resonates with the greater geographic and overall spatial and social mobility of men as compared with that of women and with the fact that compared to women, men have much more experience—and are clearly far more comfortable—dealing with various types of functionaries and officials (the vast majority of whom are male). It is noteworthy, however, that women sometimes pursue or mention the desirability of a strategy of this general sort as well, or at least make allusion to the "downside" of not doing so (for example, cases 13 and 22). What we see in these latter instances and considerations of "forum-shopping," however, are not concerns with effecting more favorable outcomes but rather hopes of avoiding the personal embarrassment and shame (*malu*) of having to deal with officials they have encountered during previous hearings or know from other contexts. The motivations for forum-shopping are thus heavily inflected by gender or, to be more precise, by the gendered differentials of power and prestige entailed in local hierarchies of virtue and value.[7]

Men's strategies and experiences as *plaintiffs* are, as one might expect, somewhat different from those involving men as defendants, though there is also a considerable degree of overlap or congruence. One reason for the convergence is that the majority of male plaintiffs are in court both to pursue divorce and to effect "damage control" with respect to their wives' accusations and financial claims; another is that over a quarter (27.27 percent) of the male plaintiffs pursuing divorce are seeking to terminate relationships with women they took as second wives in forced marriages that were effected due to compromising circumstances (illicit proximity, adultery, or rape leading to pregnancy). The strategies of male plaintiffs in these cases involve claims that they cannot support their (second) wives and are thus similar to many of the strategies encountered among male defendants. A more general observation to register here is that the narratives and overall strategies of male litigants feed into ("practical") discourses that portray men, especially men in their roles as husbands and fathers, in a strongly negative light.

PATTERNS OF RESISTANCE AND OPPOSITIONAL DISCOURSES

The material presented in previous sections of the chapter raises intriguing comparative and theoretical questions concerning patterns of resistance, oppositional discourses, and a host of related issues. This despite the fact that the data presented thus far, especially the explicit content of the seventeen dispute narratives making up the basis of the first two sections of the chapter, do not contain much in the way of elaborated or even incipient or embryonic discourse of the sort that might be termed oppositional and might not appear at first glance to be implicated in patterns of resistance bearing on kinship/gender, marriage, the state, the Islamic resurgence, or anything else. To better appreciate how these narratives and the actions to which they are keyed are relevant to the broader themes at issue here, let us consider two other cases in which patterns of (female) resistance might be said to be more clear-cut.

Case 30: *The Husband Who Pronounced a Divorce That His Wife Did Not Hear*. Present were the husband and wife (Zaleha from Kota), both of whom look to be in their fifties, the *kadi*, and Araffin.

The *kadi* begins by asking the husband a series of questions: "How long have you been married?" "Your village?" "Any children?" "Is s/he already married?" "[Your] work?" and finally, "So what's wrong with Auntie?" The husband answers all but the last question. On the subject of "what's wrong with Auntie" he testifies only that he pronounced a *talak* in front of her about nine days earlier. The wife interjects that she did not hear it, to which the husband responds, "I said it in front of her." The wife reiterates her contention, adding that she first learned of the divorce from people in the village who approached her with comments and questions like, "So, you're divorced; what's it all about?"

The *kadi* proceeds to underscore to both the husband and his wife that the husband swears he pronounced a *talak*; the wife counters with a reference to the fact that her husband subsequently "approached her," but I did not hear the specifics, only that he apparently wanted her to come to the town of Rembau with him. The *kadi* explains to both of them that husbands sometimes refuse to acknowledge that they have uttered a repudiation, but this is a case where the husband insists he did in fact do so. The *kadi*'s next question, which he addresses more to the husband than to the wife, is: "So, do you want to reconcile?" to which he adds something like, "It is best if you get back together." The husband seems uninterested in reconciling, but the wife does not appear averse to the idea.

"Excuse me, Auntie, are you menstruating?" asks the *kadi*. After she replies in the negative, the *kadi* continues, "Okay, then your *edah* period is three months and ten days. *Muta'ah* is M$100." (This seems to have been discussed by the husband and someone at the *kadi*'s office ahead of time.) *Nafkah edah* is as follows: M$100 for the first month; M$100 for the second month; M$100 for the third month. There is a reference to the *muta'ah* and the *nafkah edah* adding up to M$500 (perhaps because the husband is going to give his wife a full M$100 for the remaining ten days of the *edah* period that is left over after the three months). The wife indicates that she is not going to claim anything (else?): "If he wants to give, fine; . . . it's up to him."

The husband testifies that he will pay what he owes in installments of M$100 a month. The *kadi* then says, more or less out of the blue, that there were no witnesses to the husband's pronouncement but that the husband swore (*buat ikrar*) that he did it. The *kadi* does not add that witnesses are not necessary in such a case; nor does he come right out and state that if a husband says, "I divorce you," then it does not matter if anyone hears it; it is valid. He then figures the exact date until the end of the wife's *edah* and tells her that at that point she can come and pick up her divorce certificate. After she indicates that she is not eager to come back and get it herself, the *kadi* tells her, "Nobody else can come and pick it up for you . . . and you can't have it sent to you either. . . . If you don't come and get it, that's okay too; we will just keep it for you. . . . You may need it later."

At this juncture the *kadi* turns to the husband and remarks, "We give the husband an *edah* period, too. You can't pick up the divorce certificate before the 100 days. What if you marry in the meantime and then decide to reconcile with your wife? . . . This is just an example, but [you can see] there are problems with this. . . . We don't want lots of divorce."

The wife is not very enthusiastic about coming to get the money the husband will be forwarding to the *kadi*'s office on her behalf. She requests that the *kadi* give it to the *imam* of Gadong, who is her uncle. The *kadi* replies, "Okay, thanks," indicating that the hearing is over. The husband shakes the *kadi*'s hand and goes out, and the others leave.

Comment: In this case the wife is either resisting acknowledging that her husband repudiated her in her presence or resisting recognizing as true what her neighbors have told her: that her husband repudiated her in a setting in which she was not present. Regardless of what the wife knew or believed before coming to court, this case shows the limits of resistance; either way, the wife is repudiated (divorced). On the other hand, if her intent was merely to force the husband to appear in court, to have him deal with her directly and publicly, then clearly she has been successful, but not, however, if her hope was also that in this context he might revoke the repudation and reconcile with her; as we saw, this did not happen.

There are, then, limits to resistance. There is only so much women can and do resist, and when they push or transgress these limits their behavior can backfire in the sense of incurring potentially serious repercussions. Such is clear from the following case.

Case 31: *Aisha and Her Husband Seeking a Divorce after Thirteen Months of Marriage Because They Don't Get Along ("The Wife Won't Work, Drinks Alcohol," Etc.).* The hearing in this case involved a husband and wife (Aisha), both in their early twenties, recently married, with no children. (The wife was accompanied to the courthouse by her father, but he remained outside of the counselor's chambers for the entire session.)

The husband is from Kelantan and works in a lumber factory; the wife is from Rembau and "doesn't work." They live in a rented house and claim that they "don't get along anymore" (*tak sesuai lagi*). Apparently it was a joint decision to come to the *kadi*'s office, but it seems to have been precipitated by the wife's running away once again from the husband. (The wife petitioned at the *kadi*'s office five or six months earlier, but I have no specific information about that petition.)

The story of their meeting was quite bizarre and was one of the first issues the counselor explored after she ascertained that their marriage had been based on mutual attraction (*suka sama suka*) rather than the choice of elders. The wife recounted that she had been working as a salesgirl in a shopping plaza in Kuala Lumpur when four men—Indonesians, she made clear—approached her, asking for directions. They offered her a ride in their car, she got in, and they proceeded to hold her against her will and take her to the state of Pahang. For at least a week they kept her locked in a house and made her cook and clean for them. (I heard no reference to anything sexual, but I may have missed something.) The husband-to-be somehow heard of this, seemingly because he knew (or knew of) one of the Indonesian men who was holding her, and he rescued her from her captors. It was on this basis that they came to know and like each other.

As for the specifics of the problems they are experiencing as husband and wife: their troubles started right after they got married. The husband claimed that the wife "always runs away" (at least "six times now"), "always steals [his] money, and won't cook or wash clothes." And on at least one occasion he caught her drinking alcohol.

The wife denied that she does not cook or wash clothes, maintaining that sometimes she is simply slow getting these things done, partly because of illness that makes it difficult for her to endure contact with the cold water used to wash clothes early in the morning. As for cooking, she testified that she always cooks but is sometimes late, and that cooking and related tasks are made more difficult because the husband does not always give her oil and cooking supplies.

The wife did not gainsay running away from her husband; nor did she refute charges about taking his money. She insisted, however, that she does not steal money from him anymore. She added that the reason she runs away and can no longer stand him is that he hits (*pukul*) her. The husband, when questioned about this, admitted hitting her, "But it was because she drank liquor."

The counselor was shocked to hear about the drinking; the wife protested lamely that it was "only a tin of Shandy" (a type of "soft drink" that contains alcohol). The husband mentioned that he found her drinking at about 8:00 A.M., thus contributing to the bleak picture that both of them painted. The more general point is that the wife was extremely sultry, surly, and crass in her dealings with her husband, particularly in the counselor's office. She was reprimanded for this by the counselor (who commented on it to me later as well).

On the subject of hitting the wife, the counselor advised them that this was serious, but went on to say that it is permissable under certain circumstances, adding that there are three ways a husband can teach his wife: by giving her advice; by letting or making her sleep by herself, to remind her what it would be like if she were on her own; and if the other alternatives have failed, by hitting her, albeit not as a form of punishment or fine (*denda*), but "as one would hit a child, to teach her."

The counselor was also visibly shocked by the way the wife treated the husband and the way she behaved more generally. She lectured the wife on how it was wrong, against Islamic law, for a woman to go out of the house without the husband's permission. Interestingly, the counselor also asked the wife how many brothers and sisters she had and where she was in the birth order. This is a very frequent question in such cases. (She later told me that the wife's behavior is somewhat understandable in light of the fact that she is the fifth of six children and is thus quite spoiled.)

Toward the end of the session, the counselor inquired of them, "So, at this point, what?" The wife answered that she does not want the husband anymore, and the husband replied, "Okay, I will go along with that." The counselor then informed them, "This goes to the *kadi*," and after they signed the statements she had been preparing all the while, she told them to wait outside; they could see the *kadi* as soon as he was available.

After sitting outside the *kadi*'s office for a bit, the husband and wife went in, as did Araffin and the counselor. The *kadi* quickly read over the written statements prepared by the counselor and asked them to reiterate some basic background information. The husband testified that they previously lived with his mother-in-law but that they did not get along so now they rented a house. He also maintained, in response to the *kadi*'s questions on the subject, that he had only hit his wife "three times." The *kadi* then launched into a brief exhortation to the effect that men should not hit their wives, that he "has been all over Malaysia, India, and Egypt, and this should not be done."

The husband claimed in his defense that there had been a reason: his wife drank! The *kadi* was flabbergasted when he heard this, despite the fact that the wife added lamely in her defense (as she had done earlier with the counselor) that "it was only Shandy."

"Do you want to kill yourself? This will surely mean you'll go to hell. Do you pray?" "Before I worked," she replied, the *kadi* responding with something like, "Oh, I see; I thought so."

The *kadi* told her she had a very narrow mind (*akal sempit*). He was clearly annoyed with her, perhaps particularly with her tone and overall attitude. His own tone was rather intimidating and highly dramatic, and I couldn't help but feel that he was very conscious of the fact that he was berating and intimidating her. The *kadi* also reprimanded her for using Kelantan dialect, informing her that he wouldn't know what some of the things she said meant if he had not spent time there. He was also infuriated at the wife's tendency to mutter under her breath and at the way she kept insulting the husband and arguing with points he brought up. At one point he pounded the table and shouted at her to be silent (*diam*).

The *kadi* then asked the husband, "So, there is no other way to resolve your problems?" The husband said no. At about this time the wife inserted that the husband's elder sister interfered in their affairs; this brought a disclaimer from the husband who insisted that she had not meddled but had simply come to their house to look in on them. The wife lamented that there was no hope because even if they get back together, her husband would hit her. She did, after all, petition at the court, and of course "he will be upset with . . . that."

At this stage the *kadi* remarked that the wife's behavior was very inappropriate especially in that her name, Aisha, is the same as the wife of the Prophet. Shortly thereafter, on behalf of the *kadi*, Araffin instructed the husband to recite a statement that included the words, "with a sincere heart and without being subject to force, I hereby divorce my wife with one *talak*." He did so and proceeded to sign the statement, at which point the *kadi* sought and obtained confirmation from the wife that she accepted the divorce.

It was then decided that the total for *nafkah edah* would be M$200, a figure arrived at without much apparent thought by the husband in response to the *kadi*'s query on the matter. The husband's initial offer of M$200 appeared to be an offer of M$200 per month, but perhaps because the *kadi* responded with amazement ("M$200 a month!?"), the husband seemed to realize that this sum would be acceptable for the *edah* period in its entirety. When the wife was asked if she wanted more, she said no and her husband handed her M$200.

It had already been established that there was no *harta sepencarian*, but the *kadi* raised some additional questions on the topic: "Did you buy anything . . . a motorcycle, a bicycle?" "No." The *kadi* followed up with a series of questions, directed at the wife in particular, "Not even any clothes or shirts?" To which the wife replied, "Yes, four or five." The *kadi* then suggested that she make explicit her claims to such property, but she elected not to do so and the hearing drew to a close.

Comment: This is an especially intriguing narrative. It is also broadly allegorical, though not intended as such: the young Aisha who, as the *kadi* pointed out, shares the name of the wife of the Prophet, working as a salesgirl in a shopping complex in Kuala Lumpur, the epicenter of consumerism, vice, foreign dangers, and transgression of all kinds. Aisha is abducted by foreign (Indonesian, hence most likely Muslim) men, taken as a captive on a distant journey, and forced into domestic servitude and "illicit proximity" though not necessarily subjected to sexual assault in the Western sense of the term. She is then rescued from her plight of foreign evil, domestic servitude, and enforced moral transgression by a young Malay man who is a few years her senior and who therefore stands to her as older brother (*abang*). Recall that women use the latter term (*abang*) to refer to and address their husbands, the more germane point being that it is on this elder brother/younger sister relationship that the marriage tie is modeled. Like so many other *abang*, however, while this one offers protection that he does in fact deliver in the short term, his promises are short-lived. Worse, in his comportment we see an inversion of the ideal of the elder brother, inasmuch as he takes no heed of Aisha's physical infirmities and moral wavering (represented in her consumption of alcohol) and otherwise fails to empathize with her ailments. He does, moreover, strike her, fail to provide adequately for her, etc. More generally, we see in Aisha's husband an allegory of men as good or potentially good brothers who become husbands but not fathers (there is no reproduction here), but turn out to be bad husbands not only because of the nonreproduction at issue but also and more important because they thoroughly flaunt or violate *abang* ideals.

As the narrative progresses, Aisha's persona evolves from a variation on the theme of "damsel in distress" to one of evil woman(hood): someone who consumes alcohol, fails to pray, and is otherwise morally bankrupt, though perhaps "fallen" largely as a result of being victimized by her environment. Such is the nightmare of all Malay families whose daughters go off to nearby towns and distant cities to work, though it should be added that responsibility for preventing the realization of the nightmare, and anything short of it, falls on the men of the household and on brothers most heavily.

This moral slide becomes all the more laden with deeply disjunctive and otherwise disturbing symbolism when one recalls, as the *kadi* no doubt did, that Aisha was not simply one of the Prophet's wives, but was also very attractive sexually and was, after the death of his first wife Khadija, his "undisputed favorite" (Ahmed 1992: 51). Historians of the origins and development of Islam note that the Prophet Muhammad treated Aisha with "tender care and patience,"[8] that she was "acknowledged to have special knowledge of the Prophet's ways, sayings, and character," and that she not only rendered decisions on sacred laws and customs but is also credited with transmitting "some 2,210 *hadith* to early Muslim traditionalists."[9] Last but by no means least, even though Aisha was suspected of infidelity and found herself at the center of a storm of scandal and controversy in the early Muslim community, the Prophet was buried beneath her room, "which is now, after the Ka'aba, the most sacred spot in Islam."[10]

Much more could be said about the relationship between the young Aisha before the *kadi* and the historical Aisha, who also lived in an age of profound transition, but we shall proceed to a brief summary of what is contested or resisted in this case and what is not. In terms of what is contested or resisted: Consider, first, that Aisha has run away from her husband on various occasions; has stolen his money; and has talked back to him—all of which she basically acknowledged—and that during the hearing she was especially sultry, surly, and crass to him and to all of the court officials with whom she interacted. In some ways far worse, she occasionally consumes alcohol and is given to neglecting her daily prayers, both of which are serious offenses in Islam. That she spoke to the *kadi* in Kelantanese dialect rather than something more akin to standard Malay might also be seen as an act of resistance. Of greater analytic significance is that this latter form of resistance (if it be deemed such) earned her a reproach from the *kadi* in much the same fashion as did her muttering under her breath throughout the hearing, her tacit refusal to acknowledge the solemnity of the hearing or the practice of speaking in turns, and her refusal to let the *kadi* decide who should speak when. More broadly, judging from the way court personnel responded to her (their lack of empathy, their annoyance, the *kadi*'s pounding on his desk and demanding that she be quiet), all such behavior on Aisha's part seems to have backfired—as did her running away from her husband and leaving him to sleep by himself—and is thus indicative of the numerous ways in which resistance can be self-defeating (see Willis 1977; Scott 1985, 1990).

As for what is not contested or resisted: Note that marriage itself is not resisted; nowhere in the hearing, for example, did Aisha state anything like, "I don't want—or need—to be married." Nor, for that matter, were any sentiments along these general lines expressed even implicitly by any of the other female (or male) litigants in cases discussed thus far.[11] (The one, partial exception is case 20.) I should also underscore that neither in this case nor in others examined here do we see any evidence of female litigants articulating discourses that are critical of the legal, religious, and cultural systems that accord men certain legal prerogatives denied to women.[12]

A more general theme that emerges when Aisha's (statistically extreme) actions are viewed in relation to the behavior of women in other marriage and divorce cases we have considered, and in relation to data bearing on other domains of Malay society, is that in most social and cultural contexts, there is relatively little behavior on the part of women that might be termed resistance, let alone actual rebellion.[13] Women occasionally mock and criticize their husbands (and sons-in-law) behind their backs and to their faces, though not men in other kinship or social roles. Such mocking and criticism is usually done in a relatively good-natured way, though it is often peppered with biting sarcasm and black humor. And women sometimes intentionally embarrass their husbands in public or flee from their households, which also causes their husbands public embarrassment, to protest what they regard as extremely inappropriate behavior (such as taking a second wife).

Unlike what one finds in some other societies such as Morocco (Dwyer 1978), however, women rarely steal money, valuables, or other items (rice, other food) from their husbands or the household larders. (Aisha is one of the exceptions that proves the rule.) They don't really need to engage in such behavior since they control the household larders and administer family finances. The "bad-mouthing" of men to young children is also relatively rare, to the best of my (and Ellen's) knowledge, though I have heard Suzaini make scathing remarks in front of her youngest daughter about her second husband (the girl's father). Significantly, however, these diatribes were confined to the shortcomings of the second husband and were not generalized to other men or men as a whole. Forms of resistance that involve "talking back," refusing to speak, and/ or "withholding sex" occur as well (as in case 32 [below]) but are exceedingly difficult to characterize in terms of frequency.

One of the major arenas in which women resist official representations of femininity (and masculinity) is the *kadi*'s office. Such resistance occurs in myriad ways, the most overt of which involves direct verbal challenging of husbands and the heaping upon them of insults and other forms of verbal abuse (calling them liars, animals, etc., as in case 21). One might assume that the *kadi*'s office is relatively unreceptive to such forms of resistance, but this is not really the case or, in any event, is only partly true. The *kadi* and his staff, including especially the counselor, operate with many of the same assumptions about male and female livers, temperaments, personalities, and overall "natures" as do villagers themselves. In Rembau and elsewhere in Malaysia (Ong

1987: 131–32), such officials do, moreover, feel that most of the problems in marriage and much of the "fault" in divorce stem from men who are delinquent in their roles as husbands and fathers. Thus, many women find the relatively formal environment of the *kadi*'s office initially intimidating and otherwise off-putting, but once they begin talking with the magistrate's staff they tend both to overcome many of their inhibitions and to speak and behave in ways that indicate they are relatively free of the linguistic and other constraints that normally bear upon women (and to a lesser degree men).

The catch, of course, is that women's relatively unrestrained behavior in these (and other) contexts can easily reinforce official discourses that portray them as having more "passion" and less "reason" than men. In other words, the very recounting of narratives of male irresponsibility and female virtue sometimes conveys messages diametrically opposed to those encoded in the "contents" of the narratives in question and are, in any event, the opposite of those intended. Phrased in broader terms, female resistance of this sort, including what we saw in Aisha's case, sometimes entails what Denys Turner (1983) refers to as "performative contradictions" inasmuch as it bolsters and helps reproduce the conceptual and other legitimizing structures that undergird the gendered distribution of power and prestige in the first place (cf. Merry 1990; Hirsch 1998). The same is true of female predominance in spirit possession (*kena hantu*), which has been interpreted by some observers (Ong 1987, 1988) as forms of resistance to one or another form of men's control over women. Indeed, the predominance of spirit possession among women is frequently cited by men and women alike as evidence both of women's weaker "life force" (*semangat*) and overall spiritual nature and of their greater "passion" relative to men. These gendered differences, in turn, are typically cited as the reasons why women cannot become mosque leaders or assume other prerogatives normally restricted to men (Peletz 1996).

As for resistance on the part of men, we mentioned earlier that this too can involve performative contradictions. Note first, though, that it is not altogether apparent exactly what men are resisting when they fail to honor the contractual obligations of marriage or behave in other ways that lead their wives to press claims against them in court. Nor is it easy to determine what they are resisting when, once they are involved with the courts, they engage in foot-dragging tactics or otherwise effectively short-circuit or subvert the workings of "the system." They could of course be resisting specific claims made by or in the names of their wives, children, or in-laws; certain explicit or implicit entailments of marriage, kinship, or gender; the reach of the state; Islamic law or the resurgence of Islam (both of which are obviously heavily implicated in all of this); or some combination of these. Two points are nonetheless abundantly clear. First, such resistance (assuming that is the right term for the behaviors in question) fuels counterhegemonic discourses bearing on masculinity and gender generally. Second, these discourses not only subvert the official line on male "reason" and virtue and effectively promote views of women as the more reasonable and responsible of the two genders, but they also encourage administrative reform and the disciplinary nexus of the state gaze directed at men and, to a lesser extent, the population at large.

We should also bear in mind that there is little if any evidence that men are resisting those aspects of the definition of marriage that specify that men should support their wives; that fidelity in the context of monogamous unions (or polygynous ones) is or should be the norm; or that marriage involves a heavily contractual relationship between husband and wife. And there is no evidence indicating that men are resisting the implicit ideology underlying all of this: that conjugal bonds and parent-child relationships are encrusted primarily with— and are in this sense mainly "about"—duties, not rights.

I remarked earlier that one of the major unintended consequences of men's resistance is that it fuels counterhegemonic discourses on masculinity emphasizing that men are neither reasonable nor responsible. It remains to underscore that the latter discourses are highly elaborated and quite pervasive in many contexts and more encompassing domains of daily life *outside* the court, especially among women but also among men (see Peletz 1996), though they are also clearly present in the court itself. That men come off rather badly in the Islamic courts should not be surprising when we recall that in Rembau, in the states of Selangor and Kedah, and throughout Malaysia, the vast majority of the cases that are aired are brought by female plaintiffs on the grounds that their husbands have disappeared or otherwise abandoned them, have failed to provide them and their children with adequate support, have taken up with other women, and/or have left them in the dark as to whether or not they are still married. Remember, too, that a significant percentage of cases initiated by male plaintiffs involve men who seek to divorce women they have taken as their second wives because they were forced to do so in order to avoid prosecution and punishment for criminal transgressions such as illicit proximity, adultery, rape, etc. It is also important to recall that although court staff do not believe all claims made by female litigants, and frequently do not even try to establish "what really occurred" or even "what might have happened," they are clearly of the opinion that most of the problems experienced by married or formerly married couples are due to the behavior of men and, similarly, that men are responsible for most of the lying that occurs in their offices. Opinions of the latter sort (that men are more inclined than women both to dishonesty and to criminality) are also articulated by officials in Malaysia's secular legal system, including those who hold the highest positions in the land, as illustrated by the observation from Tun Mohamed Suffian, former Lord President of Malaysia, that serves as the first epigraph to this chapter.

In light of this situation it should not be surprising to find that many of the reforms in Islamic law and its administration that have been advocated and legislated into existence since the early 1980s have been geared primarily toward better policing and otherwise controlling the behavior of men (not women). Clear evidence of this appears not only in the prohibition on men effecting extrajudicial divorce and in the increased restrictions on polygyny, but also in the introduction of beefed-up fines and other penalties for the violations of Islamic law that are characteristically (though not necessarily exclusively) male, such as marrying under false pretenses, failing to provide *nafkah*, etc.

The idea that the Islamic courthouse, which is in many respects a core symbol of men's legal privileges and social and cultural preogatives vis-à-vis women, is simultaneously a key site in the production of counterhegemonic—and clearly disparaging—discourses concerning husbands, fathers, and masculinity in general is nicely summed up in the memorable comments of my aunt that I included as the second epigraph to this chapter ("Men, they all lie; that's what you see all the time at the *kadi*'s office"). Before discussing this perspective in greater detail, I might emphasize that Islamic courthouses are not the only symbols of male privilege implicated in the production of counterhegemonic discourses on masculinity and gender. So, too, are mosques. Villagers view the underlying rationale for the segregation of men and women during mosque services not in terms of the need to keep women apart from men in light of women's alleged capacity (especially if they are menstruating) to pollute men but as an effort to render men less susceptible to distractions that would interfere with and undermine their concentration and prayer. What is highlighted in these interpretations, in other words, is not female pollution or anything else about women that is enshrined in official discourse on gender differences but men's weaknesses and shortcomings.

My aunt's comments (that all men lie) speak volumes, but I will confine my remarks on them to a few key issues. Note, first, that she is referring to men as a whole, not simply to men in their roles as husbands or fathers, though she is of course generalizing, however unconsciously, on the basis of men's performance in these latter roles. Bear in mind also that these comments came up in an interview dealing with gender in response to questions I had raised about the similarities and differences between males and females (masculinity and femininity), not men and women in one or another kinship role. In this she is quite typical: Malays in Negeri Sembilan and elsewhere in the Peninsula, when asked to talk about men, maleness, and masculinity, commonly respond with specific reference to men in their roles as husbands or fathers. Imagery bearing on these roles, as opposed to the roles of brother, son, etc., is thus hegemonic with respect to local understandings of masculinity, though the role dimensions of such generalizations are not marked in local discourses. Also unmarked in local discourses and in those of the courts and the state generally is the fact that characterizations concerning men as a whole are made on the basis of the behavior of husbands and fathers who are situated at the bottom of the social class hierarchy.

Further complicating the picture presented here is that adult men do come off quite well in relation to women—in the sense of appearing to be benevolent, self-sacrificing, and the like—in other legal arenas, including arenas in which Islamic laws, concerning inheritance, for example, are paramount. The arenas in question, however, are found in the secular courts that deal with inheritance and other transactions of rights over "Islamic land" (*tanah faraidh*) and land that is formally endorsed as "customary" (*tanah pesaka*) or simply treated as such.

These courts are housed in the District (Land) Office (Pejabat [Tanah] Daerah), which in the case of Rembau is all the way across town from the Islamic court and the (secular) Magistrate's Court. The formal and in some respects relatively extreme administrative separation of these legal domains, which dates from the colonial era, and at least in local terms the considerable physical distance separating them sometimes works against the local intermingling of discourses of a narrowly legal nature, concerning, for example, the "Islamic fractions" into which land is to be divided. (Recall that officials associated with the Islamic courts complain that they are rarely consulted on such matters.) Similarly, but more relevant here, the administrative "domaining" effecting these distinctions and boundaries also reduces the likelihood of (but does not altogether preclude) the intermingling of discourses on gender, at least at the local level. Specifically, it decreases the chances that the relatively positive view of men in their roles as brothers and, by extension, sons (since in the Malay context being a good son [or daughter] means first and foremost being a good sibling), will rub up against and thus temper, undercut, or mute the largely negative views of men in their roles as husband/father that are produced in the Islamic courts.

Three points that are central to this study follow: state domaining is key to the types of discourses produced in the Islamic courts; an understanding of the culture of the Islamic courts thus requires that we take into account political economy (of colonial-era and postcolonial political and administrative policies, for example); and assessments of the social and cultural significance of the discourses produced within Islamic and other courts fully requires that our analytic gaze focus on but also range far beyond specifically legal arenas.

It remains to consider how and why men "come off well" in the District (Land) Office. Much of the reason has to do with the fact that dealings in these offices tend to focus on matters of inheritance involving intestate land and that men appear there in their roles as sons and brothers or clan spokesmen, not as husbands or fathers or as men in other kinship or social roles. One of the jobs of the hearing examiner, an official of the eminently secular Land and Mines Department, is to decide how to parcel up the intestate property of the deceased among survivors, who are usually adult children. The hearing examiner typically explains the Islamic "rule of thumb" that sons are entitled to receive twice the size or value of the shares allotted to daughters after prefatory remarks to the effect that, "We are all Muslims, right?" This is followed by brief informal caucusing on the part of the survivors, a common outcome of which is that sons forgo their claims to the land (or other property in question) in deference to their sisters.

The complex nexus of reasons why sons often forgo their claims in favor of their sisters need not detain us here (see Peletz 1996), though some of it has to do with the perception that females are more in need of subsistence guarantees than males for the simple reason that they are less adaptable than men (who can eke out a living in most any circumstance, as the argument goes) and may also be left in the lurch by husbands who have divorced or deserted them. To assert rights over land that could go to sisters in such a context is an inversion of proper (elder) brotherly behavior, particularly since, as the worst-case scenario has it, women without subsistence guarantees in the form of land may be forced into prostitution to support themselves and their children. According to villagers I have spoken with and many Malay writers (Jones 1994: 234–36), this is a common occurrence in the state of Kelantan because women there (and in other parts of the Peninsula outside of Negeri Sembilan) do not have the "matrilineal" guarantees that protect Negeri Sembilan women. Brothers partaking in land that might otherwise go to their sisters are thus engaging in highly ungrammatical moral behavior akin to incest and cannibalism.

In the case of land formally endorsed as *adat* or "customary" or simply treated as "ancestral" (*tanah pesaka*) and thus defined as "female property," the men who appear in the court of the District (Land) Office typically do so as clan officials (*lembaga, buapak*, etc.). Their job in such contexts is to provide guidance and official authorization on the proper procedures for transactions involving "ancestral property" and to mediate disputes involving co-heirs and those with competing or contested claims, the overwhelming majority of whom are female. It is significant that these officials are generally addressed and referred to by women and men as "elder brother" (*abang*). More relevant is that in these contexts they admirably fulfill the role of "elder brother" by looking after their charges, protecting their interests, mediating if not resolving conflicts that arise among them, and otherwise upholding sanctified values and traditions.

The fact remains, however, that men's comportment in these proceedings and in the hearings involving land subject to Islamic laws of inheritance does not inform thinking about masculinity in a major way. A partial explanation for this pattern may be the greatly reduced economic value of agricultural land in Malaysia's increasingly global economy, coupled with the contemporary economic irrelevance of adult brothers. Whatever the explanation, everyday practical constructions of masculinity, to repeat a point made earlier, are informed primarily by imagery of men in their roles as husbands and fathers.

To facilitate proceeding to more general issues, I shall summarize and elaborate briefly on some of the foregoing points. Oppositional discourses bearing on masculinity are heavily informed by perceptions of men in their roles as husbands and fathers. These perceptions are in many respects quite negative, largely because so many men are perceived as inadequate or falling short in the role of husband/father. Many men are perceived to be inadequate in the role of husband/father because the expectations entailed in the roles are not only strongly colored by ideals informing the heavily mythologized role of nurturing, protective, "elder brother" but are also rather extensive, subject to historic inflation, and unrealistic given current economic realities. More generally, oppositional discourses bearing on themes of gender, but not on topics of social class, the Islamic resurgence, or Islam as a whole, are exceptionally well developed among Malays (especially among women but also among men) both in Negeri Sembilan and in other parts of the Peninsula.[14] Even so, these discourses are still oppositional, not dominant. It thus remains to ask why the forces motivating them have not succeeded in "shattering the hegemony."

One variable that helps explain why the oppositional discourses at issue here are not more broadly elaborated has to do with the previously noted fact that male prerogatives and privileges and the discourse of male supremacy as a whole are deeply enshrined in Islamic ideology, which, for reasons discussed below (chapter 4), is largely above critical consideration, let alone explicit critique (except in the case of predominantly urban, middle-class Muslim feminists, such as those associated with organizations like Sisters in Islam). To engage in such critique is highly subversive in the most fundamental sense, on the order of incest and cannibalism; it also involves letting down the side, if not actually renouncing one's identity as a Malay. This is especially so in the current climate because of the polarized relations among the three major ethnic groups ("Malays," "Chinese," and "Indians"), the status of Islam as *the* key symbol of Malayness, and the absence of secular alternatives to Islamic modernities of the sort that exist in Indonesia, Egypt, Turkey, and many other countries with Muslim-majority populations.

A second variable is the allocation of prestige in terms of households, which tend to be, and in the case of the wealthy almost invariably are, composed of men and women alike. (In Negeri Sembilan, prestige is also allocated with respect to lineages and localized clans, but this is less directly relevant in this context.)[15] The pooling of household resources including labor for the purpose of advancing or at least maintaining the prestige standing of one's household vis-à-vis other households both presupposes and promotes day-to-day economic and other cooperation between husband and wife.[16] It also involves husband and wife conceptualizing their needs and strategies with respect to the satisfaction of subsistence concerns and the attainment of prestige, and their place(s) in the world generally, in relation to their household. Bear in mind, too, that the household is the locus of the individual's most intimate and in many respects most sustaining and meaningful social interactions. In sum, the primacy of the household in terms of the allocation of prestige and with respect to economic matters (production, consumption, and exchange) and social identity and emotional sustenance works against the development and cultural realization of gender-based interest groups, and in these and other ways inhibits the (further) elaboration of oppositional discourses, though it obviously does not preclude their existence in the first place.

A third, related variable is the historically specific construction of personhood, social adulthood, and adult womanhood especially. In order to be a full-fledged social adult, one must enter into a legitimate marriage (with a socially approved member of the opposite sex), and bear or father (or adopt) children. For women, this means not only being defined as a particular man's wife (or ex-wife or widow) and the mother of a particular man's children, but also, as mentioned earlier, a potentially extended period of economic dependence on (though not necessarily co-residence with) a particular man. The relational components of women's identity that focus on women's roles as wives and mothers have become highly salient over the course of the past century as a consequence of the historic restructuring of femininity that occurred as a result of state-sponsored changes of the sort that effected a realignment of the constituent elements of masculinity (Peletz 1996). In the case of femininity, the changes have entailed the historical deemphasis of women's roles as daughters, (natural and classificatory) sisters and sisters' daughters, and, as just noted, a foregrounding of their roles as wives and mothers. The factors responsible for such shifts include the economically and politically engendered erosion of a broadly encompassing kinship (of the sort associated with kindreds, lineages, and clans) and the attendant weakening and contraction of the siblingship undergirding it, as well as the demise of various forms of predominantly female labor exchange associated with the agricultural cycle, which, in former times, drew heavily on women as (natural and classificatory) sisters.

Clearly relevant, too, of course, is the resurgence of Islam (the *dakwah* movement), which has been animated and sustained in no small measure by ethnic and class tensions and nationalist and transnational discourse. The doctrines of Islam, like those of Buddhism, Christianity, and the other Great Religions, focus on and, more important, are interpreted locally as focusing on women's roles as wives and mothers rather than daughters and sisters. More to the point, Malaysia's Islamic resurgence, which is a largely urban-based, primarily middle-class phenomenon, has highlighted and endeavored to restrict women's sexuality and bodily processes. In these and other ways, including the endorsement of "pro-natalist programs," it has emphasized women's roles in biological reproduction along with their other "natural functions" (Stivens 1996, 1998; Frith 2001). Somewhat paradoxically, the involvement of young Malay women in high-tech factory work in Free Trade Zones and elsewhere since the 1970s has had some of the same ideological effects as the Islamic resurgence, especially since images of factory women, aside from being exceedingly negative, center on their alleged sexual promiscuity (Ong 1987, 1988; Ackerman 1991). In short, religious, economic, and attendant developments of the sort noted here have served to define women in relation to men, and as mothers, wives, and sexual hence "passionate" beings in particular, and have thus effectively promoted official discourse on gender and constrained the development and elaboration of oppositional discourses.

A fourth variable that inhibits the elaboration of oppositional discourses relates to the fact that village men and women alike espouse various features of "practical" (as well as official) views of masculinity and femininity. This may seem paradoxical and/or tautological, but the paradox and tautology, I would argue, are more apparent than real. It is in certain crucial respects much easier to conceive of and develop an oppositional discourse when those against whom it is deployed operate with a seamless, rigid, uncompromising, thoroughly self-congratulatory, and Other-despising set of assumptions about the way things are and should be. But this is not the case in Negeri Sembilan or in other parts of the Peninsula. In Negeri Sembilan and elsewhere in the Peninsula, men's and women's views of gender difference and sameness are in many regards quite similar. Men and women do, after all, operate with the same overarching framework (of "reason" and "passion") in terms of which gender is experienced, understood, and represented, and even the most extreme contrasts between men's and women's views on gender entail little more than a structural inversion of relationships among the principal signs and signifiers of the framework. More important, because many men, especially elite men, espouse views of gender that are far from seamless, uncompromising, thoroughly self-congratulatory, or Other-(female-)despising, they help put to rest suspicions on the part of women that they (men) are trafficking in thoroughly distorting or mystifying discourses. For reasons such as these and others noted earlier, the discourses of men help constrain the elaboration of oppositional discourses on the part of women, even though they simultaneously provide legitimate moral space for their existence in the first place. Phrased in broader and more abstract terms: dominant ideological formations both produce and limit the forms, scope, and force of the challenges with which they must invariably contend.[17]

The material presented in this chapter illustrates that in their kinship roles, as litigants, and in society at large, men are in a better position than women to traffic in and exploit the ambiguous and contested symbols and meanings of time, space, language, law, and "custom" (*adat*). We have also seen that men's easier manipulability of these symbols, and of uncertainty and indeterminancy in the law generally, simultaneously flows from and further amplifies power in numerous social arenas, including specifically legal ones, that women do not have. A corollary to this argument is that at the level of the individual case, men's legal strategies, including their strategies of resistance, are often more effective than women's, at least in terms of buying time and otherwise maintaining a status quo in which they can continue to make minimal if any contributions to the maintenance of their wives and children. This despite the fact that the cumulative effect of such strategies, and of men's comportment as husbands and fathers more generally, might be said to entail performative contradictions on two counts: first, it fuels counterhegemonic discourses that subvert the official line that men have more "reason" and virtue—and less "passion"—than women; and second, it has invited numerous legal reforms that have had the effect of curtailing men's autonomy (with respect to extrajudicial divorce, polygynous unions, etc.) and of more severely penalizing male incalcitrance and transgression.

We also saw that state domaining is key to the types and characteristics of discourses generated in the Islamic courts; that an understanding of the discourses and overall culture of the Islamic courts thus necessitates making analytic provision for political economy (of colonial-era and postcolonial political and administrative policies); and, similarly, that an informed interpretation of the social and cultural salience of the discourses produced within Islamic and other courts requires that our analytic gaze encompass but also range far beyond legal arenas (however broadly defined). That said, we must also acknowledge that our inquiry into resistance (and related matters) has been highly partial inasmuch as the focus in this chapter has been almost entirely on resistance involving litigants. We need also consider resistance on the part of *kadi*'s staff, for court personnel no less than litigants are caught up in webs of power, which, to cite an observation made by Ong (1995a: 1243) with respect to a very different type of state facility, simultaneously "involv[e] control and subterfuge, appropriation and resistance," and acquiescence and contestation.[18] These dynamics are among the main themes of the following chapter.

PART TWO

Modernity and Governmentality in Islamic Courts and Other Domains

CHAPTER FOUR

Reinscribing Authenticity and Identity

> The search for effective, measured, unified penal mechanisms is unquestionably
> a response to the inadequation [*sic*] of the institutions of judicial power to . . .
> new economic forms, urbanization, etc. . . . . The attempt . . . to reduce the auton-
> omy and insularity of judicial practice and personnel within the overall workings
> of the state, . . . [like] the wish to respond to emerging new forms of criminality
> . . . induce[s] a whole series of effects in the real: . . . they crystallize into insti-
> tutions, they inform individual behavior, they act as grids for the perception and
> evaluation of things.
> —*Michel Foucault, "Governmentality"*

> Given the paradoxes of modernity, there is little wrong, and perhaps a great deal
> right, with being ambivalent—especially when there is so much to be ambiva-
> lent about.
> —*Alan Wolfe,* Whose Keeper?

IN CHAPTER 1 we examined diverse facets of modernity entailed in the rationalization of law, religion, and culture generally through a focus on the history of
Malaysia's Islamic courts. We saw that especially since the nineteenth century,
the courts have been directly implicated in variously conceived projects of
modernity. Some of these projects (such as the reorganization and rationalization of the courts) were clearly of British origin and inspiration and were a
constitutive feature of colonial governance. Others are more appropriately
viewed as the outcome of modernizing projects of indigenous Malay design,
though, that said, they were in many cases inflected by symbols and idioms of
modernity derived from exogenous sources, some of which were European,
others of which were part of the culture of an increasingly transnational Islam.
In this connection we might recall Milner's important observation that ever
since early modern times "the duty of a South-East Asian raja" was "to acquire
the most *modern* spiritual doctrines and techniques"; that "*the good ruler was
always concerned with 'modernity'*"; and more generally that "in adopting [and
otherwise furthering the cause of] Islam the archipelago rulers were taking their
polities into that Muslim galaxy which must have seemed to encompass the
greater part of the *civilized* world" (1983: 45; emphases added). We have also
seen in chapters 2 and 3 that contemporary *kadi*'s concerns to maintain extant
marriages and in these and other ways help reduce traditionally high rates of

divorce are central components of their strategies to contribute to the production of modern Malay families and subjectivities, an encompassing and multi-layered project that for over thirty years now has been of central concern both to the ruling party (UMNO) and the state in its entirety.

This chapter and the next elaborate on some of these themes by dealing more explicitly with the interconnections of modernity and "governmentality" (Foucault 1991), the discursive and other techniques of power implicated in the governance of everyday behavior, and the attendant fashioning of "particular kinds of modern human beings" (Ong 2001: 9946). As with many other anthropologists, my goal is not to "arrive at some grand theory about modernity, but rather to scrutinize the concrete manifestations of emerging social practices, norms, and cultural politics in relation to the market, the nation-state, and to globalizing forces."[1] Courts of law are especially appropriate contexts in which to examine these interrelations, for as Hill and Lian (1995: 29–30) have underscored with particular reference to courts in the thriving global entrepôt of politically repressive Singapore, they make up the institutional locale for the policing that constitutes the surveillance mode associated with modern civil citizenship.

One of my specific goals in this chapter is to illuminate how the narratives of officials in Malaysia's Islamic courts aim to shore up certain symbols, idioms, and meanings of local kinship, gender, and sexuality—and to transfigure others—and in these and other ways to help constitute modern middle-class families and subjectivities and simultaneously assure that loyalties beyond the household are largely confined to the imagined community of Muslim believers (the *ummah*) and the state. I begin the discussion, however, by returning to a theme that runs throughout earlier chapters, which is that if we seek to understand the cultural logic of judicial process or other aspects of the workings of the courts, our analytic gaze needs to be focused not just on what transpires in courthouses or is contained in their written records, but also on what does not occur in court and what is absent from (or muted in) the written texts. Such themes inform the first two parts of this chapter, which draw mostly on case studies from the Islamic courts that involve Chinese converts to Islam and other non-Malay Muslims (Pakistanis, Indians). These cases raise interesting questions bearing on issues of citizenship, naturalization, and alterity. They also highlight how judicial discourses (including their elisions and silences) are involved in reinscribing certain types of authenticity and identity—or, put differently, how they are implicated in state-sanctioned efforts to bring about new ways of understanding, experiencing, representing, and otherwise being in the world.

The third part of the chapter broadens the discussion of authenticity and identity by considering the implications of rationalization processes for the cultural identities and everyday lives of "ordinary Malays" or "ordinary Muslims" (I use the two terms interchangeably) who are not in the forefront of contemporary religious or political developments.[2] One of my concerns here is to explain why ordinary Malays are not inclined to resist the rationalization at issue, especially the Islamic resurgence (the *dakwah* movement), even though many proponents of rationalization, particularly *dakwah* people, have targeted beliefs, practices, and values long central to their (ordinary Malays') cultural identities.

What's There and What's Not: The Said, the Unsaid, and the Unwritten

My interest in understanding the workings of the courts—including such issues as who uses the courts and why, and how court personnel, litigants, and others experience, understand, and represent legal processes—did of course presuppose a careful study of the actual proceedings of the court, including proceedings involving formal adjudication on the part of the *kadi*, as well as those entailing less formal processes of mediation and arbitration overseen by lower-ranking court staff like the counselor and Araffin. The realization of my research objectives also presupposed a careful study of all written records made available to me. I should emphasize, however, that I came to be just as interested in the flip side of the coin of legal texts, namely, what was left out of the proceedings or relegated to the back burner, and what was not recorded in written court documents. The lacunae and silences are in some cases of greater significance than data of a more conventional sort. The implications are far-reaching both in terms of the methodologies of archival and interdisciplinary research and for comparative and theoretical concerns. Let us take these issues one at a time.

Consider, first, a hypothetical anthropologist's or achivist's concern to answer the question: Are the cases that come before the courts more likely to be initiated by men or women? The answer to this critically important question should provide a baseline from which to begin to understand the dynamics of gender, power, and difference in the courts, and it should be straightforward, for included in the files for all cases are forms with spaces at the top to enter the names of "Petitioner" (*Sipeminta*) and "Respondent" (*Sipenjawab*). On the basis of written court records, the clear impression is that most petitioners are male. But as it turns out, even though husbands are usually listed as petitioners, wives are much more likely to initiate the legal process (as we saw in the last chapter).

The reason court staff usually list husbands as petitioners is so that husbands will have to pay the bulk of the legal fees. This strategy by court clerks, the majority of whom are male, represents a modest effort to compensate for some of the gender biases inherent in Islamic law and does, in any case, reflect local recognition that wives are more likely than husbands to find court fees burdensome. Perhaps more important, this strategy is informed by an implicit belief held by court staff and the (Malay) population at large. According to this belief, most of the problems in marriage stem from inappropriate behavior on the part of men, who, official discourse notwithstanding, are less reasonable and less responsible than women. As a male elder once explained to me, "Men are responsible for most of the problems in marriage, and they are at fault in most cases of divorce. The problem is that too many men like the good life, enjoy gambling and playing around, and basically expect to eat for free."

The ways in which court staff thus "cook the books" by reinscribing dissatisfaction and/or blame with respect to the fulfillment of conjugal responsibilities poses serious dilemmas for bureaucratic record keeping and for archivists and others who would take court documents at face value so as to better count, classify, and regulate marriage and divorce. The more general theme has been addressed by Dipesh Chakrabarty (1988), Partha Chatterjee (1993), Ranajit Guha (1994), and others in their work on Indian history and historiography—namely, that such silences and "noises in the system" lend themselves to discrepant readings and merit careful interdisciplinary research aimed at what Foucault refers to as their "archeological recovery."

Official, written records are misleading if taken at face value for other reasons as well. Forms bearing on the certification of marriage are problematic in key respects. The reason for this is that marriage payments often go unrecorded by clerks if relatives of the bride or groom are embarrassed about the sums being "too small." Small payments are stigmatizing, hence villagers do not like them widely publicized. The sizes of these payments are bound to be made public if, as required by state law, the specific amounts are written down on a form signed by two witnesses and a mosque official from the bride's community. The only way around this potential embarrassment is to "forget" to fill out the forms in their entirety.

As should be clear, people who work in the *kadi*'s office are closely attuned to and have deep empathy for villagers' sensibilities, and they are willing to dispense with a certain amount of formality if it seems that such action might avoid embarrassing those who seek their services. Official sensitivity on these issues is not all that surprising when one bears in mind that most of the employees of the *kadi*'s office hail from rural areas that are both geographically proximate and culturally similar to those of the majority of the people who come to the courthouse in search of legal assistance or state certification. More generally, officials of the court tend to orient their own behavior—and to interpret the behavior of others—in terms of the same cultural assumptions that inform the actions and understandings of the people whose interests they are enjoined to serve. Circumstances such as these suggest that the considerable powers of bureaucracy are refracted through local lenses and thus are necessarily constrained by the patterning of local sentiments and dispositions. The larger issue is that while official discourses such as those of the court are effective because of their grounding in popular language, they are by the very fact of this grounding rooted in the same cosmologies and perforce have to accommodate themselves to them.

Official records in written form are, therefore, no guarantee of great precision as to "what really happened" or even who the initial petitioners are in cases of a certain type. These examples resonate with Michael Herzfeld's (1992) observations concerning the symbolic roots of Western bureaucracy. Herzfeld has shown that the transition to literacy, which is among other things what we are dealing with here (Sweeney 1987), need not entail increased semantic fixity. This despite bureaucratic concerns with classification and attendant assertions that in the workings of the state, order, reason, and reality are necessarily always privileged or thoroughly hegemonic.

Many of these points are illustrated in the following case, which also demonstrates that marriage is heavily contractual; that the contracts at issue are increasingly construed in very narrow terms as linking only husband and wife and not their respective kin groups; and finally, that when "ethnics" (Muslims of non-Malay background) make use of the court's services, their ethnic identities (and, where relevant, their status as Muslims associated with legal schools of Islam other than Shafi'i) are clearly marked as "Other."

Case 32: *The Pakistani Wife Who Hates Her (Pakistani) Husband:* Tebus Talak *Divorce.* The first hearing in this case took place in the counselor's office and involved Fatimah B., age twenty-six, who is from Pakistan and is not very fluent in Malay, and her husband, Hamzah M., age thirty-one, also from Pakistan. A neighbor (here designated "T") served as translator/interpreter.

Counselor: Where is your house?
Wife: Rembau.
Counselor: Is it true you don't like your husband?
Wife: He causes me pain, suffering, punishment.
Counselor: Why? One day you left him. You are always leaving him. Were
    you married on the basis of mutual attraction?
Wife: Yeah.

. . . .

T: I live next door.
Counselor: The husband promised to take her back with him. The day the
    husband met Fatimah and wanted to take her back, she refused, indicating
    that she'd come by herself.
T: She's sick, she wanted to go to the clinic and stay at home for two more
    days.
Counselor: Why don't you want to follow your husband? . . . Before the
    marriage, Hamzah had never met Fatimah. They first met on the day of
    their marriage. Did he ask you if you liked him?
Wife: Yeah.
Counselor: Hamzah acknowledges that you're a quiet person.
[The wife is silent.]
T: She said on the day of the marriage that she didn't want to be with him.
    After six months she was asked if she was pregnant or not. She said she
    wasn't.
Counselor: Why don't you like him? Have you ever fought?
Wife: No.
T: Hamzah says that Fatimah is like a coolie.

Counselor: [About six weeks back] Hamzah came, but you didn't want to follow him.

T: Fatimah had not yet finished her medicine.

Counselor: Didn't you say to him that you didn't want to go back because you were still on medication?

Wife: I told him.

Counselor: What did Hamzah say in response?

T: Hamzah said it was a minor illness. Everyone at the father's house has work.

Counselor: Did you invite him to stay with you?

Wife: I did.

Counselor: Hamzah works in Tampin. It's far to go back and forth each day. That's why he doesn't want to stay in Rembau. If he invites you to stay in Tampin, do you want to or not?

Wife: I don't want to.

T: It's been ten months of marriage and they've never been together. He has never touched her.

[The husband enters.]

Counselor: Have you ever touched her?

Husband: She won't let me.

Wife: He's fierce [*garang*] with me.

Counselor: Has he ever hit you?

Wife: No.

Counselor: Why don't you like him?

Wife: [Silence.]

Husband: I don't want to divorce her, ever.

Wife: I don't like him. [To husband:] If you don't want to divorce, then I don't want to stay with you.

Counselor: You two have never been together. Hamzah still loves you. What are you unsatisfied about?

[Husband and wife argue.]

Husband: I definitely do not want to divorce her.

Counselor: Why don't you like him?

[The wife is silent.]

Counselor: Where is your marriage certificate?

Husband: Didn't bring it.

Counselor: Then this case can't be resolved [now].

T: Fatimah doesn't trust Hamzah. Fatimah's father ordered her to return to Hamzah's house but she doesn't want to.

Counselor: How about if we make a letter of agreement that Hamzah is not going to mistreat you and you must follow him back?

[The wife is silent.]

Counselor: Has he ever given you money?

Wife: Yeah.

Counselor: Your father doesn't want you to get divorced. Why don't you like him [your husband]?

Husband: If I did something wrong, I'll ask forgiveness. But I don't want to divorce her.

[The translator/interpreter goes out and Fatimah's father comes in.]

Counselor: I would like to know why Fatimah doesn't like Hamzah.

Father: She doesn't trust him.

Counselor: How come?

Husband: The first night [after the wedding] I asked her if I did something wrong.

Father: They were married [on the basis of mutual attraction], but have never slept together. At the time of the wedding, Hamzah didn't give any money, just a necklace and a ring.

Husband: I asked her if she had someone else. . . . She said nothing.

Counselor: This case can't be resolved today. I'm going to adjourn it until [next week].

The second hearing in this case did not take place on the specified date because at least one of the litigants failed to appear in court. When it did occur some days later, the *kadi* initiated it by motioning those waiting outside to come into his chambers. The wife was the first to enter, accompanied by an older man who was apparently a *haji*. The *kadi* ordered the man out without asking him anything; he wanted to speak to the wife alone. He then addressed her by asking her, "When were you married? Where's your marriage certificate?" at which point the husband came into the *kadi*'s chambers, and Araffin, entering from one of the other rooms, shouted to the *kadi*: "Hey, she doesn't speak Malaysian" and then went out to get the *haji* who had just been sent out of the room. Another man, who was to serve as an interpreter for the husband, came in and sat down. He was wearing dirty rubber boots up to his knees; it appeared from his clothes that he worked for the Public Works Department as a laborer or gardener. The *kadi* realized he was there to be an interpreter and indicated that he should come up to the desk area. He did, but he did not sit down as there were not enough chairs.

Kadi: So, what's the problem?

Translator 1 (Tr1): She doesn't like her husband, doesn't want him, no matter how much she has to suffer.

Translator 2 (Tr2): They were never together [never slept together].

Kadi: You are Hanafi, right? The wife is asking for a divorce by redemption [a *tebus talak* divorce]. What do your people do in this situation, when the wife asks for a divorce?

Tr1: This has never happened [in my experience].

Kadi: We have *tebus talak*; but your people, Hanafi law, I don't know. . . .

[Tr1 says something that makes the *kadi* think that "they" (Hanafi) have something similar to *tebus talak*.]

Kadi: Like pay back the *mas kawin*, the [money for] the feast, etc.

Tr1 [speaks to the wife and adds]: He gave *mas kawin* [in the form of a necklace] and two rings. Nothing else.

Kadi: If there is *hantaran*, etc., it should be returned.

Tr2: There were just fifteen or twenty people at the feast.

Kadi [to husband]: What do you claim from her? She doesn't want you.

Husband: It depends on the wife.

Kadi: No, no, no. This is a sin; in Islam, it doesn't depend on her. If the wife doesn't like you and you like her, what are you going to do? The husband is the one who makes the claim, not the wife. The husband can't say, "I don't want to divorce her" and leave it at that. You are still married and still responsible for her actions.

At about this time the husband voiced his view that his wife should have told him "this" (that there might be a problem, or that she would not let him touch her) before they got married. Meanwhile, Araffin asks the husband if he understands what the *kadi* is saying. The *kadi* seems to have forgotten—or not to care—that the wife does not speak any Malay and that the husband's Malay is rather minimal. Indeed, the *kadi* is speaking as fast as he usually does when he is in the midst of a hearing and is speaking in the local dialect as well.

Kadi [to husband]: You can't keep this woman. And she can't claim anything, because she doesn't want him [she is the one seeking a divorce]. [Only] if the husband doesn't want the wife, then the wife can make claims. So, what do you want to claim? Are your mother and father still alive? Your brothers and sisters?

The husband indicates "yes," and the *kadi* enjoins him to "go home and talk to them about this, about what you should claim." This is followed by discussion of the date of the next hearing. The husband makes clear he will come back later in the week. The wife remains silent, as she did during most of the proceeding.

A third hearing in this case occurred a few days later. The husband and wife and the two interpreters present during the previous hearing went into the *kadi*'s chambers. The *kadi* began after everyone took their seats.

Kadi [to husband]: What is your claim? Your wife doesn't want you.

The husband then gave the *kadi* a typed sheet he had prepared with the help of his father and one of his in-laws. The list of expenses was as follows: (1) *hantaran*—M$800; (2) *mas kawin* (necklace and two gold rings)—M$2,500; (3) rental of bus and car—M$800; (4) rental of car for the bride and groom—M$150; (5) musical troupe—M$50; (6) rental of tent—M$150; (7) printing of wedding invitations—M$200; (8) feast expenses—M$5,500. The *kadi* took the list and began reading it over, half out loud.

Kadi: This #2, the *mas kawin*; do you have a receipt for the necklace?

Husband: No.

Kadi: Bus rental, tent rental. . . . *Hantaran*? [To which someone answers, "There wasn't any."] Date of the marriage? . . . *Mas kawin*; two rings. Where did you buy them? Receipt?

Husband: My father and in-law bought them.

Kadi: Bus rental? From Melaka? M$800 to rent the bus? How many cars?

Husband: Four.

Kadi: Rental of car for the couple? Music? Wedding invitations?

At about this point in the hearing the *kadi* was given the marriage forms retrieved by one of the clerks and looked over the section pertaining to the various types of marriage payments (*hantaran*, *pemberian*, and *belanja hangus*). He remarks that if these payments were really made there would have been a record on the forms, but there isn't, adding that the marriage forms are signed and witnessed and are not accepted by his office unless they are complete. This of course is very far from the truth; as we have seen the vast majority of these forms are not filled out in their entirety.

The fact that the forms are not filled out completely poses serious problems for the husband's claims. So, too, does the fact that the husband does not have any receipts with him. When the *kadi* told him to go back and consult with his family about the marriage expenses he is claiming from his wife, he did *not* add that receipts would be necessary for the major expenses, such as the rings and necklace. So the husband is forced to go back home and return with the receipts, if they exist; everyone else is required to come back as well—all because the *kadi* did not tell the husband about the "proof" (receipts) issue.

The *kadi* also indicated the wife does not have to return the rings; if she had broken off the engagement then she would have to, but not under the circumstances of this case. He added that he would accept the letter detailing the expenses but that the husband will have to come back with the receipts and his father and in-law. He also made clear that not all the expenses will be allowed. And if I understood him correctly he specified that a portion of the *mas kawin*, *hantaran*, and feasting expenses would be given to him, but probably not the others (such as the costs of printing up invitations and renting a tent).

The wife, as it turns out, does not have a Malaysian passport but an Indian passport. The interpreter present on her behalf said that she will be getting a Malaysian passport in a few more years. Apparently she was born in Malaysia, grew up in India, and only recently moved back to Malaysia.

The rest of the discussion concerned when the next hearing would be. The *kadi* suggested some time in the next five to six weeks. The wife did not say a word throughout the hearing, but the husband still wants her and feels very upset and cheated by the whole thing. He told the counselor quite emphatically that the wife is his "forever, in this world and the Afterlife."

Comment: After everyone went out, the *kadi* and the counselor clarified some of the issues for me and elaborated on the case. The counselor speculated that perhaps the woman entered into the marriage to obtain Malaysian citizenship, and I was informed that the husband and wife are not converts but Muslims from birth. The *kadi* explained that the husband might get M$2,000–3,000 but probably not the M$9,000 or so he is seeking. As for the *mas kawin*, the husband can ask for it back since the wife is the one requesting the divorce. (Later, though, the counselor opined that he would not get the *mas kawin* back because it is the wife's.)[3] The *kadi* also clarified that there is no *edah* period if the wife was never touched.

Araffin later filled me in on *tebus talak* (also known as *khuluk*) divorce by noting that this type of marital dissolution is rare and adding that when it does occur, it is usually very early in the marriage. One of the main reasons it occurs, according to Araffin, is because some wives "won't let their husbands touch them," or refuse to have any more to do with their husbands after one or two occasions of sexual relations. A different scenario obtains if a bride has falsely claimed to be a virgin before marriage (if, for example, the husband realizes on his wedding night that his wife is not a virgin after all). In the latter circumstance he feels tricked and lied to and may demand a *tebus talak* divorce, insisting that he be repaid for what he "lost" (the marriage payments, wedding expenses associated with feasting, etc.).

The amount of money husbands demand in these cases is not automatically approved by the *kadi*, who takes into consideration the wife's background and sees what she can afford. He will not order a payment in excess of what she can manage. And he will want to know the extent of payments and other gifts to the bride, the cost of feasts, and specifically how much of the groom's own money—as distinct from his family's money—went toward all of this. The money given by others in his family is not altogether relevant. The main concern, according to Araffin, is what the husband himself paid. This is one reason why it is crucial to have accurate records of marriage expenses such as *hantaran*, *pemberian*, and so on. If there is no reliable record of these, there can be major problems in reaching settlements for *tebus talak*.

Reinscribing Authenticity and Identity

The previous case illustrates (among other things) some of the more extreme strategies deployed by women who resist one or another entailment of marriage, as well as the limitations and costs of the informal nature of judicial proceedings, of what might be termed the "downside(s)" of the cultural logic of judicial process. In the latter connection, one could perhaps argue that the husband was mistreated or poorly served by the system to a greater degree than the wife, insofar as the *kadi* gave him incomplete and contradictory information about what he needed to press his claim for reimbursement from his wife, and he was thus required to go home and return with additional, written information in the form of receipts, etc., that would serve to verify the expenses for which his wife would be liable. The case might thus constitute one of the exceptions that proves the rule that women are far more likely than men to be buffeted about by the system, in the sense that they are encouraged by the words and deeds of the court to accept delays, compromises, and uncertainties from partners who seek to foreground their own wishes and priorities.

The proceedings in this case are notable for other reasons as well, including the "to-ing and fro-ing" over written evidence; the valorization of written agreements; and the ways in which the courts ride roughshod over those who are not literate or fluent in the national language and otherwise help pull members of largely oral cultures into a world of literacy. Perhaps most significant, however, are the ways in which the proceedings highlight how the courts are implicated in the inscription of new identities, new modes of relatedness (such as companionate marriage), and new definitions of what is authentic or legitimate and what is not. The legal discourse concerning which marriage payments will be returned to the husband is especially relevant here. Recall the *kadi*'s position that not all the expenses incurred by the husband and his relatives will be made good; only those that came directly from the husband are legally salient and within his right to claim. The legal discourse here turns on a view of the institution of marriage that is clearly heavily contractual but also defines the institution in terms of an exceedingly narrow contract between husband and wife, not one involving their respective kin groups, however narrowly (or broadly) defined.

As Muslims, Pakistanis (like Malays) do of course have such a cultural conception of marriage—one that is embedded in but by no means entirely derivative from the marriage contract (*akad nikah*), for example. But they also have a contrasting and in some respects contradictory view of marriage as a union linking not just husband and wife but also—and more important—two expansive groups of kin. As this case (and many others considered earlier) suggests, the latter conception of marriage is completely irrelevant in modern-day legal arenas such as the Islamic courts. This despite the court's recognition that individuals are embedded in and sustained by kin networks (a recognition evidenced in this instance by the *kadi*'s questions and admonition to the husband: "Are your mother and father still alive? Your brothers and sisters? Go . . . talk to them about this"). Not coincidentally, the latter conception of marriage is also strongly discouraged by the system of wage labor and the modern capitalist economy generally, as well as the secular courts and countless state policies concerning subjects and citizens including, not least, the granting of voting rights, passports, and identity cards to individuals, not groups.

In these regards, it is interesting to note that the Islamic courts are operating as an ethnic or cultural (or, as it is usually expressed in Malaysian discourse, a "racial") leveling mechanism. This becomes all the more clear when one stops to consider that comparable cultural work—the devaluation of extended (consanguineal, affinal, and "fictive") kinship of all varieties—is being carried out in the secular courts whose domains of jurisdiction include matters of family law involving Chinese, Indian, and other non-Muslims. One of the great ironies of the Islamic courts in present-day Malaysia is that the courts are key components of an institutional network whose most important functions are thought to include the safeguarding of Malays and Malay culture from the real and imagined threats of Chinese, Indians, and other non-Malays, on the one hand, and the ravages of state-sponsored capitalist development, along with Western-style commercialism and moral decline, on the other. And yet at least in the arenas we are considering here, the more the courts adhere to what are regarded as authentically Islamic and modern practices that entail the refashioning of new Malay-Muslim families and subjectivities, the more they contribute to the production of a Malay-Muslim citizenry whose subjectivities and forms of kinship converge with those of the nation-state's non-Muslim population. This refashioning thus implicates the courts in the erasure of the very cultural difference they are supposed to safeguard with all of the resources at their disposal.

In order to further explore the relevant discourses and dynamics in the Islamic courts, let us recall that court personnel often jiggle or cook the books, even though this entails subverting certain classifying and ordering functions that are central to their state-defined bureaucratic charters. I should stress here that court officials are motivated to do so by deeply held moral convictions bearing on "family values" that are more compelling than the myriad interests underlying state passions to count, classify, regulate, and discipline. In other areas, of course, the actions of court officials are more consonant with state objectives. This is especially apparent with regard to the privileging of order and reason, and the impulse to regulate the disorder and passion seen as inherent in certain modalities of kinship beyond the nuclear family.

The narratives of court officials are designed to bolster certain symbols, idioms, and meanings of local kinship and to transform others and thus help ensure that allegiances beyond the household are largely limited to the global community of Muslim believers (the *ummah*) and the state. The sanctity of conjugal ties and parent-child relations are given clear precedence in terms of the overt content of exhortations and pronouncements to troubled couples, witnesses, and character references. This same priority is evident from what is conspicuously *absent* from these exhortations and pronouncements, such as positive remarks or inferences concerning collateral relatives and kin groupings like kindreds, lineages, and clans (cf. Sharifah Zaleha Syed Hassan 1986: 184). A partial explanation of these patterns lies in the tacit assumption that the smooth functioning of the courts, like the rational workings of modern states generally, presupposes narrowly defined (nuclear) family units, not an expansively construed, hence encompassing and always potentially highly unruly kinship, unless of course the latter is "merely" metaphorical as opposed to "real." This despite the court-recognized fact that the encompassing kinship at issue here has long provided local refuge from the ravages of state-sanctioned capitalist development.

I should perhaps be more explicit here and underscore that the narratives of court officials are strategic components of discourses on kinship that are advanced by the state. These discourses are keyed to concerns to enhance or at least sustain not only certain types of political legitimacy and political stability but also the economic, religious, and overall cultural development that helps underwrite political legitimacy and political stability alike. State discourses on kinship are thus crafted to effect an attenuation of the extended kinship that has long typified rural Malay society, partly because it is widely believed that such kinship is an obstacle to the consolidation of the narrowly defined political allegiances that are vital to the state's patronage machine. Forms of extended kinship, like other "backward" excesses and passions of rural society, are also construed as a drag on economic initiative, hence an impediment to the economic development of the Malay population, which trails behind the Chinese and Indian minorities in terms of overall economic standing. (Such development, as noted earlier, has been a central platform of the national ruling party [UMNO] for a full thirty years; and UMNO is quite explicit—discursively and otherwise—in its twofold campaign to eliminate rural Malay society and culture as "traditionally" constituted and "replace" it with a newly created sector of middle- and upper-middle-class urban Malay capitalists.)[4] And of course extended kinship provides potentially fertile ground for nepotism. Moreover, as already noted, extended kinship is believed to be conducive to the realization of loyalties and antagonisms that interfere with the development of the seamless brotherhood enjoined on all Muslims as members of the global Muslim community, which is, by definition, a highly valued form of family as well. In short, because "the family" is a microcosm of the moral order that underlies and helps frame the always unfinished business of nation building, it is necessarily "project, terrain, and target"[5] of state politics and competing discourses of all kinds.

In a variety of ways, then, Islamic courts are strategic players in the creation and policing of new Malay families and subjectivities. It is thus highly ironic that the language of the *kadi* and other court personnel is thoroughly infused with the symbols and idioms of the very same classificatory kinship that the courts and other institutions keyed to the workings of the state have targeted for elimination (or at least rationalization). For example, the terms of reference and address usually employed by court staff when dealing with litigants and other members of the public who are assumed to be their seniors are "elder brother," "elder sister," "uncle," "aunt," etc., rather than terms with no kin referents, such as "Mr." or "Mrs." Although this might strike the outside observer as a "performative contradiction" in Denys Turner's (1983) sense, there are two reasons why I do not think it is experienced locally in any such contradictory terms. First, in many contexts Malays do not draw a sharp distinction between "real" and "classificatory" kinship. And second, the courts' devaluation of extended kinship is not usually explicit. It tends instead to be largely unmarked and rather ambiguous. It is, moreover, encapsulated within a "pro-family" discourse that not only lends itself to divergent readings but also strongly emphasizes the value of intact families and households built around stable, or at least enduring and minimally sustaining, marriage ties. What is not usually explicit in the *kadi*'s chambers but is nonetheless obvious from initial interviewing and counseling sessions overseen by his assistant (the counselor) is that such intact marriages, families, and households are not only privileged in relation to collateral and other extradomestic kinship bonds but are also seen as very much threatened by them.

In the chambers of the counselor, husbands commonly lament that many serious marital problems stem from meddling or other interference on the part of their wives' mothers and sisters. Partly for this reason, the counselor frequently admonishes women not to overvalorize their bonds with their mothers and other blood kin at the expense of their marriage ties. Such advice is most often dispensed to young wives, who are told that it is their husbands, not their mothers, sisters, or other blood kin, who will look after them during times of hardship. Such advice is highly ideological in the sense that it refers more to an imagined or intended state than to a reality existing at present, for rates of abandonment and divorce have long been quite high. This is to say, first, that women—especially women from poor households, who constitute the main clientele of Islamic courts throughout Malaysia—cannot really count on their husbands to be there "through thick and thin," and second, that on these particular issues the discourses of the court are profoundly disjunctive with respect to many of the lived social experiences shared by these women and their female elders and other kin. Consider the following.

Case 33: *Che Tom, Who Seeks* Nafkah *and Will Not Go Live with Her Husband in Jelebu*. Present at the first hearing of this case that I observed were a thirty-two-year-old woman (Che Tom), her twenty-six-year-old husband (Said Ali), her mother (who was in and out of the office at different points in the hearing), and the couple's two children. It appeared that the wife was the first to approach the court; she claimed that her husband had been delinquent in the payment of *nafkah*.

Among the wife's principle complaints were that she had not seen her husband, who lives in Jelebu, for about eight months and that he "won't come back." As it turned out, the husband had not even returned for the birth of their second child a few months earlier; indeed, he does not even know the gender or name of the child.

The husband responded to these charges by explaining that his father is sick and that he has to look after him. Since the father lives in Jelebu, he has to be there, especially since he works there as well. He added that his wife will not go to live with him in Jelebu and that he refuses to live with her family in Rembau where she currently resides.

The wife and her mother (who spoke a great deal for the wife) said that one of the husband's relatives made or offered to make arrangements for him to get posted in Rembau instead of Jelebu but the husband did not want to go. The husband reiterated the need to take care of his father, at which point his mother-in-law interjected that the father has a wife to look after him and she is not even the husband's real mother (she is his stepmother), the implication being that there is no reason for him to be so attached to her. The husband countered with the remark that he does not get along with his (elder) sister-in-law and does not want to live with the wife's family in Rembau.

The husband admitted that he had been less than responsible, particularly inasmuch as he did not even know the name or gender of his second child, who is now more than eight months old. He promised to change his attitude and was quite open and seemingly sincere in his stated desire to be a better husband and father.

The wife's mother repeatedly answered for her daughter (the wife) and otherwise interfered in the proceedings. It was obvious, especially to the counselor, that one of the chief problems was that the mother/mother-in-law meddled in the affairs of her daughter and son-in-law and had in fact told her daughter not to follow her husband to Jelebu. One of the wife's main reasons (arguably the only one) for not following her husband to Jelebu was that she did not want to live apart from her parents.

The counselor gave the wife a long lecture on the duties and responsibilities of being a wife, the problems of getting and being divorced, making it quite clear that once she got married her primary responsibilities were to her husband and that she had to listen to what he said and asked her to do. "You must follow [your] husband's rule[s]" (*mesti ikut perintah suami*) she said on a number of occasions. "[T]his is part of religion, a basic cornerstone of Islam. . . . Forget what your parents say. . . . Don't listen to them and don't let them interfere. After all, what is going to happen when they aren't around any longer? Who is going to take care of your children? Who is going to take care of your husband's food and clothes if you don't?"

The counselor then inquired of the husband and wife if they loved one another. Both said yes, and she asked the wife if she was going to follow the husband back to Jelebu. After thinking about it for a while, the wife replied, "No." It was then that the counselor asked her over and over, "Are your parents interfering in this, telling you what to do?" Finally, it came out that her mother had forbidden her to go to Jelebu. The counselor was visibly upset with this and again lectured the wife on the importance of thinking for herself, being independent of the mother, etc., but much of what she was saying ("rely first and foremost on your husband; forget about the rest of your relatives, especially your parents") seemed to be going against the grain of local kinship.

The husband reiterated his admission of wrongdoing and his commitment to changing, adding that he had never hit his wife or gotten angry with her. The counselor then told the wife that there is no reason why they should divorce, advising the husband to try to work it out through discussions with his in-laws and instructing the wife to explain her position to her mother and tell her that she did not wish to disobey her but has to go live with her husband in Jelebu. The counselor clearly sought to promote reconciliation among all parties concerned and tried to keep the marriage intact.

In explaining her perception of the problem to the husband and wife (the mother/mother-in-law was in the room at this point), the counselor said that most of the counseling and divorce cases that reach the *kadi*'s office involve interference on the part of the wife's parents, problems with the husband's small income, etc. She also informed the wife that she wanted a decision on whether or not she was going to follow her husband to Jelebu and that she wanted the wife to come up with her own decision, uninfluenced by her mother, within four weeks. She would be in touch with her before then to set up an appointment.

During a second hearing in this case, which occurred nearly six months later, the husband and wife were present, as were the wife's parents, though only the father entered the counselor's chambers. I came into the counselor's office a few moments after the hearing had begun, so I do not know how it started, but when I entered, the main issues taken up had to do with the informal custody of the older of the two children, who is about two and a half years old. The wife's mother wants to take care of her, as she has been doing since the little girl was two months old. They are very attached to one another; indeed, the little girl does not want to be apart from her grandmother and in fact prefers her to her own mother.

A bit later in the hearing the wife announced her decision. She would go live with the husband in Jelebu on one condition: that the husband formally invite her to come live with him. The husband appeared quite patient throughout all of this, though shaking his head, smiling, and jiggling his leg quite a bit. At various points in the hearing the counselor continued lecturing the wife on the importance of making her own decisions, on the husband's rights, on the fact that the husband has a right to the child as well, and so on. The husband indicated that he would formally invite his wife to live with him within a few weeks. He also mentioned something about his in-laws (perhaps the sister-in-law), adding that he and his wife could live temporarily with his brother, if need be. The way things were left, it was up to the husband to decide whether he and his wife would raise their little girl or allow her to remain with her grandmother. The husband promised to get in touch with the counselor to let her know his final decision on this.

Comment: In a discussion concerning the first hearing in this case, the counselor made clear to me that she sees definite conflicts between Islam and *adat*, as evidenced by her statement that "*adat* should be adhered to, but with conditions," the conditions being that where *adat* and Islam prescribe or encourage different behaviors, Islam must be followed. Concerning postmarital residence, for example; while Islam says that the wife should follow the husband, *adat* encourages couples to live with the wife's family. This was clearly an issue in this case, and so far as the counselor was concerned there was no acceptable course of action other than the wife's going to Jelebu to live with her husband. The counselor also told me that when difficulties arise due to the interference of a married woman's parents, they are almost always the fault of the woman's mother as opposed to her father and that complaints of the sort at issue here usually focus on the husband's meager income or lack of steady employment.

More important in the broader scheme of things, however, are the ways in which cases such as this illustrate the role of court narratives and practices in reinforcing female roles, including not only women's religiously mandated submission to their husband's expectations and desires but also their sanctified roles as mothers. This is a pronounced theme in many of the cases I discussed in chapters 2 and 3, the more general point being that it is one of the more striking patterns I observed in the courts throughout my entire fieldwork. Patterns related to the theme of female role reinforcement are even more prominent in the ethnographic research bearing on Islamic courts located elsewhere in Malaysia, the most detailed of which, as already noted, focuses on courts in urban areas of the states of Selangor and Kedah in the early 1990s (Sharifah Zaleha Syed Hassan and Cederroth 1997; cf. Rosen 1998: 181). That said, there are significant variations on the theme of female role reinforcement. One such difference is that while the narratives and practices of Islamic courts in Selangor and Kedah tend to play up and otherwise reinforce women's roles as wives and mothers, they tend to play down—indeed, discourage—women's roles in the paid labor force and in extradomestic activities generally. Discouragement of the latter sort on the part of the court is not pronounced or at all common in Negeri Sembilan (in my experience). In fact, we have seen numerous instances (such as case 3) in which officials of the court pass over complaints from husbands that their wives work outside the home and thus have insufficient time or energy for the ("proper") performance of domestic duties. We have also seen court officials counsel husbands that such activities are vital for household maintenance.

It is difficult to say with certainty whether these contrasts between Selangor and Kedah on the one hand and Negeri Sembilan on the other derive from differences of an urban/rural or class (or intraclass) sort; from regional cultural variations (keyed to divergent *adat* and their respective implications for "customary" patterns of female inheritance, proprietorship, and production); and/or from the administrative and other (legal, political, religious) changes that occurred in the interval between my fieldwork in Negeri Sembilan courts and the research that focused on courts in Selangor and Kedah. Based on data from a wide variety of sources that indicate increased pressure on women to focus most of their time and energy on domestic roles (Ong 1995b; Stivens 1996, 1998; Chin 1998; Gaik 1999; Sloane 1999; Tan 1999; Frith 2001), it could well be that this last variable is the most relevant and that in Malaysia as a whole the Selangor/Kedah pattern is more likely to prevail in the future. Needless to say, this does not bode well either for women or for the living standards of the households and family units their incomes help sustain.

I hasten to add that it is not only in the privileging of conjugal relations at the expense of other sorts of kinship bonds that the courts are implicated in projects involving the refashioning of modern families and subjectivities. The court's valorization of blood ties over relations of formal and informal adoption makes up another facet of the modernity project, as does the foregrounding, especially in matters of inheritance, of filiation entailing shared substance. Consider, first, the following case.

Case 34: *The Indian Man Who Divorces His Malay Wife and Will Not Have to Pay Child Support Because Their Adopted Child* (Anak Angkat) *"Isn't Really Theirs."* Present at this hearing, which occurred in the *kadi*'s chambers, were a young Indian man, his Malay wife, the *kadi*, and (toward the end of the proceeding) Araffin. The husband is from the state of Perak, the wife is from a village in Rembau, and they have been married for more than four years.

Shortly after the husband and wife sat down and settled themselves, the *kadi* launched into a series of questions: How many children? Adopted children? Your own children? The problem(s)? and Where are you from? After he received answers to these queries, the *kadi* turned to the wife and asked her how long her husband had been gone, to which she replied: three months, minus a day or two. The husband had not provided *nafkah* for at least six months, perhaps closer to a year. The husband acknowledged that he had not given any money in such time because, as he put it, "I don't have any." As they continued, it became evident that they were estranged (*tak sesuai*) and that neither one wanted to remain in the marriage.

After expressing exasperation at how many divorces occur—"Ayyh, divorce, divorce, divorce"—the *kadi* moved on quickly, asking about *nafkah edah* and *sepencarian*: Motorcycle? Car? Land? The husband, who is involved in some sort of business or trade, answered in the affirmative to each of these questions, clarifying, however, that he does not have the land anymore since he sold it and is now bankrupt.

The *kadi* informed them that the *nafkah edah* is three months and ten days, adding that the husband cannot (re)marry within this period. Addressing the husband, he then asked: "How much are you going to give?" The husband replied, "M$100." *Kadi*: "M$100 a month?" "Ya." "Okay, that is M$330." The husband indicated that he would pay it next month via the *kadi*'s office, later clarifying that he would pay the first installment (rather than the entire sum) next month.

The *kadi* then raised the issue of *muta'ah* with the husband: "*Muta'ah*? . . . you've been married to your wife for four years and four months. . . . Every divorce involves *nafkah edah*, *muta'ah*, *sepencarian*, if there is any, and *nafkah anak*, if there are any children. This is written in the Quran." Based on the *kadi*'s verbal summary of the agreement a few moments later, it appeared that the husband had agreed to a *muta'ah* of M$500. The *kadi* also explained that *sepencarian* included *any* property the husband may have acquired since getting married, and that any such property would be split equally between husband and wife. But he did not go on to make clear exactly how this division would work in the case of the husband's car and motorcycle.

Because the *kadi* was very much in a hurry, apparently to go pick up one of his children, he was now rushing through the proceedings. Instructing Araffin to get the relevant form(s), he asked the husband if he could read. Since the husband replied that he could not, the *kadi* then read aloud the statement that the husband was instructed to recite, which included the words, "I . . . without being forced and with a clear mind . . . divorce my wife with one *talak*." The *kadi* added that if the husband could not read (or recite) that statement, he could say, "I divorce my wife with one *talak*," which he proceeded to do. The *kadi* went on to inquire of the wife if she accepted the divorce; she responded in the affirmative. At this point in the hearing, although the relevant fees and forms had not yet been taken care of, the *kadi* got up and basically ran out the door, trotted out to the parking area, and got in his car. Just before he drove off, Araffin rushed out with one or more forms that required the *kadi*'s signature; the *kadi* signed them on the hood of his car and drove off in a cloud of dust.

When Araffin returned, the husband asked him whether or not he was going to have to pay *nafkah anak*. Araffin did not know what to say, especially since the *kadi* had already driven away by this time, leaving this particular issue (and many other details of the case) hanging.

Comment: Later on I discussed some of the features of the case with the counselor and Araffin, who appeared quite embarrassed about the *kadi*'s abrupt departure while the hearing was still in progress. The case had come to the attention of the *kadi*'s office before this, for the *kadi* and the counselor, who did not sit in on the hearing this time around, knew many details of the case. I asked Araffin about the *nafkah anak*. He remarked that "there wouldn't be any," adding that the husband wants to raise the child but that the *kadi* and other authorities brought in on the matter will not allow this. Assuming that the wife does in fact raise the child, there will not be any *nafkah anak* because "it isn't really their child." Araffin mentioned that the transfer (of rights over the child) was not done in any official way, adding something about five years not having yet passed or elapsed. The bottom line is that Islamic law does not recognize the informal adoptions of children that are so frequent among Malays, especially in rural areas (see McKinley 1981; Banks 1983; Peletz 1988b; Carsten 1997).

Some of the same dynamics at issue in this case obtain in the administration of Islamic law bearing on inheritance and other property relations, for here too we see a devaluation of collateral ties and classificatory kinship. Not coincidentally, the foregrounding in this context of filiation entailing shared substance (blood [*darah*], flesh/meat [*daging*]) resonates with the court's nonrecognition of the exceedingly common practice of (informal) adoption. The court's refusal to recognize kinship that is not grounded in shared substance is very much out of keeping with local sensibilities, which tend to emphasize that kinship is ultimately performative, not genealogical. More generally, this refusal constitutes another example of the courts' attempt to redefine "authentic" kinship in opposition to "inauthentic" kinship, which, according to the modernity-oriented discourses of court and state alike, means kinship without legal standing or moral value.

There is considerable irony in the court's denial of legitimacy to adoption coupled with its explicit recognition of the extreme fragility of marriage ties. The irony is that such positions resonate deeply with and probably reinforce what the court regards as certain of the more parochial and problematic aspects of local distinctions between "authentic" and "inauthentic" Muslims and fly in the face of other work the courts are mandated to carry forward. To oversimplify the local view, authentic Muslims are Muslims by birth, and as such they have in common with the Muslim community not only shared substance but also the commitment to Islamic codes for conduct that is necessarily entailed in such shared substance.[6] Inauthentic Muslims, by contrast, are Muslims through conversion, who necessarily lack the shared substance characteristic of the *ummah* and, by implication, the commitment to the code for conduct as well. In short, in the local view, religious identities—like ethnic identities, gender identities, and sexual identities—are *not* chosen or achieved in the sociological sense. They are ascribed at birth because conveyed through the blood and, in this sense, profoundly "natural."

To elaborate on the irony referred to a moment ago: many of the court's perspectives on adoption and the tenuousness of marriage drive home the point that the most powerful and enduring identities, loyalties, and passions are carried in the blood and, in any case, ascribed, hence relatively immutable. And yet the courts are key components of an institutional network that serves the needs of and hopefully adds to the ranks of those who convert to Islam (*mualaf*). (Recall here that the staff of the court includes an official whose job is to provide guidance and other assistance to converts and to serve as a liaison to the national board specifically designated to serve them [PERKIM].) As such, the courts necessarily underscore a reality that is in some ways central to the achievement of civil society but is nonetheless locally unsettling. To wit, religious identities and loyalties—like identities and loyalties of many other kinds—are not ascribed at birth but are at least potentially not only freely chosen but also hybrid, fluid, and protean. Such realities are rendered all the more locally unsettling when one considers that many non-Muslims convert to Islam because of their desire to take a Muslim spouse. This fact, coupled with the high statistical probability that any local marriage will end in divorce, means that the religious identities, commitments, and loyalties of converts are seen as resting on the very shaky bed of marriage. I would suggest that on some level(s) circumstances such as these cannot help but trouble the identities—though not necessarily the commitments and loyalties—of nonconverts.[7] To appreciate some of the dynamics alluded to here, we might consider the following two cases.

Case 35: *Indian Woman Inquiring about Converting to Islam.* This inquiry occurred while I was talking to the counselor about proceedings in another case that had just come to a close. It involved a young Indian woman who came into the counselor's chambers looking rather aimless. She mumbled something to the counselor (which I did not hear) and seemed to be asking for advice on where to turn if she wanted to convert to Islam, though she also made a passing reference to a police report. The woman then left the counselor's chambers almost as quickly as she had appeared and rode off on the back of a motorcycle. The counselor proceeded to explain to me that the woman had been living with someone for a few years and that she has two children with him. It is not clear if the man with whom she has been living is a Muslim or not, but he recently drove her from the house, at which point she seems to have filed a police report. Now she is involved with an Indonesian (or a Malay) who is a Muslim, and she wants to marry him. Perhaps more precisely, the man said to her that if they are going to have a relationship then they best be married. So she wants to convert to Islam and has come to the court to look into how she should go about this.

Comment: In discussing this case with me, the counselor was clearly irritated by the fact that the woman's sole motivation to convert to Islam was so that she would be able to marry a Muslim. "What if something happens in their marriage?" the counselor asked rhetorically. "Then will she renounce Islam? We don't want this." Significantly, the counselor was far more upset about this scenario than about the very serious and obviously long-term (criminal) breaches of morality preceding the woman's visit to the courthouse.

The only other proceeding involving conversion to Islam that I observed was initiated by a young Chinese woman. This case (considered below) also underscores the cultural and institutional link between religious conversion and marriage. It emphasizes as well the contemporary relevance, so far as Malays are concerned, of an observation made by W. W. Skeat in the course of the 1899–1900 Cambridge University Expedition to the northeastern Malay states that "Malayising Siamese . . . often turned Muslim because they had a Malay wife, but *'their hearts remained untouched'* " ([1900] 1953: 113; emphasis added).

Case 36: *Marina Low (or Long) bte. Abdullah, the Chinese Convert to Islam Who Needs a* Wali Hakim. Present were two young women in their mid- to late twenties, two older men (probably in their sixties), one of whom was the *imam* in the area in which the bride-to-be resided, and two employees from the *kadi*'s office who were called in to act as witnesses. Marina, the petitioner, is Chinese and a recent convert to Islam. Like previously unmarried Muslim women in most jurisdictions of Islam, she must have a legal guardian (*wali* or *wali hakim*) to get married. The legal guardian must be a Muslim and a male, preferably (and typically) a close blood relative such as the father. In this case, however, the father is not a Muslim, and thus an official (such as a judge or *hakim*) must perform the task. Marina had come to the *kadi*'s office to have this taken care of, to get the requisite permission and formal authorization.

There was nervous, tittering laughter toward the beginning of the session when the *kadi* asked Marina what her name was. The response, though I do not think this came from Marina herself, was Marina Low (or Long), which was followed by laughter. One of the employees of the office then said something like, "Yeahlah, daughter of Abdullah [binti Abdullah]," Abdullah being the "last name" typically given to converts. More nervous laughter ensued.

The *kadi* explained to Marina that he is supposed to "marry her" (serve as the *wali hakim*), but that he is also capable of designating his authority to the *imam* of the (mosque) community of which she is a member. He went on to explain that he needed to know if she agreed to this transfer of authority. Marina consented and the *kadi* then held the *imam*'s hand, in a prolonged handshake-like gesture, reciting the relevant legal passage that effectively transferred his authority in this matter to the *imam*.

Comment: Perhaps most interesting and revealing about this case is that nervous laughter and a sense of awkwardness pervaded most of the encounter. The laughter and awkwardness seemed keyed, ultimately, to nervousness and anxiety about Marina's oxymoronic cultural identity as a Chinese Muslim. Such hybrid cultural identities are far more oxymoronic than those involving Muslims from other ethnic groups such as Indians. Indian Muslims are in fact considered "Malay" in certain contexts—which virtually never happens with Chinese converts (Nagata 1978; Frith 2001). Whether the nervousness and anxiety at issue in this case are also derived partly from explicit awareness that Marina's commitment to Islam may well be no more stable or durable than her marriage is hard to say, though I suspect that this was very much involved as was clearly true of the preceding case.

These latter two cases, along with two of the others considered earlier in this chapter, indicate that some "ethnics" do wander into the courts. But their small numbers relative to the total volume of litigants and other clients underscore that the courts are designed and construed as a decidedly Malay phenomenon, though not explicitly marked as such. (Recall here the *kadi* asking Pakistani Muslims what "your people" do in cases of *tebus talak*.) So, too, in many respects is (local) Islam in its entirety. Such social facts are abundantly obvious to Malaysian Chinese. As Donald Nonini (1998: 446–47) has noted, Malaysian Chinese not only regard Islamic courthouses as state spaces and thoroughly "Malay," but they also "associate them with police powers that are capricious and dangerous to them, and thus do their best in everyday life to avoid them." The more general theme is that Islamic courts are key players in constituting and policing ethnic and other boundaries (see Peletz 1993a, and below [chapter 5]).

The basis of local distinctions between authentic and inauthentic Muslims is more complex than suggested thus far. For even people considered "Malay" whose ascendants have been Muslims for a number of generations are, at least in certain contexts, not considered "real" or "true" Muslims. And more often than not, such people are suspect with regard to their command of Islamic knowledge and their commitment to the moral values entailed in that knowledge. The reasons for this have partly to do with Malay notions of "origin-point" (*asal-usul*) and the idea that one's origin-point is a defining feature of one's personhood and identity. Put simply, a stigmatized origin-point, like one that confers prestige, endures through time.

The courts evince strong commitment to certain entailments of the concept of origin-point (as we have seen earlier, especially in chapter 2). But as we also saw when we focused on the work of the courts and the cultural logic of judicial process in particular, the courts are at the same time committed to effecting an attenuation and transformation of the concept, such that it is more in keeping with their visions of and for the ideal future of the Muslim community. This is most apparent in the fact that while the courts are concerned to ascertain origin-point in a limited geographic or territorial sense, they are altogether silent with respect to litigants' membership in specific lineage branches, lineages, and clans and with respect to various other aspects of genealogy and pedigree, which, historically speaking, were critical features of personhood and identity. There is, in short, little concern with any such dimensions of origin-point or personhood, even though villagers, especially those over forty-five to fifty years of age, are acutely concerned with some of these other dimensions of the concept. In Negeri Sembilan, this includes the idea that seriously inappropriate marriages involving matrilineally related ancestors going back as far as seven generations may result in an individual's being deformed or exhibiting one or another form of taint (*cacat*).

Concerns of the latter sort were raised in Bogang throughout the second period of fieldwork. This was partly because an important position in the indigenous clan-based polity had become vacant and the new appointment was very much on people's minds. The *undang* and his staff were conducting interviews with numerous villagers in Bogang (and elsewhere?) who were considered viable candidates for the office, and just as the material rewards and perks were quite significant—a handsome monthly pension, a Mercedes with a driver and "flags on the hood," as some villagers put it—so too was the prestige involved. Not only did the successful candidate need to come from the appropriate clan and lineage, but he (the candidate had to be male) also needed to have exceptional knowledge of *adat* and, ideally at least, be free of disqualifying conditions. Villagers I spoke with were clearly displeased with the candidate eventually chosen for the post, a wealthy, smooth-talking man with many years of experience in the civil service. One of the reasons given for their dismay was that some four or five generations back there had been an incestuous union (*sumbang*) among his ancestors. Not surprisingly, as some confided to me, his mother had a serious skin affliction as a consequence of this inappropriate union. More directly relevant is that this ancestral incest should have disqualified him for office. That it did not was for many elders a disturbing sign of the times, driving home the point that money and other profane considerations—the man eventually chosen for the post was said to have delivered sacks full of money to the *undang* to help ensure his successful candidacy—can and increasingly do override the natural (God-given) order of things.

It remains to add that much of the work facing the courts on this particular front has already been accomplished by other modern economic and political institutions. Clear evidence that this is so comes in many forms, one being the jokes made by elders and others that while adolescent and adult men were studying up on *adat* in anticipation or hope of being called for an interview, the only *perut* they knew about—*perut* being the term both for "lineage" and for "stomach," "abdomen," and "belly"—was the one they could reach down, rub, and try to keep full of food.

To appreciate the degree to which converts to Islam are not really accepted as normal, moral people, we might consider some commentary bearing on the legally valorized and culturally acceptable (though nonetheless morally awkward) practice of prearranged, temporary marriage that is effected to enable a husband and wife to reestablish their relationship after the husband has formally and irrevocably repudiated his wife. Among other things, this practice involves finding a man who, for a fee, will agree both to marry the woman in question and to divorce her after a relatively short period, "supposedly" having consummated the marriage in the meantime. (In Islamic law the consummation is required; but in local practice and elsewhere [for example, Singapore], the temporary husband agrees, if only implicitly, to forego the consummation [Djamour 1959: 113].) Such practices are most commonly known as *cina buta*, one literal translation of which is "blind Chinese."[8] Now, according to Araffin, these practices are only morally acceptable under certain circumstances. He explained as follows:

> If a man says to another man, "This woman needs to get married so that she can get back with her husband at some point in the future," this is one thing and more or less okay. [On the other hand,] it is wrong, sinful, to make such agreements ahead of time if the parties enter the agreement with the plan of ending the relationship after a day or so. To go into specifics about marrying today, consummating, and divorcing tomorrow, with such and such a fee, and so forth, this is not acceptable.

Araffin and others I asked did not know the origins or precise meaning of the term, and they encouraged me to ask "the experts." I mentioned to Araffin that I had once read that the expression may be of Sanskrit origin and asked him if he knew anything about that. He responded that he had heard that theory but really had no idea.

A highly educated Malay woman I interviewed in the United States in 1999 told me the following regarding the origins of the term: it is because the first historical occurrence of the practice in the Malay setting involved a blind Chinese man, who because he was literally blind could not see the wife in a physical sense and was also blind/oblivious to everything else about the woman. Since he was not tempted to remain with her, he agreed to the arrangement of marriage followed quickly by divorce. Subsequent practice, however, involved Malays (not Chinese) performing this service and need not have involved someone who was blind but perhaps someone who was "*bodoh* [stupid] or something."

Kamaruddin, my research assistant, maintained that "normal people" would not perform this service, adding that it would only be done by people with "low morals." When I asked him about the specific meaning(s) of the expression *cina buta*, Kamaruddin first said that whoever performs this service must be a Muslim through birth or conversion; otherwise it would not be acceptable. More relevant was Kamaruddin's surmising that the term might refer to Chinese who had converted to Islam, who, like other converts, are commonly referred to as "new siblings" (*saudara baru*). Kamaruddin explained that Chinese converts might not have a deep knowledge of the religion. As such they might be willing to perform the service, whereas others (Malays) would feel ashamed or embarrassed (*malu*) to do so. The *buta* part, Kamaruddin continued, might be shorthand for *buta hati*, a blind follower (literally, "a blind liver") and need not refer to someone who cannot see in a literal sense.

Kamaruddin told me he did not feel that the term *cina buta* was derogatory, but the thrust of his remarks suggests otherwise. There are three points to add here. First, however one interprets Kamaruddin's exegesis, there remains conjoined in the expression *cina buta* the terms for "Chinese" and "blind." Second, Chinese are viewed by Malays as morally bankrupt because they are seen as ruled by blinding passions for gambling, for consuming large quantities of alcohol and pork, and for all varieties of making money and getting ahead, which would even include "worshipping the steps to the house" if that would get them what or where they wanted (as my adoptive mother once told me). And third, the dubious morality of Chinese does not change if they convert to Islam.

Comments such as Kamaruddin's help illustrate local understandings of the expression *cina buta* and are in my view more germane than some of the earlier debates about the meaning of the term, which focus on its etymological origins (see Djamour 1959: 113–14n. 1, 1966: 20–21n. 1). Most important for present purposes are the unambiguous and uncontested though nonetheless paradoxical features of Kamauruddin's remarks: on the one hand, Chinese and other non-Muslims can and occasionally do convert to Islam; on the other hand, the existence of conversion notwithstanding, one's religious affiliation or identity is *not* something one chooses. The upshot is that Chinese who convert to Islam are not *really* Muslims or "real [or authentic] Muslims" as far as most contemporary Malays are concerned and are, needless to say, acutely conscious of this fact (Nagata 1978; Frith 2001). Nor, for that matter, are hill-dwelling aborigines (*orang asli*), who have been subject to government-sponsored Islamization programs in recent decades (Dentan et al. 1997). The latter programs, though largely unsuccessful, have resulted in some *orang asli* communities nominally embracing Islam only to renounce it later and revert to their more traditional religious beliefs and practices owing to their experience of state-sponsored Islamization schemes as the stuff of nightmares (both literal and figurative), if not tantamount to ethnocide (Dentan n.d.). This is deeply offensive to Malays, who regard *orang asli* renunciation of Islam as a profound rejection of their unique sacred heritage, a treachery akin to treason.

A religious identity, then, is *not* a choice or an achieved status. It is, rather, something ascribed, something in the blood, in nature, hence immutable. Consequently converts, aside from being inauthentic, are also unnatural, hybrid, oxymoronic, and dangerous creatures that invert and otherwise violate the most basic moral categories of the universe. Malays throughout Malaysia were thus shocked when they heard of the widely publicized case of the two Malay men who renounced Islam, converted to Christianity, and in June 1987 boasted in the national press of the success of their missionary work among Malays. (The two men were arrested in September 1987 under the Internal Security Act for "inciting religious tension.") Media coverage of their conversion and mission-ary efforts was immediately followed by charges from PAS leadership that UMNO's failure to safeguard Islam had resulted in untold moral catastrophes that included some 66,000 Malay Muslims having renounced Islam. This claim, though never substantiated and almost certainly false, was widely interpreted (and intended) as a direct attack on the ruling party for being recklessly lax in safeguarding Islam and, by implication, Malayness as well.

Subsequent years have seen a few other high-profile cases involving Malays who have renounced Islam and converted to Christianity (see Mohammad Hashim Kamali 2000: 203–19). In this context it should not be surprising to find that some Malay religious leaders and politicians, especially but not only those associated with PAS, have sought to introduce the death penalty for apos-tasy involving Muslims who have renounced Islam (*murtad*), even while they have supported legislation allowing non-Muslim children to convert to Islam without parental consent.

State-sanctioned strategies entailing the reinscription of authenticity and identity and the domestication or "education" of passion that is often implicated in such reinscriptions are by no means confined to the Islamic courts or other domains that come within the purview of religious administrative hierarchies or (rationalized) religion as it is currently defined. This will be especially clear in the next chapter. In the meantime we might take as a case in point issues of magic and sorcery. Legal personnel at the (secular) Magistrate's court told me that cases involving magic and sorcery are not handled by the secular courts because "there is never any real evidence of such things," much as Geertz (1960: 110) found in Java. Similar points were made by staff of the Islamic courts. Interestingly, however, staff of the Islamic courts are sometimes quite adamant that certain cases do, in fact, involve one or another kind of magic or sorcery. Thus, when a woman told the court that she "couldn't stand looking at her husband's face" and that it was this way from the first day of their marriage, a court official informed me that "orang buat," literally "a person did it," per-formed "love (or affection) magic" on her. Officials of the Islamic courts do, moreover, make notations to the latter effect in the files of cases they assume involve magic or sorcery. Such informal notations—along with the dynamics to which they are keyed—have no formal evidentiary status or other legal stand-ing, but they do provide guidelines for the ways in which court staff proceed in their handling of such cases, thus partially undercutting court denials of their phenomenological reality (see also Pura 1996).

In this regard it is interesting that in 1993 some national leaders sought to have "black magic" (*ilmu sihir*) categorized as a crime under federal (statutory) law. As reported in the August 13, 1993, edition of *The Star*: "We'll have to establish what is meant by black magic and . . . then . . . [we can] begin in-depth discussions" involving, among others, police and members of the Islamic Center (Pusat Islam), the Cabinet, and the Parliament. The inspector-general of police, Tun Hanif Omar, remarked that "if a *bomoh* or one who practiced black magic were to use a body or to exhume the grave of someone or commit murder, police could take action as it was a crime." Much of this is beside the point, for committing murder is already a crime, as is exhuming a grave without the permission of authorities. In some ways most interesting in all of this is the construction of the article in question, which appears with the headline, "Police Ready for Talks on Black Magic." The first five paragraphs of the eight-paragraph piece are concerned with black magic, but the final three paragraphs focus on corruption in the (overwhelmingly Malay) police force, the stern ac-tion of the police force's disciplinary division and Anti-Corruption Agency, and proposals for a 10–20 percent increase in the salary of police personnel. There is no clear link established in the article between black magic on the one hand and corruption and low salaries in the police force on the other, though the reader could conclude that they appear in the same piece because both sets of comments emerged either in the course of a high-level police seminar or shortly after its close and the follow-up questions and comments with reporters. One obvious commonality is that both initiatives involve efforts to tame the baser side of the person (especially the Malay person) and in so doing to contribute to the production of "a particular kind of modern human being."

We see in all such dynamics clear evidence of the ways in which culturally salient and politically freighted schemes of classification are both shifting and tightening, and doing so in ways that are ultimately somewhat predictable (or at least understandable) in light of more encompassing developments in culture and political economy broadly defined. Attendant developments that merit brief mention here include the profusion since the mid- to late 1980s of local pub-lications and authoritative pronouncements (*fatwa*) concerning Islamic views, often phrased as "*the* [essential] Islamic perspective," on the donation and transfusion of blood, the transplantation of human organs, and related matters "in light of *syariah* rules and medical facts" (see Hooker 1993; Ismail Haji Ibrahim 1998; cf. Furqan Ahmad 1987; Mohammad Naaem Yassen 1990). A more general and abstract point to underscore is that paradoxes as well as ambi-guities and other types of anomalies engendered in part by new technological and other developments in medicine and other branches of science, coupled with new technologies of communication and transportation that contribute to the global circulation of discourses of all kinds, pose formidable challenges and what are perceived as dangerous threats to systems of classification and order (in all senses of the term) in *all* societies, not least in Malaysia and elsewhere in the Islamic world and the Asia-Pacific region. Equally obvious is that one of the strategies commonly deployed to cope with such challenges and threats to established orders is to attempt to rationalize and otherwise fine-tune systems of classification, even though such efforts simultaneously result in new classifica-tory anomalies that are themselves defined as threatening and dangerous. Material presented in the next chapter makes this especially—and distressingly—clear.

To summarize and conclude this section of the chapter, the discourses of court personnel evince their largely implicit but nonetheless deeply felt moral imperatives to transform and "domesticate" the always potentially unruly and disruptive sentiments keyed to local kinship, particularly local kinship that ranges beyond the household or domestic domain. These moral imperatives are part and parcel of state-sanctioned religious and political strategies geared toward reinscribing local cultural values bearing on kinship, gender, and identity. While one objective of these strategies is to constrict the domain of kinship, local legal practices that attempt to transform kinship and restrict it to a narrowly defined domestic domain are heavily constrained, highly partial, and invariably contradictory and ironic. Paradoxical circumstances such as these exist partly because the imperatives are "operationalized" by means of state charters and bureaucratic channels that transmogrify their forms and meanings. The other relevant factor is that the effectiveness of the policies and their implementation depends on their being cast in the symbols and idioms of local cosmologies and systems of knowledge to which they must ambivalently accommodate themselves.

The objective of transforming and restricting kinship is pursued partly in an effort to create modern, relatively individualized political subjects ("new Malays," *Melayu baru*) who are not beholden to potentially compromising claims and loyalties entailed in extended kinship. The realization of this objective contributes, ironically, both to the erosion of locally distinctive kinship and to the production of the Western-style nuclear families and nuclear-family households that are for a variety of reasons also increasingly common among local Chinese and Indians as well as other Malaysians. Be that as it may, this goal is pursued as part of a strategy to clear and expand the space between family and household on the one hand and state on the other and thus more easily insert disciplinary mechanisms and institutions conducive to the achievement of a particular—and highly fragmented—vision of modernity and civil society.[9]

As discussed in more detail in the next section of the chapter and in the next chapter as well, changes such as these are among the sociocultural transformations effected by state projects of modernity in conjunction with the boom-bust cycles of global capitalism to which the state projects in question are ambivalently wed; and they are simultaneously masked and legitimized by discourses about timeless Islamic, Malay, and/or "Asian (family) values" that are promoted by national leaders and other agents of the state. The problem for the state, needless to say, is that somewhat autonomous voluntary associations beyond state control can move into and effectively colonize the social spaces cleared by state laws and policies before the state's institutions and disciplinary mechanisms are in place or fully operational. Alternatively, voluntary associations that are initially under the control of the state can evolve in such a way that they come to pose real or imagined threats to the state, as has happened to some degree with opposition political parties (such as PAS) and Muslim religious organizations like Darul Arqam (which, as mentioned earlier, was banned in

1994). When this occurs, repressive measures opposed to civil society are likely to be implemented or expanded. These, too, as we have seen in the period since former Deputy Prime Minister Anwar's arrest and imprisonment in 1998, are often rationalized in terms of "Asian values."

RATIONALIZATION AND RESISTANCE REVISITED

Having concentrated in much of the preceding section on the Islamic courts' involvement in the rationalization of kinship and identity, I would like to expand the discussion by considering dynamics of (cultural) rationalization bearing more directly on religion, including the involvement in such dynamics of the Islamic courts, various state strategies, and the *dakwah* movement. I focus in this discussion, as in the volume as a whole, on ordinary Malays or ordinary Muslims who are not in the forefront of contemporary religious or political developments. A key question is why Malaysia's ordinary Muslims, who make up what Jomo K. S. and Ahmad Shabery Cheek dub the "silent constituency" (1992: 104–5), are not inclined to resist the rationalization at issue, even though many proponents of rationalization target beliefs, practices, and values long central to the cultural identities of ordinary Muslims.

Local Islamic courts are involved in the policing of Islam in a wide variety of subtle and not-so-subtle ways, many of which we have already documented. One aspect or dimension of such involvement entails the court's prosecution of individuals alleged to be guilty of what is referred to as "deviationist teaching" or, as is more common, the court's referral of such individuals to religious bureaucrats and authorities with more expansive powers with respect to the administration of Islam, such as state-level religious councils and *fatwa* committees. Such transgressions, along with cases of "religious extremism," are sometimes handled instead by the secular courts. Decisions concerning which courts have jurisdiction over these matters often depend on high-ranking state officials' views as to the gravity of the threat(s) posed by the "wayward" individuals and groups thus involved. (The cases deemed to be the most serious, such as those involving the leadership of Darul Arqam, tend to be handled by secular authorities.) More important for present purposes is that while cases such as these, along with legislative and police moves to preclude or punish the occurrence of deviationism and extremism, have received much press in Malaysia over the past few decades, they have not attracted much scholarly interest.[10] In his now classic study of resistance in the state of Kedah, for example, James Scott devotes minimal attention to such phenomena, even though he acknowledges that "rarely a month goes by without a newspaper account of the prosecution of a religious teacher accused of the propagation of false doctrines" (1985: 335n. 67). Significantly, the latter admission is relegated to a footnote, just as the "flying letter" (*surat layang*) containing subversive religious/political prophecies that circulated in Kedah in the course of his fieldwork is presented, unanalyzed, in an appendix.[11]

The media are in fact full of accounts of various types of ritual specialists (*dukun/bomoh*) and religious scholars (*ulama*) who are charged with possessing prohibited pamphlets and prayer mats or "misusing" Quranic verses for the purpose of multiplying money or predicting lottery results. Legal and political initiatives in this area are an index of the state's longstanding concern to homogenize and otherwise tidy up Malay "folk religion" by cleansing it of what state officials (and those who have their ear) define as "pre-Islamic accretions." These measures are also aimed at curbing the introduction and spread of Shi'ite (especially Iranian) teachings and stifling all dissent cast in religious terms. The state has increasingly reserved and exercised the right to define all alternative religious discourse as counterhegemonic and subversive, and thus not only an affront to the dignity of Malays, Islam, or both, but also likely to engender religious or ethnic tension, thereby threatening communal harmony and national security.

Attempts to improve policing of the Muslim community have also involved a good deal of legislation and controversy concerning the body and sexuality, particularly the ritual appropriateness of various types of food products and cosmetics and, as noted earlier, the acceptability from the point of view of Islam of blood transfusions between Muslims and non-Muslims. Similarly, state policies and discourses have extolled the virtues of Muslim women wearing veils and other types of headgear and observing one or another form of "concealment" or seclusion (*purdah*), at least in certain contexts. And of course there has been much legislation and controversy concerning matters of marriage, divorce, and the like.

A crucial question is how the legal and other initiatives outlined here have been received by ordinary Muslims. Before turning to this question, however, it will be useful to consider recent historical transformations in rural areas and among ordinary Muslims as a whole. Various changes in the fieldwork site of Bogang between my first period of research (1978–80) and my second (1987–88) serve as my point of departure. First, the public address system housed in the village mosque and used to call people to prayer was always operational (and set at a higher volume) during the second period, in sharp contrast to the situation during my first fieldwork, when it was typically out of order. Second, the quintessentially Islamic salutation *Assalam alaikum* was far more frequently used (see Milner 1986: 60, Peletz 1993a), and other Islamic symbols and idioms permeated local discourse. Third, young male *dakwah* now appeared in the village on a fairly regular basis to "spread the word." And fourth, the dress of girls and young women had become much more modest, and some of them had taken to wearing the long skirts, mini-*telekung* (head coverings like those worn by Catholic nuns in the United States), and other headgear donned by female *dakwah* in the cities.

Transformations such as these are in some respects superficial, but they are important public markers of the shifting religious climate in villages like Bogang. Other less tangible changes include the further delegitimization of spirit cults, shamanism, and other ritual practices subsumed under the rubric of *adat*, and the development of non- or arelational forms of individualism, realized by conceptualizing serious wrongdoing, such as the harboring of spirit familiars (*pelisit*), in terms of "sin" (*dosa*) rather than "taboo" (*pantang* [*larang*]). Also evident was the emergence of a more pronounced pan-Islamic consciousness, a key feature of which is greater awareness of current trends elsewhere in the Muslim world, where Islamic resurgence, efforts to forge worldwide Islamic solidarity, and radical separation between Muslims and non-Muslims is the order of the day. Germane as well were heightened concerns with demarcating local (intra-Malaysian) boundaries between Muslims and non-Muslims and, related to this last point, greater suspicions of all non-Muslims, as expressed in the intensified bodily vigilance of males and females alike.

Many of these shifts are broadly compatible with the stated objectives and overall agendas of *dakwah* leaders, but we should not jump to the conclusion that ordinary Muslims are firmly behind or centrally involved in the resurgence. Indeed, we should start with a clean slate and the most basic questions: How are the legal and other initiatives cited earlier being received by ordinary, especially rural, Malays? And, more broadly: What is the nature of ordinary, particularly rural, Malays' perceptions of and attitudes toward the resurgence? The answers to these questions are elusive for a variety of reasons, one of which is that such questions have been largely ignored in the literature. This neglect exists even though most observers acknowledge that Malaysia's Islamic resurgence is a predominantly urban, middle-class phenomenon and, more specifically, that "*dakwah* people" (*orang-orang dakwah*) are "mainly middle-level urban workers, student groups or professionals without social status or power, who are marginally involved with modern development processes and generally incapable of acquiring an important platform in decision-making concerned with the government machinery or economy" (Wazir Jahan Karim 1992: 175).

The short, admittedly imprecise answer to the question regarding ordinary, especially rural Malays' perceptions of and attitudes toward the resurgence is that while some of them support it, many, perhaps most, are clearly hostile to both various elements of the movement and the state agents and others who endorse it. This hostility exists even though ordinary Malays experience Islam as central to their daily lives and cultural identities and embrace in principle most if not all efforts to accord Islam greater primacy among Malays and in Malaysia generally. In Bogang, for example, many elders insisted that those who have sought to sanitize local religion by cleansing it of its "parochial accretions" are ignorant not only of the true teachings of Islam but also of the ways of local spirits (*jin*); some of them lamented that the nonperformance of rituals such as *berpuar* and *bayar niat* has led to repeated crop failure and, in some cases, to the demise of rice production altogether.

Others spoke scornfully of the fact that members of certain *dakwah* groups (for example, Darul Arqam) had thrown their televisions, radios, furniture, and other household commodities into local rivers to dramatize their disdain of the polluting influences of Western materialism and to underscore their commitment to returning to the pristine simplicity of the lifestyle of the Prophet. These dramatic gestures were highly publicized (and undoubtedly exaggerated) in the state-controlled national press at a time when state policymakers and UMNO leaders were actively attempting to discredit the more radical elements of the movement. Though practices such as these have never been typical of the *dakwah* movement as a whole, they loomed large in some villagers' perceptions of the resurgence in its entirety.[12] More to the point, they fly directly in the face of the most pressing concerns of rural Malays, especially the poorest among them. Rural Malays seek to improve their standards of living and, ideally, to attain middle-class status through the acquisition of more land and other wealth-generating resources, and do in any event struggle desperately to avoid further impoverishment and proletarianization (see Wazir Jahan Karim 1992: 167, 175, 184–85).

Other residents of Bogang talked about the sexual inappropriateness and hypocrisy of unspecified *dakwah* groups (Darul Arqam?) who, according to villagers' understandings of accounts in the local media, allegedly engaged in "group sex" while enjoining fellow Muslims to observe strict sexual segregation. Still others viewed the *dakwah* emphasis on sexual segregation as largely redundant, since sexual segregation has long been a feature of rural Malay society. Perhaps more important, they felt that it represented a glaring example of the resurgents' ignorance of rural Malay culture and yet another indication of their profound hostility to it (cf. McAllister 1987: 475).[13]

Bogang residents' negative perceptions of and oppositional stances toward Rembau's *kadi* are of interest here. The *kadi*, recall, is conversant in Arabic, is a graduate of the prestigious al-Azhar University in Cairo (the most esteemed institution of higher learning in the entire Muslim world), has made the pilgrimage to Mecca, and is, more generally, both a key symbol and a primary agent of the resurgence. The former headman (*ketua kampung*) of Bogang feels that the *kadi* is a "playboy" who is taken to swaggering about and being arrogant (*sombong*). Another village elder complained bitterly to me of the *kadi*'s injustice for having "publicly slandered and embarrassed" him at the local mosque. And he assured me as he did so that he was not afraid of "people in turbans," which is a shorthand reference to pilgrims (*haji*) and male *dakwah* alike. Both sets of comments are deeply allegorical. Far from being merely narratives of the self encountering an Other, they constitute highly condensed symbolic statements of the ways in which ordinary Malays as a collectivity represent the Islamic resurgents (and vice versa). That such allegorical comments depict the resurgents as arrogant or *sombong* is quite revealing, insofar as *sombong* is perhaps best translated as "unresponsive to social expectation." The perception that the resurgents are unresponsive to social expectation and to ordinary Malays' concerns with reciprocity and reproduction in particular lies at the heart of ordinary Malays' negative or at least highly ambivalent assessments of the *dakwah* movement.

More broadly, Malays throughout the Peninsula are apprehensive that the merging of secular and religious law will result in the imposition of harsher *syariah* penalties for crimes currently handled by the secular legal system,[14] just as they are concerned that if this occurs, Malays and other Muslims will be subject to punishments more severe than those meted out to non-Muslims for the same offense(s). Such apprehensions and concerns warrant brief comment, for in addition to pointing up the conundrums of ordinary Malays who raise questions about the resurgents and those who share their agendas, they help illustrate the types of discursive responses articulated by *dakwah* and those sympathetic to their visions when confronted with such concerns. Consider the introduction of legislation (brought into force in 1986) allowing the Islamic courts in Kelantan to impose corporal punishment (caning) on those guilty of certain offenses, such as the consumption of alcohol. The introduction of this legislation met with strong disfavor from some Malay jurists and from various other quarters of the Malay population on the grounds that punishments such as caning were retrograde, draconian, or out of keeping with Islam. This criticism, in turn, led supporters of the legislation to respond by equating opponents of the new laws with the "colonial masters," whose policies were said to have severely constrained the operations and overall development of the Islamic courts and by implication Islam in its entirety.[15] Similar arguments have been deployed against those who did not line up in support of the PAS efforts to introduce *hudud* laws in Kelantan in the early 1990s and, indeed, against all who have opposed PAS programs and agendas.[16]

Ordinary Malays, for their part, commonly perceive the actions and pronouncements of the resurgents as involving a direct attack on sanctified elements of their basic values and cultural identities. The value conflicts at issue are especially pronounced in the realm of feasting. The resurgents' pointed criticisms of "wasteful feasts" and of the feasting (*kenduri*) complex in its entirety pose serious dilemmas for ordinary Malays. The criticisms index searing condemnations of ordinary Malays' basic values (including many they construe as thoroughly Islamic) but are made in the name of Islam, on the grounds that feasts incorporate animistic and Hindu-Buddhist—hence pagan—elements and are, in a good many cases, sinfully wasteful (cf. McAllister 1987: 442–43). These quandaries are readily apparent when one stops to consider that the hosting of feasts in connection with weddings, funerals, circumcisions, and so forth continues to be one of the main avenues through which ordinary Malays advance their claims to status and prestige. The sponsoring of feasts is of further importance in that it enables sponsors both to reciprocate the generosity of friends, relatives, and political allies whose feasts they have attended in the past and to create ritual and other debts in others, especially potential allies. There are other benefits of feasting, such as the feelings of harmony, well-being, and safety (*keselamatan*) that feasts ideally engender among hosts and guests alike and the fact that they bring pleasure to the spirits of the deceased ancestors (*roh arwah*) and other local spirit beings (*jin*), and otherwise serve to reciprocate the assistance of all such spirits and thus help ensure social and cultural reproduction.

Some Comparative and Theoretical Implications

Nearly one hundred years ago, R. J. Wilkinson, one of the most insightful of scholar officials dealing with Malay culture, wrote, "The native of the [Malay]

Peninsula is becoming less of a Malay and more of a Mussulman [*sic*]; his national ceremonies are being discarded, his racial laws are being set aside, . . . his inherited superstitions are opposed to Moslem belief as much as to Western science, [and] his allegiance is being gradually transferred from national to Pan-Islamic ideals" (1906: 80). These words will strike anthropologically up-to-date scholars of Islam as rather dissonant. I would nonetheless contend that in formulating these thoughts Wilkinson accurately prophesied key dynamics of the historical experiences of the Malay community since the beginning of the twentieth century. Most contemporary observers, myself included, would phrase the cultural and historical dynamics at issue in terms that are less value-laden and less simplistic. Specifically, contemporary observers should object to the explicit opposition between what Wilkinson refers to as "inherited superstitions" on the one hand and what he glosses as "Moslem belief" on the other. Scholars familiar with Woodward's (1989) rereading of Javanese religion are excellently positioned to delineate the problems with such perspectives, as are those who take issue with Dutch structuralist traditions entailing dichotomous treatments of the relationship between *adat* and Islam in Malay and Southeast Asian Muslim culture generally.[17] On closer analysis, many features of Javanese and Malayan religion that earlier observers (such as Wilkinson [1906] and Geertz [1960]) interpreted as "pre-Islamic" appear to be deeply grounded in or at least highly resonant with Sufi mysticism and other Middle Eastern and South Asian Islamic traditions and thus appropriately included within the domain of "normative Islam" or "normative piety."

Revisionist contentions concerning the Islamic status of defining features of Javanese and Malayan ritual complexes such as *selamatan* or *kenduri*, shadow-puppet theater, and traditional healing are based on painstaking scholarly studies of Islamic texts (including both the Quran and the *hadith* as well as chronicles such as *Babad Tanah Jawa*) and extensive work with mystics residing in and around royal centers like Yogyakarta. These contentions along with the more encompassing debates concerning "syncretism" have encouraged a radical rethinking of our entire approach to Javanese and Malayan Islam that is highly salutary. It is important to recognize, however, that such claims and debates do not necessarily figure into the discourses of the majority of Muslims in Java or Malaysia. Javanese reformists and modernists, for example, typically appear to have little if any interest in the truth value of these types of claims, and the Javanist majority lacks access to the relevant texts and ritual specialists necessary to make such claims a foundational part of their cultural repertoire or symbolic capital (see Woodward 1989: 149–50, 237–38).[18] The distinction drawn here is essential to bear in mind, for the scholarly debates in question are in many respects cast in "etic" terms (however much they may build on "emic" categories) and appear to have little direct relevance to the "emic" experiences of the majority of the population.

This is especially so in Malaysia. Since the late nineteenth century and during the past few decades in particular, core symbols of Malayness long subsumed under the rubric of *adat*—and in some cases that of Islam as well—have been denigrated by Islamic resurgents on the grounds that they are pre- or simply un-Islamic and, as a result, have had their legitimacy undermined. In some cases, moreover, the psychological and sociological scope and force of such symbols have been drastically undercut, and the ritual and other practices associated with them have ceased to exist. At the same time there has been a dialectically related process involving the development and expansion of Islamic institutions and the heightened scope and force of Islamic symbols and idioms, a process that has clearly advanced (though it need not do so) at the direct expense of *adat* both as an institutional framework and a system of symbols and meanings.

Various aspects of this process are clear in Kelantan. During my first and second periods of fieldwork, many urban and rural Malays who no longer adhered to rural customs not only perceived Kelantanese Malays as the "most traditional" of all Malays but also regarded Kelantanese *adat* as the richest and most impressive of all Malay *adat*. Kelantanese, for their part, viewed the puppeteers (*dalang*) of the renowned shadow-puppet theater (*wayang Siam*) as the embodiment of "tradition" (Wright 1986). And yet religious authorities and others of a reformist bent, including most supporters of the Islamic opposition party, PAS (Sweeney 1972: 35), have maintained that all traditional performing arts, the shadow-puppet theater in particular, are contrary to the teachings of Islam and constitute a clear threat to the public's morality and spiritual well-being. The former *imam* of Kota Baru (Kelantan's capital) based his opposition to *wayang Siam* and related genres on the "unrestricted mingling" not only of men and women in the audience but also of male and female puppets on screen. Others have objected on the grounds that Pak Dogol, the god/clown of the *wayang Siam*, not only acts as a servant to Seri Rama, the celebrated hero of the shadow play, but is also the *dewa Sang Yang Tunggal*, the highest of all Hindu demigods (Wright 1986: 31–32). In his capacity as the One Great One and as the Kelantanese incarnation of Semar, Pak Dogol is the object of the *pujaan* (praise, adoration, worship) that is ritually enacted by *dalang* at the start of each performance. In the eyes of reformers and modernists, the ritual veneration of Pak Dogol appears distressingly close to the heinous sin of *syirik*, which refers both to polytheism generally and to the worship of idols specifically. Because the distinction between Allah and Pak Dogol has been elided by various *dalang* in the past (Sweeney 1972: 35), many reformers and modernists have found additional support for their position that *wayang Siam* performances are forbidden and sinful (*haram* and *berdosa*). Especially telling is that shortly after gaining control of the state government of Kelantan in 1990, PAS formally banned the performance of shadow-puppet theater and related genres of popular drama.[19]

Dalang have responded that all such criticism is unfounded, that their craft is both Islamic in origin and in contemporary design and that their invocations include Quranic prayers and chants. Their efforts in this regard have been largely unsuccessful, especially since, unlike the situation in the Javanese royal capitals of Yogyakarta and Solo, they lack elaborate court traditions and royal sponsorship to back them up. From some three hundred *dalang* in Kelantan in the mid-1960s, there were fewer than one hundred in the late 1970s (Sweeney 1972: 3; Wright 1986: 41n). Their numbers are in sharp decline even though the federal government, in its efforts to showcase certain features of Malay culture and counter the deracinating effects of Western-oriented modernization, has made numerous efforts to encourage the arts of *dalang* and the cultural heritage they represent, and does in any event continue to maintain an elaborate display at the National Museum (Muzium Negara) dedicated to their contributions to and embodied enactments of Malay culture. It is no exaggeration to say that the death on January 1, 2001, of the country's most famous *dalang*, Pak Hamzah Awang Amat, who acquired his knowledge and expertise from the legendary *dalang* Awang Lah and had to flee his native Kelantan and relocate in Kuala Lumpur in order to practice his art and craft, marked the end of an important era, especially one defined in cultural political terms.

Another key symbol of Kelantanese Malay culture and identity for many centuries was Main Peteri, a genre of shamanistic performance found mainly in Kelantan and Terengganu that has much in common with *wayang kulit* shadow-puppet theater and *mak yong* dance theater in its ethos, worldview, language, and basic symbolism. Carol Laderman devotes the better part of her superb (1991) monograph to analyzing the transcripts of the Main Peteri séances she attended and recorded, but she also notes at the outset of the monograph that "all the traditional healers mentioned in this book have ceased their practice, due to death, infirmity, or religious considerations" (xvi). In later pages we learn that although death and infirmity are partly responsible for the cessation of some shamanistic performances, the chief factor in the decline of Main Peteri (the genre is more or less defunct) and all other traditional theatrical performances is "religious opposition" from those alternatively referred to as "the Islamic establishment," the "Islamic hierarchy," "pious folk," or simply "religious people." They oppose Main Peteri and related genres on the grounds that these performances are pre-Islamic and therefore sinful, especially because they attest to the continued significance in contemporary Malay culture of Hindu-Buddhist and pre-Indic (animist) motifs that stand as highly condensed symbols of "pre-Islamic days of ignorance." More specific objections are raised because shamans are seen by "pious folk" as trafficking in various Hindu, ancestral, and chthonic spirits and deities—some of whom are expressly sought out as alternatives to Allah when He fails to respond to ritual specialists' requests.[20]

Laderman's book thus presents us with an enigma. On the one hand, owing largely to opposition cast in Islamic terms, certain long-established rituals are no longer performed. On the other hand, many of the sanctified beliefs and postulates encoded in such rituals retain their wide currency and are, for many villagers at least, still thoroughly compelling. The more general dilemma is that while Islamic opposition to local *adat* has intensified in recent decades, these very same *adat* (or certain features of them) still make up important, if increasingly devalued, components of cultural identity among ordinary Malays in Kelantan, Negeri Sembilan, and elsewhere, particularly inasmuch as they help demarcate and reinforce the boundaries of local communities and differentiate locally defined groups of Malays both from one another and from outsiders as a whole. Bear in mind here that Malays in Kelantan have generally low regard for and certainly do not want to be identified with Malays in Negeri Sembilan (and vice versa), let alone Javanese, Minangkabau, etc. Kelantanese and other Malays differentiate themselves from one another on the basis of their *adat*, since Islam, in their view, is essentially the same wherever it is found. To grind down and obliterate distinctions of *adat* is to render Kelantanese Malays equivalent to Negeri Sembilan Malays, Javanese, and Minangkabau. This flattening and evisceration of locally defined *adat* and cultural identities may be the price that has to be paid for the cultural and political unification of Malays and their continued political supremacy vis-à-vis Chinese, Indians, and others. But it is a price paid with considerable ambivalence.

Ordinary and other Malays increasingly refer to themselves as "we Muslim people" (*kita orang Islam*) rather than "we Malay people" (*kita orang Melayu*; Nash 1991: 698)—thus providing additional support for Wilkinson's early twentieth-century remarks about Malays becoming "more Muslim" and "less Malay." But ordinary Malays clearly experience profound ambivalence both about the overall trajectory and cultural cost of twentieth-century change and about the resurgents, state policies, and agencies most directly implicated in the transformations—most notably, the perceived losses—in question. This ambivalence would undoubtedly be less pronounced if the state-sponsored institutional changes associated with the resurgence responded more directly to the basic needs of rural Malays. As it stands, however, many of these measures are geared toward meeting the twin objectives of state building (centralizing and consolidating state power) and responding to the concerns of certain segments of an urban, middle-class constituency.

In light of ordinary Malays' negative perceptions of and attitudes toward the resurgence, one might reasonably expect to find some organized protest against the resurgence or at least a range of behavior that might plausibly be interpreted as overt or covert resistance to it. In the latter connection I have in mind those everyday forms of resistance that James Scott has documented for rural Malays opposed to the Green Revolution and the New Economic Policy: character assassination, slander, backbiting, gossip, shunning, foot-dragging, noncompliance, and the like (1985; see also Scott 1990). Such everyday forms of resistance do exist, though, all things considered, they are not common. It is not only everyday forms of resistance that are relatively unelaborated but also what Scott refers to in his more recent work as "the hidden transcript," that is, "the discourse that takes place 'offstage,' beyond direct observation by powerholders" (1990: 4). Why, then, despite ambivalence and hostility of the sort mentioned earlier, is there relatively little evidence of either everyday resistance to the resurgence or an elaborated or even incipient alternative (let alone an explicitly counterhegemonic) ideology that critiques the movement in religious or other terms?

There are at least four variables that constrain the elaboration of resistance and oppositional ideologies, including those largely confined to hidden transcripts.[21] The first two fit more or less comfortably within the scope of (can be accommodated by) contemporary resistance studies. The third and fourth do not and partly for this reason will be discussed in greater detail.

First, as already noted, ordinary (and other) Malays incur potentially grave political risk if they publicly question or cast aspersions on the increasingly hegemonic discourses of the *dakwah* movement. Trafficking in alternative religious discourses is dangerous. The state not only reserves and increasingly exercises the right to define all alternative discourses as counterhegemonic and therefore an affront to the dignity of Malays and/or Islam; it also holds that such alternative religious discourses are liable to engender religious or ethnic tensions and thus threaten communal harmony and national security. In the worst-case scenario, trafficking in alternative religious discourses, even those that are not counterhegemonic, can land one in jail for an extended period of time.

A second variable, inextricably related but not reducible to the first, has to do with the fact that village society and culture are in many respects encapsulated within a national political order in which, in the words of Bourdieu, there is "total . . . [and in some ways] totally invisible censorship on the expression of the specific interests of the dominated . . . [such that the latter] can only choose between the sanitized words of official discourse and inarticulate grumblings" (1984: 462). In fact, such encapsulation is both incomplete and highly uneven, and although official discourse is "highly sanitized," the alternatives are by no means invariably confined to "inarticulate grumblings." "Grumblings" bearing on race, ethnic, and gender relations, for example, are in many instances both highly articulate and trenchant.

The third variable has relatively little to do with fears of political reprisals, material losses, or censorship—concerns that relate ultimately to inequities of power and domination and to the real or imagined experiences of discipline and punishment and that all too often are privileged in the cross-cultural literature on resistance as *the* primary impediments to resistance. The variable to which I refer is a broadly moral or existential constraint emanating from the constitution of Malay cultural identity. To wit: ordinary Malays experience profoundly disconcerting moral and existential dilemmas if they register any form of dissent with the movement insofar as it claims as its primary objective the spiritual and material betterment of all Malays (Muslims), and likewise appears to be the only vehicle capable of protecting Malays from Chinese and Indian infidels and from the ravages and vicissitudes of government policies, state-sponsored capitalism, and the global economy (cf. McAllister 1987: 476).

Put simply, albeit in a mixed metaphor, it is not kosher and is in many contexts a morally treasonous offense akin to incest and cannibalism for Malays to come out publicly against the Islamic resurgence, particularly inasmuch as doing so is tantamount to "letting down the side" if not actually renouncing one's identity as a Malay (see Jomo K. S. and Ahmad Shabery Cheek 1992: 104–5). This is especially true because many of the rituals and symbols that long constituted Malay cultural identity have been eviscerated by nationalist and transnationalist discourses emphasizing Islamic nationalism and reform as well as "science," "progress," and "secular education." At this point in history, in other words, the rituals and symbols that are central to Malay cultural identity are so thoroughly enmeshed in a translocally and transnationally defined Islam that there is little if any space for the development of a moral vocabulary that allows Malays to resist the resurgence or construct an alternative vision of or for the future. Exacerbating the situation is the absence of meaningful secular movements, of the sort found in Indonesia and other countries with Muslim majorities, with the capacity to serve as alternative vehicles for the realization and canalization of reformist sentiments conducive to redemptive change. In the absence of such movements, there is hardly any room for "fence sitting," and very little middle ground generally, in the increasingly politicized religious and other social arenas in which Malays act out and create meaning and order in their lives. In this respect the situation in contemporary Malaysia differs in significant ways both from what one finds in much of Indonesia and many other countries with sizable Muslim populations and from the situation in Malaysia (Malaya) during the heyday of the Kaum Muda movement in the early twentieth century.

The moral constraints at issue here are of comparative and theoretical interest, particularly since moral variables are typically given insufficient analytic attention in the literature on resistance. In this connection we might consider Scott's (1985) incisive analysis of everyday forms of peasant resistance in the state of Kedah, which is in many respects the locus classicus of contemporary resistance studies. Scott does make provision for moral variables such as ties of kinship, friendship, patronage, and ritual commensality that impede poor Malays' resistance to the Green Revolution and the New Economic Policy. In Scott's view, and that of many other students of resistance (like Taussig [1980]), however, such variables are relevant only insofar as they "muddy the 'class waters'" or otherwise impinge on relations of power and domination that obtain between major status groups (landlords and tenants, rich and poor, and so forth). Conversely, moral variables that do not impinge on relations of the latter sort are largely overlooked by Scott and many other students of resistance. Thus, while scholars like Scott distance themselves from Marxist theories of exploitation and class, they often preserve one of Marxism's hidden premises: the tendency to see class as somehow the most "essential," natural, or unfetishized of all social groupings and thus to see class interests as the most important or rational of all social interests.

Of broader concern, as Ortner (1995) points out, is that scholars such as Scott give short shrift to religiosity and culture as a whole.[22] Even though Scott, especially in his 1990 work, discusses various culturally specific forms of personal humiliation and degradation that are associated with domination and are on occasion resisted on religious grounds or in religious terms, these instances of personal submission and humiliation are linked with what are ultimately narrowly defined variants of political, economic, or racial domination and exploitation. Scott makes no provision for instances of cultural domination or cultural disenfranchisement that are not part of relatively fixed forms of domination tied to class-based or feudal hierarchies or to systems of caste, apartheid, slavery, and the like. (The same is true, albeit to a lesser degree, of Taussig [1980]; see Edelman [1994].) I emphasize this point partly because in the larger scheme of things, ordinary Malays are not deeply concerned with the political and economic implications of the resurgence, though some such implications are certainly bothersome and threatening to many of them (see also Jomo K. S. and Ahmad Shabery Cheek 1992: 99).[23] It is rather the symbolic and overall cultural domination—particularly the religiously cast moral critique of their cultural identities—entailed in the movement, which is, recall, supported primarily by "middle-level urban workers, student groups . . . [and] professionals without [significant] social status or power" (Wazir Jahan Karim 1992: 175), that is most offensive and troubling for them. Note that many of the everyday forms of resistance undertaken by ordinary Malays to "fend off" the resurgence are directed primarily at institutional infringements on their autonomy and social control. The analytically and culturally distinct dimensions of the resurgence that ordinary Malays find most *morally* offensive are much more troubling for them to confront, directly or otherwise, and are, partly for this reason, all the more vexing than the institutional encroachments mentioned earlier.

A fourth variable that constrains the elaboration of resistance and oppositional ideologies has to do with the fact that most ordinary (and other) Malays feel that they live in something of a Panopticon in which all social relations are hierarchical and power-laden and all social activities are assiduously scrutinized and evaluated by intimate and not so intimate Others. This is not the famed Panopticon of Foucault (1977), where Big Brother and his agents are ubiquitous, omniscient, and all-powerful, with their unrelenting gazes and disciplinary mechanisms penetrating the most intimate recesses of personal and social space. Rather, the Panopticon to which I refer is more like what Unni Wikan (1987, 1989) has described for rural Bali, where endemic status rivalries are matters of life and death both in the metaphorical sense delineated by Geertz in his celebrated (1973a) analysis of the Balinese cockfight and in a literal sense as well. In Bali, the systematization of doctrine and the intensification of religious concern that are part and parcel of religious rationalization ("internal conversion") have only to a limited degree involved the "disenchantment of the world," the removal of "the locus of sacredness . . . from the rooftrees, graveyards, and road-crossings of everyday life" (Geertz [1964] 1973: 174)[24] or, put differently, the "displacement of magical elements of thought." That the Balinese have by no means bid adieu to the "garden of magic" is clear from Wikan's findings that Balinese "live in a world where murder or attempted murder resulting in sickness from sorcery is the order of the day" (1989: 300) and, more generally, that "around, 50 percent of all deaths . . . are thought to be caused by black magic or poison" (295). Wikan emphasizes that most of this evil and misfortune is believed to be caused not by witches, sorcerers, or other local repositories of esoteric knowledge but by "intimate others" who are motivated by envy, jealousy, greed, or concerns to retaliate against those who have rebuffed their advances or overtures, or otherwise given offense. As they make their daily rounds, according to Wikan, Balinese live feeling "forever vulnerable," even in the relatively "private" contexts of their yards, kitchens, and bedrooms. In contrast to the domination and powerlessness experienced by prisoners and others trapped within the Panopticons of Foucault, however, the perennial feelings of vulnerability experienced by Balinese are only minimally (if at all) related to their positions in class or other relatively fixed status hierarchies and are only minimally (if at all) keyed to the presence within their environs of Big Brother or his agents. These feelings stem instead from the hundreds if not thousands of big *and* little brothers and sisters peopling their social universes, good numbers of whom are assumed to be deploying all of the social and cultural resources at their disposal to enhance their own prestige and simultaneously undercut the prestige claims of all others.

Most ordinary (and other) Malays appear to feel that they live in the same type of Panopticon, one in which (to paraphrase Miranda and thus overstate the case) anything they say or do can and will be used against them. In the Malay Panopticon, Islamic symbols and idioms are among the most strategic—and clearly the most sanctified—of the social and cultural resources available to people to articulate their claims to high status discursively and, as is more commonly done, to make direct or indirect allusions to the status inferiority of others. The symbols and idioms of *adat* and modernity are in many cases altogether irrelevant as criteria to rank oneself vis-à-vis others and, in any event, do not resonate with the shifting religiosity characteristic of rural communities or the nation as a whole. In contexts such as these, questioning anything cast in Islamic terms, like specific legislative measures or one or another aspect of the *dakwah* movement, increases one's vulnerability both to homegrown social criticism and to loss of prestige in locally defined hierarchies of value. Put differently, even in local communities made up entirely of ordinary Malays, it is always risky to be perceived as "insufficiently Islamic" or a "bad Muslim." Erring on the side of being "too Islamic," in contrast, generally carries little risk and does, moreover, bring many potential social and cultural rewards.

These Panopticon-like features of the social and cultural universes of ordinary Malays thus serve to constrain the elaboration of strategies and ideologies of resistance to the Islamic resurgence. More generally, they indicate that an understanding of resistance and oppositional ideologies (including hidden transcripts) requires an analysis of the political dynamics of the presentation of self in everyday life that goes far beyond investigation of the politics of the major lines of cleavage associated with the relatively fixed hierarchies of class, race, and gender. In the highly mercurial topographies of everyday social life, all discourses have multiple uses and are, among other things, both sources of constraint (and personal, social, and cultural mooring) as well as potentially valuable resources that can be deployed in the pursuit of social actors' culturally defined interests. The multiple and in many cases contradictory uses and entailments of discourses including, most notably, religious discourses account for a good measure of the ambivalence surrounding them. Studies of culture and politics that focus on domination and resistance or accommodation thus need to devote greater analytic attention to the phenomenon of ambivalence. If they fail to do so, they run the risk of being both "ethnographically thin" (to borrow Ortner's term) and highly anemic with respect to their treatment of the cultural psychology of the social actors who are at the center of their inquiries.

Malaysia's Islamic resurgence is an urban-based, middle-class phenomenon. The movement has been supported and constrained by a wide variety of dynamics, including legislation and state policies aimed partly at encouraging it along relatively moderate lines and otherwise controlling and co-opting it in an effort to undercut religious and political opposition and shore up support for the ruling party. The effects of the resurgence in the countryside and among ordinary Malays merit far more attention than they have received thus far, especially since most Malays live in or hail from rural areas and conceptualize and enact their religiosities and cultural identities in terms that are distinct from (and in some cases mutually incompatible with) those of the resurgents.

The discourses of the resurgence, though not usually represented as monolithic in the scholarly literature, are nonetheless far less hegemonic than most accounts of the resurgence suggest. Many rural and urban Malays are extremely ambivalent and hostile toward the movement, even though they do embrace and experience Islam as central to their daily lives and identities. The fact remains, however, that their ambivalence and hostility are not necessarily realized in everyday forms of resistance or even in the elaboration of "discourses that take place 'offstage,' beyond direct observation of powerholders" (Scott's hidden transcripts). An accurate sense of the impact of the resurgence and the support it receives in rural areas and among ordinary Muslims thus requires that our investigations extend beyond clandestine sabotage, foot-dragging, noncompliance, slander, character assassination, and the like and focus much more closely on the sentiments and dispositions of the rural Malay populace, many of which are not realized in practice or in hidden transcripts. A given population's refusal or reluctance to engage in practices of resistance along with its failure or unwillingness to elaborate hidden transcripts does not necessarily reflect its fears of political reprisals or material losses, its befuddlement or mystification by charismatic leaders or some other form of "false consciousness," or, more generally, the efficacy of one or another type of politically motivated hegemony. Such refusals, reluctance, and failures (to phrase the issue in arguably problematic negative terms) may stem instead from moral constraints and ambivalences that are both analytically and culturally distinct from variables typically highlighted in resistance studies.

Neither the state nor its policies are monolithic; similarly, ideologies propagated by the state or elites of various kinds, however hegemonic, are never thoroughly dominant or absolutely controlling. For these and other reasons we need to be more attuned both to the existence and reproduction of sentiments and dispositions that are contrary to official hegemonies and to the moral and other variables that constrain (or, alternatively, promote) their elaboration in alternative (including explicitly counterhegemonic) discourses. In the latter connection in particular, constraints and other entailments of a moral nature merit far more attention than they have received thus far. So, too, does the phenomenon of ambivalence, which is a key variable both in the religious and political arenas of contemporary Malaysia and in contexts of social and cultural change generally—indeed, in all of social life.[25]

In the Malay case, rationalization and other religious changes have involved the emergence of diverse currents of Islamic nationalism and reform, the rise of *dakwah* sensibilities, and the decline, though not the disappearance, of spirit cults and most types of shamanism and traditional midwifery. They have also witnessed spiritual power and energy being increasingly concentrated in God rather than simply held by Him for the most part but also diffused among sacred shrines, graveyards, traditional curers and exorcists, and various local spirits. Even so, many beliefs and practices associated with what Weber ([1922] 1963: 13) refers to as the "chthonic deities of the peasantry" are alive and well, and there is still considerable demand for highly syncretic, largely pre-Islamic rituals geared toward healing victims of poisoning and sorcery. Despite their increasingly dubious legitimacy by local standards, these latter rituals, and the institution of *dukun* (healer) more generally, still flourish largely because Malays continue to be extremely fearful and anxious about being poisoned and sorcerized (Provencher 1979: 48; Peletz 1988a, 1993b). Such rituals are in fact thriving in urban areas because urban Malays appear to be even more fearful of mystical attack and poisoning than do their rural counterparts.

These fears and anxieties attest to heightened concerns with bodily vigilance, the integrity of the Malay social body, and the stability of the Malaysian body politic (see Ong 1988; Frith 2001). So, too, do many other late twentieth-century developments within the Malay community: outbreaks of spirit possession ("mass hysteria") on the shop floors of modern factories in Free Trade Zones and elsewhere; women wearing more modest clothing (including head-gear and the veil) and being subject to more restrictive controls on their bodily functions and sexuality; and public debates about giving and receiving blood as well as the ritual appropriateness of various food products and the ingredients used in perfumes, cosmetics, and other preparations for care of the body. These and attendant developments point to important shifts in the sources, loci, and meanings of danger and marginality discussed below (chapter 5) and elsewhere.[26] The broader relevance of such developments, aside from their obvious demonstration that cultures are not seamless wholes and are in fact characterized by far more disjunctions, paradoxes, and contradictions than are allowed by Geertzian and other Parsonian formulations of Weberian theory, is twofold. First, they indicate that processes of rationalization are far less uniform, linear, and mechanical than is widely assumed. And second, they provide poignant testimony to the darker, apocalyptic side of rationalization, such as the depersonalization and alienation that result from politically sustained rationalization and the attendant politicization and reinscription of categories of understanding and experience, bearing on authenticity and identity, for example, that were previously taken for granted. This theme figures prominently in Weber's scholarship but is frequently obscured in the work both of Weber's intellectual disciples and of a good many religious modernists (Muslims, Christians, and others) who sound the clarion call for rationalization and reform. Processes of religious rationalization and reform are not all purification and enlightenment. In Malaysia, Bali, other parts of Indonesia, and many other contexts where such processes are well underway, they have some decidedly invidious and otherwise divisive ("antirational") consequences for basic human social relations.

Producing Good Subjects, "Asian Values," and New Types of Criminality

> Nowadays, with people moving into the city and with modern change and such, there are all sorts of things going on. . . . People think they can do anything.
> —*Sheikh Gazali bin Haji Abdul Rahman, chief judge, Islamic Court of the Federal Territory of Kuala Lumpur, 1998*

> Parents [need] to take up parenting skills and adopt the zero tolerance concept in family life, religion and law. . . . Zero tolerance means parents will not endure or allow room for waywardness in the family. They will not adopt the *tak apalah* (it doesn't matter) attitude. . . . UMNO branches, religious departments, schools, parent-teacher associations and the media . . . [will all] be utilized to spread the message on proper parenting skills.
> —*Datuk Abdul Hamid Othman, minister in the prime minister's department, 1997*

IN PREVIOUS CHAPTERS I have demonstrated that in terms of their everyday discourses and actual practices, Malaysia's Islamic courts are centrally involved in producing a modern Malay middle class composed of relatively individualized and responsive political subjects who are not beholden to potentially compromising claims and loyalties entailed in extended kinship that might undercut their allegiances to the nation-state and the global community of Muslim believers. I have also made clear that the court's efforts in these areas resonate with state concerns to clear and expand the space between family (household) and state, and thus more easily insert disciplinary mechanisms and institutions conducive to the furtherance of the always unfinished project of nation building in accordance with a particular vision of modernity and civil society in an age of ever-increasing globalization.

In this chapter I pursue some of these themes in greater detail by examining the production of mutually constituting and otherwise dialectically related discourses concerning purportedly traditional "Asian values" and new types of criminality. I should perhaps reiterate here that in the course of my fieldwork in the Islamic courts, these latter discourses were not evident in a register of specifically "Asian values," though they were articulated in the highly congruent registers of Islamic and/or Malay values. Such narratives are nonetheless pressed into service with respect to the very same reinscription of authenticity and identity that occurs in the Islamic courts, and as components of discursive strategies to constitute "good subjects" and define new types of criminality, they resonate deeply with the narratives produced by these courts. No less significant is that some of the political and cultural crises that have heightened the centrality of discourses on "Asian values" in recent years have helped bring about the passage of Islamic laws bearing on "sodomy," "homosexuality," and "lesbianism." Such developments allow us to see a legal and more encompassing cultural "discourse in the process of constituting itself" (Foucault 1980: 38)—or more accurately, a variety of such discourses in the making. They also provide compelling empirical support for one of Foucault's (1977, 1978) more insightful critiques of received wisdom. To wit: that much of what appears to be "straightforward repression" is not merely negative in the sense of curtailing, denying, and proscribing but also, and more important, that it has "positive" or productive dimensions in that it is centrally implicated in the creation, reproduction, and circulation of new symbols, meanings, and more encompassing discourses—new forms of knowledge and power. This is clearly the case in Malaysia, where the last few decades, the 1990s especially, have seen not only the repression of all varieties of transgender practices but also the creation of entirely new discourses bearing on perversions and "homosexuality" in particular, which is defined in nationalist and transnational discourse as a thoroughly "Western disease." For these and other reasons these discourses are germane to the work and overall missions of the Islamic courts in recent years and well into the foreseeable future.

In terms of case material, much of the chapter is devoted to a discussion of two celebrated criminal cases that rocked Malaysia in the mid- to late 1990s. The first involved a woman (Azizah) from the state of Kelantan, who in December 1996 was found to have "passed" as a male in order to marry her female lover, creating public controversy on such a scale that she was referenced in some media accounts as "the woman who shook the nation." The second case involves nationally eminent and internationally revered politician Anwar Ibrahim, who has been held in prison since September 1998, which is when he was stripped of his official titles (which included deputy prime minister and minister of finance) and charged with numerous counts of sodomy, corruption, and bribery. To help establish some context for these cases and the myriad issues they raise, I first provide brief remarks on the cultural history of gender pluralism in Southeast Asia.

A NOTE ON GENDER PLURALISM, TRANSGENDER PRACTICES, AND THE LONG DURÉE

Among the more interesting features of Southeast Asia as a "culture area" are the deeply entrenched and broadly institutionalized traditions of pluralism with respect to gender and sexuality. Put differently, Southeast Asians have long exhibited considerable tolerance and respect for numerous variants of gendered behavior. In the present context I cannot elaborate on the reasons for these patterns, their scope, or historical origins, though I can direct attention to a few relevant dynamics that prevailed during the period of Southeast Asia's early modern history that is sometimes referred to as the "Age of Commerce" (1450– 1680). Perhaps most important to note is that during the first half of the Age of Commerce (and for many centuries prior to it), religious traditions throughout Southeast Asia were "profoundly dualistic, with male and female elements both needing to be present to give power and effect. Female gods of the underworld, of the earth or crops (especially rice), and of the moon balanced the male gods of the upper world, the sky, iron (that which ploughs the earth, cuts the rice stalk), and the sun" (Reid 1993: 161–62). Women predominated in a good many ritual contexts associated with agriculture, birth, death, and healing, per- haps because their reproductive capacities were seen as giving them regenera- tive and other magical powers that men could not match.

This was a period in Southeast Asia's history that was characterized not only by relatively egalitarian relations between males and females but also by rela- tive tolerance and indulgence with respect to things erotic and sexual, at least among the commoner majority. Indeed, Portuguese observers of the sixteenth century reported that Malays were "fond of music and given to love," the broader themes being that "pre-marital sexual relations were regarded indul- gently, and [that] virginity at marriage was not expected of either party" (Reid 1988: 153). Other European observers emphasized similar patterns when writ- ing about Javanese, Thais, Burmese, and Filipinos.

Such being the case, it should not be surprising to find that transgendered behavior of various kinds has a long and venerable history in the region.[1] Dur- ing the first half of the period 1450–1680, and presumably in earlier times as well, Southeast Asians typically accorded enormous prestige to men who per- formed certain ritual services dressed in female attire ("ritual transvestites"). Such individuals, along with female ritual specialists (who apparently did not usually engage in transvestism or in any other variety of transgendered behav- ior) served as sacred mediators between males and females, and between the spheres of humans and the domains of spirits and nature (Reid 1988, 1993; B. Andaya 1994, 2000a; L. Andaya 2000; Brewer 2000). Unfortunately we know very little about the extent to which ritual transvestites—or anyone else—may have engaged in same-sex sexual relations in sacred or secular contexts; may have been inclined toward sexual relations with persons of both sexes; or may have participated in transvestism in nonritual settings. Similarly, we do not know if the tranvestism at issue was eroticized in any way; if we are dealing with one or another variant of transsexualism; and perhaps most important, if the transvestism under consideration represents a quarantined exception to the general sexual ethos that prevailed in the societies in question. And needless to say, we have no information on the subjectivities or desires of the individuals who were involved in or simply observed the rituals at issue. Even so, it is extremely important to bear in mind, both for immediate purposes and so as to have some historical context in which to understand the shifting discourses and dynamics discussed momentarily, that with reference to the Malay world broadly defined (to include Java, Borneo, the Celebes, other parts of Indonesia, as well as the Philippines, etc.) scholars of this era of Southeast Asia's history speak of "the respect accorded bisexualism" and go on to characterize the evidence for this pattern as "particularly pronounced" (B. Andaya 1994: 105). One reason for this pattern may be that bisexualism, like ritual transvestism, combined elements from and simultaneously transcended the male-female duality that helped structure and animate the universe in its entirety. Another may be that in combining elements of male and female, institutionalized bisexualism and transvestism symbolized wholeness, purity, and gender totality (L. Andaya 2000: 35–36) and thus the unfractured universe posited to exist before the advent of humanity and difference.[2]

Of more immediate concern than the variables that may have served to engender and reproduce such patterns is their transformation during the second half of the Age of Commerce. This era in Southeast Asia's history witnessed dramatic changes associated with dialectically related processes involving not only the intensification of commerce and state building but also the heightened centrality in courtly realms and beyond of Islam, Buddhism, and Christianity. Due to the spread and consolidation of these "male oriented, legalistic, and hierarchical world religions" (B. Andaya 1994: 106), none of which makes any scriptural provision for women's public ritual centrality, the previously sacrosanct role of women and transvestites in public ritual and religion was subject to processes of questioning and ultimately to a loss of prestige, status, and overall legitimacy. So, too, was much of the sexual license and gender pluralism that had long characterized the region, though this is not to say that at the local level (in terms of locally grounded systems of belief and practice) any of these phenomena were necessarily systematically stigmatized per se (Reid 1988, 1993).

These trends, which are best documented for the Philippines (Brewer 1999, 2000), continued in subsequent centuries. Such was due in no small measure to the pronounced (albeit regionally variable) impact of colonial rule, Western missionary activity, and increasingly muscular states committed to ideologies and projects of high modernity (Scott 1998). These and attendant developments helped stimulate the growth of religious nationalisms, which, to oversimplify, also tended to constrict the public (especially religious and ritual) spaces accorded women and those involved in one or another variant of transgendered behavior.

Even so, anthropologists in the 1960s could still report that

[b]asically, S.E. Asians are far more tolerant of personality deviation, abnormality, and disorder than we are. *Homosexuals and transvestites are treated with kindness and an amused tolerance; they are seldom considered a menace to society, blamed for being what they are, or made to feel that they must be kept in separate places from other people, ostracized or confined to institutions.* Physical imperfection or mental abnormality are [also] regarded as something bestowed by God, as an act of fate (*adjal* or

nasib), and accepted as such by kinsmen and the community. (Jaspan 1969: 22–23; emphasis added)

Consistent with but in many ways more striking than the latter observations are reports from the Malaysian state of Kelantan based on extensive field research conducted in the late 1960s by anthropologist Douglas Raybeck. In Kelantan, long considered by Malays and others a bastion of "traditional" and "authentic" Malay culture as well as an epicenter of "Islamic conservativism" (chapter 4), Raybeck found that Malays "regard[ed] homosexuality as peculiar, different, and even somewhat humorous, but they [did] *not* view it as an illness or a serious sin" (1986: 65; emphasis added). Raybeck also discusses "the institution of male transvestite performers," underscoring not only that these performers were viewed by other villagers as highly skilled and professional, but also that they could outearn other villagers, who made up the bulk of their audience.

In some ways more revealing are Raybeck's findings that there were several "specialized homosexual villages" in or near the state capital, Kota Baru, the best known of which adjoined the sultan's palace. These were not segregated ghettos to which explicitly homosexual gender-transgressors were banished. Movement to and residence in such villages seems to have been altogether "voluntary,"[3] and there is no evidence of anyone "raiding" these communities or otherwise harassing or bothering their members. And of course the fact that these communities came to the attention of the visiting anthropologist means that they were certainly known as well to other villagers, to local as well as regional and state-level religious and secular authorities at all levels (including the sultan of Kelantan), and to Malay (and Malaysian) society at large, especially in the case of the community that abutted the sultan's palace.

There is clearly more to say about Raybeck's valuable ethnographic data, which are all the more significant for the subsequent historical shifts they allow us to elucidate. For the time being, suffice it to underscore two themes. First, due largely to religious and other developments since the 1970s, such villages no longer exist. And second, while I know of no such communities (past or present) in Negeri Sembilan or other areas of the Peninsula, Raybeck's material on Malay attitudes toward transgendering resonates with the findings of other scholars who have worked among Malays since the 1970s and is also entirely consistent with my findings in Negeri Sembilan during the 1970s and 1980s. I have discussed these elsewhere (Peletz 1996, n.d.), and will simply note a few points here.

During the 1970s and 1980s, Malays in Negeri Sembilan still exhibited considerable tolerance and respect for individuals involved in transgender practices, who tend to be referred to as *pondan*, a term which covers much the same semantic field as the terms *bapok* and *banci* encountered in Singapore and Indonesia, respectively. *Pondan* and corresponding terms in other parts of Southeast Asia have multiple (sometimes mutually contradictory) referents, but they typically denote an adolescent or adult male who either dresses or adorns himself like a woman, walks like a woman, behaves sexually like a woman (has sex with men), or acts like a woman in other ways. In keeping with the relative deemphasis of sex and gender in local societies and cultures throughout the region, the encompassing nature of the *pondan* concept works against the cultural elaboration of distinctions—found in English and many other languages—among transvestism, transsexualism, hermaphroditism (intersexuality), homosexuality, and effeminate behavior. It merits emphasis as well that an individual's real or imagined proclivities with regard to "sexual-object choice," his or her "sexual orientation," has never been a primary marker of the *pondan* category, which is, in any event, a mediating rather than supernumerary category.

The fact remains, however, that at present the sole ritual activity specifically linked with transgendering is that of the bridal attendant (*mak andam*). Legislative and other measures that will be discussed in the context of broader social and political changes in due course may well eliminate the link between transgendering and *mak andam* in the not too distant future. They are, in any case, contributing to a further secularization, stigmatization, and criminalization of the role—resulting in its redefinition as a contaminating, as opposed to sacred, mediator perversely muddling and enmiring the increasingly polar terms of a gender system long characterized by pluralism.[4] More generally, recent political and legal developments are contributing to a heightened dichotomization of gender, especially since they seem to have as their central goals the elimination of all mediating categories such as *pondan* and *mak nyah* (transsexuals), the simultaneous cleansing ("defeminization") of locally defined masculinities, and the "tidying up" of local masculinities and femininities alike.

To appreciate the discursive context in which such dynamics are unfolding, let us turn to a consideration of contemporary discourses concerning purportedly traditional "Asian values" (and "the West") that have been promoted in recent years by national leaders, public intellectuals, and others on both sides of the Pacific Ocean. We shall pay particular attention to the ways in which such discourses are pressed into service to advance certain political agendas and wars of position. I shall also focus attention on some of the sentimentalizing features, silences, and ironies of these discourses, including the ways they define transgender practices of all varieties as perversions that are both thoroughly Western in origin and profoundly threatening with respect to the health and reproduction of all locally valued forms of family, race, and nation—hence a "deep categorical treachery" in Appadurai's (1996: 154) sense.

NARRATIVES OF "ASIAN VALUES" AND THE RISE OF SOCIAL INTOLERANCE

In the present context it is perhaps most useful to examine discourses of "Asian values" by taking as our point of departure some of the more encompassing narratives (and narrative products) in which they are embedded. In this regard, we are fortunate that in 1999 Mahathir published yet another highly controversial and deeply revealing book, titled *A New Deal for Asia*, which contains a good deal of material on "Asian values." Before turning to some of the arguments in this volume, we might situate the book in relation to other important events of 1999, such as the first phase of the fractious trial of Anwar Ibrahim, and the fallout, domestically and in foreign quarters, from the trial, the arrests leading up to it, and the way that Mahathir's security forces handled those who protested these developments. Bear in mind, too, that notwithstanding all of this, the year 1999 also saw Mahathir's triumphant reelection as prime minister.[5]

A New Deal for Asia is perhaps best assessed in relation to two of Mahathir's earlier volumes, namely, *The Malay Dilemma*, published in 1970, and *The Challenge*, which first appeared in 1976 in a Malay-language edition as *Menghadapi Cabaran*.[6] *A New Deal for Asia* is also profitably viewed in relation to a 1995 book Mahathir coauthored with prominent Japanese politician (and current governor of Tokyo) Shintaro Ishihara titled *The Voice of Asia*. The two volumes are remarkably similar in at least two ways: first, they espouse more or less identical discourses of "Asian values," a phrase that I set off in quotes throughout the discussion here; and second, they are both works of cultural production that are appropriately viewed as models of and for liberal economic reasoning in Asia as it heads into the new millenium (Ong 1999a). A key difference is that *The Voice of Asia* appeared in 1995 at the height of the Asian economic boom and is, as might be expected, highly triumphant; Mahathir's *A New Deal for Asia*, in contrast, was written after the financial crisis that began in Southeast Asia in 1997 and is far more humble, though still thoroughly infused with Mahathir's trademark race-chauvanism and Manichean obsessions.

One of the central arguments of both books is that Asians should "just say no" to Western models of development and democracy. (The original title of *The Voice of Asia* was, in fact, *The Asia That Can Say No*.)[7] Both books cite "adaptability, flexibility, and tolerance" as quintessentially Asian values; and both explain that in the Asian view of things, "society, state, and family are more important than the individual." Similarly, both books contend that "Asian values" are diametrically opposed to the values of "the West," which is said to have witnessed the "separation of religion from secular life and the gradual replacement of religious with hedonistic values." In the words of Mahathir, the result is that

> [m]aterialism, sensual gratification, and selfishness are rife. . . . [There is] diminished respect for marriage, family values, [and] elders, and . . . [a proliferation of] single-parent families, . . . incest, . . . homosexuality, . . . [and] unrestrained avarice. [More generally, people's] . . . moral foundations [are] crumbling, . . . and they are suffering all kinds of psychological . . . decay, . . . stress, and . . . fear. (80–81)

Many of Mahathir's remarks about "Asian values" are, at base, about Asian "family values" and are curiously reminiscent of the so-called family-values debates in this country involving public intellectual figures and not so intellectual public figures like former Vice President Dan Quayle. I make this point for two reasons: first, to cut across the Kiplingesque divide between East and West undergirding Mahathir's comments, and second, to draw attention to the fact that exceedingly underspecified references to "family values," Asian or otherwise, necessarily involve what semioticians and linguists refer to as "floating signifiers." Such signifiers have multiple, often contradictory referents and are thus capable of being harnessed to wildly divergent political agendas. Of more immediate concern here is that like Lee Kuan Yew and his successor (Goh Chok Tong) in Singapore, Mahathir has made it clear in interviews and public speeches that human rights, democracy, and civil society of the sort held up as Western ideals simply do not work in Asian countries like Malaysia, Singapore, and Indonesia. Indeed, Mahathir maintains that Western ideals should not be viewed as values to strive for and that those who suggest otherwise are arrogantly ethnocentric, if not overtly racist, and bent on seeing Muslims fail in Asia and elsewhere.

Having sketched out a few features of the narrative of "Asian values," I would like to turn to a historical question: Where did this discourse on "Asian values" come from? Or, put differently, what are the variables that have served to promote the discourse? In answering this question I focus on the Malaysian and Singaporean variants of the discourse and on the dynamics most relevant in those contexts.

Among the most obvious factors that contributed to the emergence of recent discourse on "Asian values" are the phenomenal postwar economic growth of Japan, South Korea, Taiwan, and Hong Kong, as well as the more recent and in some ways more spectacular economic success stories, at least through July 1997, of Thailand, Malaysia, Singapore, and Indonesia. As is well known, politicians, scholars, and others on both sides of the Pacific invoked one or another set of "Asian values" to help explain these phenomena.

The specific discourse of "Asian values" that has been retailed by Mahathir in recent years is also an outgrowth of his "Look East Policy," inaugurated in 1981. As such, it merits note that while the moral and material entailments of the policy were notoriously unclear to many government spokesmen, Mahathir apparently had in mind "The East" as represented only by Japan and South Korea.[8] Conspicuously excluded from promotions and discussions of the policy were references to Taiwan and Singapore, most likely because of their ethnic Chinese majorities and the resulting political dis-ease that this might create on the home front, particularly in light of the local cultural politics of race. In any case, the policy, which was offered as an antidote to blind emulation of the West, meant not so much trading only with Japan and South Korea but adopting certain of their characteristics: their hard work and diligence, and their much touted valorization of the group over the individual. One reason the policy was quietly discontinued after awhile is that its architects never really studied the extent to which the Japanese and Korean patterns were in fact transferable to Malaysia. And in the end, Japanese reluctance to engage in technology transfer led Mahathir to accuse them of favoring a "colonialist relationship" with Malaysia.

We might also consider Mahathir's views concerning the origins of Japan's phenomenal postwar economic success. Mahathir has long credited this success to Japan's "slavish imitation of things Western." Appearances, then, are not always what they seem, which is to say that from Mahathir's point of view, the

"Look East Policy" entailed looking to two particular East Asian countries that had either successfully imitated the West or successfully reworked their emulations of things Western into locally meaningful patterns ostensibly suitable for export to other Eastern countries.

The discourse on "Asian values" has also been fueled by a variety of political crises, all of which were arguably related to issues of globalization and sovereignty. One such crisis developed from the 1993 Vienna Conference on Human Rights, which witnessed extensive Western critiques of Malaysia's record on issues of human rights and a spirited counterargument cast partly in terms of "Asian values." A somewhat similar crisis unfolded as a consequence of Singapore's arrest, detention, and subsequent caning of the all-American Michael Fay. As the crisis began to unfold in late 1993 and early 1994, politicians, public intellectuals, and media figures on both sides of the Pacific invoked what were heralded as "traditional values" to justify their allegiances in the war of positions that developed. Lee Kuan Yew, for example, repeatedly cited the need to defend "Asian values" against Western incursion. He also insisted that Westerners do not understand Asians, who place the interests of the group over the interests of the individual, and who are quite content to be ruled by what he euphemistically referred to as "strong governments" as long as they deliver economic prosperity.[9]

As it turned out, Michael Fay did survive both the flogging and the media frenzy he encountered on his return to the States. More important for present purposes is that the discourse on "Asian values" enunciated by Lee Kuan Yew survived and prospered in Singapore, elsewhere in Asia, and far beyond. This should be particularly clear to those who have followed events in Malaysia since September 1998 and will in any case be evident when we discuss the cases of Azizah and Anwar (below).

There is much to say about this discourse, but I will confine my immediate remarks to two sets of issues. The first has to do with matters of heterogeneity. Not all Asian leaders agree with the Mahathirs, the Lee Kuan Yews, and the others who traffic in the discourse of "Asian values." Martin Lee, for example, chairman of Hong Kong's Democratic Party, has argued that we need to "put to rest the myth of 'Asian values': that democracy and human rights are 'Western concepts' inimical both to Asia and to economic growth."[10] In this view, the notion of "Asian values" is a sloppy and ideologically loaded term. Many scholars, student leaders, and others in mainland China would appear to feel the same way and are highly critical of the ways the concept of "Asian values" has been invoked by government leaders in Beijing to rationalize the oppressive activities of the state, including the tragedy of Tiananmen. In much the same fashion, former opposition leader Kim Dae Jung, who is now President of South Korea, has repeatedly emphasized that "Asian values" have never precluded democracy.[11] On this front, Megawati Sukarnoputri, the new president of Indonesia, also offers hope, especially in light of the fact that Indonesia, with a predominantly Muslim population of 215 million people, is the largest Muslim country in the world.

The second issue has to do with the deeply ironic fact that Asian leaders, like

Mahathir, Ishihara, and Lee Kuan Yew, espouse an essentializing Orientalism of the sort that literary critic Edward Said excoriated in his now classic (1978) study of Western literary representations of "the Orient." Said was dealing primarily with the literature on the Middle East, as opposed to East Asia, but his basic argument is relevant in the present context as well. Much like the nineteenth-century construction of "the Orient" produced in the West, the notion of "Asian values" articulated by Mahathir and others is not only cast in wildly unqualified, absolute terms; it also presupposes a monolithic, eternally unchanging, homogenized "Asian" (as well as an undifferentiated, immutable, sexually anarchic, and terminally decadent "Western"), whose essential features transcend time, space, gender, class, occupation, and local cultural identity. Another of Said's arguments, that Orientalism is both a product of domination and a key resource deployed to help effect and reproduce that domination, is also relevant here. Indeed, the very same argument could be made about the new variant of Orientalism subsumed under the rubric of "Asian values." Like its predecessor, it is, to paraphrase a point made by Sylvia Yanagisako (1995) in another context, an incomplete, selective, and in many ways deeply nostalgic and sentimentalizing narrative that renders invisible various types of experiences and meanings in the name of forging unity out of diversity. More ironic still is that this discourse accepts as given the very imperial-era and thoroughly Kiplingesque chasm between East and West that millions of people in "the Orient" have fought to eradicate, owing to its inherently racist and dehumanizing features, to say nothing of its ideological functions (see Syed Husin Alatas 1977; Said 1993; Ong 1999a). It also helps reproduce the invidious imperial legacy (intellectual, cultural, and political) that those who articulate it are so loathe to own in many public contexts.

There are many other ironies and curious features of this discourse, some of which appear as silences, elisions, and conflations. Consider, for example, the cultures and countries that are conspicuously absent from the discourse. In the Southeast Asian context, the Philippines would seem to be the most glaring omission, explicable, perhaps, by the relatively poor showing of the Philippine economy in recent decades, though an arguably more likely explanation is that for Mahathir, the notion of a Christian Asian is both an oxymoronic hybrid and a deep categorical treachery. Also generally absent from the discourse is any mention of Myanmar, Cambodia, Laos, or Vietnam. Moving beyond Southeast Asia, one is struck by the lack of references to South Asia and west Asia (the Middle East). Clearly, then, as Ong (1999a) has also discussed, both the timeless and the "new Asians" touted in this discourse are either Muslims or people who adhere to a mélange of Confucianism and Buddhism. As suggested a moment ago, however, only certain types of Muslims (Shi'ites are definitely out) and certain types of Buddhists and Confucists are potential candidates for this discursively privileged status of "Asian," new or otherwise.

It is equally important to consider the flip side of the coin of "Asian values." Where, in other words, might one find repositories of " 'traditional' Asian values"? And how do they figure into Mahathir's narratives? If we confine ourselves to the Malaysian setting, and to what Mahathir has written about Malay culture in its rural, ostensibly "more traditional" forms, the deeply ideological nature of this discourse becomes all the more evident. So, too, do the enormous "development" challenges that Mahathir and like-minded politicians have set for themselves and their countrymen since the early 1970s.

In *The Malay Dilemma*, Mahathir depicts "Malay character" in the following terms: Malays are "courteous," "gentle," "formal yet tolerant," "self-effacing," "passive," and "withdrawn" but with "a clear sense of righteousness"; they are also "resigned," "complacent," "soft," "weak," and "indolent"—"afflicted by a seemingly permanent stupor," "uninterested in work," and, more generally, "fatalistic . . . feudalists . . . in the grips of unadjusted minds" that are "in need of rehabilitation." Malays also exhibit "a complete failure to relate cause and effect," and "are never committed to anything."

In these comments we see an example of "self-Orientalizing" that is far more extreme than anything Mahathir has been disseminating in recent speeches and publications like *A New Deal for Asia*. As alluded to earlier, we also see the enormous challenges—associated with economic "development," with the forging of a national identity, and with the creation of a viable nation—that Mahathir and others have sought to identify and overcome during the last thirty years. To fully appreciate these points, we need to consider Mahathir's attitudes toward local Chinese. All I can say in this context is that in *The Malay Dilemma*, the Chinese are depicted in stark, racialist terms as "adventurous," "hard," "aggressive," "predatory," and "inherently good at business" because they are "instinctively thrifty" and given to "secret deals, private arrangements and water-tight family" and guild organizations. Perhaps most revealing in light of Mahathir's current emphasis on the cultural kinship said to obtain among the "new Asians" are the following remarks, which appear toward the very end of *The Malay Dilemma*: "In Malaysia we have three major races; . . . their physiognomy, language, culture, and religion differ;" *"there is no dialogue. . .* "[they] have practically *nothing in common"* (175; emphases added).

Particularly when viewed in light of *The Malay Dilemma*, Mahathir's contemporary ruminations on "Asian values" provide clear illustration of Yanagisako's previously noted point that Orientalist discourses are selective and sentimentalizing narratives that render invisible various types of experiences and meanings in the name of forging unity out of diversity. If such is the case, we might then ask: At whose expense is such unity forged? Put differently, which societies or sectors of society are marginalized in—or as a consequence of the deployment of—this discourse on cultural kinship?

I have already provided a partial answer to these questions in my comments about those regions of Asia (including the Philippines, Vietnam, South Asia, etc.) that are conspicuously absent from the discourse on "Asian values." Of more immediate relevance here are sectors of society such as women and ethnic minorities like the Penan of Sarawak (East Malaysia) who, as a consequence of globalizing forces, are subject to new forms of discrimination and new constraints on sovereignty that vary considerably from one group to the next. Ong examines some such groups and their variegated predicaments in her highly original and in many ways brilliant book, *Flexible Citizenship* (1999), which presents deeply incisive analyses of contemporary state practices, citizenship regimes, and "systems of graduated sovereignty" in Malaysia and elsewhere in Asia and the Pacific. Some of the same groups are discussed in another important volume on the region also published in 1999, Milne and Mauzy's *Malaysian Politics under Mahathir.*

Curiously absent from both of these texts, however, are even brief considerations of the communities of subalterns that are arguably *most* subject to discrimination and marginalization in the particular variants of modernity and "Asian values" that Malaysian officialdom have embraced. I refer to gays, lesbians, bisexuals, transvestites, and all others engaged in transgendering of a homegrown and/or more cosmopolitan variety—who may number more than 20,000 in Kuala Lumpur alone.[12] Suffice it to note that while modern-day trends involving the stigmatization and criminalization of transgender practices and identities might be said to date from the early 1980s, they became much more pronounced beginning around 1994 and have been especially intense since the onset of the Asian financial crisis in mid-1997. Some of the relevant developments and trends since the mid-1990s merit brief consideration here. (Others will be discussed further along.)

Two of the main objectives of the NEP and many other state programs implemented in the last thirty years have been to eliminate poverty, especially among Malays, and to effect a restructuring of the relationship between "race" and economic function. The realization of these twin objectives has entailed (among other things) effectively encouraging Malays to abandon their rural economic traditions (rice farming, fishing, rubber tapping, and the like) so as to become increasingly involved in small-scale trade and business activities as well as the larger-scale entrepreneurial endeavors and other urban economic niches that are (also) conducive to the creation of a new middle class of urban Malays (*Melayu baru*, or "new Malays"; see Shamsul A. B. 1999b; Andaya and Andaya 2001: 333–36). Such programs have been successful in many respects, not least in terms of encouraging mass Malay migration from rural areas to state capitals throughout the country (for example, Penang, Melaka, Johor Baru) but also, and more important, to the extremely cosmopolitan federal capital, Kuala Lumpur, which, like certain other urban centers in the region (Bangkok, Jakarta, Manila) has long had a reputation for sexual license of different kinds. For a variety of reasons, many of which are relevant to an understanding of the growth of "subcultures" of transgendered individuals (including cosmopolitan gays and lesbians) in urban areas in the United States like San Francisco and New York City, these patterns of migration and urbanization contributed to the increased visibility of Malaysian gender-transgressors, particularly homosexuals, especially during the economic boom years of the 1980s. So, too, albeit in different ways, did the phenomenal growth of the global sex industry in neighboring Thailand, the peaking of the AIDS crisis there during the period 1992–93, and the resultant attention that the latter crisis came to receive from Thai officials, various governments in the region (including Malaysia's), and world health organizations and NGOs of various kinds (Bishop and Robinson 1998). Such heightened visibility could have resulted in a number of very different outcomes; the effect in Malaysia, however, was that the transgendered encountered more organized opposition that included redoubled efforts not only to undercut their visibility and legitimacy but also to eliminate them altogether, all in the name of "Asian (family) values."

As one example, in the second half of 1994, the state-run radio and television network Radio and Television Malaysia (RTM) banned transvestites and gays from appearing on its programs.[13] According to Information Minister Mohamed Rahmat, the action was taken "in line with the national policy which focuses on the importance of health and family values," the bottom line being, "*We do not want to encourage any form of homosexuality in our society*" (emphasis added). Shortly thereafter, Prime Minister Mahathir, in a statement critical of Western countries that provide one or another degree of legal recognition to lesbian and gay couples, said: "*Such a concept of the family is crazy and contrary to religious teachings. It will only produce illegitimate children who may, in turn, have incestuous marriages with their siblings*" (emphasis added).[14] Not surprisingly, by year's end (December 1994) a "seven-man" jury in Penang freed a Malay factory woman who had been held in jail since the 1991 killing of her housemate on the grounds that she did so in self-defense after the housemate "made lesbian advances at her and tried to rape her."[15]

The next few years saw the appearance of numerous accounts in the government-owned and -controlled media—typically short but alarmist—of "gay clubs," such as the one that appeared in the June 22, 1995, issue of *The Sun* (a Malaysian daily), which carried the headline "Gay Clubs Not Allowed." The gist of the story was that "gays clubs" were illegal ("not allowed to be registered in the country"). The main objective of the piece, however, seems to have been to invite readers to participate in and thus broaden and enhance efforts to eliminate homosexuality by providing intelligence to the authorities, for it included the line, "If you have information on any gay club, inform Deputy Home Minister Ong Ka Ting." Similar headlines—"Gay Clubs Are Not Allowed to Be Reigstered in Malaysia," "69 Held in Raid at Club for Gays"— have become commonplace. According to one of the stories appearing beneath such a headline, "Police detained 69 men, including 12 foreigners, at an exclusive club believed to be for gays in Jalan Raja Laut [Kuala Lumpur] here yesterday. . . . The club, which is operating without a license, is a shophouse which was converted into an exclusive club equipped with a gymnasium, sauna, and rooms specially for gays. All the detainees were taken to the headquarters for urine tests. Four club employees were also detained." Like many others of this ilk, the account excerpted here draws attention to or at least raises the spectre of multiple illegalities—operating a business establishment without a license; using illicit drugs (to be detected by urine tests); and engaging in homosexual encounters in gymnasiums, saunas, and "rooms specially for gays." Of comparable if not greater significance, it also draws explicit ties among homosexuality, drug use, and foreigners.

In light of this kind of negative publicity, it is not surprising that subsequent years saw the Kuala Lumpur Town Council and the Malaysian Youth Council beseeching the government to take strict measures to abolish any form of homosexual activity in the city.[16] One such appeal occurred in connection with a Gay Pride Event that had been scheduled for June 28, 1998. Invitations to the event had been distributed and promoted via the club's website, which, as the appeal emphasized, was used for "international exposure." As might be expected, the event was cancelled.[17]

In recent years, moreover, the police have raided *pondan* beauty contests in Kuala Lumpur and elsewhere. In one celebrated case a few years ago, the police arrested the Malay (Muslim) contestants but not the non-Muslim *pondan* in the pageant. Such partisan behavior was also evident during a "more conventional" all-female beauty contest held in Selangor in June 1997. In that case (the Miss Malaysia Petite Pageant), the Malay winner and two other Malay contestants were arrested at the end of the show. Middle-class Malays and other Malaysians I spoke with in 1998 felt that it was highly ironic, to say the least, that the police sat through and presumably enjoyed the entire performance before arresting any of the participants. They also argued that it was unfair that the Malay contestants were singled out in these cases, some of them adding that the authorities "surely have better things to do." Similar arguments were advanced by members of Malaysia's leading Muslim feminist organization, Sisters in Islam, whom I also interviewed in 1998. Moreover, as noted by Mohammad Hashim Kamali (2000: 280), a highly respected professor of Islamic law and jurisprudence at the International Islamic University Malaysia, "within two weeks of arrest, the three young women were charged, found guilty and each fined M$400 . . . a display of efficiency that the Syariah Courts are hardly known for."

A decidedly different perspective emerged in the course of an interview I conducted in 1998 with the chief judge who presides over the Islamic court system of the Federal Territory of Kuala Lumpur. The gist of his comments on the subject, which are included as one of the epigraphs to this chapter—"Nowadays, with people moving into the city and with modern change and such, there are all sorts of things going on. . . . People think they can do anything"— implies that the massive flow of villagers and rural culture into the city is disorderly and unsettling; that "we have to draw a line somewhere"; and that "we really mean business." These comments resonate deeply with the perspectives of Mary Douglas (1970), Gayle Rubin (1984), Kath Weston (1998), and others, who argue that sexualities are particularly politicized and contested during times of rapid and unsettling sociocultural change. They also suggest that non-normative ("deviant") sexualities are an easy target for politicians and others who seek to exert control over the circumstances of such change and to maintain or broaden their constituencies in the process.

NEW TYPES OF CRIMINALITY: AZIZAH, ANWAR, AND BEYOND

At present, homosexual behavior is heavily criminalized throughout Malaysia. Oral and anal sex between same-sex partners, for example, which are covered by Section 377 of the national Penal Code, are categorized under the rubric of "carnal intercourse against the order of nature." Such acts are liable to punishment by imprisonment for up to twenty years as well as whipping, even if they are consensual. Moreover, any act defined as "gross indecency" between two men or two women, whether public or private, is a criminal offense that can lead to two years' imprisonment. This includes attempts to establish contacts between same-sex partners (that is, "cruising"). Partly because such cases are prosecuted by the police and thus usually require the filing of reports from someone directly involved, there have been few "successful" prosecutions of gay men and even fewer of lesbian women. It is essential to bear in mind in any event that these are secular laws, *not* religious laws. Contrary to the assumptions of many Westerners, in other words, we are not dealing with yet another example of "medieval Islamic rigidity" with respect to gender and sexuality. Indeed, the precedents for these particular laws and many of the specifics of their language were introduced by the British during colonial times, initially in the Indian Penal Code of 1860, which was subsequently incorporated with slight amendments into the penal codes of the Straits Settlements (1872), the Federated Malay States (in stages, beginning in 1874), the Unfederated Malay States, the Federation of Malaya, and so on.[18]

The Case of Azizah

One prosecution leading to the conviction of a lesbian woman that merits consideration in this context was widely covered in the Malaysian press on a more or less daily basis from December 1996 to March 1997. This case, which is the subject of extremely insightful work by Tan Beng Hui (1999) to which I am much indebted, involved two young women (Azizah Abdul Rahman, age twenty-one, and Rohana Mat Isa, age twenty) residing in the state of Kelantan. Azizah, described in many accounts as a "tomboy," habitually dressed in male attire and according to press accounts "otherwise looked and behaved like a man."[19] Partly because Azizah had also taken a man's name and possessed a male identity card, she succeeded in convincing the local religious authorities (among others) that she was a male and could thus marry her partner. Azizah is also said to have fooled her bride and the witnesses at her wedding and, more seriously, to have "disgraced Islam."

Although or perhaps because this case was the "first instance of its kind in Malaysian history,"[20] Azizah was charged on two relatively pedestrian criminal counts: "impersonating a man," and "using a false identity card." These offenses fall within the jurisdiction of the secular courts. Perhaps more relevant is that such offenses were the most clear-cut and least complicated transgressions to prosecute, since the question of proof is less vexing and exacting than would be the case if charges of a specifically sexual nature were heard in the religious courts. These charges carried the additional advantage that their prosecution could be overseen by the federal government, something which would not occur if the charges had been of a religious nature and had thus been tried in the Islamic courts, especially since the latter are under state (rather than federal) jurisdiction.

Upon learning Azizah's true (female) identity, Rohana's father sought to have the marriage annulled—an issue that, significantly, was never pursued by Rohana herself, even though Rohana claimed that throughout the course of their relationship she had been deceived as to Azizah's real (female) identity and was not herself a lesbian. But there were complications with respect to an annulment, since under the circumstances it was not altogether clear that a valid marriage had been contracted in the first place. Similarly, although Azizah and Rohana did engage in sexual contact (involving, among other things, mutual caressing and Azizah's applying her hands to Rohana's vagina) that was construed as illicit (as *zina*, hence actionable), their possession and use of "sexual aids" in the form of a dildo, though apparently outrageous to public sensibilities, was more problematic as a specifically religious offense since in the eyes of many Islamic jurists penetration by a dildo does not constitute "real sexual intercourse." Issues such as these prompted state authorities in Kelantan and elsewhere to tighten their Islamic Family Law Enactment(s) so as to prevent—or at least more clearly criminalize and penalize—unions of this sort (as discussed below).[21] They also resulted in the local *kadi*'s threatening to bring charges of a specifically religious nature against Azizah. Though he never did so, he did eventually annul the marriage, apparently having decided that it had been a valid union in a narrow legal sense.

In this context it merits emphasis that in the state of Kelantan, where the two lived, there were no laws currently in force specifically prohibiting sexual relations among women, though such had been proposed by the PAS–controlled state government a few years earlier in its attempt to institute the Islamic criminal laws and punishments specified in the Quran (*hudud*). The actual implementation of such laws, which was stalled and ultimately scuttled by the federal government, could have resulted in Azizah's (and Rohana's?) being found guilty of offenses subsumed under the rubric of *musahaqah*, this being defined as "a ta'zir offense consisting of an act of sexual gratification between females by rubbing the vagina of one against that of the other . . . [the punishment . . . for which] shall be at the discretion of the Court" (Rose Ismail 1995: 116–17). The penalty proposed for this crime is not altogether clear, although the punishment for its "male counterpart," that is, *liwat*, which is construed as an offense "consisting of carnal intercourse between a male and another male or between a male and a female other than his wife, performed against the order of nature, that is through the anus," might be the same as that for *zina*: one hundred lashes and a year's imprisonment, or stoning to death with stones of medium size.[22]

Investigation of Azizah's background revealed that she was a Malay Muslim whose citizenship status was that of a Thai national permanently resident in Malaysia. She had apparently been born in Malaysia and was in any case raised by an aunt, not by her mother (or parents). At age thirteen she had gotten pregnant by a (young Malay?) man with whom she eloped to Thailand. He turned out to be a poor husband, and rather than suffer abuse at his hands, Azizah proceeded to divorce.[23] Even though she had a child to raise, she subsequently decided that she did not want to be supported by or dependent on any man and that she would have relationships with women instead. Information released in the course of the trial revealed in addition that she had married Rohana "for love" but also partly because Rohana, facing family pressure, had threatened to break off their eight-year relationship if they did not get married.

The sentence Azizah received from the judge who heard the case resulted in her serving twenty-four months in prison. According to media accounts, "the demonic son-in-law" was eventually "rehabilitated." She later appeared in Islamic headgear (a *tudung*), proclaiming, among other things, that "she regretted her erroneous ways," and that her future plans and desires included "conventional marriage."

Significantly, though not surprisingly, press accounts of the case repeatedly emphasized a number of related themes bearing on Azizah's biography, most notably her lower-class background; the fact she had been adopted and raised by an aunt and was thus deprived of her "real" mother's ("natural") love, affection, and guidance; and that she was of foreign (Thai) origins if only in the sense that she had lived in Thailand for a number of years since eloping there at age thirteen upon learning that she was pregnant. The more general message driven home by media accounts and official pronouncements about the case was that Azizah's misguided and misspent youth and waywardness had resulted not merely in a failed, "broken" (heterosexual) marriage, a subsequent turn toward homosexuality, massive deception, and criminal illegality that shocked the entire nation. It also landed her in prison, effectively orphaned her son, and disgraced both her family and Islam alike.

At the height of the dramatic, sensationalistic, and in many respects salacious media coverage of this incident (more specifically, just a month after Azizah's conviction and some two weeks before the *kadi* annulled the marriage), a somewhat similar incident of "cross-dressing" came to light in the neighboring state of Terengganu. A key difference, however, is that this case involved a male couple, who, it should be noted, received but a fraction of the media coverage accorded Azizah and Rohana (a mere five days, as opposed to three solid months). The headlines concerning this case underscored that "a *transvestite* tried to marry a man by posing as a woman" (emphasis added). The accompanying articles explained that "the marriage was called off after the bridegroom . . . discovered the true gender of his prospective wife." State Criminal Investigation Division Chief Assistant Commander Abdul Halim Abdul Hamid reported that the boy "went into hiding when news of his failed attempt to marry his lover . . . [hit] the press," and that he was "detained for investigation under the Penal Code for 'using a forged document'."[24]

It is not merely that the media coverage of this incident paled in comparison to the media attention lavished on Azizah and Rohana. The sentence meted out to the offending cross-dresser in this instance—an illiterate fifteen-year-old shop assistant by the name of Fauzi Yaacob, who was wearing a shirt, jeans, women's shoes, and two earrings in his left ear when arrested and was apparently so attractive and so convincingly "female" that he had already received five marriage offers—was also much lighter (a jail term of roughly seven as opposed to twenty-four months). This despite the fact that on at least two previous occasions Fauzi had been arrested by the police on similar if not identical grounds ("posing as a woman").

The differences in the media coverage and sentencing in these incidents are pronounced, and they make very clear that when cross dressing or other transgendered behavior of this sort involves men it is far less offensive to legal and sociocultural sensibilities than such behavior on the part of women. But we should also note the similarities in these cases and the way they were handled by the media. One obvious implication of the media coverage in both instances is that homosexuals resort to transvestism to marry and deceive and, conversely, that transvestism is merely a "cover" for homosexuality. Another is that "gender woes" of all varieties have come to plague Malaysia; that insufficient vigilance on the part of parents and others is partly to blame; and that parents, teachers, schools, and religious and political leaders and their associations need to be pressed into service to prevent the further spread of such sinful, unnatural, and profoundly corrosive and threatening behavior. It is thus not surprising that during the media circus surrounding these incidents a minister in the prime minister's department, Datuk Abdul Hamid Othman, offered a detailed public commentary on the Fauzi case, in which he "link[ed] gender woes to upbringing":[25]

> *Boys brought up as girls has been the main reason they become transvestites. . . . Some parents who have sons and yearn for a daughter end up dressing one of their sons as a girl, buying him bangles and allowing him to develop female characteristics.* They fail to realise the danger because the child, confused about his gender, grows up thinking he is a woman trapped in a man's body.

> Parents need to be told the importance of bringing up their children according to the child's *natural gender*. A daughter should realize she will eventually become a wife and a son should know he will be a husband someday, not the other way around. . . . Parents [need] to take up parenting skills and adopt the *zero tolerance* concept in family life, religion and law.

> Zero tolerance means parents will not endure or allow room for waywardness in the family. They will not adopt the *tak apalah* (it doesn't matter) attitude.

> UMNO want[s] to *wipe out the problems of transvestites* in its war against social ills. The religious and social welfare bureaus of UMNO . . . [will] meet . . . to discuss the

matter. . . . *UMNO branches, religious departments, schools, parent-teacher associations, and the media . . . [will all] be utilized to spread the message on proper parenting skills.* (emphases added)

I shall return to some of Datuk Hamid's comments shortly. In the meantime it merits emphasis that partly because of the notoriety and backlash generated by such cases—some felt that they were "a sign that the world is coming to an end"—but also because of the (almost always tense) political climate and the resultant tendency to find groups on whom to place blame for society's ills, various jurisdictions in Malaysia have sought to increase the penalties for same-sex relations and to outlaw sexual contact between women that involves "rubbing the vagina of one against that of the other." The more general point is that gays, lesbians, and others whose sexual orientations constitute a significant departure from stereotypical gender roles are increasingly subject to discrimination and harassment in the form of verbal and physical abuse, detention and arrest, and curtailment or loss of educational, employment, and other economic opportunities.

In May 1998, for instance, the state of Johor, following the example set by the Federal Territory of Kuala Lumpur, passed legislation, which was subsequently approved by the sultan and became official law in 1999, that introduced whipping as an additional penalty to punish Muslims convicted of sexual offenses such as "sodomy," "lesbianism," and "extramarital sex." State Executive Councillor and Islamic Affairs Committee Chairman Datuk Abdul Kadir Annuar explained that the move was to check growing social problems and moral decadence in the state, and that whipping and increased fines would henceforth be provided for under amendments to the Syariah Criminal Procedure Code Enactment 1997 and the Syariah Criminal Offenses Enactment. Specifically, the new enactments, which also apply to "those spreading deviationist teaching, pimps and purveyors of promiscuous relations," provide for a mix of six strokes of the rotan, fines up to M$5,000, and imprisonment of up to three years upon conviction.[26] Similar enactments have been introduced in other states.

As for some of the broader trends, transgendering has become heavily stigmatized, criminalized, and medicalized and has come to be defined increasingly in terms of sexuality and sexual pathology in particular, whereas even in the 1980s this was not the case. The criminalization of *pondan, mak nyah,* homosexuality, and transgendering generally is not only a strategy geared toward the cleansing of locally defined masculinities, feminities, and sexualities. I would argue that moves along these lines and attendant strategies are also central components of more encompassing schemes of governmentality (Foucault 1991; see also Ong 1999a) and that the latter schemes have three analytically distinct though related objectives: the creation and policing of modern middle-class families and subjectivities that will help bring about a transnational Asian renaissance; the reinscription of various types of authenticity and identity that are held to be conducive to this renaissance; and the promotion of an array of nationalist and transnational narratives bearing on "Asian values" that empha-

size a timeless, tradition-bound, patriarchal, strongly heterosexual, and otherwise essentialized "Orient" (which is cast in sharp relief to an equally timeless
and essentialized "West" that is represented as bereft of traditions other than
those entailing sexual anarchy and terminal decadence). I would also contend
that efforts to stigmatize and criminalize transgender practices in Malaysia,
Singapore, and elsewhere in Southeast Asia in the name of "Asian values" are
key features of contemporary strategies aimed at legitimizing and easing the
profoundly dislocating sociocultural transformations effected by state projects
of modernity in conjunction with the boom-bust cycles of global capitalism to
which the state projects in question are ambivalently wed. To help illustrate
these arguments we shall proceed to the case of Anwar.

Anwar and Beyond

Nationalist and transnational discourses on "Asian values" have frequently been
invoked by Malaysian politicians and others in connection with the case of
Anwar Ibrahim. This case dominated Malaysian politics and mediascapes from
September 1998 through mid-2000 and is widely viewed as one of the most
severe political crises in the nation's history since the devastating postelection
"race riots" of May 13, 1969, that resulted in the deaths of hundreds of people
and the destruction of the homes and property of about six thousand residents
of Kuala Lumpur. Setting aside for the moment the structural tensions, political
disputes, and personal differences between Anwar and Mahathir (and their respective supporters) that helped foment the crisis,[27] we might say that it began
on September 2, 1998, when Anwar, Mahathir's extremely popular heir apparent, was stripped of his official titles and duties, which included deputy prime
minister and minister of finance. Shortly thereafter Anwar, who is also the
former head of both the International Islamic University and the Malaysian
Islamic Youth Organization (ABIM), was detained under the Internal Security
Act. He was subsequently charged with five counts of sodomy (under Section
377 of the national Penal Code) and other sexual impropriety (adultery), and
various counts of bribery and corruption, all keyed, ultimately, to the accusations of sodomy. During the initial months of his incarceration, he suffered life-
threatening injuries at the hands of his jailors, much as he and many others
predicted would happen when he was first arrested. Indeed, Malaysia's attorney
general eventually acknowledged that the police were responsible for at least
some of Anwar's serious head and other injuries. The former chief of police
(Abdul Rahim), for that matter, went on record with the admission that he was
personally responsible for inflicting some of the blows on Anwar.[28]

There are three quick points to register before getting into the specifics of
this case and the fallout to which it (and the developments leading up to it)
gave rise. First, the majority if not all of the charges against Anwar seem politically motivated if not altogether bogus—at least three of the five men who
supposedly acknowledged having been sodomized by Anwar, for example, have
since emphasized that their "confessions" were coerced. Second, generally

peaceful marches and rallies protesting Anwar's treatment have been met with truncheons, tear gas, plastic bullets, water cannons, police brutality, a large number of arrests, and pronouncements from Mahathir and his supporters that the repressive measures at issue are clearly necessary and altogether in keeping with "Asian values." And third, the mockery of a trial that resulted in Anwar's conviction was characterized by gross discrepancies in the accounts of government prosecutors and "witnesses," and by all varieties of other "irregularities."

The first phase of Anwar's trial, focusing on charges of bribery and corruption, began on November 2, 1998, and eventually resulted in conviction on four different charges of "corruption" in the form of "abuse of power," specifically that Anwar illegally used his powers of office to thwart the police investigation of the sodomy charges against him. This phase of the trial formally ended on April 14, 1999, at which time Anwar was sentenced to six years in jail. The hearings lasted a full seventy-eight days, thus making this phase of the proceedings alone the longest criminal trial in Malaysian history.

The second phase of the Anwar trial began on June 7, 1999, and was concluded on August 8, 2000, at which point Anwar was sentenced to an additional nine years in prison. This phase focused on allegations of sexual crimes; the alleged offenses include an adulterous liaison (Anwar is married) with one of his private secretary's female in-laws, which falls under the category of *zina*. Far more widely publicized, indeed, the most frequently referenced charges, are the accusations that he engaged in homosexual relations with five different men and that he is thus guilty of multiple counts of sodomy or *liwat*. This (second) phase of the trial was suspended at various points in the fall of 1999 due partly to Anwar's illness, widely thought to be caused by arsenic poisoning at the hands of his jailors, and partly to the presiding judge's decision that a temporary suspension of the hearings would be conducive to the climate leading up to the "snap-elections" held on November 29, 1999, which, not suprisingly, resulted in Mahathir's reelection as prime minister.

At first glance the charges against Anwar might seem quite disparate and variegated. But there is a common logic underlying and linking them, for just as each of them entails an allegation that Anwar transgressed one or another cultural code of fidelity or moderation, so too does each transgression constitute treason (*derhaka*). To elaborate on the issue of fidelity: Anwar stands accused (and has been convicted) of engaging in corruption and bribery and thus of being unfaithful to his office, to his political patron (the prime minister, who was absolutely central to his attainment of office), and to idealized political traditions (that brook neither corruption nor bribery), as well as to the ruling political party (UMNO), the electorate, the Malay "race," the Muslim community, and the nation. Similarly, we have seen that Anwar has been charged with various counts of (heterosexual) adultery and numerous counts of (homosexual) sodomy, and thus obviously stands accused of being unfaithful not only to his wife but also both to his family as a whole (whose trust he is said to have betrayed) and to the nation generally, especially since the nation is held to be built up and to depend for its very survival on strong families formed around stable, enduring conjugal bonds that are ideally monogamous and otherwise exclusivistic.

As for the theme of moderation, the issues here are perhaps more straightforward. To be charged with and convicted of corruption and bribery is obviously to be held out as someone who wields illegal and otherwise excessive power, a crime of immoderation and excess that is all the more serious in the case of an elected official who is vested with more power and authority than anyone else in the entire country save the prime minister. The charges of (heterosexual) adultery might be said to speak for themselves insofar as they, too, clearly suggest immoderation and excess, in the sense of someone who is not capable of satisfying their ("more than moderate," "excessive") sexual urges within the context of marriage, and thus must turn to other women and to illegality for their satisfaction. It is no small matter here that the extremely widespread counterhegemonic discourse suggesting that the official line notwithstanding, men have more (not less) "passion" (*nafsu*) than women and are for this reason ultimately less (not more) responsible than women, is fueled by precisely this type of immoderate behavior on the part of men. Such behavior (men "playing around," needing more than one mate, etc.) is specifically cited by many women (and some men) as the grounds upon which they base their view that compared to women, men are ultimately more *gatal* ("scratchy," "itchy," or "horny") and ultimately less responsible (see Peletz 1996). To the extent that this discourse impacts all men negatively, it also involves "letting down the (male) side," hence a form of betrayal and infidelity.

The charges of homosexuality also raise the specter of immoderation and excess, particularly since homosexual sex, not being seen by Malays as reproductive, is viewed as a form of self-indulgent and gratuitous sex and, at least in the official discourse disseminated in the present-day context, as behavior that is sinful as well as pathological in both the social and medical senses of the term in that it is pursued only for perverse pleasure. It is noteworthy in this connection that one of the widely publicized (though undoubtedly coerced if not altogether manufactured) statements attributed to one of the men (Azizian Abu Bakar) said to have been sodomized by Anwar proclaimed, "His [Anwar's] insatiable lust shows that he is someone who could be classified as chronic, . . . [that] this [chronic insatiable lust] exerted intense pressure on my spirit and mind," and it was this "intense pressure" that was responsible for the fact that he (Azizian) unwittingly and ultimately unwillingly (given his compromised willpower) became Anwar's "homosexual slave" (*hamba homoseksual*). The image of Anwar as extremely immoderate (excessive) is further reinforced by the foregoing reference to slavery, which in the Malay context necessarily brings to mind images of royalty, who kept slaves in former times and continue to enjoin their subjects to refer to themselves, when addressing royalty, by a term whose principal meaning is that of slave (*hamba*), though it also means something like "your humble servant." The clear implication here is that Azizian was a slave to the royal Anwar, royal in any case being associated in the current political climate with all varieties of increasingly contested excesses and immunities, including those associated with otherwise criminalized sexuality.

In official Malay culture all such immoderate behavior is highly inappropriate and extremely transgressive, particularly in light of the proper/moderate conduct expected of a national leader who is vested with the title of minister of finance and whose mandates obviously include proper ("rational") stewardship of national (including natural) resources in the broadest sense of the term. To greatly oversimply (and to mix metaphors), Anwar's transgressions amount to his having indulged and inflamed his passions (*nafsu*) to the point of a Dionysian frenzy that is altogether unacceptable in light of the Appollonian moderation expected of political leaders and of men generally.

The charges of homosexual offenses become all the more serious and overdetermined when one looks more closely at some of the particulars of the men Anwar is said to have sodomized, especially those of the two men whose statements and overall circumstances received the most extensive and unrelenting press coverage (partly because they were, according to press accounts, the first to be charged after government probes into some of the allegations made in a book that was widely circulated by Anwar's detractors in June and July 1998).[29] The two men are Sukma Darmawan Sasmitaat Madja, age thirty-seven, an Indonesian by birth who, in addition to being Anwar's adopted brother, is an interior designer and businessman and currently a permanent resident in Malaysia, thanks in no small measure to Anwar's having facilitated his application for Malaysian citizenship, and Munawar Ahmad Anees, age fifty, from Pakistan, a friend and former speechwriter and lecturer. The fact that the first of these men is Anwar's adopted brother and is thus related to Anwar through ties of kinship necessarily raises the specter of incest (*sumbang*). Incest is among other things an offense against keeping separate that which should be separate, of failing to maintain proper boundaries, and in former times it could eventuate in capital punishment. The alleged incest is all the more serious in this instance since it confounds, in addition, the most basic of all boundaries—male and female. The fact that both of these men are foreigners (Indonesian and Pakistani, respectively) raises additional, deeply unsettling questions about inappropriate mixing, breaches of national security, and "letting down the side" (Malays), especially since one of them enlisted Anwar's help in obtaining much coveted Malaysian citizenship.

Another of the five men, Mior Abdul Razak bin Yahya, a fashion designer specializing in bead work for women's clothes, who is friends with Sukma and has worked for Anwar's wife (Wan Azizah), has also been accused of engaging in "group sex" with Anwar at the Hilton Hotel in Petaling Jaya,[30] a satellite community of Kuala Lumpur.[31] The fact that the first and third of the men mentioned here are involved in the design industry, which is linked in popular thinking with *pondan* and other variants of gender-transgressors, and that one of them is said to have engaged in "group sex" raises questions about gatherings of *pondan* and their associations as well as Islamic organizations such as Darul Arqam. Islamic groups like Darul Arqam have been banned by the government on various grounds, including the charge that their communal activities have included one or another variant of "group sex," which is thus subversive in multiple (overdetermined) ways.

Whether or not Anwar is guilty of any of these crimes (and most Malaysians, along with most foreign observers, have very strong doubts about the veracity of the charges, to say nothing of the process by which they have been adjudicated), it is clear from many indications that Anwar is also being charged, albeit unofficially, with treason (*derhaka*) and that the case for treason is in many ways difficult to refute. To clarify what I mean here, I need to explain that while the Malay term *derhaka* has meanings which include certain Western understandings of the term "treason" (violation of allegiance to one's country or sovereign, especially the betrayal of one's own country by waging war against it or by consciously or purposely acting to aid its enemies), it also evokes images of the most unheard-of breaches and inversions of the divinely ordained and simultaneously naturalized social order, such as incest (*sumbang*) and cannibalism, both of which (also) involve an unacceptable partaking of "one's own." More than that, incest, cannibalism, and treason are explicitly linked in Malay culture through myths, customary sayings, and aphorisms, including the expression, "like a chicken eating its own flesh" (*macam ayam makan daging sendiri*), which is sometimes invoked when people talk of incestuous unions. Such unions are seen as involving a preying on and consuming of one's own, much like domesticated chickens consuming the flesh of their consociates when they eat the scraps of cooked chicken that have been tossed out to them through the windows or the floorboards after a meal (see Peletz 1988b: 53–58); and, at least in former times, they were regarded as treasonous violations of *adat*.

We may summarize the main points here as follows: (1) in Malay culture, publicly criticizing a patron or a father-like figure, and/or rising at his expense, thus "eating off" him, is a form of disloyalty and treason that can also entail symbolic cannibalism; (2) Anwar has publicly differed with and criticized his former patron and father figure Mahathir on a variety of issues relating to economic and other policy matters, including but by no means limited to International Monetary Fund (IMF) guidelines issued to Malaysian ministries in the wake of the Asian financial crisis, and if only in this restricted sense is thus susceptible to charges of disloyalty, treason, and symbolic cannibalism; (3) offenses of treason and cannibalism are conjoined in Malay political culture with acts of incest, the latter being but one category of "bad sex"; and (4) those believed to be guilty of treason and/or cannibalism are thus likely to be—or might as well be—guilty of one or another form of "bad sex" such as homosexuality, especially if they are allied with or conceptually linked to the West, which, in official Malaysian discourses and in popular culture generally, is *the* main source of the "bad sex," perversion, and moral turpitude that exists both in Malaysia and in the world as a whole.

Rather than elaborating on the legal and political aspects of this trial, including the cultural-political dimensions of the specific charges against Anwar and the overall portrait of him that the government has tried to paint, I shall proceed to two other sets of dynamics, one of which has to do with the international and domestic fallout from Mahathir's handling of the issues associated with the trial and the verdict. The other concerns the society-wide effects of the government's construction of Anwar's alleged criminality.

Mahathir's handling of the affair met with sanctions in the form of censure not only from the United States and other Western nations but also from various Asian countries, including friendly neighbors such as predominantly Muslim Indonesia and the Philippines, an overwhelmingly Catholic country with a sizable Muslim population. It is notable that much of the censure from these very different nations was embedded in a shared discourse keyed to increasingly international standards of due process and human rights.

Far more detrimental to Mahathir's legitimacy as the Muslim leader of a predominantly Muslim nation is that his handling of the affair also met with sharp condemnation from the heads of Muslim groups, both domestic and international. Some of the Muslim protest from local and international quarters stemmed from the belief that the proceedings against Anwar should have been held in the Islamic courts. One of the more strongly worded of these international condemnations came from Shaikh Taha Jabir Al-Alwani, whose impeccable credentials include having obtained an advanced degree in Islamic law and jurisprudence (*fiqh*) from al-Azhar University in Cairo; having taught for many years at Imam Muhammad ibn Sa'ud Univeristy in Riyadh, Saudi Arabia; and being a founding member of the Muslim World League, Mecca, and a member of the International Fiqh Council of Jeddah. Shaikh Taha Jabir's condemnation of the sodomy trial is contained in a document that was circulated on the Internet shortly after the sodomy verdict against Anwar was announced on August 8, 2000. It is also widely available in pamphlet form from sidewalk vendors and bookstores in Kuala Lumpur and elsewhere.[32]

The shaikh states that based on Islamic law, "one could write volumes on the violations of the rights of the accused"; he then goes on to enumerate a series of violations that render both the verdict and the trial as a whole illegal. The latter enumeration invokes numerous passages from the Quran and various *hadith* by way of substantiation and includes the following: that "the alleged offense, sodomy, is a crime of honor and character, like *zina* [that] requires four credible eyewitnesses who have witnessed the act first hand, with no barrier or obstruction"; that "if there is the slightest discrepancy in their testimony the whole case is to be dismissed and the witnesses or accusers are guilty of slander or libel"; that Anwar was denied the opportunity to "call and cross-examine a key witness in the person of the Prime Minister," who had privileged access to a good deal of material evidence and was a critically important character witness; that the government denied Anwar's request to have all of the alleged "victims" of his acts "medically examined for signs of sodomy"; that the government's case lacked specificity as to the precise dates of the alleged crimes; and that the government was guilty of numerous counts of witness tampering and attorney intimidation.

The shaikh's overall assessment of the trial and verdict is summed up in his remarks that it was "an embarrassing conviction to the Malaysian Judiciary System. It has disgraced the great name of Malaysia. The judge should have upheld the values of Justice and *Shari'a* and the ethics of his profession by dismissing the case outright. It is judges like him who are the subject of the *Hadith* of the Prophet . . . 'two out of every three judges ends up in Hell fire'."

The shaikh continues by emphasizing that the judgment was a "violation of justice, the *Shari'a* law in form and substance . . . [and] a gross violation of the defendant's Human Rights." Lest anyone miss the bottom line of his professional, *syariah*-based judgment, he concludes his statement by underscoring, on the one hand, that "Anwar Ibrahim should be declared innocent . . . [and] released immediately" and, on the other, that "his accusers [including Prime Minister Mahathir?] should be tried for slander and libel."

Especially significant in light of my concerns with the interplay of multiple legal sensibilities and the challenges that a multiplicity of legal sensibilities pose to the legitimacy and sovereignty of those who hold or seek the reins of state power (chapter 2) is that although the pamphlet from which I quote is offered as "a *syariah* review"—and *syariah*-based condemnation—of the trial and verdict, its subject matter, logic, and appeal range well beyond *syariah* as it is generally understood. This is particularly evident in the nature of the shaikh's language and his explicit references to illegalities in the form of "withholding evidence," "tampering with witnesses," "obstructing justice," and "intimidating [defendants'] attorneys," all of which are familiar to anyone conversant with common-law based legal traditions in Western nations such as the United States. The pamphlet's extra-*syariah* framing is also apparent in the way the shaikh explicitly valorizes the "agreement of international observers" as well as evidence derived from modern scientific medical examination and, perhaps most important, "the defendant's Human Rights" (note the capital H and the capital R).

The shaikh's references to these phenomena might be seen as consonant with the centuries-old Islamic mandate enjoining those involved in adjudication to render evaluations and judgments based (partly) on consensus with "fellow legal specialists" and/or "local custom," particularly if, as seems especially appropriate in the Malaysian context, we interpret "fellow legal specialists" and "local custom" broadly to include common-law lawyers and the common law, respectively. But what is most interesting about the shaikh's document is that it interweaves language and key symbols of *syariah* and Western law, invokes criteria of legitimacy that are of radically disparate origin, and thus greatly expands the grounds on which the trial and, by implication, the regime of Prime Minister Mahathir are to be judged illegitimate. In doing so it not only helps guarantee that the document will resonate with the legal and attendant ethical and overall moral sensibilities of a large segment of the world's population; it also increases the likelihood that at some future point these latter sensibilities might be galvanized and mobilized into a broadly multilateral ("transcivilizational") sanctioning of the Mahathir regime.

Mahathir's treatment of Anwar did in any case forever change the Malaysian political landscape. This is partly because the Anwar affair, especially the blatant perversion of the judiciary for narrowly political purposes, not only created and "mobilized domestic groups that then influence[d] authority structures within the state," as Stephen Krasner (1999: 32–33) has put it with respect to analogous dynamics elsewhere in the world; it also "altered domestic conceptions of legitimate behavior, [and] subjected domestic institutions and personnel to external influence." Having already mentioned some of the external pressure brought to bear on domestic institutions and personnel in the wake of Anwar's arrest, I would underscore that the Anwar affair also gave rise to all varieties of other phenomena. These include new national-level political parties (most notably, Parti Keadilan Nasional [the National Justice Party], generally known as Keadilan, which is headed by Anwar's wife, Wan Azizah); new national-level political coalitions (the Alternative Alliance [Barisan Alternatif], composed of Keadilan and PAS, among others); a multitude of local NGOs with transnational connections; and a plethora of new books, articles, periodicals, websites, chat rooms, and other media products—each insisting in its own way that business as usual (corruption, cronyism, nepotism, and "money politics") is no longer acceptable and that new standards of transparency, accountability, and efficiency are vital to the nation's institutional (particularly economic) health and well-being, as well as its political standing and prestige in the international community.

More generally, the Anwar affair seriously alienated large segments of the Malaysian population, polarized the Malay community, and politicized Malay women and youth in particular, one immediate result of which was that many Malays, including disproportionately large numbers of women, voiced their opposition to Mahathir and UMNO in the general elections held in November 1999 by casting their votes for Keadilan or the major Islamic opposition party, PAS. One consequence of the shift away from UMNO, which has also occurred in more recent by-elections, is that PAS gained control of the state government in Terengganu, which borders the state of Kelantan, the other major PAS stronghold. These dynamics, in turn, encouraged Mahathir to take women's concerns more seriously, or at least to create a Ministry of Women's Affairs. It is too soon to tell if this is a pyrrhic victory for women, as many suspect. It is indicative of the shifting political landscape, however, that official announcements concerning the creation of this ministry in January 2001 were immediately followed by widely publicized press releases from leaders of the transsexual (*mak nyah*) community, who expressed the hope that state-sponsored efforts to promote greater public awareness of issues of gender would lead to their formal recognition and acceptance as a "third sex."

The electorate's swing toward PAS in the last few years is usefully viewed in the context of changes that have occurred in the PAS–controlled state of Kelantan since the early 1990s. Since that time the state government there has introduced a variety of legal, administrative, and policy proposals aimed at making the judicial and other institutions of their states "more Islamic," the more encompassing objective being to encourage their Muslim residents and ultimately Malaysia's entire Muslim population—and some would say all non-Muslims as well—to adopt a "more Islamic" way of life. In some cases, the changes that have been implemented or proposed seem heavily laden with symbolism but relatively inconsequential in "real-life" terms, such as separate supermarket checkout lines for males and females and the abolition of unisex hair salons. In other instances, the measures at issue have far broader social and cultural consequences or potential implications. I would include in the latter category the Kelantan government's 1990 banning of shadow-puppet theater and related genres of popular dramatic art that were long central to local Malay cultural identities, as well as the legislative and other measures pursued by Kelantan authorities in the early 1990s in an effort to implement *hudud* laws, which bear on various criminal offenses and some of the more severe penalties for their transgression specified in the Quran.[33] The formal implementation of these laws was stalled and ultimately scuttled by the national government, but many Malays and non-Malays fear that it is only a question of time before such laws are introduced in Kelantan and elsewhere in the Peninsula. Such fears have been heightened since late 1999, when authorities in the newly PAS–controlled state of Terengganu floated a proposal, later rescinded, to impose a tax (*kharajat*) on the economic activities of all non-Muslims in the state.

Not surprisingly, recent years have also witnessed enhanced legitimacy and prestige accorded to Islamic scholars and men of learning (*ulama*), especially in Terengganu and Kelantan, but elsewhere as well, along with greatly stepped-up activity on the part of the increasingly high-profile Islamic Center (Pusat Islam), which is based in Kuala Lumpur and has as one of its key mandates the reduction of vice among Muslims and the upgrading of Muslim morality generally. These developments have gone hand in hand with the apparent upsurge in support among Malays, particularly youth, for Islamization programs of various kinds. Some Malaysians feel that trends such as these are responsible for the increase in censorship and self-censorship that characterizes contemporary political and social discourse, and for the overall constriction of the discursive spaces commonly associated with civil society.

For mostly obvious reasons, developments of the latter sort have exacerbated the conundrums of legitimacy and sovereignty facing Mahathir (especially since UMNO is seen as relatively secular compared to PAS), just as they will almost certainly exacerbate the quandaries facing his successors, however Islamist, accommodationist, or secular they may be. The same is true of other dynamics that have contributed to divisions and polarization among Malays. More generally, political and other disunity among Malays is seen by many Malays and other Malaysians as a grave threat to Malaysia's sovereignty, as are the processes of economic and political globalization over which a more sovereign Malaysia might be able to exercise a modicum of control. In this connection it merits emphasis that many Malaysians view economic and political globalization as more or less synonymous with neocolonial domination by Western powers that differs from its colonial-era counterparts primarily by being more invidious, pervasive, and hegemonic. In the local view of things, then, disunity among Malays necessarily poses multiple (overdetermined) threats to Malaysian sovereignty.

Mahathir's handling of the affair, including, especially, his government's construction of Anwar's alleged criminality, changed the political landscape in other ways as well, partly by exploiting sentiments and dispositions that are in some respects quite distinct from those we have already discussed. Perhaps most obvious has been the highlighting of homosexuality, and its stigmatization, criminalization, and medicalization, in the myriad contexts that make up public culture. It is not simply the case that local papers have been filled with what are, in the Malaysian setting, shockingly detailed and lurid accounts of the charges against Anwar and the evidence introduced by the government to prosecute him; such evidence has included stained mattresses, samples of blood, pubic hair, and semen, and scientific reports detailing the findings of anal probes, all of which have been front-page news. Equally shocking to the sensibilities of many Malaysians has been the constant bandying about—in government speeches, newspapers, and radio and television broadcasts—of terms such as *liwat*, the latter being the (Arabic-origin) Malay term for sodomy that prior to Anwar's arrest was generally unknown even to highly educated Malays.[34] The term has become so widely circulated and invoked that at least some Malaysians given to linguistic play have jokingly substituted one vowel for another (an "i" for an "a") so as to refashion the government slogan, "The Year for Visiting Malaysia" (*Tahun Melawat Malaysia*) as "The Year for Sodomizing Malaysia" (*Tahun Meliwat Malaysia*).[35]

Similarly, much media attention has been lavished on Mahathir's repeated reminders that homosexuality is a disease of Western origin that is criminalized in Malaysia.[36] Extensive media play has also been accorded Mahathir's pronouncements that "[i]n Malaysia we reject such extreme acts" and "We accept men as men and women as women," the factually erroneous implication of which is that Malaysians have never tolerated or accepted men or women who deviate from normative definitions of masculinity or femininity, respectively. Needless to say, the state-controlled media also made much of Mahathir's very public, bottom-line position(s), articulated as: Malaysians need to "distance themselves from misguided Western ideas, such as accepting homosexuality as a human right," and "I cannot accept a man who is a sodomist as leader of the country."[37]

It remains to consider the consequences of the media frenzy surrounding the Anwar case and some of the dynamics it has fueled. Most relevant here are the deployment of discourses and the whipping up of public sentiment against homosexuality and, by extension, transgendering of all varieties. Manifestations of these discourses and sentiments include the increased frequency of police raids on certain parks, malls, restaurants, bars, parking lots, and other locales seen as friendly to gays, lesbians, and other transgendered individuals. Such raids on the part of the overwhelmingly Malay police force typically result in the widely publicized arrest, detention, and drug testing of their patrons, especially the foreigners among them, who, as is typically emphasized in press accounts, are usually *Western* men. They also commonly involve the publication in the newspapers of photos of those arrested, resulting in serious repercussions of various kinds. Such raids are also partly responsible for the waves of fear and panic currently experienced by members of Malaysia's gay, lesbian, and transgendered communities who, especially if they are members of one or another ethnic minority (Chinese, for example), rightfully fear discrimination and harassment in the form of verbal and physical abuse, detention and arrest, and the curtailment or loss of educational, employment, and other economic opportunities.

Another consequence of these developments is in some ways much more ominous. I refer to the formation of community-based vigilante groups, made up largely of Malays, who have taken to monitoring activities in their neighborhoods that they deem to be "immoral" or "un-Islamic." Such groups, which apparently began forming around 1994, assisted in the arrests of some seven thousand people from 1994 to 1995 alone and have been encouraged by government officials to "fight homosexuals" and wipe out homosexuality in its entirety. As one high-ranking government official put it, "We certainly do not want to see our country turning into another replica of Western countries."[38]

One of the groups that is explicitly antihomosexual was launched on October 21, 1998, not coincidentally a mere seven or eight weeks after the first broadly public airing of sodomy charges against Anwar. From the outset this group, known as the People's Anti-Homosexual Volunteer Movement (PASRAH), disclaimed any political motivation, even though most of its members appeared to belong to the inner circle of the ruling UMNO party and its founding chairman, Ibrahim Ali, was both a member of the UMNO Supreme Council and a staunch supporter of Prime Minister Mahathir. One of the group's self-described goals is to bring about the closing of all bars, recreational centers, and other establishments frequented by gays, lesbians, and bisexuals (PASRAH cited some thirteen such spots in Kuala Lumpur), who are estimated by PASRAH to number approximately twenty-four thousand in Kuala Lumpur alone.[39]

The more general goal of PASRAH, which claims the existence of some fifty like-minded organizations, is to press for legislation and other measures that will eliminate homosexuality in its entirety, on the grounds that it is a defiling Western import that is profoundly threatening with respect to race and nation because it jeopardizes the reproduction and strengthening of Islamic and Malaysian values specifically and "Asian values" in general. In this connection we might recall that some of the more "puritanical" and "conservative" Malay Muslims in Malaysia, many but not all of whom are associated with PAS, seek the passage of legislation that would result in homosexual sexual activity being penalized with the punishment sometimes meted out in Islamic countries for heterosexual adultery/fornication (*zina*), which can include caning or whipping (involving as many as one hundred lashes) and, in some cases, capital punishment.

The formation of PASRAH in October 1998, coupled with the emergence of numerous like-minded organizations, is but one manifestation of a type of cultural cleansing that has been going on in Malaysia during the past few decades. Such cultural cleansing is geared toward purging Malaysia of what are perceived to be contaminating and otherwise unacceptable cultural influences, in this instance, of foreign, especially Western, origin. These are very disturbing developments for a variety of reasons and have in fact been condemned by local human rights organizations, such as SUARAM (Suara Rakyat Malaysia [The Voice of the Malaysian People]), which insists that attempts by PASRAH members to incite discrimination and condemnation of a minority group is a "misguided form of support for the Prime Minister."[40] The establishment of organizations such as PASRAH has also been decried by certain prominent individuals, such as Marina Mahathir, who is a highly respected journalist, author, and businesswoman, as well as the daughter of Prime Minister Mahathir and the president of the Malaysian AIDS Council and the Malaysian AIDS Federation. Marina Mahathir has publicly articulated the well-founded fears that such "hate campaigns" might promote intolerance, "inflame public prejudice" against gays and lesbians, and "make anti-social acts such as harassment of certain groups acceptable."[41] The daughter of the prime minister is clearly one of the very few individuals in the country who can safely criticize developments of this sort, and she may be partly responsible for the fact that PASRAH's formal, "above-ground" existence appears to have been short-lived.

In this context it is relevant that some of those I interviewed in January 2001 insisted that PASRAH continues to operate but not in an official or "above-ground" capacity. Others I interviewed, including Marina Mahathir, told me that PASRAH no longer exists in any form, not even as a shadow organization, and that its founding members have likewise ceased to hold important political positions of any variety. Many who are of the latter opinion, along with some who feel that PASRAH is indeed alive and well (though underground), hastened to emphasize the following themes. Whatever its present status and scope of operations, PASRAH is but one example of an increasingly common type of "morally corrective" organization and cultural-political sensibility. And in some ways more germane, each and every urban and rural community in the country has as part of its system of local governance at least one committee or council charged with upholding public morality and bringing morally suspect or "wayward" individuals to the attention of local government authorities or their superiors.

There is, I believe, a more important point in all of this, which is that those threatened by dynamics involving the formation of the many PASRAH–like vigilante groups that continue to operate are not simply individuals involved or believed to be involved in homosexual activities. Also very much threatened are men and women involved in transgendering who are *not* homosexual, as well as *all men perceived to be effeminate* and *all women perceived to be masculine*, especially since being effeminate in the case of a male and masculine in the case of a female is increasingly construed as a major sign or symbol of being "a homosexual" (*seorang homoseksual*).

Developments and dynamics of the latter sort are increasingly evident in various spheres and regimes of governmentality—including national and state legislatures, the secular and religious courts, as well as other subsystems of law and administration—and in other public institutions and agencies that have come to exercise ever greater control over the most intimate of private domains. Here we might recall the speech made by Minister Datuk Abdul Hamid Othman in February 1997 at the height of the public controversies surrounding the cases of Azizah and Fauzi. Reassuring his audience of the government's redoubled efforts to combat transvestism, other "gender woes," and "social ills" more generally, he announced new plans to draw on and actively recruit the personnel and other resources of political parties (UMNO branches), religious departments, schools, parent-teacher associations, and the media to "spread the message on proper parenting skills" including, in particular, the message that parents need to *learn* "proper" parenting skills. In this context, as we have seen, "proper" parenting means adopting a *"zero tolerance* concept" in "family life, religion and law," which is to say that parents should neither "endure [n]or allow room for waywardness in the family" nor "adopt the *tak apalah* (it doesn't matter) attitude" when it comes to the gendered and potential sexual(ized) proclivities of their children.

Thus targeted by these new campaigns is not only the social tolerance long exhibited by Malay parents toward certain types of gendered conduct (such as male experimentation with female dress, adornment, and comportment), but also children's "polymorphous" behavior with respect to sex (what Freud referred to as their "polymorphous perversity") and gender alike. But much more is at issue. Indeed, what is involved here are at least four broadly encompassing and critically important developments: (1) the targeting and, more important, the problematizing of childhood and adolescent sexualities; (2) the harnessing of pedagogical institutions to better supervise and regulate "the problem" of childhood and adolescent sex, what Foucault spoke of as the "pedagogization" of childhood and adolescent sex (1978:104); (3) the tacit and unmarked admission, which is highly subversive with respect to much of the official discourse on the subject, that at least in the case of transvestism, local "gender woes" are *not* entirely or even primarily of Western origin and may in fact be the direct result of the particular parenting traditions long enshrined in *local* culture; and (4) the equally tacit and unmarked though ultimately far more subversive admission that gender identities and sexual orientations are not the direct, unmediated by-product of one's genital constitution or otherwise ascribed at birth (in a sociological sense), but are achieved (also in the sociological sense) and thus capable of being malleable, hybrid, and protean, much like religious, ethnic, and other identities.

Attendant developments have entailed the emergence of entirely new discourses which concern and are simultaneously cause and effect of the production of "a whole machinery for speechifying, analyzing, and investigating" (Foucault 1978: 32) a related series of themes. These include but are not limited to the following: "sodomy" and "homosexuality"; "sodomy and homosexuality as perversion"; and "sodomy and homosexuality as perversion of Western origin"—all of which are related through complementary opposition to and are otherwise deeply constitutive of the discourses on "Asian values" that have proliferated in Malaysia, Singapore, and elsewhere in Asia since the early to mid-1990s. The highly politicized "incitement to discourse" that has given rise in mediascapes and elsewhere to the "veritable discursive explosion" (Foucault 1978: 17) bearing on sodomy, homosexuality, and perversion bears a loose "family resemblance" to some of the historical trajectories that Foucault has described for France and other parts of Europe in the eighteenth and nineteenth centuries. So, too, does the transposition of certain categories that has occurred in the course of the "discovery of sexuality" and the "invention of homosexuality" in particular. To paraphrase Foucault's (1978: 43) observation that in France, whereas "the sodomite had been a temporary aberration, the homosexual was now a species," we might say that in Malaysia, whereas the gender-transgressive *pondan* had long been seen (and in many respects still is regarded) as a temporary aberration, "the homosexual," like "the sodomist" (the two terms tend to be used interchangeably in Malaysia), is clearly a species, "a personage, a past, a case history, and a childhood, in addition to being a type of life, a life form, and a morphology, with an indiscreet anatomy and possibly a mysterious physiology" (Foucault 1978: 43), though some of this occurs with certain types of *pondan* as well. A key difference from France is that the *pondan* was never sexualized in the way that the French sodomist was, which is to say that in the Malaysian context we see a move from an aberration that was gendered though neither sexualized, stigmatized, nor criminalized, to a species, which, in addition to being (homo)sexualized, is also stigmatized and criminalized.

One other comparison with France worth noting here has to do with Foucault's observation that in sixteenth- and seventeenth-century France, moral categories of "excess" and "debauchery" were of considerable cultural elaboration and broad sociopolitical concern. This is because they were seen as cause and effect of "heredity" and thus always implicated in potentially anxious discourses on "the health of the race" and, by implication, that of the nation, including those discourses focusing specifically on fears and anxieties about racial—and/or national—degeneration. Of additional interest here is Foucault's (1978: 118) point that in eighteenth- and nineteenth-century France, the moral category of "perversion" superseded that of "excess/debauchery" such that the series "excess/debauchery, heredity, degeneration" was superseded by the series "perversion, heredity, degeneration." Obvious differences in time frame aside, here too we see a loose "family resemblance" to the Malaysian case, though the latter might be said to be in the midst of an epistemic or discursive transition, one highlighted most visibly by the combination of charges against Anwar, which, as we have seen, include (if only implicitly) accusations of excess, debauchery, *and* perversion. That charges of perversion are meant to be the most damning of all accusations is additional evidence of the trajectory to which we have alluded, especially since, as various prominent Malaysian observers have noted, allegations that officials have engaged in adultery, corruption, and the like have become so commonplace in the Malaysian political setting that something "truly scurrilous" (because "truly perverse") had to be concocted in order to have the desired result of destroying Anwar's spiritual and religious credentials and overall moral character, hence his political legitimacy.

In the French context, as Foucault has shown, the appearance in the nineteenth century of an extensive series of psychiatric, jurisprudential, and literary

> discourses on the species and subspecies of homosexuality, inversion, pederasty, and "psychic hermaphrodism" [not only] made possible a strong advance of social controls into this area of "perversity"; . . . it also made possible the formation of a "reverse" discourse: homosexuality began to speak in its own behalf, to demand that its legitimacy or "naturality" be acknowledged, often in the same vocabulary, using the same categories by which it was medically disqualified. (1978: 101)

We might thus ask if something along these lines has also occurred in Malaysia, or, put differently, if there is any Malaysian evidence bearing on such matters that might support Foucault's frequently cited observation, which I paraphrase, "where there is knowledge/power, there is resistance." Before answering such questions it is well to add a bit more complexity to Foucault's position by underscoring, as Robert Hefner has done, that "reverse" discourses "emerge not as phenomena contained within discourse alone" but also as a result of more sociological variables such as "the creation of new landscapes of human agency [like] the city, [the] Internet, business enterprises [that are] not dependent on state patrons," etc.[42] Some of these landscapes invite heightened control and repression at the hands of different categories of elites, but "others allow for the quotidian practices of anonymity, autonomy, and self-determination" (in selecting a place to live, a career, or a mate, for example) that ultimately lead some people to articulate and enact alternative definitions of their selves and their futures. This argument resonates with my earlier elucidation of the fact that modernity has both bright sides and dark ones. It is not out of keeping with the Foucauldian emphasis on discourse, but it adds another more complex layer than Foucault offers, one that is consistent with Malaysia's historical and contemporary experience of "institutional differentiation, spatialization, and movement."[43]

Malaysian evidence of these dynamics and discourses does in fact exist, as Malaysian expert Tan Beng Hui (1999) has noted with respect to the discourse on "Asian values" and the particular ways it has singled out homosexuality, cross-dressing, and transgendering of all varieties as being "unAsian."

> *The discourse on Asian values has also "benefited" the homosexual (female and male) community in Malaysia. The constant cautions against homosexuality and other forms of social "evil" have given these various phenomena—as well as the actors behind them—a prominence never before seen in Malaysia. The Asian values discourse has inadvertently ended up publicly acknowledging and naming the presence of homosexuality in Malaysian society. Furthermore, the very idea of needing to contain homosexuality and to "get rid" of it is premised on a recognition that homosexuality not only exists but that it can also be promoted. This is extremely significant*

since it implies that sexual identities are not natural, fixed, and immutable as they are commonly made out to be. (287; emphasis added)

In the essay cited here Tan does not go as far as saying that either home-grown or more cosmopolitan gender-transgressors have also begun speaking publicly on their own behalf, to demand that their legitimacy or "naturality" (to use Foucault's term) be acknowledged. But the very existence of her work is a clear indication of burgeoning developments along these lines. Additional evidence of such trends appears in the related work published by Malaysian scholars and activists in 1996 under the pseudonyms of "Rais Nur and A.R.", which provides an overview of the lesbian movement in Malaysia and the ways that lesbians and gays are persecuted by the state;[44] and in articles posted on the Internet in 1998 and 1999 by Alina Rastam and Nadiah Ba-madhaj, which discuss the Anwar case in the context of the need for Ma-laysians to lobby for the legal and cultural recognition of sexual rights—especially the sexual rights of gays, lesbians, and transsexuals—as human rights.[45] More generally, the Internet has facilitated a veritable explosion of discourses concerning not only sexual orientation and sexual rights in the Malaysian setting but also the experiences of gay and lesbian Malaysians living abroad, increasing numbers of whom have sought and been granted political asylum in the United States and Canada on the grounds that, as homosexuals, they are subject to persecution in Malaysia. Anwar's conviction on sodomy charges, coupled with his August 8, 2000, sentencing to an addi-tional nine years in prison, may well help ensure that at least in the short run, some of these discourses remain relatively "underground" in Malaysia—or largely confined to cyberspace. But there is every reason to believe that these discourses will multiply exponentially in the months and years ahead, and that those involved in their production and dissemination will eventually seek more public venues to assert their legitimacy and naturality.

Both in this chapter and in chapter 4 I have been concerned with modernity and governmentality in Islamic courts and other domains. In chapter 4, much of which focused on the refashioning of authenticity and identity in the Islamic courts, we saw that the narratives of Islamic courts are key ingredients of state strategies geared toward reinscribing certain types of authenticity and identity—or, put differently, new ways of understanding, experiencing, representing, and otherwise being in the world. And we saw that these strategies in turn are central components of state agendas aimed at constituting modern middle-class families and subjectivities and simultaneously guaranteeing that loyalties be-yond the household be largely restricted to the imagined community of Muslim believers (the *ummah*) and the state. We have also seen that since the early 1970s the ruling party (UMNO) has been explicit in its goal of eradicating rural Malay society and culture as "traditionally" constituted as part of the ground-work necessary for creating an altogether new sector of middle- and upper-middle-class urban Malay capitalists that will ideally be able to hold its own if not excel in competition against local Chinese and Indians as well as other Asians *and* Westerners in increasingly global economic and political arenas.

The realization of these agendas has entailed social engineering and cultural cleansing that has been extremely dislocating and otherwise deeply painful for rural Malays and all ordinary Muslims (see Peletz 1993a, 1997; Kahn and Loh Kok Wah 1992; Stivens 1996; Lee and Ackerman 1997). It is thus highly ironic, though perhaps not at all surprising as a strategic countermove, that political and religious leaders have taken such pains in recent years to formulate a discourse on "Asian values" that emphasizes a timeless, eternally unchanging, and otherwise strongly tradition-bound and essentialized "Oriental," whose basic subjectivities and family values transcend time, space, gender, class, occupation, and local cultural identity. The latter discourse is all the more ironic in light of all the explicit and in many respects intense antagonism among Malaysia's three main "races," to say nothing of the highly disparaging attitudes of locals to hill-dwelling aborigines as well as migrant workers and illegal immigrants of Asian background.

Since the production and worldwide circulation of all such discourses (like those of Muslim feminists, local and Western NGOs, and specifically human-rights organizations that we considered earlier) are very much part and parcel of processes of globalization, I would like to turn, finally, to a few remarks on globalization and nation-state sovereignty. Saskia Sassen (1996, 1998) has written insightfully on the subject, but as Ong (1999a) correctly points out, Sassen sometimes gives the impression that she conceives of the dynamics in essentially zero-sum terms; that is, "more" globalization is said to lead inexorably to "less" nation-state sovereignty. Ong suggests that we transcend zero-sum problematics and look instead at the ways that globalizing phenomena pose new challenges to nation-states and thus help elicit new strategies of governmentality, new regimes of citizenship, and new systems of graduated sovereignty— all of which can be pressed into service to negotiate globalizing forces in a variety of different ways. This is a vital corrective I thoroughly endorse. But I would also register a friendly caveat and underscore that it is a theoretical or analytic perspective, what anthropologists, drawing on the distinction that linguists make between phonetics and phonemics, used to call an "etic" perspective. "Etic" perspectives need to be distinguished from their "emic" counterparts (the perspectives articulated by the people whose social lives and cultural products we aim to describe and interpret). It seems crucial to maintain the distinction in the present context. I say this because Mahathir and other Southeast Asian leaders (and, I would guess, most of their countrymen) do seem to experience, understand, and represent forces of globalization—including the financial meltdown and the myriad economic, political, and moral crises to which it gave rise—as a devastating assault on their multiple sovereignties, including the integrity of their imagined communities, bodies politic, and invariably sexed and gendered bodies.

According to Mahathir's widely retailed worldview (*A New Deal for Asia*), forces of globalization have unleashed on Southeast Asia the unbridled greed and other base passions of unruly herds of foreign currency traders and speculators like George Soros. Mahathir is explicit in insisting that such groups, along with the IMF and related organizations, have totally undercut the rights of Asian leaders to defend their countries and control their destinies, and have in these and other ways completely disregarded principles of national sovereignty. Mahathir's nationalist discourses since mid-1997 are in fact strikingly reminiscent of the narratives of women who have been subject to (date) rape. They are in any case redolent with symbols, idioms, and overt imagery of victimization through theft, assault, and humiliation; of the laws of the jungle; of fault lines that can be widened and prised open; of shattered certainties and stolen futures; and perhaps most revealingly, of the violent penetration that necessarily results from having been unwittingly open and receptive to id-driven, wanton foreigners hell-bent on the creation and subsequent domination of a borderless world. In this connection we need also bear in mind that Anwar has been widely depicted in the press and elsewhere as a supporter of the IMF and an ally of the West in general. Given this overall discursive context, the allegations that Anwar illegally penetrated and otherwise violated a variety of Malaysian and other men, at least one of whom was related to him through bonds of kinship, are deeply allegorical. Indeed, it is hard to think of a political narrative that is more conducive to exploiting local fears and anxieties about being insufficiently vigilant in safeguarding the integrity and sovereignty of bodies, families, and the body politic from the real or imagined onslaught of globalization.

CONCLUSION

Islam, Modernity, and Civil Society

TOWARD THE BEGINNING of this book I remarked on the wane of the cold war, the demise of the former Soviet Union and various socialist economies in Eastern Europe and elsewhere, and the ways in which the world's Muslim communities and their religious beliefs and practices have emerged in the Western imagination as the predominant threat to world order and security. I also noted that the promulgation of disparaging and otherwise negative views of Muslims and their traditions is best viewed historically, and that such imagery has a long established (though uneven) genealogy, represented in a good deal of eighteenth- and nineteenth-century literature, for example, and in many other spheres of cultural production extending back to, even predating, the Crusades. The leitmotivs in the literary and other cultural domains at issue here have varied considerably over time in terms of their relative emphasis and hegemony as well as the scope and force of their core symbols and meanings. Beneath the surface diversity, however, one can discern profound historical continuity in Western imagery of Muslims and Islam: excess, debauchery, cruelty, and, more recently, perversion, violence, and savage brutality—the underlying theme in all of this being irrationality. The latter was of course the Ur-theme that both animated and framed Max Weber's Victorian-era critique of "*kadi*-justice" and Islamic legal systems as a whole. It was also a central component of his explanation for why Muslim societies failed to develop systems of capitalism comparable to those found in the West. Clearly central to Weber's vision of these East-West contrasts is the idea that Islamic courts and the values and subjectivities associated with them are "backward looking," if not caught in a time warp dating from the tenth century, and that for these and other reasons they pose fatal obstacles to the attainment of the rational ("progressive" and "enlightened") modes of government, economy, and social organization held to be conducive to modernity's holy trinity—urbanization, industrialization, and bureaucratization.

Against all such views and attendant imagery I have advanced a twofold thesis and a series of corollary arguments. The first part of the thesis is that there is a very clear cultural logic informing judicial process in Islamic courts both in Malaysia and elsewhere, though like all cultural logics (legal and otherwise), it is informed by contrasting discourses and the play of mutually contradictory elements—and is more accessible and transparent, or at least more beneficial, to some (for example, men) than to others (women). Perhaps most central to the cultural logic of judicial process is the valorization of negotiation, compromise, and reconciliation, which are key themes both in the formal and informal ideology and everyday practice of Malay and other Malaysian interpersonal relations, and in the official theory and actual conduct of Malaysian politics at all levels (local, regional, and national). These findings are consistent with Dale Eickelman and James Piscatori's recent (1996) survey of politics in the Muslim world. Ranging well beyond the usual geographic foci (the Middle East and North Africa), their survey illustrates that far from being either mono-lithic or prone to conflict and violence, Muslim politics are extremely hetero-genous; that they usually proceed via negotiation, compromise, and bargaining; and that they typically make provision for diversity and pluralism. My findings also resonate deeply with the recent work of Bruce Lawrence (1998) and Rob-ert Hefner (1993, 1998a, 1998b, 2000), which, in different ways, illuminate the rich variety of generally flexible and accommodationist political traditions char-acteristic of the Muslim world in general and of Indonesia in particular (the world's largest Muslim nation).

The second part of the main thesis running throughout this volume is that Islamic courts, far from being major obstacles to social, cultural, or economic change, are in fact strategic loci in the projects of modernity that the leaders of Malaysia, and in former times Malaya, have set for themselves and their coun-trymen. (This despite the fact that the particular way their mandates and desti-nies were defined by the shifting fortunes of British-backed Malay elites as a result of the Pangkor Engagements of 1874 helped ensure that they would not pose serious challenges to basic political hierarchies.) Such has been true of the Islamic courts since (and perhaps even before) their reorganization under the British beginning in the late 1800s. Throughout the colonial era and well into the early postcolonial period, the courts have been instrumental in promoting change, though they were of course simultaneously concerned to safeguard var-ious traditions deemed vital to the contemporary constitution and reproduction of the Malay and more encompassing Muslim community. Indeed, from the early 1970s through the 1990s, the courts were strategically involved in the furtherance of the New Economic Policy, which had as its twin goals the elim-ination of poverty and a severing of the link between "race" and "economic function." Practically speaking, the NEP sought the ultimate elimination of the rural Malay agricultural sector and its "replacement" with a sector of middle-class urban Malay capitalists (*Melayu baru*) who could compete successfully— economically and otherwise—both with local Chinese and Indians and with other Asians and Westerners alike. The Islamic courts have been key players in the attainment of these goals in that they have actively contributed to the cre-ation and policing of modern middle-class families and subjectivities. The same could be said of the role of the courts in the years following the superseding of the NEP by the NDP in the early 1990s and the latter's replacement by Vision 2020, which seeks full industrialization within the first twenty years of the new millennium.

The larger theme is that the Islamic courts, and local institutions of Islam as a whole, have encouraged a certain type of modernity and civil society that is characteristically Asian and distinctively Malaysian. The courts help establish the foundations for Malaysian-style modernity and civil society in at least four ways. First, they provide a legitimate, state-sanctioned, and relatively confidential forum—one of the very few available *anywhere* in Malaysia—that allows people to articulate an important range of their intimate experiences and to thrash out some of their deeply felt differences and conceptions of moral injustice, all in a frank, "no holds barred" sort of way. It is no small matter that the forum provided by the Islamic court comes with at least implicit guarantees of protection from many of the repercussions that would normally result from any such expressions of discontent or challenge to institutionalized authority. To fully appreciate the uniqueness of this, we might recall that it is a heavily sanctioned criminal offense to publicly discuss most other forms of difference, inequality, and injustice, such as those keyed to ethnic relations, the prerogatives of sultans, and the constitutional privileges accorded the Malay population; and that failure to abide such proscriptions can easily result in prolonged (indeed, indefinite) detention under the dreaded Internal Security Act. Reliance on fora such as the Islamic courts may well have cathartic and therapeutic dimensions, but the more significant point here is that the mere existence of such fora both allows for and encourages the type of direct verbal exchange and empassioned airing of difference prohibited in most other contexts in Malaysia but nonetheless integral to a modern-day citizenry, a state that is responsive to democratic sentiment, social and cultural pluralism, and a vibrant marketplace alike.

A second way in which the courts encourage modernity and civil society is by emphasizing the contractual responsibilities—though not so much the rights—of the individual. The dynamics at issue here help foreground the idea that while individuals necessarily move through the life course as members of status- and identity-conferring groups of various kinds (households, more encompassing groups of kin, village communities, and the like), they are both able and advised to enter into written, contractual relationships (such as marriage) of their own accord, albeit with the formal approval of a father (or another male kinsman) in the case of women. Also central to these dynamics is the notion that individuals have recourse when the contracts into which they have entered have been violated, although the violations are phrased more in terms of the other party not fulfilling his or her responsibilities than such behavior resulting in a denial of the individual's rights. The discourses and practices surrounding marriage payments, their return in the case of certain forms of divorce (for example, *tebus talak*), and of course Islamic notions of sin (*dosa*) likewise place a premium on the concept of the individual and the idea that, second to God, ultimate responsibility for one's fate both in this world and in the Afterlife lies with the individual, not with some larger group (such as a kindred, lineage, or clan).

Third, the courts encourage and otherwise help bring about both the further erosion of extended kinship and the democratization of family relations and marriage in particular. These goals are pursued partly through morally corrective advice and more encompassing discourses (including their silences, elisions, and conflations) geared toward freeing individuals from some of the constraints of extended kinship, or (at least) toward endorsing such freedom. The realization of these goals is also sought through efforts to dilute some of the gendered inequalities that obtain in Islamic law (though the court's activities in these areas are not explicitly marked as such). Recall, too, that the courts engage in practices premised on the assumption that men cause most of the problems in marriage and are at fault in much (even most) divorce and do, moreover, resort to dishonesty much more than women. In this the courts are, in effect, contributing to the destabilization of one of the most basic fulcrums of Islamic and state-sanctioned inequality. Put differently, in these and other ways the courts are simultaneously creating space for the emergence and growth of sentiments, dispositions, and embryonic ideologies that are a direct challenge to one of the most fundamental of the official lines shared by Islam and the state.

The potential for widely ramifying subversion here is enormous, especially in light of Claude Lévi-Strauss's altogether reasonable ([1949] 1969) contention that gendered differences and inequalities were the first forms of difference and inequality that were institutionalized in pre-historic times and that partly for this reason they are foundational to *all* subsequently developed systems of difference and inequality, including, not least, those based on race and class. In fact, one need not grant either dimension of the Lévi-Straussian argument to recognize that Islamic courts are implicated in the production of counterhegemonic ideologies of gender that have the potential to destabilize all other systems of hierarchy and prestige. To appreciate my position, one need only bear in mind that while men control political, religious, and administrative hierarchies of all kinds (be they local, regional or national), they are also seen as more prone to lying and criminal activity, as well as other varieties of moral transgression. One of the more general points here is that the courts are in many ways unwittingly implicated in the production and circulation of discourses that encourage a healthy skepticism about the basis of privileges accorded to men, including but not limited to men in political office. Another is that such skepticism has the potential to temper hierarchies both in the household and far beyond, and thus to check the predatory impulses of those who might prey on those making up one or another category of subaltern.

Fourth, the courts emphasize that identities, rather than being carried in the blood or otherwise ascribed at birth and thus in some sense "natural," are in a very basic sense freely chosen and thus at least potentially thoroughly hybrid and protean. More generally, by moving toward policies and practices that make more room (but certainly do not always allow) for choice—including, no small matter, the choice to go against one's parents' wishes in selecting, staying with, or leaving a spouse, and the choice to give up on and exit a marriage if it does not fulfill one's emotional needs—the courts are according sanctified legitimacy to the exercise of theoretically uncoerced judgments and decision-making processes of the sort that are essential to modernity and civil society alike.

On the basis of material presented in earlier chapters, one could easily extend this summary list of ways in which the courts are implicated not only in projects of modernity but also in the gradual albeit highly uneven expansion of civil society. The foregoing should suffice, however, to counter the assumptions and contentions found in Western popular culture and in certain streams of Western academic discourse as to the inherently regressive and "backward-looking" (medieval, tribal) nature of Islamic courts. The summary list provided above should also be useful as a corrective to the widespread views that states, especially in the Muslim world and elsewhere in Asia, are always thoroughly repressive. While not gainsaying the importance of efforts to describe and analyze state repression (including exclusionary policies) of various kinds, we also need to recognize the "liberatory dimensions of states," just as we need to unravel the conditions that make each possible (Hefner 1998a; see also Eickelman 1996; Eickelman and Piscatori 1996). The most relevant (in the sense of intellectually productive) question, in any case, is not whether Islam is compatible with modernity, civil society, or democracy (or vice versa), but rather the extent to which the ideologies and practices of states, including states that include Islamic elements or inflections, are conducive to the growth of democratic sentiments and cultures (White 1996). We should perhaps be more specific here and emphasize that the questions to which anthropologists can most usefully address their inquiries have to do with the ways in which the discourses and practices of various components and more encompassing subsystems of states, including those that for one or another reason may be "semi-autonomous" with respect to the others, nourish democratic or civic culture. In attempting to address issues bearing on the promise or future of civil society, it is this nourishing of civic culture that is most critical, not simply a "body count" of NGOs arrayed in opposition to the state, as Hefner (1998a, 2000) also argues.

Before turning to comments bearing more directly on matters of the latter sort, I need to underscore a few points that will serve to temper the arguably celebratory tone of the summary comments offered thus far. The political and other conditions outlined here are fragile and contingent, and late twentieth-century processes involving the centralization of the Islamic courts and their increasingly bureaucratic "corporate" style do not necessarily bode well for the growth of civil society or the expansion of women's rights in particular and may, at least in the short run, work in the opposite direction. That said, there are clear limits to the degree of centralization that can be accomplished since each state in Malaysia is theoretically autonomous with respect to the regulation of Islamic affairs, which rests in theory with the "traditional" head of each state (typically the sultan).

It is also imperative to recognize that by opening up spaces for women, by providing them with resources and allies capable of being called on to negotiate and, in some instances, to terminate their relations with their husbands, the state, through the courts, is also making itself more indispensable to women by increasing their reliance on the judiciary, and is thus further intruding into their lives. There is an appreciable trade-off here and elsewhere where such processes have occurred, as is clear from Sally Engle Merry's (1990) incisive descriptions and analyses of working-class women's increased use of lower courts in contemporary America. Similarly, by restricting men's prerogatives to enter into extrajudicial divorce (which in former times could be effected with complete legitimacy in the privacy of one's bedroom), both the courts and the state are intruding into and thus further whittling away at private domains—a process we also see in the recent criminalization of domestic violence and non-normative sexual and gendered behavior. Such being the case, women and men who turn to the courts to help them resolve matrimonial and other domestic matters might be seen as inadvertently complicit in the state's colonization of social space. In registering such observations I am not "blaming the victim." Rather, I am underscoring that in terms of citizenship and participation in modern-style polities, rural and other Malays are not merely "passive spectators who vote" but are in fact engaged in the making of history, albeit, to paraphrase Marx's famous observation, not necessarily as they wish, choose, or imagine.

These are some of the "downsides" that need to be taken into consideration when assessing the impact of projects of modernity (including rationalization) and civil society. More generally, we have seen (especially in chapter 4) that in Malaysia, Indonesia, and elsewhere, rationalization and other processes of modernity are not all liberation, freedom, purification, and enlightenment. There is a dark side to these processes that often takes the form of anomie, alienation, and increased repression. Put simply, there are some decidedly "anti-human" dimensions of rationalization and modernity as a whole. One reason for this is that, as numerous scholars including Tocqueville, Weber, Foucault, and, most recently, James Scott (1998) have noted, projects of modernity need not give rise to or involve liberatory movements or even tentative steps toward the positive institutional arrangements of civil society. (Another is the Janus-faced nature of civil society, addressed below.) The classic projects of "high modernity" that Scott (1998) examines, for example, include Stalinist programs of forced collectivization and "compulsory villagization" in Tanzania, both of which were disastrous in terms of their human toll. Clearly relevant in the Malaysian context is the recent emergence of decidedly "uncivil" associations such as PASRAH, whose explicit agenda of purging Malaysia of homosexuality and transgender practices of all varieties is very much at odds with pluralistic visions of the sort usually associated with the concept of civil society. For these and other reasons, some bearing on gender, kinship, and related matters, others bearing more on its applicability in non-Western settings, it will be useful to consider the latter concept in greater detail.

KINSHIP MATTERS IN THE DIALECTICS OF CIVIL SOCIETY AND THE STATE

Discourses on civil society have a long and complicated genealogy, and it is beyond the scope of my remarks here to delve into such matters in any substantive way. Suffice it to say that the concept is clearly of Western origin and in its modern sense is often traced to the Scottish Enlightenment (though it has Aristotelian roots), whence it spread to and through the works of Toqueville, Hegel, Gramsci, Parsons, Habermas, Foucault, and many others. There has been a pronounced resurgence of interest in the concept since the collapse of both the former Soviet Union and various socialist economies in Eastern Europe. Many scholars, especially political scientists and political philosophers, have argued that when it comes to imagining and planning for the futures of countries in these and other areas, the concept is "good to think with," even—or particularly—when its visions are out of keeping with, or out of the reach of, local lived realities.

At the same time, various Western intellectuals such as anthropologist Chris Hann (1996), have claimed that as it stands or is generally understood, the concept is inapplicable to non-Western societies and thus of little value to anthropologists in light of its European roots, its positing of an highly atomized, agentic individual, and its superficial attention to kinship. That said, some of the same figures, including Hann, are quite equivocal as to the value of the concept in that they proceed to utilize a slightly modified form of it to help them organize and interpret ethnographic data from non-Western societies. Certain Muslim scholars, such as Turkish sociologist Şerif Mardin (1995), have likewise suggested that the Western origins of the concept render it inapplicable to Muslim and other non-Western societies for the simple reason that in the traditions of such societies there are no institutional or other provisions for the open spaces, freedoms, and uncoerced choices of civil society—or anything like them (cf. T. Asad 1993). I hasten to add, however, that a good many Muslim and other non-Western intellectuals have both lobbied for and otherwise made extensive use of the concept in their own milieus. Indeed, there is a burgeoning literature produced by Muslims and non-Muslims alike dealing with the institutions that encourage or, alternatively, discourage, civil society in Islamic and other societies in the Middle East, Southeast Asia, East Asia, and elsewhere (see, for example, Norton 1995, 1996; Eickelman and Piscatori 1996; Rabo 1996; White 1996; Hefner 1998a, 2000; Kasaba 1998). This is especially apparent in Malaysia, where local NGOs of various stripes articulate discourses bearing on human rights and civil society (see, for example, Noraini Othman 1994, 1999; Rose Ismail 1995; see also Shamsul A. B. 2000; Sharifah Zaleha Syed Hassan 2001). The more general point is that just as markets and states are here to stay, so too are the discourses and debates about civil society that they have spawned.

Most scholars agree that the concept of civil society refers to the conceptual space occupied by public institutions and associations that can help safeguard the interests of individuals and groups by serving as a bulwark against the powerful and dominating political and economic bureaucracies of states and markets, respectively. Many accept Gramscian definitions of civil society as "the public space between large-scale bureaucratic structures of state and economy on the one hand, and the private sphere of family, friendships, personality, and intimacy on the other."[1] This is more or less the position of philosopher Kai Nelson, who writes that civil society is "located in a conceptual space distinct from, and between, the state and the at least supposedly private sphere of the family and spousal arrangements and the like."[2] Nelson notes further that "in locating civil society we must look for those organizations or practices that are not directly governmental or economic but which generate opinions and goals, in accordance with which people who partake in these practices and are a part of these organizations seek not only to influence wider opinion and policies within existing structures and rules, but sometimes also to alter the structures and rules themselves."[3]

Many others adopt a view that is somewhat similar, except for the fact that they *include* rather than exclude familial institutions ("the family") within the domain of civil society. Thus, political scientist Jean Cohen sees civil society as "a sphere of social interaction distinct from economy and state, composed above all of associations (*including the family*) and publics" (emphasis added). In her view, "modern civil society is created and reproduced through forms of collective action, and it is institutionalized through laws, especially subjective rights that stabilize social differentiation."[4] We have also seen that she regards civil society as "a project, a terrain and target of democratic politics."

Literature of the sort cited here is of interest to me for a number of reasons having to do with kinship, which is obviously (though variably) central to definitions of civil society but woefully disregarded in both the actual investigation and the theorization of civil society. One matter of no small significance in this context is that "the family" is *excluded* from some definitions of civil society and *included* in others. Another more general point is that whether or not "the family" is included in conceptions of civil society, there is an unmarked and unwarranted assumption in much of the civil society literature, especially in the contributions of political philosophers and political scientists, that at least in American and Western European societies and their Eastern European counterparts "the family" is more or less the same if not identical. This overly homogenous and essentialized view of what constitutes "the family"—of its forms, discourses, practices, symbols, and meanings—like the unwarranted conflation of the distinction between families and households, is very much out of keeping with what anthropologists, sociologists, and historians of the family know to be the case when they look at such matters closely. One is reminded here of Rayna Rapp's (1987) important, self-critical observation concerning her "blindspots" with respect to synchronic variations and temporal changes in household patterns in her field site in rural France. She writes that we are so accustomed to thinking that ostensibly modern families are all alike that we are desensitized to and inadvertently inclined to gloss over many of their regional, class, ethnic, racial, and other differences, along with the multitudes of ways in which they change over time.

Embedded in much of the literature at issue is not only a static, Rousseauean, and otherwise essentialized and outmoded view of "the family" but also extremely strong and optimistic support of civil society. The mutually constitutive nature of these thematic emphases will be taken up in due course. In the meantime we might consider two incisive observations made by Hefner.[5] The first is that in many respects "civil society" has been accorded much of the semantic authority and cachet that "the people" used to have among those who supported progressive causes. The second is that neither of these two concepts clarifies very much about "the conditions of the possibilities of democratic, egalitarian, or civil politics." I would add a third observation here, which is that neither concept is all that helpful in specifying the real or imagined conditions of family life, kinship, or sociability that might serve in important ways as the template, model, or other basis for a sustaining social or moral order.[6]

Especially optimistic, romantic, and utopian in the senses noted above is political philosopher Michael Walzer (1995), whose work on civil society is in many other respects extremely insightful and nuanced. For Walzer, civil society refers to "the space of *uncoerced human associations* and also the set of relational networks—formed for the sake of family, faith, interest, and ideology— that fill this space" (1995: 7; emphasis added).

> The picture here is of people freely associating and communicating with one another, forming and reforming groups of all sorts, not for the sake of any particular formation—family, tribe, nation, religion, commune, brotherhood or sisterhood, interest group or ideological movement—but *for the sake of sociability itself.* For we are by nature social, before we are political or economic beings. (1995: 16; emphasis added)

Particularly when taken together, such views evince rather Pollyanna conceptions of "the family" and of sociability in general and seem to me to entail visions of civil society that are wildly optimistic and just as wildly unrealistic. Perhaps more to the point is that the notion of "uncoerced human associations" appears to derive from some heavily mythologized ideal of "the family." As a corrective, I would draw attention to the findings of scholars of kinship and social organization—including but not limited to anthropologists, sociologists, and family historians—that bonds and other associations of kinship are frequently infused with coercion that is psychological, moral, and economic, and all too commonly physical as well, and are otherwise shot through with all kinds of ambivalences.[7] The more general theme is well put by Alan Wolfe (1989: 18), who has argued that we need to avoid the temptation, when confronted with "the limits of the market and the state as moral codes, to reject both in favor of some pre-exisitng moral community that may never have existed, or if it did exist, was so oppressive that its members thought only of escape" (see also Wolfe 1989: 207; cf. Stacey 1991, 1996; Coontz 1992). These kinds of correctives and cautionary notes with respect to our disciplinary "*Gemeinschaft* longings" have far-reaching policy implications.[8] This is especially so in light of the export of Western models of civil society to Eastern Europe, Asia, Africa, and Latin America and the unspoken assumption, both in the West and in areas encouraged to develop or expand civil society, that Western *models* reflect Western *realities* (Sampson 1996).

Elsewhere Walzer points to an important paradox: "[T]he state itself is unlike all the other associations" in that it "both frames civil society and occupies space within it" (1995: 23). He goes on to aver that in the former ("framing") capacity "it fixes the boundary conditions and the basic rules of all associational activity." But is this latter statement really, or entirely, true? For instance, might this be said, too, albeit in a different way, of "the family" or, more accurately, of institutions of kinship; namely, that such institutions fix, frame, or ground the basic rules of much associational activity, or at least provide key templates and models of and for such activity? And might we also say that institutions of kinship provide the contexts within which many experiences, understandings, and representations of sociality—as well as the obviously malleable foundations of notions of self, other, difference, inequality, time, place, etc.—are initially generated? If such is the case, and there are century-long accumulations of scholarship in anthropology, sociology, and history indicating that it is, then two things are clear: informed understandings of the possibilities and challenges of civil society in the context of specific nation-states will require looking much more closely at the domains of kinship that obtain in the nation-state entities in question; and informed understandings of the sort alluded to here will also require that we devote much more analytic attention to state-mediated dialectics of kinship and civil society.

In the latter connection one is reminded of previously noted observations concerning the symbolic roots of Western bureaucracy. In order for local bureaucracies to be effective, they must speak to some degree in locally meaningful languages. This, in turn, requires taking on or accommodating themselves to key aspects of local cosmologies and subjectivities. And most relevant here, it means that the considerable powers of state bureaucracies are necessarily mediated by local cosmologies and subjectivities (as discussed in chapter 4). To a certain degree this is true of kinship as well, in that local kinship can put its stamp on the workings of the state. The more general point is that what states do to—and with—the symbols, idioms, practices, and institutions of kinship is of widely ramifying significance not only for the proficiency and meanings of state operations at the local level but also for civil society as a whole.

Some scholars have directed attention to these matters, if only by raising a series of provocative questions. For example, in his discussion of Britain, anthropologist Peter Loizos has asked whether changes in kinship have implications for civil society:

> Does Britain have weaker kinship ties than it did 100 years ago? Do high divorce rates mean "the decline of the family" or, more plausibly, the appearance of more complex family relations? . . . What do such changes imply for civil society, governance, social order, and the quality of our lives? Does the greater involvement of women in the labour force leave fewer look-outs to curb delinquency in urban neighbourhoods, and fewer carers for elderly relatives? . . . Is the shift to an activist, do-it-yourself citizenry (including anti-crime networks, some authorised by the police and some unauthorised) one of the particular effects of the decline in deference? (1996: 62; emphasis added)

Historians have on occasion posed these types of questions as well, and in some instances have been able to answer them with considerable if chilling precision.

Ben Kiernan's (1996) work on the ground-level political strategies of the Khmer Rouge during the Pol Pot regime (1975–79) is a case in point. Kiernan elucidates the ways in which the Khmer Rouge systematically extirpated all "bourgeois," "reactionary," "feudal," "tribal," and other "conventional" forms of kinship and marriage—indeed, all private spaces—in order to "wipe the slate clean" and begin to build up what to their mind was a truly pure and revolutionary society and culture. Of course it was not only kinship and marriage as generally understood that was eradicated. So too were Buddhist monastic orders, other religious associations, many types of secular institutions, and various ethnic groups (especially Vietnamese and "tribals"), though the majority of the 1.6 million people who were killed or died due to starvation, exhaustion, or disease were, in fact, ethnic Khmers.

There are many other similar though less extreme examples of these dynamics that one could cite from formerly socialist countries like Romania, East Germany, and the Soviet Union,[9] and from nonsocialist settings discussed in the works of Foucault (1977, 1978, 1980, 1991) and Ong (1999a). But three points should be clear. The first is that in most societies, regardless of whether people are heavily exploited subjects without codified rights or modern, rights-bearing citizens, the forces of market and state constrict and devalue private lives; this is all the more true when national elites and others pursue projects of modernity, civil society, ethnic cleansing, or racial or religious purification. The second is that those who authorize projects of modernity—whether or not they include visions of civil society, ethnic cleansing, or purification—construe the domain of kinship and the invariably gendered and sexed bodies and selves that help constitute that domain as project, terrain, and target in all senses of these terms. The third is that anthropologists can make enduring contributions both to the scholarly literature and to the world as a whole by describing and interpreting the on-the-ground realities of modernity and civil society from the point of view of those who live within them and must perforce negotiate them in order to sustain themselves materially and create order and meaning in their individual and collective lives.

BACK TO THE MALAYSIAN FUTURE

In Malaysia, as we have seen, Islamic courts are not simply key players in the state's widely touted projects of modernity; they are also imbricated in and thus provide valuable windows on the state's highly ambivalent commitment to civil society. Put differently, while the courts help to fashion middle-class families and subjectivities conducive to the attainment of a certain type of modernity, they are also helping clear a space that state agencies, along with various NGOs (some state-friendly and/or progressive, others not), have targeted in light of their own passions, preoccupations, and agendas. The short- and long-term effectiveness of the state's use of the courts with respect to the attainment of its goals and fragmented visions of governmentality, modernity, and civil society will depend in no small measure on whether relatively autonomous voluntary associations that are to one or another degree beyond state control are able to move into and effectively define the parameters and meanings of the social spaces made available by state laws and policies before the state's institutions and disciplinary regimes are in place and up and running. Another relevant variable is that voluntary associations that are initially subject to the control of the state can develop in such a way that they come to pose real or imagined dangers to the state, as has occurred to some degree with political party organizations such as PAS and Muslim religious organizations like Darul Arqam. When this happens, repressive laws, policies, and ad hoc measures opposed to the institutional arrangements and cultural sensibilities of civil society are likely to be implemented or expanded.

The case of Darul Arqam, including, especially, its banning by the state in 1994, illustrates two broad and exceedingly important issues that are relevant far beyond Malaysia. First, a truly pluralistic society would make provision for Darul Arqam, even though its leader (Ashaari Muhammad) is reported to have been exclusionary in his visions of and for the future (Abdullahi A. An-Na'im 1999). Second, most of the space being "closed off"—or, more generally, the constriction of civil society—is occurring at the hands of secular officials (who often bypass the secular courts) under pressure and initiative from one or another faction in the executive branch, even or especially when such moves are ostensibly undertaken in the name of Islam or on behalf of Muslim subjects. Ashaari Muhammad was detained and imprisoned in 1994 *not* on the basis of any specifically religious laws but because state authorities deemed him to be engaged in "deviationist" activities that were held to be "a threat to national security," and he was held under the provisions of the thoroughly secular Internal Security Act (which dates from the 1948–60 communist insurgency, "The Emergency"). Recall, too, that the concept of "deviationism" as such does not exist either in the Shafi'i legal school of Islam that is institutionalized in Malaysia (and in many other parts of the Muslim world) or in any other orthodox school of Islamic law; and that the concept of "deviationism" has no clear basis in *any* realm of Malaysia's present-day legal system (ibid.).

The stigmatization and criminalization of homosexuality and other transgender practices is somewhat more complicated in that the Quran does forbid homosexual activity. That said, historians and other scholars have documented considerable social tolerance for homosexuality and transgendering throughout the history of the Islamic world.[10] Such tolerance is especially apparent in the history of Malaysia and the rest of Muslim (and non-Muslim) Southeast Asia. We need to bear in mind, too, that in recent years most of the legal cases and other official actions that have been taken against Malaysians accused of being involved in gender-transgressive activities have been pursued by *secular* authorities, have involved charges of a *secular* nature, and have been prosecuted in *secular* legal arenas. More generally, *secular* authorities have made the most noise on these fronts, not least by spearheading efforts aimed at purging Malaysia of untoward ("contaminating") elements as part of a campaign of rein-scribing purportedly traditional "Asian values."

In Malaysia, then, the largest threats to civil society lie not with one or another facet of Islamic jurisprudence (such as "*kadi*-justice") or with some other aspect of Islam, but with the thoroughly secular state (which is of course not only of British design but also modeled on British institutions). The same is true not only of Indonesia, as Hefner's (1993, 2000) incisive and detailed an-alyses have shown, but also of a great many other states with Muslim-majority populations or significant Muslim minorities (Eickelman and Piscatori 1996; Lawrence 1998; Gerges 1999). Indonesia, for example, has seen more than its share of bloodshed and violence since the mid-1960s and during the last few years in particular, especially in connection with East Timor's move toward independence, Aceh's desire for increased autonomy, deteriorating relations among Christians and Muslims in Ambon and elsewhere, and of course the fall of former President Suharto and subsequent efforts to hold him and his family and their supporters accountable for their excesses and criminality. Much of the bloodshed and violence has been represented by political authorities and their allies and spokesmen as the result of an unbridled "primordialism" unleashed by or otherwise associated with Islamic sentiments or some other narrowly construed religious or ethnic loyalties. Such representations are often conjoined with arguments to the effect that the "primordialism" at issue threatens stability, development, and prosperity, and thus fully requires the continued existence of severe restrictions on basic associational freedoms and a bloated military appa-ratus with more or less unrestricted license to kill. In fact, however, in many parts of Indonesia, the lion's share of the turmoil and murder has been tacitly encouraged and more often than not incited and sustained by military and para-military forces loyal to Suharto, to one or another faction of his supporters, and/or to those currently seeking to consolidate power in his absence.

In Malaysia, military and paramilitary forces are relatively minor players in political arenas and enjoy nowhere near the political or other institutional clout they do in Indonesia. The similarity with Indonesia, and with much of the rest of the world where religion and "primordial sentiments" of various kinds are invoked to further govermentality and repression, lies in the fact that much of the exclusionary and other antidemocratic sentiment in Malaysia is encouraged if not engendered in the first place by secular leaders who either enjoy one or another degree of control over an overwhelmingly secular state apparatus or harbor dreams of capturing it.

To look at the present and future of Malaysia and to locate the main threats to Malaysian civil society within the Malaysian state (to contend, for example, that it is not sufficiently self-limiting and that far too much of its authority is vested in the executive branch)—and to wish for Malaysians that their future might include "more" civil society and "less" state—is not to adopt an uncriti-cal stance toward civil society. (Nor is it to espouse the naïve view that Malay-sians or others can nowadays do without the presence of a strong state to regulate social relations and help safeguard their interests.) Not all aspects of civil society are positive; it does allow for "horizontal nastiness" as Hefner (1998b) points out, PASRAH and similarly oriented vigilante groups in Malaysia being prime examples. In Wolfe's apt words, "[I]t is important that th[e] same ambivalence" that modern-day liberal democrats exhibit "toward markets and states be carried over into an ambivalence toward civil society" (1989: 207). Though there are many reasons for this, a particularly compelling one for anthropologists is that many of the people whose communities we live in and try to understand do, in fact, experience civil society—and modernity (including rationalization)—in decidedly ambivalent ways.

N O T E S

1. For information on these matters, I am indebted to Omid Safi (2001) who has helped construct a website that contains links to many other relevant sites. See: <*http:// groups.colgate.edu/aarislam/response.htm*>.

2. Southern (1962: 22, 42n. 10).

3. A notable exception to this generalization is the work of Robert Hefner (1993, 1998a, 1998b, 2000); see also Hefner and Horvatich (1997).

4. There is a voluminous literature on Islamic law in Malaysia (see, e.g., Ahmad Ibrahim [1965] 1975, 1997a, 1997b and the relevant sections of Hooker 1978, 1984; see also Hooker 1983a, 1983b). But very little of the literature deals directly with the "on the ground" dynamics of judicial process, past or present, or with the overall culture or political economy of the Islamic courts. Exceptions to some of these generalizations include Sharifah Zaleha Syed Hassan (1986); Sharifah Zaleha Syed Hassan and Cederroth (1997); Horowitz (1994); and Mohammad Hashim Kamali (2000).

5. Peletz (2000).

6. The first of these figures derives from Andaya and Andaya (2001: 1); the second is from the Department of Statistics, Malaysia (p. 35), and is the mid-year estimate for 2000.

7. Department of Statistics, Malaysia (p. 35).

8. While all Malays are Muslims, not all Muslims in Malaysia are Malays; the country's Muslim population includes a small number of Muslims from South Asia, particularly India.

9. The Malays of Negeri Sembilan are usually treated in the literature as a "special class" of Malays since their social structure includes descent units of matrilineal design. Elsewhere I have argued that the contrasts between Negeri Sembilan and other Malays are greatly overdrawn and that the underlying similarities merit far more analytic attention than they have received thus far (Peletz 1994, 1996; cf. Peletz 1988b; Stivens 1985, 1991; and McAllister 1987).

10. Peletz (1988b).

11. Some of the material in the next few pages is adapted from Peletz (1996).

12. Peletz (1996).

13. IKIM is the acronym for the Institut Kefahaman Islam Malaysia (The Malaysian Institute of Islamic Understanding), a government think tank located in Kuala Lumpur.

14. The phrase comes from Alan Wolfe (1989: 143).

15. I borrow the phrase "civil pluralism" from Hefner (1998a, 2000).

1. For discussions of the use of the term "early modern" with reference to Southeast Asia from the fifteenth through the eighteenth centuries, see Rafael (1993); and Andaya and Andaya (1995).

2. See, for example, Liaw Yock Fang (1976: 38).

3. The wide range of legal options available in the most high-profile case of illicit sexual relations in Bogang in the late 1970s included bringing in outside authorities and having both the young man and his teenaged girlfriend incarcerated. It is notable that the

negotiated settlement that was actually pursued (a "shotgun marriage") involved no such authorities and was the most "face saving" of all alternatives (see Peletz 1996: 132–54).

4. In Hefner's words: "In Java, the Malay Peninsula, and southern Sulawesi [throughout the early modern period], . . . the concern for Islamic orthodoxy was *relaxed*, allowing localized or syncretic traditions to survive in court ritual and folk religion. At a few times and in a few places, of course, some Muslim rulers promoted a strict application of Islamic law. . . . *In most of the early modern archipelago, however, the law was applied with a gentler and more pluralistic hand* (2000: 29; emphasis added).

5. He does, in fact, devote nearly two full pages of text to "the singular appearance of a Malay . . . albino," whom he observed "under the shade of a tree on the river bank" (2: 160–61).

6. A more extensive consideration of the context in which Clifford prepared his comments would be useful here but is largely beyond the scope of my discussion. It should suffice to mention that Clifford's derogation of Malays, along with his position that Britain was justified in using whatever means were necessary to extend control over and "save" the people of Malaya, was articulated at a time when there was considerable doubt in some British quarters as to the wisdom of Britain's recent efforts to acquire the state of Pahang, especially after the outbreak in 1891 of the Pahang War, which continued intermittently until 1895, and Clifford's involvement shortly before the war's end in a well-publicized and controversial crossing of international boundaries "in hot pursuit" (Andaya and Andaya 2001: 172; see also Clifford 1929). Since Clifford had ambitions well beyond Malaya and did in fact move on to important posts in the colonial service in Trinidad and Ceylon as well as the Gold Coast and Nigeria (he served as governor in the latter two settings), his remarks were probably intended to have a broad audience and wide application. A more detailed (albeit heavily psychological) reading of Clifford's writings against the backdrop of contemporary developments appears in Tidrick (1990: chap. 3).

7. Clifford (1899: 369).

8. Ibid., 370.

9. Ibid., 375.

10. Ibid.

11. Clifford (1899: 376).

12. Ibid., 377.

13. Ibid.

14. Clifford (1899: 378). As Tidrick makes clear, "Violence stimulated his [Clifford's] imagination to a degree which ought indeed to have concerned his employers, though there is no evidence that it did" (1990: 100). By the mid-1920s Clifford suffered from a "manic depressive illness . . . that eventually cut short his career" (88, 127–29).

15. Clifford (1899: 378–79).

16. Ibid., 372.

17. Ibid., 385.

18. Ibid.

19. Clifford (1899: 380).

20. Ibid., 380–81.

21. Ibid., 381.

22. Ibid., 381–82.

23. Ibid., 396.

24. Ibid.

25. Bird (1883: 142).

26. Ibid., 81–82.
27. Ibid., 84, 85.
28. Ibid., 80, 81.
29. Ibid., 145, 146.
30. Ibid., 146.
31. Ibid.
32. Ibid.
33. Bird (1883: 148).
34. Ibid.
35. Ibid.
36. Bird (1883: 81).
37. Sadka (1968: 252).
38. Ibid., 255.
39. Ibid.
40. Sadka (1968: 252).
41. Cited in ibid.
42. Sadka (1968: 258–59).
43. Ibid., 262.
44. Ibid., 256. The rarity of Malays appearing as offenders in criminal cases has received insufficient attention from scholars dealing with this period in history. Some questions that we should at least raise include: Is the relative rarity of Malays being charged in criminal cases due to the fact that Malays were "more law-abiding" than Chinese or Indians (or others)? Were they instead or in addition less subject to the colonial judiciary's gaze by virtue of their greater tendency to reside in rural enclaves of their own design, as opposed to the more visible urban settlements of the Chinese and the highly visible rural plantation communities inhabited by Indians—all of whom were more "legible" to the state (to borrow Scott's [1998] terminology)? Or was it because criminal transgressions such as were perpetrated by Malays (e.g., drunkenness, breaches of the peace, stabbing, homicide, theft, burglary, arson, rape) were less likely to come to the attention of colonial authorities because of the Malay preference to handle such matters within their own communities and by means of their own—usually informal—sanctions, such as shaming and shunning? Other partial answers suggest themselves to some of the questions raised here: for example, that crimes of drunkenness were relatively few and far between in a population to which alcohol was forbidden, a population that by all accounts generally observed the prohibition; that crimes of vagrancy tended to be more urban phenomena, as did breaches of the peace; and that forgery and coining might be more common in urban settings or in those sectors of society most entangled in the money economy. Also relevant is that Malay crimes of the moment tended to be related to adultery, which came under the jurisdiction of the *kadi*'s courts, as opposed to the criminal courts overseen by the British.
45. Sadka (1968: 262).
46. Ibid., 264.
47. Ibid.
48. Ibid.
49. Sadka (1968: 264–65).
50. Ibid., 265.
51. Ibid.
52. Ibid.
53. See Sadka (1968: 265n. 3).

54. Islamic law specifies a one-hundred-day period following a divorce or a husband's death during which time a woman may not remarry and is normally entitled to support from her husband or his estate. This is referred to as the *edah* period. One of the chief rationales for the *edah* period is to determine if the woman is pregnant; another, if she is pregnant, is to help establish both the paternity of her child and who is legally responsible for supporting it.

55. Sadka (1968: 266–67).

56. Ibid., 267.

57. Cited in ibid., 270.

58. Ibid., 270.

59. Ibid.

60. Ibid.

61. Ibid.

62. See Yegar (1979: 152–53) for an enumeration of the types of courts the British established and the nature of the fines *kadi* could impose in the 1890s.

63. Yegar (1979: 155). In Negeri Sembilan at the turn of century, the *kadi*'s court was held at Sri Menanti; but the *kadi* was apparently "a mere figurehead", and the *yang dipertuan besar* is said to have decided the cases. Things changed after the 1901 enactments; for example, regular meetings and warrants were executed by the police, not by the *yang dipertuan besar*'s bailiffs. It seems that *kadi* could order imprisonment beginning around 1900 or 1901.

64. Yegar (1979: 155).

65. Ibid., 157.

66. Some of the material in this section is adapted from Peletz (1988b).

67. *LNS* 1:1.

68. Such themes receive detailed treatment in Roff (1967), Kessler (1978), and Milner (1995). Also relevant is Geertz's (1960) analysis of similar processes in Indonesia.

69. Quoted in A. Azmi Abdul Khalid (1990: 159).

70. Dato Sedia Raja Abdullah (1927: 313).

71. Dato Sedia Raja Abdullah (1925: 104).

72. For a discussion of these matters, see Laitin (1986); Hefner (1987, 1990); and Peletz (1993a). Significantly, villagers' responses to my questions concerning why certain syncretic (largely animist/Hindu-Buddhist) rituals, such as *berpuar*, are no longer performed and why many of the beliefs associated with these rituals have likewise declined in force and scope were frequently couched in expressions such as "We're modern now," "This is the age of science," and "We're not stupid anymore." These responses are strikingly similar to those documented for the Yoruba of Nigeria (Laitin 1986). In short, there is not much evidence among either Malays or the Yoruba that the religious changes in question were motivated by factors associated with what Weber refers to as the "theodicy of suffering encounter[ing] increasing difficulties" (1946: 275).

73. See *NSGG* (1904, 9:337–38).

74. This was a key development with far-reaching implications, especially in light of the post-colonial state's widespread use of the provisions to suppress (real and imagined) political opponents (see chapter 5 and conclusion).

75. *NSAR* (1915: 3).

76. What types of penalties, if any, clan figures had the authority or power to impose on individuals violating Ramadan prohibitions prior to British rule is unclear.

77. *SUSCP* (of 7/7/1888), 62–63.

78. The Quranic prohibition against homosexuality also finds expression in the fif-

teenth-century Laws of Melaka, but there is no evidence to suggest that the punishments specified in the latter codes were ever regularly or systematically imposed on those presumed guilty of engaging in homosexual liaisons. (Indeed, as discussed in chapter 5, various types of transgender practices have long been socially accepted, even revered, in the Malay Peninsula and Southeast Asia as a whole.) In presenting a version of the Laws of Melaka, Newbold (1839, 2: 298) refers to the "Hukum Liwateh, . . . the law against sodomy, or bestiality," noting that the penalty for this crime is the same as that for *zina*. Unfortunately, however, Newbold does not specify the type or category of *zina* to which he refers and thus leaves unclear whether, in theory, the punishment would have included stoning to death or one hundred blows with a rattan and a year's expulsion from the city or community.

79. The individuals with whom sexual union and marriage are forbidden by Islam due to considerations of consanguineal or affinal relatedness are, from the perspective of a male, as follows: mother, grandmother, daughter, granddaughter, full and half-sister, niece, great-niece, aunt, great-aunt, wife's ascendants and descendants, and the wives of ascendants and descendants. (A female is prohibited from entering into sexual relations and marriage with her father, grandfather, son, grandson, and so on [Fyzee (1949) 1974: 105–6].) The Malay concept of *sumbang* embraces a much broader range of offenses, including sexual relations among those of common descent group membership as well as other kinds of moral impropriety. In the case of an adolescent or adult male, these improprieties include sitting in a secluded or confined area alongside a woman other than one's wife, particularly a woman with whom *adat* forbids marriage, and walking side by side or conversing with such a woman (see Peletz 1988b: 53–58, 243–44, 1996: 116–23).

80. See Roff (1967: 8, 84–85) and Gullick (1958: 140); cf. Banks (1976).

81. *SUSCP* (4/27/1893: 86).

82. Yegar (1979: 200).

83. A concise introduction to the Malayan Union, UMNO's origins, and Malaya's independence in 1957 appears in Andaya and Andaya (2001: chap. 7).

84. Hizbul Muslimin was short-lived, partly because within a few months of its formation "its national and regional leaders were arrested and detained under the Emergency Regulations"; of broader significance is that it provided "the ideological and organizational foundation for the PMIP" (Pan-Malayan Islamic Party; PAS) (Firdaus Haji Abdullah 1985: 47), which was established in 1951 and has played a key role in Malaysian politics since the mid-1950s.

85. See Hooker (1972) for a thorough treatment of issues pertaining to Negeri Sembilan's state constitution and the juridical relationship between *adat* leaders and district- and state-level authorities charged with secular and religious administration.

86. *FMGGNS* (1949, no. 2, vol. 25: 257–58).

87. *FMGGNS* (1950, no. 3, vol. 3: 65–66).

88. Elsewhere I provide a more detailed discussion of the ways in which colonial policies contributed to these processes (Peletz 1988b, 1993a, 1994).

89. See Kahn (1976) for a similar approach to *adat* and tradition among the Minangkabau of Sumatra.

90. The legislation is commonly referenced in the literature under the heading, "Islamic Family Law Enactment [or Act], 1984," 1984 being the year the legislation began to be enforced in the Federal Territory of Kuala Lumpur. In certain states, such as Melaka, the new laws began to be enforced as early as 1983; in other states, however, the enactments in question did not become effective law until 1991. To avoid confusion

arising from regional variation and from discrepancies between the official dates of the enactments and their actual implementation as law, I sometimes refer to the legislation in question as the "Islamic Family Law Enactments of 1983–91."

CHAPTER 2

1. I might also make clear that for purposes of description and analysis what I take to be a "case" does at times differ from that of court personnel. In a few instances, I have treated preliminary inquiries at the courthouse as a case, even though the members of the *kadi*'s office did not regard the inquiry as a case (*kes*) in a technical sense (by formally creating a file, etc.). In most instances, the cases described below are also treated as cases by the courts.

2. Although Weber is usually credited with popularizing the notion of "*kadi*-justice," the term appears to have been coined by Richard Schmidt, one of Weber's colleagues at Freiburg University (Weber 1968, 2:1003n. 2).

3. For a discussion of the possible reasons for ambiguities in law generally, see Kress (1992: 201); see also Moore (1978). For analyses of ambiguity and ambivalence in Islamic cultures and Islamic legal systems, see Ewing (1988); Haeri (1989); and Peletz (1996); see also Peletz (2001) and the sources cited there.

4. According to Islamic law, a man who repudiates his wife with one *talak* and then experiences a change of heart has one hundred days from the pronouncement of the *talak* to formally reconcile with her (*rujuk*). If the husband and wife do not reconcile during this time but decide later that they want to resume their relationship, they are free to remarry one another. The same generalizations apply in the case of a man who utters a second *talak* either at the time of the first pronouncement or on a subsequent occasion. However, if a man has repudiated his wife with three *talak*, the couple is irrevocably divorced and may not "take up where they left off" or remarry until after the wife has married someone else, consummated the union, and obtained a divorce (or become widowed). Some of these matters are discussed in more detail in chapter 4. (See also note 11, below.)

5. I did not observe the hearings associated with any of these cases, but I do know that in one of the cases, categorized as "marriage without the permission of the *kadi*" (*nikah tanpa izin kadi*), the couple claimed that they were married and had a marriage certificate but were not able to produce it. The clerk I spoke with about the case said that they might have been living together as man and wife without having actually been married. The case was set in motion (via formal complaint) by an *imam*, presumably the *imam* of the community in which the couple resides. If they had gone through a marriage ceremony but simply failed to obtain the *kadi*'s permission to marry, then they could have been fined M$100. If no marriage ceremony was involved, the consequences would be more severe (e.g., jail time).

6. As noted below, laws passed since my interview with Zul have ruled out the possibility of appealing a *kadi*'s decision in a secular court.

7. Classical Islamic law prescribes the death penalty for apostasy but only under certain very specific conditions—for example, when it entails "blasphemy and rebellion against the [Islamic] community and its legitimate leadership" (Mohammad Hashim Kamali 2000: 209 passim). Even in such circumstances, however, it does not mandate the guillotine.

8. Except where modified by legislation making provision for the substitution of law(s) from other legal schools of Islam (see Horowitz 1994).

9. The extensive household survey I conducted in Bogang in 1979 and 1980 revealed that roughly two-thirds of all completed marriages had ended in divorce (Peletz 1988b). Similar patterns have been reported by scholars working in other regions of the Peninsula, but as Jones (1994) notes, recent decades have seen a decline in divorce in most areas of the country.

10. The phrase is Hochschild's (1983: 172).

11. Many jurisdictions in the Islamic world do not regard the more or less simultaneous utterance of three *talak* as an irrevocable divorce. But in Shafi'i Islam such an utterance is held to constitute an irrevocable divorce (Horowitz 1994: 550).

12. Ortner's "nature/culture" thesis has of course generated a great deal of debate. Elsewhere I discuss many aspects of the controversies along with the ways in which a substantially refined version of the original thesis helps illuminate data bearing on Malays and other Muslim societies and cultures (Peletz 1996).

13. Legal scholars, lawyers, and others involved in drafting the Islamic Family Law Enactments of 1983–91 argued that "Islamic law, properly understood, is a regime of rights"; they were thus out to rectify those aspects of the system that tended to emphasize responsibilities to the relative neglect of rights (Donald Horowitz, personal communication, June 27, 2001).

14. Jones (1994: 53).

15. See Azizah Kassim (1984); Sharifah Zaleha Syed Hassan and Cederroth (1997); Horowitz (1994); and Mohammad Hashim Kamali (2000).

16. Horowitz has observed that in addition to the "mediatory" style of local *kadi* and the "inquisitorial" style of the chief *kadi* I have described here, there is a third style, the "passive" style that sometimes predominates in Kuala Lumpur and Petaling Jaya, when lawyers are involved on both sides and the *kadi* essentially sits back and lets them try their cases, merely ruling from time to time on objections to evidence that one or the other of the lawyers seeks to have admitted. Horowitz suggests that this style, typical of both British courts and secular courts in Malaysia, may be the one the reformers were really aiming at when they sought to overhaul various aspects of the Islamic judiciary. The latter interpretation is supported by evidence from a wide variety of sources, not least that one of the ways reformers sought to "upgrade" Islamic courts was by sending *kadi* to England to obtain English law degrees as well as firsthand familiarity with the workings of British judicial process (Donald Horowitz, personal communication, June 27, 2001).

17. I cite examples for which we have exceptionally nuanced studies: for Singapore, see Djamour (1966); for Indonesia, see Lev (1972) and Nakamura (1983); for Yemen, see Messick (1988, 1993); for Morocco, see Rosen (1980–81, 1989a, 1989b), Dwyer (1978, 1979), and Powers (1992); for Kenya, see Hirsch (1998); and for Ottoman Syria and Palestine, see Tucker (1998).

18. Some of these points have also been raised by Merry (1994: 54n. 2); cf. Just (1992: 399–400). For additional views on some of the limitations of Geertzian (1983a) perspectives on law as a cultural system, see Moore (1989); and Thompson (1995).

19. The figure for the number of countries at issue here is taken from Eickelman and Piscatori (1996: 111–12).

20. Cited in Seth Mydans, "Blame Men, Not Allah, Islamic Feminists Say," *New York Times*, October 10, 1996.

21. For an excellent discussion of these points, see Horowitz (1994).

22. On the important role of transnational linkages in contemporary Islam, see Eickelman and Piscatori (1996: esp. chap. 6).

CHAPTER 3

1. The development of the critical legal studies movement beginning in the 1970s has played a key role in drawing scholarly and public attention to issues bearing on the ambiguity in law and the ways in which such ambiguity is often exploited at the expense of those whose voices and concerns are typically unvoiced. But as Conley and O'Barr (1990: 11–12) point out in their pioneering work on legal discourse, the critical legal studies literature makes little if any provision for the voices of those on whose behalf they speak. One goal here is to make provision for such voices and to demonstrate the concrete ways in which ambiguity is exploited in the discourses of plaintiffs and defendants alike (see also chapter 2, n. 3 [above].)

2. FELDA is the acronym for the Federal Land Development Authority, which was established in 1956 to help poor and landless Malays.

3. This problem is exceedingly widespread: for example, "1997 statistics from the Selangor Syariah Court . . . revealed that out of 2,165 cases of divorce registered with the court, there were only 29 cases of *muta'ah*" (Mohammad Hashim Kamali (2000: 226).

4. Donald Horowitz, personal communication, August 20, 2001.

5. For a recent discussion of some of these discourses, see Frith (2001).

6. Making matters more complicated for women is that with the passage of the 1983–91 enactments, husbands and wives must participate in counseling sessions at the court before *kadi* will authorize divorce; men's refusal to participate in such sessions adds to the delays that women experience when they approach the court for divorce.

7. We have also seen that men are less concerned than women with paying court fees. This may be because men are more able to afford these fees than women, but it also reflects their lesser concern with expenditures, which is a heavily elaborated theme in local discourse on kinship and gender. The fees are in any case rather minimal, even by local standards, though they can add up. At the time of my second fieldwork, the main fees in Negeri Sembilan were as follows: initiating proceedings (or arranging to have a discussion [*perbicaraan*]) was M$3; a summons was usually about M$5, though it could be higher, depending on the distance between the office issuing the summons order and the home or office of the person being summoned; registering a divorce involved a M$5 fee; and reconciliation, M$1.

8. Ahmed (1992: 51); cf. Rodinson (1971).

9. Ahmed (1992: 73).

10. Ibid., 58.

11. But see the case of Azizah discussed in chapter 5 (below).

12. That said, discourses of the sort at issue here do exist in more urban settings and are partly responsible for the equalizing thrust of the 1983–91 enactments.

13. But see Ong (1987, 1988); see also the assessments of her arguments on spirit possession as resistance that appear in Peletz (1996: esp. chap. 5).

14. Not all of the relevant literature supports my view that oppositional discourses bearing on social class are relatively unelaborated in the Malay setting; see, for example, Scott (1985).

15. Some of the material in the next few pages is adapted from Peletz (1996).

16. There is some debate as to the precise extent to which husbands and wives actually intermingle their funds; see Li (1989).

17. See Williams (1977: 114); see also Willis (1977); and Scott (1985).

18. Ong's observations derive from research on providers of health care services to Cambodians residing in the San Francisco Bay Area.

CHAPTER 4

1. Ong (2001: 9946).

2. Concerning terminology, terms such as "ordinary Muslims" (and "ordinary Malays"), on the one hand, and "Muslim resurgents" ("*dakwah* people" and so forth), on the other, are defined largely through contrast and are employed to refer to "religious orientations or modes of piety [rather] than . . . fixed sociological categories" (Woodward 1989: 8). There are potential problems with the use of such terms, but they are, to my mind, less pronounced than the dilemmas associated with other terms that might be employed in their place. A more fine-grained terminological distinction than the one used here would be more consistent with the nuances of the data presented in this volume, but I assume the reader will keep in mind that there is considerable variation in religious orientations among ordinary Muslims and Muslim resurgents alike.

3. Araffin also maintained that *mas kawin* is not returned in instances of *tebus talak* unless the wife has refused to consummate the marriage, in which case the husband is entitled to petition to have half of it returned.

4. For a particularly clear if disturbing example of such thinking, see Mahathir Mohamad (1970). For an excellent discussion of the broader issues, see Ong (1999a).

5. I borrow this phrase from political scientist Jean Cohen (1995: 39), who utilizes it with reference to civil society (as "a project, a terrain and target of democratic politics").

6. For a discussion of the somewhat analogous cultural assumptions that exist in the American setting, see Schneider (1977, 1984).

7. Unfortunately I cannot pursue such matters in the present context.

8. They are also known in the literature by the Arabic-origin term *muhallil*, but I never encountered this usage in the field.

9. On this point see Joel Kahn and Francis Loh Kok Wah (1992).

10. Sharifah Zaleha Syed Hassan (1989) is a notable exception.

11. I am indebted to Ortner (1995) for underscoring the significance of these oversights and for delineating some of the more general problems with resistance studies of the sort undertaken by Scott (1985, 1990). See also Gal (1995) and the sources cited in note 22 below.

12. At the time of my second fieldwork, Darul Arqam was a master trope for the resurgence, at least for ordinary Muslims. In fact, members of Darul Arqam were a very small minority of those who identified with or were otherwise involved in the *dakwah* movement.

13. In the late 1980s, Bogang villagers' reactions to increasing numbers of urban women donning veils and other headgear were also ambivalent at best (Peletz 1997: 243; see also Wazir Jahan Karim 1992: 185–87; cf. Scott 1985: 196n. 190).

14. For a brief discussion of some of these concerns, see "Going Back to the Book," which appears in the August 11, 1989, edition of *Asiaweek* (cited in Banks 1990: 545n. 21).

15. See, for example, the conclusion of Ahmad Ibrahim's (1987) article on the "caning controversy."

16. The terms *hudud* and *hudud* laws refer to certain criminal laws and some of the more severe punishments for their transgression as specified in the Quran. (See also note 33, chap. 5.)

17. See, for example, Roff (1985); Ellen (1983); and Peletz (1988a: esp. chap. 3).

18. There are important exceptions to this generalization (see Hefner 1993, 2000).

19. Not surprisingly, all the *dalang* interviewed by Sweeney in the mid-1960s opposed PAS and supported UMNO (Sweeney 1972: 35). Almost all of the *dalang* interviewed by Wright a decade later professed the same allegiances (Wright 1986: 33, 41n. 33).

20. Although the texts Laderman analyzes contain numerous references to Betara Guru (Shiva of the Hindu pantheon) and characters derived from the Hindu epic the Ramayana, none of these figures is explicitly linked in local thought either to Hindu deities or to any other Indic or otherwise non-Islamic traditions.

21. Limitations of space preclude a lengthier discussion. Another variable to which I should perhaps draw attention, if only in passing, is that ordinary Malays undoubtedly find it difficult to challenge the resurgents on theological grounds, especially since, compared to the resurgents, they have relatively limited access to key religious texts and their meanings.

22. I realize I run the risk of essentializing studies of resistance by citing Scott's work as typical of all such studies. There are important differences between the approaches and perspectives of Scott, on the one hand, and those of Jean and John Comaroff, Aihwa Ong, Gayatri Chakravorty Spivak, and Paul Willis and others associated with British cultural studies, on the other. See Ortner (1995) for an incisive discussion of some of these differences and various problems with the study of resistance generally; see also Abu-Lughod (1990); Sholle (1990); Brown (1991); Edelman (1994); and Kaplan and Kelly (1994).

23. Others are viewed in strongly positive terms.

24. Recent research in Bali reveals not only that spirit cults of various kinds continue to flourish but also that there has been a revitalization of ritual activity associated with ancestral spirits and ancestor temple ceremonies. As Boon (1979: 288–89) suggests, these developments indicate that the "disenchantment of the world" has not made all that much headway in Bali and that for these and other reasons it is more appropriate to speak of the situation in Bali in terms of processes involving a "*re*enchantment of the world or, put somewhat differently, remystification rather than demystification." The more general point here is that the "rationalization of religious organization and intensification of ritualism keyed to a hierarchical cosmology are not intrinsically opposed; nor need either necessarily advance by denying the legitimacy of the other."

25. See Weigert (1991); Peletz (1993a, 1993b, 1995, 1996, 2001); Ortner (1995).

26. Ong (1988); Peletz (1988a, 1993a, 1993b); compare Taussig (1980); Zelenietz and Lindenbaum (1981).

CHAPTER 5

1. A note on terminology may be in order here, especially since the meanings of portmanteau concepts such as "transgender" are not clearly bounded or stable and are employed by different scholars in different ways (much like "cross-gender" in earlier times). I take my reading of the prefix "trans" from Aihwa Ong, who writes, "*Trans* denotes both moving through space or across lines, as well as changing the nature of something" (as in transformation or transfiguration) or going beyond it (as in transcend), be it a bounded entity or process, or a relationship between two or more phenomena; it also "alludes to the transversal, the transactional, the translational, and the transgressive aspects of . . . behavior and[/or] imagination that are incited, enabled, and regulated" by

the logics of culture and political economy (1999a: 4). As for transgender, Riki Ann Wilchins has observed, "*Transgender* began its life as a name for those folks who identified neither as crossdressers nor as transsexuals—primarily people who changed their gender but not their genitals. . . . The term gradually mutated to include any gender-queers who didn't actually change their genitals: [such as] crossdressers, . . . stone butches, [and] hermaphrodites; . . . and people began using it to refer to transsexuals [some of whom do change their genitals] as well" (1997: 15–16). A similar view of the concept informs Joanne Meyerowitz's work: "In . . . [today's] popular lingo, . . . '*transgendered*' people . . . [is] an umbrella term used for those with various forms and degrees of crossgender practices and identifications. 'Transgender' includes, among others, some people who identify as 'butch' or masculine lesbians, as 'fairies,' 'queens,' or feminine gay men, and as heterosexual crossdressers as well [as] those who identify as transsexual. The categories are not hermetically sealed, and to a certain extent the boundaries are permeable" (2002: 10). Evelyn Blackwood's conceptualization of transgender, which I find especially helpful, builds on Wilchins's definition, though she also employs the term transgendered in "its broadest sense to refer to anyone who is 'transgressively gendered'" (to borrow Kate Bornstein's [1994] phrase) (Evelyn Blackwood, personal communication, February 11, 2002; see also Blackwood and Wieringa 1999: ix–xi, passim). Blackwood also correctly underscores that all such umbrella terms have certain meanings and connotations in the United States and the West generally that might not be relevant elsewhere, and that we should thus utilize the terms with caution when we are labeling, grouping, and interpreting practices and identities in non-Western settings.

2. There is a voluminous literature on transgender practices in Southeast Asia, though most of it pertains to the twentieth century. See, for example, Peacock (1968); Johnson (1997); Boellstorff 2000; and the relevant essays in Atkinson and Errington (1990); Murray (1992); Murray and Roscoe (1997); Reinfelder (1996); Sears (1996); Manderson and Jolly (1997); and Blackwood and Weiringa (1999). For recent discussions of transgender behavior in the early modern era, see Brewer (1999); and L. Andaya (2000).

3. That said, the question of volition and agency is a complicated one, especially in light of heterosexual villagers' objections to the overt practice of homosexual sexual activity within predominantly heterosexual communities, coupled with the absence in the latter communities of opportunities for those inclined toward same-sex relations to pursue their erotic interests.

4. I am indebted to Stallybrass and White (1986: 110) for some of the phrasing here.

5. Some Western press accounts represented the election returns as a landslide victory for Mahathir; in fact, Mahathir lost a good deal of the Malay support he had previously enjoyed.

6. Due to limitations of space I focus my comparative remarks on the first of these volumes.

7. The precedent for this volume was Ishihara's (1990) *The Japan That Can Say No.*

8. For a comprehensive discussion of these and related matters, see Milne and Mauzy (1999).

9. For an insightful and evenhanded overview of the Michael Fay affair, see Asad Latiff (1994).

10. See M. Lee (1998).

11. See Rosenthal (1997).

12. This is an estimation derived from January 2001 interviews in Kuala Lumpur with gay activists and other knowledgeable individuals. The estimates ranged from 10,000–

15,000 at the lower end of the scale, to 150,000 at the upper end. Most estimates were in the range of 15,000–25,000.

13. Reuters News Service, August 17, 1994.

14. Cited in *The Washington Blade*, August 24, 1994.

15. *Sunday Star*, December 18, 1994.

16. *Sunday Metro*, June 28, 1998.

17. Ibid.

18. I am indebted to M. B. Hooker for this information (personal communication, December 13, 2000).

19. Tan (1999: 289).

20. Ibid.

21. *The Star*, January 22, 1997.

22. For clarification of the variation in punishment, see Rose Ismail (1995: 114).

23. Tan (1999: 295).

24. *The Star*, February 19, 1997.

25. Ibid.

26. Prior to these amendments, the maximum penalty for the sexual offenses at issue involved a fine of M$1,000 and six months' imprisonment.

27. See Funston (1999); Milne and Mauzy (1999).

28. He has since been convicted and sentenced on some of the lesser charges, but not the more serious illegalities stemming from this abuse.

29. The book bore the title *50 Dalil Mengapa Anwar Tidak Boleh Jadi PM* (50 reasons why Anwar cannot become PM).

30. See *<http://www.freemalaysia.com>*, May 13, 1999.

31. The other two men Anwar has been accused of sodomizing are Azizian Abu Bakar, who was formerly employed by Anwar's wife as a driver, and Hairany Mohd. Naffis, a former lecturer in political science at the Universiti Kebangsaan Malaysia.

32. The Malaysian version (complete with Arabic and English translation) that I purchased in Kuala Lumpur in January 2001 bears the title *Pendirian Syari'at Terhadap Hukuman Bersalah Ke Atas Dato' Seri Anwar Ibrahim* (*Syariah Review of the Guilty Verdict Passed on Dato' Seri Anwar Ibrahim*).

33. As far as many Muslim scholars are concerned, the *hudud* laws enforced in much of the Muslim world are based on questionable interpretations of Quranic injunctions. See, for example, Rose Ismail (1995); Mohammad Hashim Kamali (2000).

34. As Shamsul A. B. (2000: 229) has noted, "terms like 'sodomy', 'homosexuality', 'anal sex', 'pubic hair', 'semen', 'bodily liquids', 'masturbation', 'sexual intercourse', and 'DNA' came to be defined and discussed in graphic legal and scientific detail in the court, almost non-stop for weeks on end."

35. To the best of my knowledge, the latter expression does not double as an index of local views concerning Western leaders' responses to Mahathir's handling of the Anwar case, for example, that Mahathir or Malaysia has been or is being sodomized by the West. Compare Asad Latiff's (1994) volume on Singapore's caning of Michael Fay, its international repercussions for Singapore, and Singaporeans' reactions to Western criticism, which is summed up in the book's title, *The Flogging of Singapore: The Michael Fay Affair*.

36. Mahathir would no doubt be horrified to learn that some villagers from eastern Indonesia who have immigrated to East Malaysia in search of work have not only contracted AIDS there but have also come to view the disease as a scourge of *Malaysian* origin and have in fact begun speaking about it in somewhat euphemistic terms as "immigration sickness" (Sydney Jones, personal communication, September 7, 2000).

37. *News Planet*, September 25, 1998.

38. *Sydney Star Observer*, February 23, 1995.

39. PASRAH spokesmen have not clarified how they arrived at this figure.

40. *New Straits Times*, October 23, 1998.

41. Ibid.

42. Robert Hefner, personal communication, June 6, 2001.

43. Ibid.

44. The article, titled "Queering the State: Towards a Lesbian Movement in Malaysia," appears in Reinfelder (1996).

45. See Alina Rastam (1998); and Nadiah Bamadhaj (1999).

CONCLUSION

1. Walter Adamson (1987/1988: 320) cited in Nelson (1995: 44).

2. Nelson (1995: 42).

3. Ibid., 45–46.

4. Cohen (1995: 37).

5. Robert Hefner, personal communication, May 20, 2000.

6. Nor is the enormously important corpus of Foucault's work, though I cannot pursue the point here.

7. For a recent discussion of some of the literature on ambivalence in kinship, see Peletz (1995, 2001); cf. Peletz (1996).

8. The phrase is Wolfe's (1989: 193).

9. For a particularly compelling example from East Germany, see Spülbeck (1996).

10. Some of the literature is reviewed in Murray and Roscoe (1997); see also Murray (1992), the relevant sections of Boswell (1980), and material cited in the bibliographies of the sources referenced in chap. 5, n. 2 (above).

GLOSSARY OF FREQUENTLY USED MALAY TERMS*

adat — tradition, custom, customary law.

akal — reason; rationality.

alim — religious scholar; man of learning (pl. = *ulama*).

asal-usul — place of birth, origin-point, origins.

assalam alaikum — peace be with you.

cerai — divorce (technically, termination of marriage).

cerai hidup — divorce (technically, termination of marriage by divorce).

cerai mati — termination of marriage by death.

dakwah — to invite or call or answer the invitation or call; missionary work; Islamic resurgence.

edah — the one-hundred-day period following a divorce or a husband's death during which time a woman may not remarry and is normally entitled to support from her husband or his estate.

fasakh — divorce by judicial proceedings; judicial rescission or voiding of marriage contract; annulment.

fitrah — tithe; alms in the form of rice, etc., given at the end of the fasting month.

haji — a man who has made the pilgrimage (*haj*) to Mecca (fem. form = *hajjah*).

hantaran — obligatory cash payment or other gift due to be paid under *adat* by the bridegroom to the bride at the time the marriage is solemnized.

harta sepencarian — joint acquisitions, conjugal property.

hudud — laws bearing on various criminal offenses and some of the more severe penalties for their transgression as specified in the Quran.

kadi — judge or magistrate in an Islamic court.

kadi besar — chief judge or magistrate in an Islamic court.

khalwat — illicit proximity.

liwat — sodomy.

mas kawin — obligatory marriage payment due under Islamic law by the bridegroom to the bride at the time the marriage is solemnized; literally, "marriage gold."

mufti — juriconsult.

muta'ah — an obligatory consolatory gift payable to a wife divorced without fault.

nafkah — material maintenance and support that a man is normally required to provide his wife and children.

nafkah anak — mandatory child support.

*Includes foreign (e.g., Arabic-origin) terms that are in common usage in Malaysia's Islamic courts or among Malays generally.

nafkah edah — normally mandatory material maintenance and support for a divorcée through her *edah* period (usually three months and ten days).

nafsu — passion; lust.

pemberian — gift(s); marriage gift(s) other than cash made by the bridegroom to the bride at the time the marriage is solemnized (clothes, handbag, makeup, etc.).

penghulu — leader.

rogol — rape.

rujuk — reconcile; reconciliation.

sepencarian — see *harta sepencarian*.

sumbang — incest; improper or repugnant behavior or conditions.

syariah — Islamic law.

taklik — conditions attached to a marriage contract which, if broken, entitle a woman to divorce.

talak — divorce of a wife through repudiation; pronouncement of divorce formula.

tangkap basah — catch or arrest for illicit proximity; literally, "wet catch."

tebus talak — a type of divorce in which the wife compensates her husband for agreeing to release her (also known as *khuluk*).

ulama — religious scholars; men of learning (sing. = *alim*).

ummah — follower of a certain religion; community of Muslim believers.

undang — district chief; supreme lord and lawgiver.

wali — legal guardian (*wali hakim* = judge or other official who serves as *wali*).

yang dipertuan besar — title of traditional ruler of Negeri Sembilan.

zakat — tithe payable at the end of the fasting month.

zina — illicit sexual intercourse; fornication; adultery.

BIBLIOGRAPHY

OFFICIAL RECORDS

Buku Tahunan Perangkaan Malaysia (Yearbook of Statistics Malaysia) 2000. Jabatan Perangkaan Malaysia (Department of Statistics, Malaysia). Kuala Lumpur: Government of Malaysia, 2000.

Buletin Perangkaan Sosial (Social Statistics Bulletin). Malaysia, 1991. Jabatan Perangkaan Malaysia (Department of Social Statistics, Malaysia). Kuala Lumpur: Government of Malaysia, 1991.

FMGGGNS (Federation of Malaya Gazettes, Government of Negri Sembilan). 1949, 1950. Public Record Office, London.

LNS (The Laws of Negri Sembilan, 1883–1902). Singapore, 1904. Public Record Office, London.

NSAR (Negri Sembilan Annual Report). 1899, 1915. Public Record Office, London.

NSGG (Negri Sembilan Government Gazettes). 1904. Public Record Office, London.

PKDR (Pejabat Kadi Daerah Rembau). 1963–88. Kadi's Office, Rembau, Negeri Sembilan.

SUSCP (Sungei Ujong State Council Proceedings). 1888, 1893. Public Record Office, London.

SELECTED STATUTES

Administration of Muslim Law Enactment, 1960 (Negeri Sembilan)
Federal Constitution of Malaysia, 1957
Islamic Family Law Enactment (Negeri Sembilan), 1983
Islamic Family Law Enactment of Kelantan, 1983
Islamic Family Law (Federal Territories) Act, 1984 (Act 303)
Islamic Family Law (Federal Territories) (Amendment) Act, 1994
[National] Penal Code (Act 574) [2000]
Selangor Administration of Islamic Law Enactment, 1989
Selangor Islamic Family Law Enactment, 1984
Syariah Criminal Offenses (Federal Territories) Act, 1997 (Act 559)
Syariah Criminal Procedure Code Enactment, 1997 (Johor)

BOOKS, ARTICLES, AND THESES

A. Azmi Abdul Khalid. 1990. "Dato' Abdullah Bin Haji Dahan: Undang Rembau, 1922–38." In *Negeri Sembilan Dahulu Dan Sekarang* [Negeri Sembilan in the past and at present], ed. Norazit Selat, 157–64. Kuala Lumpur: United Selangor Press Sdn. Bhd.

Abaza, Mona. 1991. "The Discourse on Islamic Fundamentalism in the Middle East and Southeast Asia: A Critical Perspective." *Sojourn* 6 (2): 203–39.

Abdul Rahman bin Haji Mohammad. 1964. *Dasar-Dasar Adat Perpateh* [The Foundations of adat perpateh]. Kuala Lumpur: Pustaka Antara.

Abdullahi A. An-Na'im. 1999. "The Cultural Mediation of Human Rights: The Al-Arqam Case in Malaysia." In *The East Asian Challenge for Human Rights*, ed. Joanne R. Bauer and Daniel A. Bell, 147–68. New York: Cambridge University Press.

Abu-Lughod, Lila. 1990. "The Romance of Resistance: Tracing Transformations of Power through Bedouin Women." *American Ethnologist* 17 (1): 41–55.

Ackerman, Susan. 1991. "*Dakwah* and *Minah Karan*: Class Formation and Ideological Conflicts in Malay Society." *Bijdragen tot de Taal-, Land-, en Volkenkunde* 147 (2/3): 193–215.

Adamson, Walter. 1987/1988. "Gramsci and the Politics of Civil Society." *Praxis International* 7 (3/4): 320–39.

Ahmad Ibrahim. [1965] 1975. *Islamic Law in Malaya*. Kuala Lumpur: Malaysian Sociological Research Institute.

———. 1973. "The Law Reform (Marriage and Divorce) Bill, 1972." *Malayan Law Journal* 1:vii–ix.

———. 1987. "Caning for Shariah Court Offences." In *The Law Majallah*, 101–5. Petaling Jaya, Selangor: The Law Society, International Islamic University.

———. 1997a. *Family Law in Malaysia*. 3d ed. Kuala Lumpur: Malayan Law Journal Sdn. Bhd.

———. 1997b. *Pentadbiran Undang-undang Islam di Malaysia* [The administration of Islamic law in Malaysia]. Kuala Lumpur: Institut Kefahaman Islam Malaysia.

Ahmad Ibrahim and Ahilemah Joned. 1987. *The Malaysian Legal System*. Kuala Lumpur: Dewan Bahasa dan Pustaka.

Ahmed, Leila. 1992. *Women and Gender in Islam: Historical Roots of a Modern Debate*. New Haven: Yale University Press.

Alexander, Jeffrey C. 1989. *Structure and Meaning: Relinking Classical Sociology*. New York: Columbia University Press.

Ali E. Hillal Dessouki, ed. 1982. *Islamic Resurgence in the Arab World*. New York: Praeger.

Alina Rastam. 1998. "Out of the Closet and Into the Courtroom? Some Reflections on Sexuality Rights in Malaysia." *Saksi*, no. 2, <*http://www.saksi.com/novdec98/alina.htm*>.

Andaya, Barbara Watson. 1994. "The Changing Religious Role of Women in Pre-Modern Southeast Asia." *South-East Asia Research* 2 (2): 99–116.

———. 2000a. "Delineating Female Space: Seclusion and the State in Pre-Modern Island Southeast Asia." In *Other Pasts: Women, Gender, and History in Early Modern Southeast Asia*, ed. Barbara Watson Andaya, 231–53. Honolulu: Center for Southeast Asian Studies, University of Hawaii.

———. 2000b. "States, Laws, and Gender Regimes in Early Modern Southeast Asia." Paper presented at the Humanities Research Center, Australian National University, Canberra, September 15, 2000.

Andaya, Barbara Watson, and Leonard Y. Andaya. 2001. *A History of Malaysia*. 2d ed. Honolulu: University of Hawaii Press.

Andaya, Barbara Watson, and Yoneo Ishii. 1992. "Religious Developments in Southeast Asia, circa 1500–1800." In *The Cambridge History of Southeast Asia*, ed. Nicholas Tarling, 508–71. Cambridge: Cambridge University Press.

Andaya, Leonard Y. 2000. "The Bissu: Study of a Third Gender in Indonesia." In *Gender and History in Early Modern Southeast Asia*, ed. Barbara Watson Andaya, 27–46. Honolulu: Center for Southeast Asian Studies, University of Hawaii.

Andaya, Leonard Y., and Barbara Watson Andaya. 1995. "Southeast Asia in the Early Modern Period; Twenty-Five Years On." *Journal of Southeast Asian Studies* 26 (1): 92–98.

Anderson, Benedict R.O.'G. 1983. *Imagined Communities: Reflections on the Origin and Spread of Nationalism*. London: Verso.

Appadurai, Arjun. 1996. *Modernity at Large: Cultural Dimensions of Globalization.* Minneapolis: University of Minnesota Press.

Asad, Talal. 1993. *Genealogies of Religion: Discipline and Reasons of Power in Christianity and Islam.* Baltimore: Johns Hopkins University Press.

Asad Latiff. 1994. *The Flogging of Singapore: The Michael Fay Affair.* Singapore: Times Books International.

Atkinson, Jane, and Shelly Errington, eds. 1990. *Power and Difference: Gender in Island Southeast Asia.* Stanford: Stanford University Press.

Awang Sudjai Hairul and Yusoff Khan. [1977] 2000. *Kamus Lengkap* [Complete dictionary]. 3d ed. Petaling Jaya: Pustaka Zaman.

Azizah Kassim. 1984. "Women and Divorce among the Urban Malays." In *Women in Malaysia,* ed. Hing Ai Yun, Nik Safiah Karim, and Rokiah Talib, 94–112. Kuala Lumpur: Pelanduk.

Bakhash, Shaul. 1984. *The Reign of the Ayatollahs: Iran and the Islamic Revolution.* New York: Basic Books.

Banks, David J. 1976. "Islam and Inheritance in Malaya: Culture Conflict or Islamic Revolution?" *American Ethnologist* 3 (4): 573–86.

———. 1983. *Malay Kinship.* Philadelphia: Institute for the Study of Human Issues Publications.

———. 1990. "Resurgent Islam and Malay Rural Culture: Malay Novelists and the Invention of Culture." *American Ethnologist* 17 (3): 531–48.

Bateson, Gregory. 1936. *Naven: A Survey of the Problems Suggested by a Composite Picture of a New Guinea Tribe Drawn from Three Points of View.* Stanford: Stanford University Press.

Bird, Isabella. 1883. "Sketches in the Malay Peninsula." *Leisure Hour,* 17–23, 80–86, 142–51, 194–204.

———. [1883] 1969. *The Golden Chersonese and the Way Thither.* Reprint, Kuala Lumpur: University of Malaya Press.

Bishop, Ryan, and Lillian Robinson. 1998. *Night Market: Sexual Cultures and the Thai Economic Miracle.* New York: Routledge.

Blackwood, Evelyn, and Saskia Wieringa, eds. 1999. *Female Desires: Same-Sex Relations and Transgender Practices across Cultures.* New York: Columbia University Press.

Bloch, Maurice. 1989. *Ritual, History, and Power: Selected Papers in Anthropology.* London: Athlone Press.

Boellstorff, Thomas. 2000. "The Gay Archipelago: Postcolonial Sexual Subjectivities in Indonesia." Ph.D. diss., Stanford University.

Boon, James A. 1979. "Balinese Temple Politics and the Religious Revitalization of Caste Ideals." In *The Imagination of Reality: Essays in Southeast Asian Coherence Systems,* ed. A. L. Becker and Aram A. Yengoyan, 271–91. Palo Alto: Ablex.

Bornstein, Kate. 1994. *Gender Outlaw: On Men, Women, and the Rest of Us.* New York: Vintage/Random House.

Boswell, John. 1980. *Christianity, Social Tolerance, and Homosexuality.* Chicago: University of Chicago Press.

Bourdieu, Pierre. 1977. *Outline of a Theory of Practice.* Cambridge: Cambridge University Press.

———. 1984. *Distinction: A Social Critique of the Judgment of Taste.* Cambridge, MA: Harvard University Press.

Bowen, John. 1986. "On the Political Construction of Tradition: *Gotong Royong* in Indonesia." *Journal of Asian Studies* 45 (3): 545–61.

———. 1993. *Muslims through Discourse: Religion and Ritual in Gayo Society*. Princeton: Princeton University Press.

Bowrey, Thomas. [1680] 1905. *A Geographical Account of Countries Round the Bay of Bengal, 1669 to 1679*. Ed. R. C. Temple. Cambridge: Hakluyt Society.

Brenner, Suzanne. 1995. "Why Women Rule the Roost: Rethinking Javanese Ideologies of Gender and Self-Control." In *Bewitching Women, Pious Men: Gender and Body Politics in Southeast Asia*, ed. Aihwa Ong and Michael G. Peletz, 19–50. Berkeley: University of California Press.

Brewer, Carolyn. 1999. "Baylon, Asog, Transvestism, and Sodomy: Gender, Sexuality, and the Sacred in Early Colonial Philippines." *Intersections: Gender, History, and Culture in the Asian Context* 2 (May 1999), <*http://www.sshe.murdoch.edu.au/intersections/issue2/carolyn2.html*>

———. 2000. "From Animist Priestess to Catholic Priest: The Re/gendering of Religious Roles in the Philippines, 1521–1685." In *Other Pasts: Women, Gender, and History in Early Modern Southeast Asia*, ed. Barbara Watson Andaya, 47–68. Honolulu: Center for Southeast Asian Studies, University of Hawaii.

Brown, Michael F. 1991. "Beyond Resistance: A Comparative Study of Utopian Renewal in Amazonia." *Ethnohistory* 38 (4): 388–413.

Burchell, Graham, Colin Gordon, and Peter Miller, eds. 1991. *The Foucault Effect: Studies in Governmentality*. Chicago: University of Chicago Press.

Carsten, Janet. 1997. *The Heat of the Hearth: The Process of Kinship in a Malay Fishing Community*. Oxford: Oxford University Press.

Caton, Steven C. 1999. *Lawrence of Arabia: A Film's Anthropology*. Berkeley: University of California Press.

Chakrabarty, Dipesh. 1988. "Conditions for Knowledge of Working-Class Conditions: Employers, Government and Jute Workers of Calcutta, 1890–1940." In *Selected Subaltern Studies*, ed. Ranajit Guha and Gayatri Chakravorty Spivak, 179–230. New York: Oxford University Press.

Chandra Muzaffar. 1987. *Islamic Resurgence in Malaysia*. Kuala Lumpur: Fajar Bakti.

Chatterjee, Partha. 1993. *The Nation and Its Fragments: Colonial and Post-Colonial Histories*. Princeton: Princeton University Press.

Chin, Christine B. N. 1998. *In Service and Servitude: Foreign Female Domestic Workers and the Malaysian "Modernity" Project*. New York: Columbia University Press.

Clifford, Hugh. 1899. "Life in the Malay Peninsula; As It Was and Is." In *Proceedings of the Royal Colonial Institute*. Vol. 30 (1898–1899). London: Royal Commonwealth Society.

———. 1929. *Bushwhacking and Other Asiatic Tales and Memories*. New York: Harper and Brothers.

Cohen, Jean. 1995. "Interpreting the Notion of Civil Society." In *Toward a Global Civil Society*, ed. Michael Walzer, 35–40. Providence: Berghahn Books.

Comaroff, John, and Simon Roberts. 1981. *Rules and Processes: The Cultural Logic of Dispute in an African Context*. Chicago: University of Chicago Press.

Conley, John M., and William M. O'Barr. 1990. *Rules and Relationships: The Ethnography of Legal Discourse*. Chicago: University of Chicago Press.

Coontz, Stephanie. 1992. *The Way We Never Were: American Families and the Nostalgia Trap*. New York: Basic Books.

Cowan, C. D. 1961. "Ideas of History in the Journal of the Malayan (Straits) Branch of the Royal Asiatic Society, 1874–1941." In *Historians of Southeast Asia*, ed. D. G. E. Hall, 279–85. Kuala Lumpur: Oxford University Press.

Daniel, Norman. 1993. *Islam and the West: The Making of an Image*. Oxford: Oneworld Publications.

Day, Anthony. 1996. "Ties that (Un)Bind: Families and States in Pre-Modern Southeast Asia." *Journal of Asian Studies* 55 (2): 384–409.

de Casparis, J. G., and I. W. Mabbett. 1992. "Religion and Popular Beliefs of Southeast Asia Before c. 1500." In *The Cambridge History of Southeast Asia*, vol. 1, pt. 1, ed. Nicholas Tarling, 276–339. Cambridge: Cambridge University Press.

de Josselin de Jong, P. E. 1960. "Islam versus Adat in Negri Sembilan (Malaya)." *Bijdragen tot de Taal-, Land-, en Volkenkunde* 116:158–203.

Dentan, Robert K. n.d. "How Semai Folktales Construe Ethnocide: Ambiguity, Ambivalence, Helplessness and Fear in West Malaysia." Department of Anthropology, SUNY Buffalo.

Dentan, Robert K., Kirk Endicott, Alberto G. Gomes, and M. B. Hooker. 1997. *Malaysia and the Original People: A Case Study of the Impact of Development on Indigenous Peoples*. Boston: Allyn and Bacon.

Dirks, Nicholas, Geoff Eley, and Sherry Ortner, eds. 1994. *Culture/Power/History: A Reader in Contemporary Social Theory*. Princeton: Princeton University Press.

Djamour, Judith. 1959. *Malay Kinship and Marriage in Singapore*. London: Athlone Press.

———. 1966. *The Muslim Matrimonial Court in Singapore*. London: Athlone Press.

Douglas, Mary. 1966. *Purity and Danger: An Analysis of the Concepts of Pollution and Taboo*. London: Routledge.

———. 1970. *Natural Symbols: Explorations in Cosmology*. New York: Pantheon.

Dwyer, Daisy H. 1978. *Images and Self-Images: Male and Female in Morocco*. New York: Columbia University Press.

———. 1979. "Law Actual and Perceived: The Sexual Politics of Law in Morocco." *Law and Society Review* 13 (3): 739–56.

Edelman, Marc. 1994. "Landlords and the Devil: Class, Ethnic, and Gender Dimensions of Central American Peasant Narratives." *Cultural Anthropology* 9 (1): 58–93.

Eickelman, Dale. 1982. "The Study of Islam in Local Contexts." *Contributions to Asian Studies* 17:1–16.

———. 1996. Foreward to *Civil Society in the Middle East*. Vol. 2. Ed. Augustus Richard Norton, ix–xiv. Leiden: E. J. Brill.

Eickelman, Dale, and James Piscatori. 1996. *Muslim Politics*. Princeton: Princeton University Press.

Ellen, Roy F. 1983. "Social Theory, Ethnography and the Understanding of Practical Islam in South-East Asia." In *Islam in South-East Asia*, ed. M. B. Hooker, 50–91. Leiden: E. J. Brill.

Englund, Harri, and James Leach. 2000. "Ethnography and the Meta-Narratives of Modernity." *Current Anthropology* 41 (2): 225–48.

Evers, Hans-Dieter, and Sharon Siddique. 1991. "Religious Revivalism in Southeast Asia: An Introduction." *Sojourn* 8 (1): 1–10.

Ewing, Katherine. 1988. *Shari'at and Ambiguity in South Asian Islam*. Berkeley: University of California Press.

Firdaus Haji Abdullah. 1985. *Radical Malay Politics: Its Origins and Early Development*. Petaling Jaya: Pelanduk Publications.

Fischer, Michael. 1980. *Iran: From Religious Dispute to Revolution*. Cambridge, MA: Harvard University Press.

Foucault, Michel. 1977. *Discipline and Punish: The Birth of the Prison*. Trans. Alan Sheridan. New York: Vintage.

———. 1978. *The History of Sexuality, Volume 1: An Introduction*. New York: Vintage.

———. 1980. *Power/Knowledge: Selected Interviews and Other Writings, 1972–1977*. New York: Pantheon.

———. 1991. "Governmentality." In *The Foucault Effect: Studies in Governmentality*, ed. Graham Burchell, Colin Gordon, and Peter Miller, 87–104. Chicago: University of Chicago Press.

Frith, Tabitha. 2001. "Reflexive Islam: The Rationalisation and Re-enchantment of Religious Identity in Malaysia." Ph.D. diss., Monash University.

Funston, John. 1999. "Malaysia: A Fateful September." *Southeast Asian Affairs 1999*, 165–84. Singapore: Institute of Southeast Asian Studies.

Furqan Ahmad. 1987. "Organ Transplant in Islamic Law." *Islamic and Comparative Law Quarterly* 7 (2): 132–36.

Fyzee, Asaf A. A. [1949] 1974. *Outlines of Muhammadan Law*. 4th ed. Reprint, Delhi: Oxford University Press.

Gaik Cheng Khoo. 1999. "Gender, Modernity, and the Nation in Malaysian Literature and Film (1980s and 1990s)." Ph.D. diss., University of British Columbia.

Gal, Susan. 1995. "Language and the 'Arts of Resistance.'" *Cultural Anthropology* 10 (3): 407–24.

Geertz, Clifford. 1960. *The Religion of Java*. Glencoe, IL: Free Press.

———. [1964] 1973. "'Internal Conversion' in Contemporary Bali." In *The Interpretation of Cultures*, 170–89. New York: Basic Books.

———. 1973a. "Deep Play: Notes on the Balinese Cockfight." In *The Interpretation of Cultures*, 412–53. New York: Basic Books.

———. 1973b. *The Interpretation of Cultures*. New York: Basic Books.

———. 1983a. "Local Knowledge: Fact and Law in Comparative Perspective." In *Local Knowledge: Further Essays in Interpretive Anthropology*, 167–234. New York: Basic Books.

———. 1983b. *Local Knowledge: Further Essays in Interpretive Anthropology*. New York: Basic Books.

George, T. J. S. 1980. *Revolt in Mindanao: The Rise of Islam in Philippine Politics*. Kuala Lumpur: Oxford University Press.

Gerges, Fawaz. 1999. *America and Political Islam: Clash of Cultures or Clash of Interests?* Cambridge: Cambridge University Press.

Gerth, H. H., and C. Wright Mills. 1958. "Introduction: The Man and His Work." In *From Max Weber: Essays in Sociology*, ed. H. H. Gerth and C. Wright Mills, 3–74. New York: Oxford University Press.

Guha, Ranajit. 1994. "The Prose of Counter-Insurgency." In *Culture/Power/History: A Reader in Contemporary Social Theory*, ed. Nicholas Dirks, Geoff Eley, and Sherry Ortner, 336–71. Princeton: Princeton University Press.

Gullick, J. M. 1958. *Indigenous Political Systems of Western Malaya*. London: Athlone Press.

———. 1987. *Malay Society in the Late Nineteenth Century: The Beginnings of Change*. Singapore: Oxford University Press.

Gupta, Akhil. 1995. "Blurred Boundaries: The Discourse of Corruption, the Culture of Politics and the Imagined State." *American Ethnologist* 22 (2): 375–402.

Haeri, Shahla. 1989. *Law of Desire: Temporary Marriage in Shi'i Iran*. Syracuse: Syracuse University Press.

Halim Salleh. 1999. "Development and the Politics of Social Stability in Malaysia." *Southeast Asian Affairs 1999*, 185–203. Singapore: Institute of Southeast Asian Studies.

Hallaq, Wael B. 1997. *A History of Islamic Legal Theories: An Introduction to Sunni Usul al-Fiqh*. Cambridge: Cambridge University Press.

Hann, Chris. 1996. "Introduction: Political Society and Civil Anthropology." In *Civil Society: Challenging Western Models*, ed. Chris Hann and Elizabeth Dunn, 1–26. London: Routledge.

Hann, Chris, and Elizabeth Dunn, eds. 1996. *Civil Society: Challenging Western Models*. New York: Routledge.

Hefner, Robert W. 1985. *Hindu Javanese: Tengger Tradition and Islam*. Princeton: Princeton University Press.

———. 1987. "The Political Economy of Islamic Conversion in Modern East Java." In *Islam and the Political Economy of Meaning*, ed. William R. Roff, 53–78. London: Croom Helm.

———. 1990. *The Political Economy of Mountain Java: An Interpretive History*. Berkeley: University of California Press.

———. 1993. "Islam, State, and Civil Society: ICMI and the Struggle for the Indonesian Middle Class." *Indonesia* 56:1–35.

———. 1998a. "On the History and Cross-Cultural Possibility of a Democratic Ideal." In *Civil Society: The History and Cross-Cultural Possibility of a Democratic Ideal*, ed. Robert W. Hefner, 3–49. New Brunswick, NJ: Transaction Publishers.

———, ed. 1998b. *Democratic Civility: The Historical and Cross-Cultural Possibility of a Modern Ideal*. New Brunswick, NJ: Transaction Publishers.

———. 2000. *Civil Islam: Muslims and Democratization in Indonesia*. Princeton: Princeton University Press.

Hefner, Robert W., and Patricia Horvatich, eds. 1997. *Islam in an Era of Nation-States: Politics and Religious Renewal in Muslim Southeast Asia*. Honolulu: University of Hawaii Press.

Herzfeld, Michael. 1992. *The Social Production of Indifference: Exploring the Symbolic Roots of Western Bureaucracy*. Chicago: University of Chicago Press.

Hill, Michael, and Lian Kwen Fee. 1995. *The Politics of Nation Building and Citizenship in Singapore*. London: Routledge.

Hiro, Dilip. 1989. *Holy Wars: The Rise of Islamic Fundamentalism*. New York: Routledge.

Hirsch, Susan F. 1998. *Pronouncing and Persevering: Gender and the Discourses of Disputing in an African Islamic Court*. Chicago: University of Chicago Press.

Hochschild, Arlie Russell. 1983. *The Managed Heart: Commercialization of Human Feeling*. Berkeley: University of California Press.

Hooker, M. B. 1972. *Adat Laws in Modern Malaya: Land Tenure, Traditional Government, and Religion*. Kuala Lumpur: Oxford University Press.

———. 1978. *A Concise Legal History of Southeast Asia*. Oxford: Oxford University Press.

———. 1983a. "Introduction: The Translation of Islam into South-East Asia." In *Islam in South-East Asia*, ed. M. B. Hooker, 1–22. Leiden: E. J. Brill.

———. 1983b. "Muhammadan Law and Islamic Law." In *Islam in South-East Asia*, ed. M. B. Hooker, 160–82. Leiden: E. J. Brill.

———. 1984. *Islamic Law in South-East Asia*. Singapore: Oxford University Press.

———. 1989. Review of *Malaysia's National Language Policy and the Legal System*, by Richard Mead. *Journal of Asian Studies* 48 (1): 227–28.

————. 1993. "Fatawa in Malaysia, 1960–1985" (Third Coulson Memorial Lecture). *Arab Law Quarterly* 8:93–105.

Horowitz, Donald. 1994. "The Qur'an and the Common Law: Islamic Law Reform and the Theory of Legal Change." *American Journal of Comparative Law* 62 (2 and 3):233–93, 543–80.

Horton, Robin. 1971. "African Conversion." *Africa* 41 (2): 85–108.

Huntington, Samuel. 1996. *The Clash of Civilizations and the Remaking of World Order.* New York: Simon and Schuster.

Husin Mutalib. 1990. "Islamic Revivalism in ASEAN States: Political Implications." *Asian Survey* 30 (9): 877–91.

————. 1993. *Islam in Malaysia: From Revivalism to Islamic State?* Singapore: Singapore University Press.

Ishihara, Shintaro. 1990. *The Japan That Can Say No.* Trans. Frank Baldwin. New York: Simon and Schuster.

Ismail Haji Ibrahim, ed. 1998. *Islam dan Pemindahan Organ* [Islam and organ transfer]. Kuala Lumpur: IKIM.

Jaspan, M. A. 1969. *Traditional Medical Theory in Southeast Asia.* Hull, England: University of Hull.

Johnson, Mark. 1997. *Beauty and Power: Transgendering and Cultural Transformation in the Southern Philippines.* London: Berg.

Jomo K. S. and Ahmad Shabery Cheek. 1992. "Malaysia's Islamic Movements." In *Fragmented Vision: Culture and Politics in Contemporary Malaysia,* ed. Joel S. Kahn and Francis Loh Kok Wah, 79–105. Honolulu: University of Hawaii Press.

Jones, Gavin. 1994. *Marriage and Divorce in Islamic South-East Asia.* Kuala Lumpur: Oxford University Press.

Just, Peter. 1986. "Let the Evidence Fit the Crime: Evidence, Law, and 'Sociological Truth' among the Dou Donggo." *American Ethnologist* 13 (1): 43–61.

————. 1990. "Dead Goats and Broken Betrothals: Liability and Equity in Dou Donggo Law." *American Ethnologist* 17 (1): 75–90.

————. 1992. "History, Power, Ideology, and Culture: Current Directions in the Anthropology of Law." *Law and Society Review* 26 (2): 373–411.

Kahn, Joel S. 1976. "'Tradition,' Matriliny, and Change among the Minangkabau of Indonesia." *Bijdragen Tot de Taal-, Land-, en Volkenkunde* 132:64–95.

Kahn, Joel S., and Francis Loh Kok Wah, eds. 1992. *Fragmented Vision: Culture and Politics in Contemporary Malaysia.* Honolulu: University of Hawaii Press.

Kalid Jafri. 1998. *50 Dalil Mengapa Anwar Tidak Boleh Jadi PM* [50 reasons why Anwar cannot become PM].

Kaplan, Martha, and John D. Kelly. 1994. "Rethinking Resistance: Dialogics of 'Disaffection' in Colonial Fiji." *American Ethnologist* 21 (1): 123–51.

Kasaba, Resat. 1998. "Cohabitation? Islamist and Secular Groups in Modern Turkey." In *Civil Society: The History and Cross-Cultural Possibility of a Democratic Ideal,* ed. Robert W. Hefner, 265–84. New Brunswick, NJ: Transaction Publishers.

Katz, June, and Ronald Katz. 1975. "The New Indonesian Marriage Law: A Mirror of Indonesia's Political, Cultural, and Legal Systems." *American Journal of Comparative Law* 23 (4): 653–81.

Kessler, Clive. 1978. *Islam and Politics in a Malay State: Kelantan, 1839–1969.* Ithaca: Cornell University Press.

————. 1980. "Malaysia: Islamic Revivalism and Political Disaffection in a Divided Society." *Southeast Asia Chronicle* 75:3–11.

Kiernan, Ben. 1996. *The Pol Pot Regime: Race, Power, and Genocide in Cambodia under the Khmer Rouge, 1975–1979*. New Haven: Yale University Press.

Knight, John. 1996. "Making Citizens in Post-War Japan." In *Civil Society: Challenging Western Models*, ed. Chris Hann and Elizabeth Dunn, 222–41. London: Routledge.

Krasner, Stephen. 1999. *Sovereignty: Organized Hyprocrisy*. Princeton: Princeton University Press.

Kress, Ken. 1992. "Legal Indeterminacy and Legitimacy." In *Legal Hermeneutics: History, Theory, and Practice*, ed. Gregory Leyh, 200–215. Berkeley: University of California Press.

Laderman, Carol. 1991. *Taming the Wind of Desire: Psychology, Medicine, and Aesthetics in Malay Shamanistic Performance*. Berkeley: University of California Press.

Laitin, David D. 1986. *Hegemony and Culture: Politics and Religious Change among the Yoruba*. Chicago: University of Chicago Press.

Lawrence, Bruce B. 1998. *Shattering the Myth: Islam beyond Violence*. Princeton: Princeton University Press.

Lazarus-Black, Mindie, and Susan F. Hirsch, eds. 1994. *Contested States: Law, Hegemony, and Resistance*. New York: Routledge.

Lee, Martin. 1998. "Testing Asian Values." *New York Times*, January 18.

Lee, Raymond, and Susan Ackerman. 1997. *Sacred Tensions: Modernity and Religious Transformation in Malaysia*. Columbia: University of South Carolina Press.

Lev, Daniel. 1972. *Islamic Courts in Indonesia: A Study in the Political Bases of Legal Institutions*. Berkeley: University of California Press.

Lévi-Strauss, Claude. [1949] 1969. *The Elementary Structures of Kinship*. Reprint, Boston: Beacon Press.

Li, Tania. 1989. *Malays in Singapore: Culture, Economy, and Ideology*. Singapore: Oxford University Press.

Liaw Yock Fang. 1976. *Undang-Undang Melaka* [The Laws of Melaka]. The Hague: Martinus Nijhoff.

Lister, Martin. 1887. "The Negri Sembilan: Their Origin and Constitution." *Journal of the Royal Asiatic Society, Straits Branch* 19:35–53.

———. 1890. "Malay Law in Negri Sembilan." *Journal of the Royal Asiatic Society, Straits Branch* 22:299–319.

———. 1891. "Pantang Larang of Negri Sembilan." *Journal of the Royal Asiatic Society, Straits Branch* 23:142–44.

Loewith, Karl. 1970. "Weber's Interpretation of the Bourgeois-Capitalistic World in Terms of the Guiding Principle of 'Rationalization.'" In *Max Weber*, ed. Dennis Wrong, 101–22. Englewood Cliffs, NJ: Prentice-Hall.

Loizos, Peter. 1996. "How Ernest Gellner Got Mugged on the Streets of London, Or: Civil Society, the Media, and the Quality of Life." In *Civil Society: Challenging Western Models*, ed. Chris Hann and Elizabeth Dunn, 50–63. London: Routledge.

Low, James. 1850. "Observations on Perak." *The Journal of the Indian Archipelago and Eastern Asia* 4:497–504.

Madale, Nagasura. 1986. "The Resurgence of Islam and Nationalism in the Philippines." In *Islam and Society in Southeast Asia*, ed. Taufik Abdullah and Sharon Siddique, 282–314. Singapore: Institute of Southeast Asian Studies.

Mahathir Mohamad. 1970. *The Malay Dilemma*. Singapore: Donald Moore/Asia Pacific Press.

———. 1976. *Menghadapi Cabaran* [Meeting the challenge]. Kuala Lumpur: Pustaka Antara.

———. 1986. *The Challenge*. Kuala Lumpur: Pelanduk Publications.

———. 1999. *A New Deal for Asia*. Kuala Lumpur: Pelanduk Publications.

Mahathir Mohamad and Shintaro Ishihara. 1995. *The Voice of Asia: Two Asian Leaders Discuss the Coming Century*. Tokyo: Kodansha International.

Manderson, Leonore, and Margaret Jolly, eds. 1997. *Sites of Desire, Economies of Pleasure: Sexualities in Asia and the Pacific*. Chicago: University of Chicago Press.

Marcus, George. 1995. "Ethnography in/of the World System: The Emergence of Multi-Sited Ethnography." *Annual Review of Anthropology* 24:95–117.

Mardin, Şerif. 1995. "Civil Society and Islam." In *Civil Society: Theory, History, Comparison*, ed. John Hall, 278–300. Cambridge: Polity Press.

Marsden, William. [1788] 1966. *A History of Sumatra*. 3d rev. ed. Kuala Lumpur: Oxford University Press.

McAllister, Carol. 1987. "Matriliny, Islam, and Capitalism: Combined and Uneven Development in the Lives of Negeri Sembilan Women." Ph.D. diss., University of Pittsburgh.

———. 1990. "Women and Feasting: Ritual Exchange, Capitalism, and Islamic Revival in Negeri Sembilan, Malaysia." *Research in Economic Anthropology* 12:12–51.

McKenna, Thomas M. 1998. *Muslim Rulers and Rebels: Everyday Politics and Armed Separatism in the Southern Philippines*. Berkeley: University of California Press.

McKinley, Robert. 1981. "Cain and Abel on the Malay Peninsula." In *Siblingship in Oceania: Studies in the Meaning of Kin Relations*, ed. Mac Marshall, 335–87. Ann Arbor: University of Michigan Press.

Mead, Richard. 1988. *Malaysia's National Language Policy and the Legal System*. New Haven: Yale University Southeast Asian Studies.

Merry, Sally Engle. 1990. *Getting Justice and Getting Even: Legal Consciousness among Working-Class Americans*. Chicago: University of Chicago Press.

———. 1994. "Courts as Performances: Domestic Violence Hearings in a Hawai'i Family Court." In *History and Power in the Study of Law: New Directions in Legal Anthropology*, ed. June Starr and Jane F. Collier, 35–58. Ithaca: Cornell University Press.

Messick, Brinkley. 1988. "Kissing Hands and Knees: Hegemony and Hierarchy in Shari'a Discourse." *Law and Society Review* 22 (4): 637–59.

———. 1993. *The Calligraphic State: Textual Domination and History in a Muslim Society*. Berkeley: University of California Press.

Meyerowitz, Joanne. 2002. *How Sex Changed: A History of Transsexuality in the United States*. Cambridge, MA: Harvard University Press.

Milne, R. S., and Diane Mauzy. 1999. *Malaysian Politics under Mahathir*. London: Routledge.

Milner, Anthony C. "Islam and the Muslim State." In *Islam in South-East Asia*, ed. M. B. Hooker, 23–49. Leiden: E. J. Brill.

———. 1986. "Rethinking Islamic Fundamentalism in Malaysia." *Review of Indonesian and Malaysian Affairs* 20 (2): 48–75.

———. 1995. *The Invention of Politics in Colonial Malaya: Contesting Nationalism and the Expansion of the Public Sphere*. Cambridge: Cambridge University Press.

(Tun) Mohamed Suffian. 1988. *An Introduction to the Legal System of Malaysia*. Kuala Lumpur: Penerbit Fajar Bakti.

Mohammad Hashim Kamali. 2000. *Islamic Law in Malaysia: Issues and Developments*. Kuala Lumpur: Ilmiah Publishers.

Mohammad Naaem Yassen. 1990. "The Rulings for the Donation of Human Organs in the Light of Shari'a Rules and Medical Facts." *Arab Law Quarterly* 5:49–87.

Moore, Sally Falk. 1978. *Law as Process: An Anthropological Approach.* Boston: Routledge and Kegan Paul.

———. 1986. *Social Facts and Fabrications: "Customary" Law on Kilimanjaro, 1880–1980.* Cambridge: Cambridge University Press.

———. 1989. "History and the Redefinition of Custom on Kilimanjaro." In *History and Power in the Study of Law: New Directions in Legal Anthropology,* ed. June Starr and Jane F. Collier, 277–301. Ithaca: Cornell University Press.

Muhammad Abu Bakar. 1981. "Islamic Revivalism and the Political Process in Malaysia." *Asian Survey* 21 (2): 1040–59.

———. 1987. *Penghayatan Sebuah Ideal: Suatu Tafsiran Tentang Islam Semasa* [Appreciation of an ideal: An interpretation of contemporary Islam]. Kuala Lumpur: Dewan Bahasa dan Pustaka.

Mundy, Peter. [1667] 1919. *The Travels of Peter Mundy in Europe and Asia, 1609–1667.* Vol. 3. Ed. R. C. Temple. Reprint, London: Hakluyt Society.

Munson, Henry. 1988. *Islam and Revolution in the Middle East.* New Haven: Yale University Press.

Murray, Stephen O., ed. 1992. *Oceanic Homosexualities.* New York: Garland.

Murray, Stephen O., and Will Roscoe. 1997. *Islamic Homosexualities: Culture, History, and Literature.* New York: New York University Press.

Mydans, Seth. 1996. "Blame Men, Not Allah, Islamic Feminists Say." *New York Times,* October 10.

Nader, Laura, and Harry Todd, eds. 1978. *The Disputing Process: Law in Ten Societies.* New York: Columbia University Press.

Nadiah Bamadhaj. 1999. "The Hot Potato: Sexuality Rights Advocacy in Malaysia." *Saksi,* no. 3, <http://www.saksi.com/jan99/nadiahb.htm>.

Nagata, Judith. 1978. "The Chinese Muslims of Malaysia: New Malays or New Associates? A Problem of Religion and Ethnicity." In *The Past in Southeast Asia's Present,* ed. Gordon P. Means, 102–14. Ottawa: Secretariat, Canadian Society for Asian Studies/Canadian Council for Southeast Asian Studies.

———. 1982. "Islamic Revival and the Problem of Legitimacy among Rural Religious Elites in Malaysia." *Man* 17:42–57.

———. 1984. *The Reflowering of Malaysian Islam: Modern Religious Radicals and Their Roots.* Vancouver: University of British Columbia Press.

Nakamura, Hisako. 1983. *Divorce in Java.* Jogjakarta: Gadjah Mada University Press.

Nash, Manning. 1984. "Fundamentalist Islam: Resevoir for Turbulence." *Journal of Asian and African Studies* 19:73–79.

———. 1991. "Islamic Resurgence in Malaysia and Indonesia." In *Fundamentalisms Observed,* ed. Martin E. Marty and R. Scott Appleby, 691–739. Chicago: University of Chicago Press.

Nelson, Kai. 1995. "Reconceptualizing Civil Society for Now: Some Somewhat Gramscian Turnings." In *Toward a Global Civil Society,* ed. Michael Walzer, 41–68. Providence: Berghahn Books.

Newbold, T. J. 1839. *Political and Statistical Account of the British Settlements in the Straits of Malacca.* 2 vols. London: John Murray.

Nonini, Donald. 1998. "Chinese Society, Coffee-Shop Talk, Possessing Gods: The Politics of Public Space among Diasporic Chinese in Malaysia." *Positions* 6 (2): 439–73.

Noraini Othman, ed. 1994. *Shari'a Law and the Modern Nation-State: A Malaysian Symposium.* Kuala Lumpur: SIS Forum (Malaysia) Berhad.

———. 1999. "Grounding Human Rights Arguments in Non-Western Culture: Shari'a and the Citizenship Rights of Women in a Modern Islamic State." In *The East Asian Challenge for Human Rights*, ed. Joanne Bauer and Daniel A. Bell, 169–92. New York: Cambridge University Press.

Norton, Augustus Richard, ed. 1995. *Civil Society in the Middle East.* Vol. 1. Leiden: E. J. Brill.

———. 1996. *Civil Society in the Middle East.* Vol. 2. Leiden: E. J. Brill.

Ong, Aihwa. 1987. *Spirits of Resistance and Capitalist Discipline: Factory Women in Malaysia.* Albany: SUNY Press.

———. 1988. "The Production of Possession: Spirits and the Multinational Corporation in Malaysia." *American Ethnologist* 15 (1): 28–42.

———. 1995a. "Making the Biopolitical Subject: Cambodian Immigrants, Refugee Medicine, and Cultural Citizenship in California." *Social Science and Medicine* 40 (9): 1243–57.

———. 1995b. "State versus Islam: Malay Families, Women's Bodies, and the Body Politic in Malaysia." In *Bewitching Women, Pious Men: Gender and Body Politics in Southeast Asia*, ed. Aihwa Ong and Michael G. Peletz, 159–94. Berkeley: University of California Press.

———. 1999a. *Flexible Citizenship: The Cultural Logics of Transnationality.* Durham: Duke University Press.

———. 1999b. "Muslim Feminism: Citizenship in the Shelter of Corporate Islam." *Citizenship Studies* 3 (3): 355–71.

———. 2001. "Modernity: Anthropological Aspects." In *International Encyclopedia of the Social and Behavioral Sciences*, vol. 15, ed. Neil J. Smelser and Paul B. Baltes, 9944–49. New York: Elsevier.

Ong, Aihwa, and Donald Nonini, eds. 1997. *Ungrounded Empires: The Cultural Politics of Modern Chinese Transnationalism.* New York: Routledge.

Ong, Aihwa, and Michael G. Peletz. 1995a. Introduction to *Bewitching Women, Pious Men: Gender and Body Politics in Southeast Asia*, ed. Aihwa Ong and Michael G. Peletz, 1–18. Berkeley: University of California Press.

———, eds. 1995b. *Bewitching Women, Pious Men: Gender and Body Politics in Southeast Asia.* Berkeley: University of California Press.

Ortner, Sherry. 1974. "Is Female to Male as Nature Is to Culture?" In *Woman, Culture, and Society*, ed. Michelle Rosaldo and Louise Lamphere, 67–87. Stanford: Stanford University Press.

———. 1995. "Resistance and the Problem of Ethnographic Refusal." *Comparative Studies in Society and History* 37 (1): 173–93.

———. 1996. *Making Gender: The Politics and Erotics of Culture.* Boston: Beacon Press.

———, ed. 1999. *The Fate of "Culture": Geertz and Beyond.* Berkeley: University of California Press.

Parr, C. W. C., and W. H. Mackray. 1910. "Rembau, One of the Nine States: Its History, Constitution, and Customs." *Journal of the Royal Asiatic Society, Straits Branch* 56:1–157.

Parsons, Talcott. 1963. Introduction to *The Sociology of Religion*, by Max Weber. Trans. Ephraim Fischoff, xix–lxvii. Boston: Beacon Press.

Peacock, James. 1968. *Rites of Modernization: Symbols and Social Aspects of Indonesian Proletarian Drama.* Chicago: University of Chicago Press.

———. 1978. *Muslim Puritans: Reformist Psychology in Southeast Asian Islam.* Berkeley: University of California Press.

Peletz, Michael G. 1988a. "Poisoning, Sorcery, and Healing Rituals in Negeri Sembilan." *Bijdragen Tot de Taal-, Land-, en Volkenkunde* 144 (1): 132–64.

———. 1988b. *A Share of the Harvest: Kinship, Property, and Social History among the Malays of Rembau.* Berkeley: University of California Press.

———. 1993a. "Sacred Texts and Dangerous Words: The Politics of Law and Cultural Rationalization in Malaysia." *Comparative Studies in Society and History* 35 (1): 66–109.

———. 1993b. "Knowledge, Power, and Personal Misfortune in a Malay Context." In *Understanding Witchcraft and Sorcery in Southeast Asia*, ed. C. W. Watson and Roy F. Ellen, 149–77. Honolulu: University of Hawaii Press.

———. 1994. "Comparative Perspectives on Kinship and Cultural Identity in Negeri Sembilan." *Sojourn: Journal of Social Issues in Southeast Asia* 9 (1): 1–53.

———. 1995. "Kinship Studies in Late Twentieth-Century Anthropology." *Annual Review of Anthropology* 24:343–72.

———. 1996. *Reason and Passion: Representations of Gender in a Malay Society.* Berkeley: University of California Press.

———. 1997. "'Ordinary Muslims' and Muslim Resurgents in Contemporary Malaysia: Notes on an Ambivalent Relationship." In *Islam in an Era of Nation-States: Politics and Religious Renewal in Muslim Southeast Asia*, ed. Robert W. Hefner and Patricia Horvatich, 231–73. Honolulu: University of Hawaii Press.

———. 2000. "'Asian Values' in Southeast Asia." Paper presented at the Association for Asian Studies Annual Meeting, San Diego.

———. 2001. "Ambivalence in Kinship since the 1940s." In *Relative Values: Reconfiguring Kinship Studies*, ed. Sarah Franklin and Susan McKinnon, 413–43. Durham: Duke University Press.

———. 2002. "Judicial Process and Dilemmas of Legitimacy and Sovereignty: The Malaysian Case in Comparative Perspective." In *Sovereignty under Challenge: How Governments Respond*, ed. John D. Montgomery and Nathan Glazer, 221–58. New Brunswick, NJ: Transaction Publishers.

———. n.d. *Sex and the State: Transgender Practices, State Strategies, and "Asian Values" in Southeast Asia.* New York: Routledge.

Pinault, David. 1992. *The Shiites: Ritual and Popular Piety in a Muslim Community.* New York: St. Martin's Press.

Powers, David. 1989. "Orientalism, Colonialism, and Legal History: The Attack on Muslim Family Endowments in Algeria and India." *Comparative Studies in Society and History* 31:535–71.

———. 1992. "On Judicial Review in Islamic Law." *Law and Society Review* 26 (2): 315–41.

Provencher, Ronald. 1979. "Orality as a Pattern of Symbolism in Malay Psychiatry." In *The Imagination of Reality: Essays in Southeast Asian Coherence Systems*, ed. A. L. Becker and Aram A. Yengoyan, 43–53. Norwood, NJ: Ablex.

Pura, Raphael. 1996. "A Malaysian Morality Tale for the 1990s: Control of Renong Could Be Up for Grabs in Spellbinding Divorce Battle." *Asian Wall Street Journal*, July 30.

Rabo, Annika. 1996. "Gender, State and Civil Society in Jordan and Syria." In *Civil Society: Challenging Western Models*, ed. Chris Hann and Elizabeth Dunn, 155–77. London: Routledge.

Rafael, Vicente. 1993. "Preface to the Paperback Edition." *Contracting Colonialism: Translation and Christian Conversion in Tagalog Society under Early Spanish Rule*, ix–xvi. Durham: Duke University Press.

————, ed. 1999. *Figures of Criminality in Indonesia, the Philippines, and Colonial Vietnam.* Ithaca: Southeast Asia Program, Cornell University.

Rais, Nur, and A.R. 1996. "Queering the State: Towards a Lesbian Movement in Malaysia." In *From Amazon to Zami: Towards a Global Lesbian Feminism*, ed. Monika Reinfelder, 70–85. London: Cassell.

Ranger, Terence. 1983. "The Invention of Tradition in Colonial Africa." In *The Invention of Tradition*, ed. Eric Hobsbawm and Terence Ranger, 211–62. Cambridge: Cambridge University Press.

Rapp, Rayna. 1987. "Toward a Nuclear Freeze? The Gender Politics of Euro-American Kinship Analysis." In *Gender and Kinship: Essays toward a Unified Analysis*, ed. Jane F. Collier and Sylvia Yanagisako, 119–31. Stanford: Stanford University Press.

Raybeck, Douglas. 1986. "The Elastic Rule: Conformity and Deviance in Kelantan Village Life." In *Cultural Identity in Northern Peninsular Malaysia*, ed. Sharon Carstens, 55–74. Monographs in International Studies, Southeast Asia Series, no. 63. Athens: Ohio University Press.

Reid, Anthony. 1988. *Southeast Asia in the Age of Commerce, 1450–1680.* Vol. 1: *The Lands below the Winds.* New Haven: Yale University Press.

————. 1993. *Southeast Asia in the Age of Commerce, 1450–1680.* Vol. 2: *Expansion and Crisis.* New Haven: Yale University Press.

Reinfelder, Monika, ed. 1996. *Amazon to Zami: Towards a Global Lesbian Feminism.* London: Cassell.

Rodinson, Maxime. 1971. *Mohammed.* New York: Penguin.

————. 1973. *Islam and Capitalism.* Austin: University of Texas Press.

Rofel, Lisa. 1999. *Other Modernities: Gendered Yearnings in China after Socialism.* Berkeley: University of California Press.

Roff, William R. 1967. *The Origins of Malay Nationalism.* Kuala Lumpur: University of Malaya Press.

————. 1974. "The Origin and Early Years of the Majlis Ugama." In *Kelantan: Religion, Society and Politics in a Malay State*, ed. Willliam R. Roff, 101–52. Kuala Lumpur: Oxford University Press.

————. 1985. "Islam Obscured? Some Reflections on Studies of Islam and Society in Southeast Asia." *Archipel* 29:7–34.

Rose Ismail, ed. 1995. *Hudud in Malaysia: The Issues at Stake.* Kuala Lumpur: SIS Forum (Malaysia) Berhad.

Rosen, Lawrence. 1980–81. "Equity and Discretion in a Modern Islamic Legal System." *Law and Society Review* 15 (2): 217–45.

————. 1989a. "Islamic 'Case Law' and the Logic of Consequence." In *History and Power in the Study of Law: New Directions in Legal Anthropology*, ed. June Starr and Jane F. Collier, 302–19. Ithaca: Cornell University Press.

————. 1989b. *The Anthropology of Justice: Law as Culture in Islamic Society.* Cambridge: Cambridge University Press.

————. 1998. "Review of *Managing Marital Disputes in Malaysia: Islamic Mediators and Conflict Resolution in the Syariah Courts*, by Sharifah Zaleha Syed Hassan and Sven Cederroth. *Journal of Legal Pluralism* 40:179–81.

Rosenthal, A. M. 1997. "On My Mind: Lessons of the Asian Collapse." *New York Times*, December 23.

Roy, Olivier. 1994. *The Failure of Political Islam.* Cambridge, MA: Harvard University Press.

Rubin, Gayle. 1984. "Thinking Sex: Notes for a Radical Theory of the Politics of Sexuality." In *Pleasure and Danger: Exploring Female Sexuality*, ed. Carole S. Vance, 267–319. New York: Routledge and Kegan Paul.

Sadka, Emily. 1968. *The Protected Malay States, 1874–1895*. Kuala Lumpur: University of Malaya Press.

Safi, Omid. 2001. "An American Muslim Grappling with the Events of 9/11." Paper presented at the Hamilton Forum, Hamilton, New York, October 3, 2001.

Safie bin Ibrahim. 1981. *The Islamic Party of Malaysia: Its Formative Stages and Ideology*. Kuala Lumpur: Nuawi bin Ismail/University of Malaya Press.

Said, Edward. 1978. *Orientalism*. New York: Vintage.

———. 1993. *Culture and Imperialism*. New York: Vintage.

Sampson, Steven. 1996. "The Social Life of Projects: Importing Civil Society to Albania." In *Civil Society: Challenging Western Models*, ed. Chris Hann and Elizabeth Dunn, 121–42. London: Routledge.

Sanders, Paula. 1991. "Gendering the Ungendered Body: Hermaphrodites in Medieval Islamic Law." In *Women in Middle Eastern History: Shifting Boundaries in Sex and Gender*, ed. Nikki R. Keddie and Beth Baron, 74–95. New Haven: Yale University Press.

Sassen, Saskia. 1996. *Losing Control? Sovereignty in an Age of Globalization*. New York: Columbia University Press.

———. 1998. *Globalization and Its Discontents*. Cambridge, MA: Harvard University Press.

Schluchter, Wolfgang. 1979. "The Paradox of Rationalization: On the Relation of Ethics and World." In *Max Weber's Vision of History*, ed. Guenther Roth and Wolfgang Schluchter, 11–64. Berkeley: University of California Press.

Schneider, David M. 1977. "Kinship, Nationality, and Religion in American Culture: Toward a Definition of Kinship." In *Symbolic Anthropology: A Reader*, ed. Janet L. Dolgin, David Kemnitzer, and David M. Schneider, 63–71. New York: Columbia University Press.

———. 1984. *A Critique of the Study of Kinship*. Ann Arbor: University of Michigan Press.

Scott, James C. 1985. *Weapons of the Weak: Everyday Forms of Peasant Resistance*. New Haven: Yale University Press.

———. 1990. *Domination and the Arts of Resistance: Hidden Transcripts*. New Haven: Yale University Press.

———. 1998. *Seeing Like A State: How Certain Schemes to Improve the Human Condition Have Failed*. New Haven: Yale University Press.

Sears, Laurie, ed. 1996. *Fantasizing the Feminine in Indonesia*. Durham: Duke University Press.

Seda-Poulin, Maria Luisa. 1993. "Islamization and Legal Reform in Malaysia: The *Hudud* Controversy of 1992." *Southeast Asian Affairs 1993*, 224–42. Singapore: Institute of Southeast Asian Studies.

(Dato) Sedia Raja Abdullah. 1925. "The Leading Saints in Rembau." *Journal of the Royal Asiatic Society, Malayan Branch* 3 (3): 101–4.

———. 1927. "The Origin of the Pawang and the Berpuar Ceremony." *Journal of the Royal Asiatic Society, Malayan Branch* 5 (2): 310–13.

Shaikh Taha Jabir Al-Alwani. [2000]. *Pendirian Syari'at Terhadap Hukuman Bersalah Ke Atas Dato' Seri Anwar Ibrahim* [Syariah review of the guilty verdict passed on Dato' Seri Anwar Ibrahim].

Shamsul A. B. 1983. "A Revival in the Study of Islam in Malaysia." *Man* 18:399–404.

——. 1986. *From British to Bumiputera Rule: Local Politics and Rural Development in Peninsular Malaysia.* Singapore: Institute of Southeast Asian Studies.

——. 1997. "Identity Construction, Nation Formation, and Islamic Revivalism in Malaysia." In *Islam in an Era of Nation-States: Politics and Religious Renewal in Muslim Southeast Asia*, ed. Robert W. Hefner and Patricia Horvatich, 207–27. Honolulu: University of Hawaii Press.

——. 1999a. "Consuming Islam and Containing the Crisis: Religion, Ethnicity, and Economy in Malaysia." In *Southeast Asian-Centered Economies or Economics?* ed. Mason C. Hoadley, 43–61. Copenhagen: Nordic Institute of Asian Studies.

——. 1999b. "From *Orang Kaya Baru* to *Melayu Baru*: Cultural Constructions of the Malay New Rich." In *Culture and Privilege in Capitalist Asia*, ed. Michael Pinche, 86–110. London: Routledge.

——. 2000. "Making Sense of Politics in Contemporary Malaysia: Resisting Popular Interpretation." In *Trends and Issues in East Asia 2000*, ed. Ng Chee Yuen and Charla Griffy-Brown, 227–48. Tokyo: Idris and Fasid.

Sharifah Zaleha Syed Hassan. 1985. "From Saints to Bureaucrats: A Study of the Development of Islam in the State of Kedah." Ph.D. diss., Cornell University.

——. 1986. "Women, Divorce, and Islam in Kedah." *Sojourn* 1 (2): 183–98.

——. 1989. "Versions of Eternal Truth: Ulama and Religious Dissenters in Kedah Malay Society." *Contributions to Southeast Asian Ethnography* 8:43–69.

——. 2000. "Islamic Revivalism and Social Cleavages in an Urban Community in Malaysia." *Bulletin of the Royal Institute for Inter-Faith Studies* 2 (2): 33–47.

——. 2001. "Islamization and the Emerging Civil Society in Malaysia." In *Islam and Civil Society in Southeast Asia*, ed. Nakamura Mitsuo, Sharon Siddique, and Omar Farouk Bajunid, 76–88. Singapore: Institute of Southeast Asian Studies.

Sharifah Zaleha Syed Hassan and Sven Cederroth. 1997. *Managing Marital Disputes in Malaysia: Islamic Mediators and Conflict Resolution in the Syariah Courts.* Richmond, Surrey: Curzon Press.

Sholle, David. 1990. "Resistance: Pinning Down a Wandering Concept in Cultural Studies Discourse." *Journal of Urban and Cultural Studies* 1 (1): 87–105.

Simmel, Georg. [1908] 1971. "The Stranger." In *Georg Simmel on Individuality and Social Forms*, ed. Donald N. Levine, 143–49. Chicago: University of Chicago Press.

Skeat, W. W. [1899–1900] 1953. "Reminiscences of the Cambridge University Expedition to the North Eastern Malay States, 1899–1900." *Journal of the Malayan Branch of the Royal Asiatic Society*, vol. 26, pt. 4, 9–147.

Sloane, Patricia. 1999. *Islam, Modernity and Entrepreneurship among the Malays.* New York: St. Martin's Press.

Southern, R. W. 1962. *Western Views of Islam in the Middle Ages.* Cambridge, MA: Harvard University Press.

Spülbeck, Susanne. 1996. "Anti-Semitism and Fear of the Public Sphere in a Post-Totalitarian Society: East Germany." In *Civil Society: Challenging Western Models*, ed. Chris Hann and Elizabeth Dunn, 64–78. London: Routledge.

Stacey, Judith. 1991. *Brave New Families: Stories of Domestic Upheaval in Late Twentieth-Century America.* New York: Basic Books.

——. 1996. *In the Name of the Family: Rethinking Family Values in a Postmodern Age.* New York: Basic Books.

Stallybrass, Peter, and Allon White. 1986. *The Politics and Poetics of Transgression.* Ithaca: Cornell University Press.

Starr, June, and Jane F. Collier, eds. 1989. *History and Power in the Study of Law: New Directions in Legal Anthropology*. Ithaca: Cornell University Press.

Stivens, Maila. 1985. "The Fate of Women's Land Rights: Gender, Matriliny, and Capitalism in Rembau, Negeri Sembilan, Malaysia." In *Women, Work, and Ideology in the Third World*, ed. Haleh Afshar, 3–36. London: Tavistock.

———. 1991. "The Evolution of Kinship Relations in Rembau, Negeri Sembilan, Malaysia." In *Cognation and Social Organization in Southeast Asia*, ed. J. Kemp and E. Husken, 71–88. Leiden: Koninklijk Instituut voor Taal-, Land-, en Volkenkunde.

———. 1996. *Matriliny and Modernity: Sexual Politics and Social Change in Rural Malaysia*. St. Leonards: Allen and Unwin.

———. 1998. "Sex, Gender, and the Making of the New Malay Middle Classes." In *Gender and Power in Affluent Asia*, ed. Krishna Sen and Maila Stivens, 87–126. London: Routledge.

Strange, Heather. 1981. *Rural Malay Women in Tradition and Transition*. New York: Praeger.

Sullivan, Patrick. 1983. "A Critical Appraisal of Historians of Malaya: The Theory of Society Implicit in Their Work." In *Southeast Asia: Essays in the Political Economy of Structural Change*, ed. Richard Higgett and Richard Robson, 65–92. Melbourne: Routledge.

Sweeney, P. L. Amin. 1972. *The Ramayana and the Malay Shadow Play*. Kuala Lumpur: National University of Malaysia Press.

———. 1987. *A Full Hearing: Orality and Literacy in the Malay World*. Berkeley: University of California Press.

Swettenham, Sir Frank. [1895] 1984. *Malay Sketches*. Reprint, Singapore: Graham Brash.

Swift, Michael G. 1965. *Malay Peasant Society in Jelebu*. London: Athlone Press.

Syed Husin Alatas. 1977. *The Myth of the Lazy Native*. New York: Frank Cass.

Tan Beng Hui. 1999. "Women's Sexuality and the Discourse on Asian Values: Cross-Dressing in Malaysia." *Female Desires: Same-Sex Relations and Transgender Practices Across Cultures*, ed. Evelyn Blackwood and Saskia Wieringa, 281–307. New York: Columbia University Press.

Taussig, Michael. 1980. *The Devil and Commodity Fetishism in South America*. Chapel Hill: University of North Carolina Press.

Thompson, Richard H. 1995. "Common Sense and Fact-Finding: Cultural Reason in Judicial Decisions." *Legal Studies Forum* 19 (2): 119–37.

Tidrick, Kathryn. 1990. *Empire and the English Character*. London: I. B. Taurus Company.

Tucker, Judith E. 1998. *In the House of the Law: Gender and Islamic Law in Ottoman Syria and Palestine*. Berkeley: University of California Press.

Turner, Bryan S. 1974. *Weber and Islam: A Critical Study*. London: Routledge and Kegan Paul.

Turner, Denys. 1983. *Marxism and Christianity*. New York: Barnes and Noble.

von der Mehden, Fred. 1980. "Islamic Resurgence in Malaysia." In *Islam and Development: Religion and Socio-political Change*, ed. John Esposito, 163–206. Syracuse: Syracuse University Press.

———. 1988. "Malaysia and Indonesia." In *The Politics of Islamic Revivalism: Diversity and Unity*, ed. Shireen T. Hunter, 247–61. Bloomington: Indiana University Press.

Walzer, Michael. 1995. "The Concept of Civil Society." In *Toward a Global Civil Society*, ed. Michael Walzer, 7–27. New York: Berghahn Books.

Wazir Jahan Karim. 1992. *Women and Culture: Between Malay Adat and Islam*. Boulder: Westview Press.

Weber, Max. [1922] 1963. *The Sociology of Religion*. Trans. Ephraim Fischoff. Boston: Beacon Press.

———. [1925] 1968. *Wirtschaft und Gesellschaft. Grundriss der Verstehenden Soziologie*. Reprinted as "Economy and Law (Sociology of Law)." In *Economy and Society: An Outline of Interpretive Sociology*. Vol. 2. Ed. Guenther Roth and Claus Wittich, 641–900. Berkeley: University of California Press.

———. 1946. *From Max Weber: Essays in Sociology*. Trans. by H. H. Gerth and C. Wright Mills. Oxford: Oxford University Press.

———. 1968. *Economy and Society: An Outline of Interpretative Sociology*. 2 vols. Ed. Guenther Ross and Claus Wittich. Berkeley: University of California Press.

Weigert, Andrew. 1991. *Mixed Emotions: Certain Steps toward Understanding Ambivalence*. Albany: SUNY Press.

Weston, Kath. 1998. *Long Slow Burn: Sexuality and Social Science*. New York: Routledge.

Weyland, Petra. 1990. "International Muslim Networks and Islam in Singapore." *Sojourn* 5 (2): 219–54.

White, Jenny B. 1996. "Civic Culture and Islam in Urban Turkey." In *Civil Society: Challenging Western Models*, ed. Chris Hann and Elizabeth Dunn, 143–54. London: Routledge.

Wikan, Unni. 1987. "Public Grace and Private Fears: Gaiety, Offense, and Sorcery in Northern Bali." *Ethos* 15:337–65.

———. 1989. "Managing the Heart to Brighten Face and Soul: Emotions in Balinese Morality and Health Care." *American Ethnologist* 16 (2): 294–312.

Wilchins, Riki Anne. 1997. *Read My Lips: Sexual Subversion and the End of Gender*. Ithaca: Firebrand Books.

Wilkinson, Richard J. 1906. *Malay Beliefs*. London: Luzac.

———. [1908] 1970. "Malay Law." Reprinted in *Readings in Malay Adat Laws*. Ed. M. B. Hooker, 6–47. Singapore: Singapore University Press.

Williams, Raymond. 1977. *Marxism and Literature*. Oxford: Oxford University Press.

Willis, Paul. 1977. *Learning to Labor: How Working Class Kids Get Working Class Jobs*. New York: Columbia University Press.

Wolfe, Alan. 1989. *Whose Keeper? Social Science and Moral Obligation*. Berkeley: University of California Press.

Woodward, Mark R. 1989. *Islam in Java: Normative Piety and Mysticism in the Sultanate of Yogyakarta*. Tucson: University of Arizona Press.

Wright, Barbara. 1986. "The Role of the Dalang in Kelantanese Malay Society." In *Cultural Identity in Northern Peninsular Malaysia*, ed. Sharon A. Carstens, 29–45. Athens: Ohio University Center for International Studies, Center for Southeast Asian Studies.

Wrong, Dennis. 1970. Introduction to *Max Weber*, ed. Dennis Wrong, 1–76. Englewood Cliffs, NJ: Prentice-Hall.

Yanagisako, Sylvia. 1995. "Transforming Orientalism: Gender, Nationality and Class in Asian American Studies." In *Natural Symbols: Essays in Feminist Cultural Analysis*, ed. Sylvia Yanagisako and Carol Delaney, 275–98. New York: Routledge.

Yegar, Moshe. 1979. *Islam and Islamic Institutions in British Malaya, 1874–1941: Policies and Implementation*. Jerusalem: Magnes Press.

Yengoyan, Aram A. 1983. "Transvestism and the Ideology of Gender: Southeast Asia and Beyond." In *Feminist Re-visions: What Has Been and What Might Be*, ed. Vivian Patraka and Louise Tilly, 135–48. Ann Arbor: Women's Studies Program, University of Michigan.

Zainah Anwar. 1987. *Islamic Revivalism in Malaysia: Dakwah among the Students.* Kuala Lumpur: Pelanduk Publications.

Zelenietz, Marty, and Shirley Lindenbaum, eds. 1981. *Sorcery and Social Change in Melanesia*. Special issue of *Social Analysis*, vol. 8.